THE PSYCHOLOGY
OF HUMAN
MEMORY

THE PSYCHOLOGY
OF HUMAN
MEMORY

ARTHUR WINGFIELD
Brandeis University

DENNIS L. BYRNES
University of Massachusetts, Boston

ACADEMIC PRESS
New York
London
Toronto
Sydney
San Francisco
A Subsidiary of Harcourt Brace Jovanovich, Publishers

Cover photo by Dan Lenore
Original cartoon illustrations by Catherine Wingfield

Academic Press, Inc.
111 Fifth Avenue, New York, New York 10003

United Kingdom Edition published by
Academic Press, Inc. (London) Ltd.
24/28 Oval Road, London NW1

ISBN: 0-12-759650-X
Library of Congress Catalog Card Number
80-619

Printed in the United States of America

PREFACE

F.C. Bartlett once noted that nothing is so practical as a good theory. Bartlett was also a devoted advocate of the view that the best theories were constructed in the process of trying to solve practical problems. For many students who approach the study of memory, this plea for "ecological validity" rings a sympathetic bell. There are few of us who do not want to know why we forget and how we can prevent—or at least retard—this disastrous state of affairs called "forgetting." But there is more to the question of memory than its occasional failures. We also want to know how memory supports our knowledge of the world, how it permits us to answer questions and to solve problems. The question of memory, then, is at its most fundamental, a practical one.

Psychology's search for answers, however, approached the study of memory from a very different perspective. From the very beginnings of memory research, the goal was to develop a "pure" theory, one "uncontaminated" by real-world applicability and problems. One can see this tendency in older handbooks of experimental psychology, in which the topic of memory might be confined to a single chapter on the reproduction or recognition of well-defined sets of learning materials. Such an approach may have been a necessary beginning, but it could not be more than that.

The past decade of research has seen an increasing recognition that the study of memory implies a necessary interdependence with the study of learning, perception, language, problem solving, and the process of reasoning. Largely under the impetus of the so-called information processing approach to cognitive function, terms like "memory," "perception," and "cognition" began less and less to delimit particular areas of research, or particular kinds of research questions. The human information processing system operates as a whole and one part of this system cannot be studied, or understood, without the involvement of the whole. Indeed, the point has been reached where a good text on memory shows an extraordinary topic overlap with the material ordinarily covered in a good text on cognitive psychology.

The reason for this shift in approach lies in the theoretical changes which have been necessary to accomodate an ever-expanding research literature. The information processing viewpoint began this movement with the influential structural approach, which conceptualized the memory system in terms of three distinct and independent stores: sensory memory, short-term memory, and long-term memory. By the early 1970s this too gave way to a more pluralistic notion of the nature of memory representations, their construction, and retrieval. The emphasis gradually shifted away from memory *structures* to memory *processes;* the questions about memory thus broadened to include such issues as whether coding processes in memory demand attentional effort, and how recall interacts with the process of inference.

This text is intended as an introductory survey of these changing concepts. We expect our student readers, whether undergraduate or in some cases graduate students, to have had little background in psychology beyond, perhaps, an experimentally oriented introductory course in general psychology. To meet our goal with this readership in mind, we have organized this book to track and describe the intriguing changes in explanatory metaphors used by research investigators, and to show how these changes had direct consequences in their research and theory building. Viewing the study of memory in this way leads us to take some of the earlier approaches, such as that of verbal learning and interference theory, as more than simply a quaint "prehistory" of modern approaches. In short, we see not simply change, but evolution.

In Chapter 1 we discuss this development of metaphor and theory in greater detail. This is followed in Chapters 2 and 3 by a discussion of associationist views of memory, and certain theoretical problems that led to the gradual acceptance of increasingly elaborate and more cognitive explanations. Chapter 4 continues this theme with a consideration of how the meaning of events, and the contexts in which we derive this meaning, both complicates and enriches our notions about the structure of memory. It is here that the field of semantic memory receives its major attention.

In Chapters 5 and 6 we describe the contemporary development of the dual concepts of sensory storage and of selective attention. We introduce the current notions of how mental activities require effort, or capacity, and how the manifest limits on capacity guide our ability to store and process memory information.

Chapters 7 and 8 more directly confront the evolving shift from the structural stores notion of a distinct short-term and long-term memory (Chapter 7), to the modern "levels of processing" framework (Chapter 8), which attempts in its own way to do justice to the variety of encoding and retrieval strategies that the average person has under his or her command.

If Bartlett's goal was a study of memory that has applicability to our understanding of everyday problems and practical applications, we cannot leave memory theory without a serious look at how well current memory theory translates into applied areas. Chapter 9 makes just such an attempt.

Throughout this book we have attempted to provide an up-to-date account of the current status of memory theory and research. At the same time we have also tried to provide the student reader with a good feeling for the interaction between experimental data and theory and the way conceptual changes have nourished promising progress in the field.

Our task throughout the development of this text was made immeasurably easier by James D. Anker, our sponsoring editor at Academic Press, and by Richard Christopher, our project editor, and the entire production staff. We are also grateful for the criticisms, suggestions, and advice from a number of people who read and commented on earlier versions of our manuscript. Douglas Nelson, Glenn Meyer, John Hovancik, and Douglas Herrmann deserve special acknowledgement and gratitude. Joan Roy has our thanks for her speed and efficiency in typing the entire manuscript, as do the many students who read and commented on our early drafts from their own unique but essential perspective.

Arthur Wingfield
Dennis Byrnes

June 1980

CONTENTS

ASSOCIATIONS AND FORGETTING IN LONG-TERM MEMORY

MEANING AND KNOWLEDGE: STUDIES OF SEMANTIC MEMORY

CODING PROCESSES: I. SENSORY MEMORY

THE PSYCHOLOGY
OF HUMAN
MEMORY

INTRODUCTION AND OVERVIEW

1

TOPIC QUESTIONS

1. What Is Memory?
Why has the study of memory been so important to psychology? Why has memory research concentrated on memory for words? How does motivation and effort affect memory performance?

2. Memory Processes.
What is the distinction often made by psychologists between *memory structures* and *memory processes*? What are the three basic processes involved in memory performance? What is a *memory code*?

3. Memory Structures.
What is *sensory memory*, and how is it distinguished from *short-term memory*? How do we characterize *long-term memory*? What is a major alternative to emphasizing these memory structures?

4. Theoretical Approaches to Memory.
What was the early *associationist* approach to memory? How did *Gestalt psychology's* view of memory differ from this? What elements form the more recent *cognitive* or *information processing* approaches to memory?

5. The Search for Memory.
To what extent are memory theories truly different, or are they different ways of talking about the same phenomena? How will this question be addressed in the remainder of this book, and what is the goal of our search?

The explanation of human memory has been called the "supreme intellectual puzzle of the century," (Anderson & Bower, 1973, p. 1). This may seem something of an exaggeration in the context of the possibilities of nuclear war, the energy crisis, and the population explosion, but, at least for psychologists, memory and learning are at the core of all other problems. Questions about the effects of experience, how they are produced, and their consequences for competence and performance have enormous importance for developmental psychology, personality, education, social relationships, perception, and thought. In fact, one can view most of the areas of psychology as involving variations on this theme and differing only in the content to be studied.

Having painted such a wide vista, this book lays claim to only a small but important part of the territory. We will be primarily concerned with theories and experiments that ask how people acquire and use information. Since its inception, the experimental psychology of memory has concentrated on the learning and recall of language materials. This preoccupation with language is not surprising given that learning to use language to categorize experience is probably our most important human skill. All other behaviors are affected by the fact that we are a linguistic animal. Because of this, much of the work on memory that we will review assumed that what we find out about learning and memory for words can be applied to the acquisition and use of other behavioral skills. This may have been a mistake; we will talk about some of the problems in generalizing results even across different tasks in which language is used.

WHAT IS MEMORY?

No one has ever seen a memory and no one is ever likely to see one. In our everyday conversation we use that word to talk about things we *do*. We *remember* our first day in class, or *forget* where we parked the car. We *recognize* an old friend, or *recall* a pleasant day at the beach. All these things have to do with memory. The term as we use it in this book, and as you probably use it now, has to do with the capacities human beings have to retain information, to recall it when needed, and to recognize its familiarity when they later see or hear it again. The study of memory is the attempt to describe how these capacities are exercised and why, in the case of forgetting, attempts to exercise these capacities may be frustrated.

If what we *do* could always be relied upon to reflect what we *know*, the study of learning, memory, and knowledge would be a much simpler chore. The fact is that what we do (our performance or behavior) is not always a true measure of what we have learned (our knowledge), nor even less is it a measure of what we could have learned or done under ideal circumstances (our capacity).

On the one hand, memory can be a very creative process in which good "memory" performance may often reflect the result of logical inference as much as stored facts, per se. Students often do well on an

TABLE 1-1 Fourteen reasons why I failed the last examination.

Group	Responses
I. Performance/Behavior	
	1. My pencil kept breaking (I broke my glasses), so I wrote too slowly.
	2. I was tired (sick) when taking the examination.
	3. I knew the answers, but I just couldn't think of them.
	4. I was too nervous during the exam, and had a mental block.
	5. The questions misled me as to what was wanted for an answer.
	6. I was preoccupied with personal problems and just couldn't think.
II. Knowledge/Capacity	
	1. I was tired (sick) when trying to study for the exam.
	2. I just didn't study enough.
	3. I learned the individual facts, but couldn't see how they related to each other.
	4. I couldn't understand the material.
III. Uncategorizable	
	1. I didn't know the exam was today.
	2. I just wasn't up for it.
	3. A flying saucer landed in my bedroom and . . .
	4. I never do well on objective exams.

examination, not because they know the answer through study, but because they can logically deduce what the correct answer must be. These are our occasional success stories. On the other hand, how often have you done poorly on an examination, even when you felt you were well prepared? In a not very scientific survey, we have come up with two main groupings of explanations one often hears following a midterm or final examination (see Table 1-1). The first group implies a performance deficit and the second, an admission that the knowledge was not there in the first place. In evaluating excuses, as well as in memory research, it is often difficult to specify the source of poor performance; hence, our Group III.

The point we wish to make is that memory research, and our explanations of memory based on this research, must often confront the distance between what may actually be represented in memory versus our behavioral measures of the consequences of this representation. Indeed, much of the experimental work you will be reading about in subsequent chapters is based on psychologists' continuing attempts to devise more and more ingenious ways to find external measures of our internal representations.

The distinction between capacity and performance, or knowledge and behavior, is also frequently made because we must distinguish between the factors that affect what we do at a particular time and those that affect what we are able to do under the most favorable circumstances. You will be more likely to remember the answers on a completion test if you try hard than if you do not. We also know poor results will accompany too much stress or anxiety. Your grade on the exam may tell us as much about your motivation or mood as it does about your capacity to remember.

If you are very tired, your memory performance will be less accurate than if you are alert. Again, this provides information about the effects of fatigue on performance and may not be very informative about what you may be capable of remembering under more favorable circumstances. Both of these factors, your observed performance and your actual knowledge or capacity, are of interest to us in memory research. We are concerned with a very complex system whose operation can be affected in a variety of ways. One of our fundamental problems in making inferences from studies of memory will be to separate and distinguish among these separate effects.

MEMORY PROCESSES

One way of distinguishing different kinds of questions about memory is to separate those which concern processes from questions that concern memory structures (Atkinson & Shiffrin, 1968). Questions about memory processes have to do with the mental activities we perform in order to put information into memory and the activities that later make use of that information. Questions about structure have to do with the nature of memory storage itself: how this information is represented, how long the representation may last, and how memories may be organized. That is, questions about memory structures can concern either *what* is represented (the content of the representation), or the *characteristics* of these representations (their durations, their relationships to other representations, and so forth). We will analyze the act of remembering as dependent on at least three logically distinct processes: acquisition, retention, and retrieval.

Acquisition　Information that is to serve as the basis for remembering must first be acquired. A failure of recall or recognition may be the result of inattention during the original experience or a misunderstanding of the experience. Contemporary students of learning think of this as the encoding problem.

We can view experience as producing some mental representation. This representation is the *memory code*. The content of a memory representation, then, may be determined by the nature of the acquisition process. Not all information that was available to you will necessarily be incorporated into the memory code. The code will represent only part of the information that could have been derived from the situation. For example, you may remember that you saw Professor X in class today, but do you remember what color shirt the professor was wearing? Did you encode this information at all?

A substantial part of the problem in the study of acquisition is to determine what has been encoded and why. These problems lead us to inquire about selective attention, the effects of understanding on learning, and into trying to describe the many possible strategies a person may use to encode the information presented to them. These, according to our previous definitions, are questions about memory processes. Further, these processes may vary in their efficiency, depending on past knowledge or experience. When material is meaningful, fitting well with our prior knowledge, the code is quickly established and invariably effective. When verbatim rote learning is required, acquisition is often slow, and nothing short of hard work.

The most obvious variable affecting acquisition in such cases is practice. The earliest studies of verbal learning concerned themselves mostly with how the conditions of practice affected later performance on the same or similar materials. For example, what kind of practice is best? Should you study the same materials over and over for a prolonged period of time, or is it better to have short study periods with frequent rest breaks (massed versus distributed practice)? Should you practice the material in its entirety, or should you practice it in parts and put it all together after you have learned the pieces (whole versus part learning)? The interpretation of practice effects and how these effects are produced is of considerable importance to the different theoretical views we discuss in later chapters.

Retention　The second logically separable process contributing to the success or failure of a memory performance is retention. Information acquired from experience must be retained if we are to use it as the basis of a later act of remembering. Retention problems are problems in the storage of information that has been adequately coded. Ironically, the study of storage historically focused mainly on negative conditions, i.e., why do people forget? This work has specified a number of factors that interfere with maintenance of the memory code over time. The most important of these conditions is the acquisition of new information. Again, how new learning affects the retention of old is a controversial and difficult problem. We will later discuss these findings in the context of interference theory.

Retrieval   If information has been adequately encoded at the time of presentation and successfully retained over time, we may still have a problem in retrieving this information when we try to remember. Most people have had the experience of knowing that they know something, but for some reason being unable to "get at it." That feeling of knowing is validated by the fact that you often remember the information long after there is any occasion to use it. It is also the case that you can usually recognize the right answer on a multiple-choice test even though you could not recall that answer without the "hints" such tests supply. Both these examples are problems of retrieval. The information has been correctly encoded and retained, but there is a failure to correctly reactivate that code.

Retrieving stored information is preeminently a strategic process. When trying to recall your social security number, you would never make the mistake of recalling a letter. Your attempts to get at the correct information are not random draws from a pile of memories. You seem to *search* on the basis of certain principles or rules. Retrieval is orderly and what is stored seems to be well organized rather than a jumble of memory codes one on top of the other.

The schemes or strategies one uses to search through memory are as varied as the number of possible ways events can be described. For example, in trying to describe some long-past conversation you might systematically think of the physical environment in which that conversation took place ("Let's see, you were sitting there, and I was sitting here, and you said . . . "). Or you might organize your search in terms of the significance of the conversation for some other series of events ("This was the first time I realized Suzie liked me."). The perennial question concerning these organizations is whether they owe their effectiveness to events at the time of acquisition, or whether they are properties of the retrieval process itself. In other words, is it the case that the storage of information is organized during encoding, and retrieval merely makes use of this established organization? Or, on the other hand, is coding much like entering words into a dictionary or facts into an encyclopedia? In the latter case, organization occurs in the way we look through the stored information to find what we need; that is, in strategies of retrieval.

Like most dichotomies this question need not be answered in only one way. It is probably true that successful memory performance depends on a compatibility between the strategies of retrieval and the strategies of the original encoding. For example, the encoding strategies of early childhood may be incompatible with adult strategies for retrieving information. Many of us cannot remember our earliest years at all, or we may remember them in distorted or inconsistent ways. As a child you looked up at doorknobs and could not reach the refrigerator handle. Events could be interpreted only in a very limited frame of reference. You, in effect, lived in a different world than you do as an adult. The distortion that comes about as a simple result of your change in size would become apparent if you visited a childhood haunt to find that it had seemed to shrink over the years. Organization of encoding and retrieval are of major importance to any view of memory. We will talk about these issues at length in later chapters.

The three memory processes we have described, acquistion, or "encoding," retention, or "storage," and recall, or "retrieval," form the repeating themes of this book. The theories and experiments we will describe can be arranged along a variety of different dimensions, but the issues addressed are always questions or controversies concerning this division of processes. It is particularly important that the student see how these processes are logically separable components of the memory performance. Much of the arguments presented hinge on the effects of varying conditions on one or the other of these fundamental memory activities.

MEMORY STRUCTURES

When we investigate memory structures we are interested in the form and nature of information storage as a product of the memory processes we have just described. In what form is information stored? Do we, for example, store visual information exactly as experienced, such that in remembering we have access to a kind of image of the original event? Or, on the other hand, is all information stored in some very abstract form that nonetheless allows us to derive an image of what the experience must have been? This problem may be unsolvable (Anderson, 1978) since many different kinds of representation could lead to the same memory performance. This controversy over the nature and existence of mental images is an ancient and fascinating one that will be reviewed as we discuss the variety of memory codes.

The structural problem that has attracted the greatest experimental and theoretical interest is the hypothesis that there are distinctly different kinds of memory systems that (1) are retained for different periods of time and are potentially subject to different causes of forgetting, (2) contain different kinds of memory codes, and (3) have different limitations on the amount of information retained. For example, let us take the question of duration. Are your memories of last night's dinner menu, or of the page numbers for tomorrow's reading assignment a different kind of memory than that of your address, or the names of your high school friends?

The first memories mentioned are retained only as long as they are useful. It is unlikely that you will be able to remember last month's dinner menu or the reading assignment for the second week of last semester. However, you probably can recall the address of the home you lived in as a child and the names of many of the people you knew then. Do these differences in retention represent differences in the kind of memory storage in which they are represented?

Sensory Memory

If you watch a glowing cigarette move in the dark, you will see an orange trail following the movement. This trail could be thought of as a kind of memory—the visual sensation is retained for some period of time after the object is no longer there. As you watch, the trail quickly fades. The persistence of the visual sensation lasts for much less than a second. The same phenomenon can be observed for the other senses. If you touch the back of your hand lightly with the point of your pencil and then quickly pull the pencil away, you should be able to notice that the sensation of being touched persists for an instant after the pencil is withdrawn.

The very brief persistence of unprocessed sensory information has been thought of as representing the first of three different kinds of structural stores. It is called a *sensory memory*, or sometimes a *sensory register*. Many theorists believe that this form of memory acts as something like a sensory "echo" of just received visual and auditory information, and perhaps for other senses as well. Further, such sensory storage may briefly hold more information than one can in fact ever use or remember.

This ability to retain sensory information, even for a very brief duration, gives us additional time to process and code this information into some more enduring form. Thus, sensory memory has been seen as a distinct memory structure, distinguished from others by its sensory content, its very brief duration, and the large amount of information it can temporarily hold.

Short-Term Memory

Some memories seem to last much longer than the instant that character-izes a sensory image, but these also seem to be transient. When you look up an address or phone number for the first time, you are unlikely to retain it for very long unless you continue to repeat it to yourself. Telephone numbers seldom outlast the time it takes to dial them. However, unlike sensory memory, we can rehearse a telephone number or grocery list and retain that information indefinitely.

Information stored in *short-term memory* is usually considered to have been reacted to or coded into some form of language. We have stored at this stage not simply a record of the visual sensation of numbers on a page, but we now have the names for those numbers and can say them to ourselves. As we think about looking up and dialing a telephone number, we also see that the amount of information we can hold without extensive rehearsal is sharply limited.

Another way of thinking about this second stage is to say that the sensory information at the previous stage has now been related to something that we know, such as how our knowledge of visual forms relates to number names. Considerable early research seemed to show that memory after brief intervals is invariably coded as names or verbal descriptions of experience. We now make such a statement with considerably more caution since, as we shall see, some form of visual memory often appears in our research.

Long-Term Memory

In the scheme of structural components of memory we are presenting here, if you were shown the word AUNT, you would first have a visual trace of the word, storing only its visual form for a brief instant. You would then form a short-term trace of the word which you might try to retain by repeating it to yourself. Given a little time, you might summon up memories of your own aunt or of other associations you may have to this word.

This final form of memory storage is presumed to be of the longest duration and involves the coding of the true meaning of an event. Usually referred to simply as *long-term memory*, events are placed in the context of other related events or concepts. If events are related meaningfully to what we know, those events can be remembered much longer than, for example, a list of nonsense syllables. Some theorists have made an additional distinction between the long-term memory for general knowledge, such as the meanings of words, and our memory for long-past experiences. We will discuss this distinction in our coverage of semantic memory.

Levels of Processing

In describing these three structurally distinct memory stores, we have been faithful to two decades of fruitful memory research which had found an advantage in separating three qualitatively different forms of memory and studying each in considerable detail. The reality of human memory is, of course, one of dynamic quality. Information is not so much shifted from one store to another as it is continually processed through deeper and deeper levels of analysis. Many of the phenomena of short-term memory can be described as the product of "shallow" processing at one end of a continuum, with "deep" processing to a semantic level, at the other. Rather than seeing memory storage in terms of distinct systems, this view suggests that memory codes be characterized by the degree of processing that produced them (Craik & Lockhart, 1972; Craik & Tulving, 1975).

The theoretical distinction between structural components of memory and their relationship to retention has been the subject of one of the major debates in experimental psychology. Whether or not these ideas survive in the ultimate explanation of human memory, they have proven useful in organizing the various kinds of questions students of memory have asked and the kinds of experiments they have used to provide their answers. Each of these hypothetical structures will be examined in the course of this book, together with the recent "levels of processing" approach to human memory.

THEORETICAL APPROACHES TO MEMORY

Theories in psychology, as well as in other disciplines, begin with some assumptions about what is to be explained, what kind of events are important, and what techniques will be most useful in asking questions about these events. There are several different theoretical and experimental approaches to the psychology of memory, but we will categorize them here under two broad headings that seem to us to represent very different orientations.

These orientations emphasize different characteristics of human memory and employ different ideas about what a successful theory of memory should look like. For the sake of this distinction we can begin with a rather stereotyped view of these orientations. In practice, the boundaries are less easy to draw. There has been a borrowing of concepts and a merging of ideas between the viewpoints that may at first appear clearly different ways of thinking about memory.

Associationism

Aristotle is usually given credit for first articulating the laws of association (Tulving & Madigan, 1970). The British Empiricist philosophers of the seventeenth century expanded and elaborated these ideas into a broad conception of human nature. Ebbinghaus, the first person to experimentally examine human memory, used these ideas as the basis for his investigations. When animal learning and behavior became a central topic in experimental psychology in the 1920s, the ideas of the associationists were adapted to describe these phenomena. While the early philosophers spoke of connections between elementary sensations or ideas, the students of animal behavior spoke of connections between elementary stimuli and responses.

The language of associationism in the study of human memory is predominantly the stimulus–response (S–R) language of animal learning and conditioning. Words and sentences presented to the subjects are the stimuli; words and sentences emitted by the subject are the responses. Of course, it is more complicated than this. Responses also serve as stimuli, as when you hear your own voice or read what you are writing. In addition, there may be *covert stimuli* and *responses* that occur within the person. Talking this way about memory performance led many to a description of memory as a sequence, or "chain," of discrete events. In acquiring an association, a stimulus becomes connected to a response. The study of acquisition thus becomes the attempt to discover laws governing the formation of these connections. Retention is the persistence of these connections over time, and retrieval is the reactivation of these connections for recall.

The concept of associations has been used in several different ways that must be kept separate in order to think clearly about these issues. The most important and common use of the word is descriptive. When you say that the words KING and QUEEN are associated, you are simply saying that when one of these words occurs, you tend to think of the other. If we ask people to say the first word that comes to mind when we say KING, most will say QUEEN. Here we are just using the word "association" to refer to the fact that one thing tends to follow the other. Any theory of memory will have to explain associations in this sense.

The word association can also be employed in a theoretical sense. When used in this way, the term proposes an explanation of why one word tends to follow another. The theoretical use of the term explains memory as a vast network of interconnected elements. The connections between elements are the associations. Experiments from this point of view attempt to establish what conditions are necessary for the formation of these connections, how the connections interfere with one another, and the circumstances that lead to their reactivation. The descriptive use of association simply names what we observe: one thing follows another. The theoretical use claims to name some internal connection that is the basis of our observations.

For association theorists, *contiguity* was the fundamental condition for the formation of connections. Indeed, contiguity has been cited as the basic cause of associations since the time of Aristotle. Two events become associated because they occur together in time. In our example, KING and QUEEN become associated because they have frequently occurred together in our experience. According to this principle, we learn the alphabet as a sequence of associations. The response of one letter name serves as the stimulus for the next letter name. Since we practice the letters as a sequence, particular letters consistently occur together in time.

The most important property of an association is its *strength*. The more often two elements occur together the stronger will be the association between them. Stronger associations tend to crowd out and interfere with weaker ones. It is very difficult to recite the alphabet in any but the familiar order. Associations in any other order are weaker because they have not occurred frequently together in time. The interference of the stronger associations inhibit attempts at recitation in any other order. Contiguity, then, according to the associationists, is the necessary condition for the formation of associations. Interference is the major cause of forgetting.

People obviously do not always produce the response that has occurred most often in the past to a particular stimulus. Responses sometimes occur that have never been paired with the stimulus at all. In order to explain the occurrence of associations without prior contiguity, association theory makes use of the idea of *mediation*. A mediated association between two elements results from associations between these two elements and a third element. For example, a person asked to give an association to the word COFFEE might respond with the word CHAIR. CHAIR is an unusual response and is not likely to have been heard frequently in conjunction with COFFEE. However, association theory explains this unlikely occurrence by claiming that other, more likely, responses intervene between the stimulus and the overt response. For example, the person may associate COFFEE with TABLE, which immediately elicits CHAIR. The mediator TABLE is a silent participant in this chain. The varieties of mediation possible and the difficulties of demonstrating mediation will be discussed later.

In summary, associationism takes the sequential dependencies between words to be the primary problem in the explanation of human memory. All other problems of remembering, and recalling can be reduced to problems in the acquisition, retention, recognizing, and retrieval of associations. This view of human learning and memory has been the most well-developed and powerful view for several decades. It is only within recent times that associationism has received serious challenge in this area of study. The challenge has come from an old rival, the cognitive approach to human functioning.

Cognitive Psychology

In an older experimental psychology, "cognition" referred to the study of thinking and problem solving. It was a general term that dealt with attempts to describe how people reacted in new ways to find solutions to novel problems. Beginning in the late 1960s, the term cognitive psychology began to be used to describe the experimental psychology of how people acquire, store, manipulate, and use information (Neisser, 1967). Cognitive psychology, in short, could be said to have staked a claim to being a psychology of knowledge.

Although modern cognitive psychology derived from many sources, one can see the beginnings of a dynamic integration of perception, learning, and thinking in, for example, the early Gestalt school of psychologists (Bartlett, 1932; Koffka, 1935). For this group of psychologists, learning could not be described as the formation of associations among elements. Perception, memory, and thinking are all part of one dynamically organized system. New information is not simply added to the system; it also modifies the organization of that system. This structure in turn may distort or alter the information to fit the prevailing conditions.

The important contribution of this approach was an emphasis on organization and the idea that new and old learning have reciprocal effects on each other. On the one hand, new information alters the organization of old learning. The organization will change so as to produce the simplest and most regular new organization that can accommodate the new information. On the other hand, new information may be altered somewhat to conform to the organization into which it has introduced some change.

New information can also result in a radical restructuring, as when practicing the material suddenly produces an insight or a new understanding. In Gestalt terms, the system has been reorganized to permit problem solution. The analogy can be made to perception, in which the object of one's search may suddenly seem to "jump out" from a visual scene. Practice and new information can produce different effects depending on the tensions within the memory organization and the stability of that organization.

Gestalt psychology is not a contemporary theory, in the sense that few experiments are conducted to contrast predictions of this theory with alternative views. It would be misleading to suggest that cognitive psychology is a rebirth of the Gestalt tradition. On the other hand, many of the ideas present in contemporary memory theory were originally championed by the Gestalt school. Its emphasis on organization has become one of the major focal points in the study of memory.

Information Processing

Events outside the field of psychology also had a substantial impact on the development of a cognitive point of view. The rapid development of digital computers after World War II led many people to see an analogy between the processing of information by machines and by people. The computer is an electronic device whose fundamental unit has a relatively simple logic. By connecting these units in different ways computers are capable of acquiring, storing, and retrieving considerable amounts of information at great speeds. A description of how this is accomplished in the computer, it was thought, might be a precise way of talking about how information might be handled by human beings. By programming a computer to perform a particular task, we might discover what functions were necessary for a human being to accomplish the same thing.

Taking the computer as a model, theorists represented memory, learning, and perception as various aspects of the "processing of information." Mental processes, from this point of view, function much like a computer program. A program manipulates data in a series of stages or levels. The program selects appropriate information and then uses this information to perform a sequence of operations. This sequence is often drawn in the form of a *flow chart,* a series of boxes connected by arrows. Each box represents an operation or function performed by the computer. The arrows represent the order in which the operations are carried out. Many cognitive theorists adopted this technique to describe the sequencing of mental operations. The organization of the chart—the labels for each box and the direction of the arrows—would describe the flow of information in mental activity. We will have occasion to see examples of this approach as we proceed.

Note that this representation emphasizes the flow of time as well as the flow of information. Mental processes are not instantaneous. They take time and follow each other in an orderly way. Experiments generated within the information processing approach to cognitive psychology often manipulate time, or measure the time course of a memory performance. By measuring how much time is taken to perform different memory activities, these investigators hoped to discover how the different stages might be arranged and how one level affects others. Of course, we can never directly observe the operation of a single stage by itself. Like the Gestalt psychologists, cognitive theorists see the mind operating as an interdependent system. Memory, perception, and thought are not independent, and thus any experimental observations we make must be seen as a consequence of interactions within this single complex system.

Structure, Codes, and Levels. Information processing theorists have often distinguished between *structural components* and *control processes*. We have described analogous concepts earlier. For these theorists, the concept of a structural component is similar to the notion of a computer's "hardware"—the wiring and electronic components that are the same regardless of how the computer is used. By analogy, the structural components of human memory are the sensory register, short-term memory, and long-term memory. Each of these is considered to play a particular role in the overall functioning of the system. However, even among like-minded theorists, there is disagreement about the characteristics and defining properties of these components. They even disagree about whether it makes sense to talk about components at all.

Some theorists prefer to speak about different kinds of codes left behind by cognitive activities that differ in the depth to which the information was processed. We saw this earlier in our reference to "levels of processing" as an alternative way of viewing memory operations. Deeper processing will generally result in better memory performance because such processing permits us to establish what is unique about a particular event. The more unique the encoding of an event, the more easily it can be discriminated from other codes. Levels of processing provides a convenient framework in which to discuss the various questions about memory codes and their relationship to cognitive operations like retrieval. Although this framework is not without critics and controversy (Eysenck, 1978; Nelson, 1977), we will frequently adopt this way of talking in order to organize and clarify the theories and experiments described in the following chapters.

THE SEARCH FOR MEMORY

Having presented a variety of distinctions and conceptual possibilities, where then do we begin the study of this complex capacity of human beings called memory? We will begin first with a look at the historical development of attempts to bring this capacity under the scrutiny of experimental laboratory methods. This approach will present the basic elements of the associationist position.

Our next step will be to describe the evolution of current theories of conceptual memory as they developed from, and in reaction to, these earlier approaches. With this as a background, we will examine the analysis of memory in terms of the structural components described earlier (sensory memory, short-term memory, and long-term memory) and alternatives to this structural view. Finally, we will describe the implications of all of this work for the practical purposes of improving human learning and performance, and our understanding of certain pathologies that produce disorders of memory.

In reading this introduction, you may have suspected that these differences in orientation toward the study of memory are only verbal differences. It might appear that some positions could be converted to others simply by translation. This would be a mistake. We should not underrate the importance of differences in how one talks about remembering. Talking about things in different ways very often leads one to ask different kinds of questions, perform different kinds of experiments, and to pay attention to different aspects of a given phenomenon. While one point of view may eventually explain all the discoveries of another, some of these discoveries might not have been made had the contrasting points of view not been expressed.

We must reinforce our cautionary note about the sharp contrasts drawn to this point. Like most contrasts, these are most useful in helping one to get one's bearings before plunging into very complex questions. In practice, the divisions become easily blurred. Each theory incorporates aspects of some of the others as the result of new data and new criticism. Psychologists have not been very successful in describing modes of thought. We may have to be satisfied to say that the differences among the points of view to be described amount to differences in the feel and flavor of the theories and concepts employed. We hope that you will gain an appreciation for that metaphor from the pages of this book.

CHAPTER SUMMARY

1. *What Is Memory?*

   A. The term memory is an inclusive one that deals with our ability to acquire and retain information, to recall it when needed, and to recognize its familiarity when we see it or hear it again. Questions about the effects of experience, how they are produced, and their consequences for competence and performance have enormous importance for developmental problems, personality, education, social relationships, perception, and thought. Indeed, the subject of memory lies at the very core of modern experimental psychology.

   B. Learning to use language to categorize experience is a uniquely important human skill, and much of our total behavior is influenced by the fact that we are "linguistic animals." For this reason, early memory research concentrated heavily on acquisition and retention of verbal materials.

   C. We can distinguish between our potential competence at a particular task and our actual performance in a particular situation. This distinction might be described as a difference between what we could do under optimal conditions and what we actually do. Motivation and effort affect our performance, rather than our competence.

2. *Memory Processes*

    A. Memory processes refer to the mental activities involved in acquisition and recall. Memory structure refers to the manner of storage of the information, its duration, and its organization.

    B. The basic processes that affect performance are acquisition, retention, and retrieval. Failures of recall often result from failures in initial acquisition due to inattention or misunderstanding of the original experience. Retention refers to our ability to store information for a period of time after it has been coded. Forgetting, as the term is ordinarily used, refers to the loss of stored information due primarily to the acquisition of new, competing material. Retrieval can be described as a search process amenable to any one of a number of recall strategies. Recall is usually best when the cues used in retrieval most closely match those used in initial encoding.

    C. The mental representation of experience is called a memory code which, in turn, is heavily influenced by the conditions of acquisition.

3. *Memory Structures*

    A. Sensory memory refers to the brief retention of visual, auditory, or other sensory information in an unanalyzed form just long enough for its potential encoding. Short-term memory, on the other hand, is longer lasting than sensory memory, contains predominantly verbal rather than sensory information, and is sharply limited in the amount of information it can hold. Retention of material in short-term memory not amenable to the immediate formation of a semantic code, such as remembering a telephone number, can be maintained for a few seconds in verbal form, or longer, if maintained through verbal rehearsal.

    B. Long-term memory refers to the more permanent storage of information where material is placed in the context of related events or previously acquired concepts. The duration of this form of memory far exceeds the transient stores of sensory and short-term memory.

    C. To view the processing of information as a progression through a sequence of distinct memory stores can fail to emphasize the dynamic quality of memory. An alternative view, "levels of processing," sees a continuum from shallow to deep processing with no clear terminal points separating one form of storage from another. Rather than storage in distinct systems, this view suggests that memory codes be characterized by the degree of processing that produced them.

4. *Theoretical Approaches to Memory*

    A. Associationism was an early attempt to extend studies of animal learning and conditioning to the analysis of human learning. Contiguity in time was seen as a basic element in the formation of associations. Storage of complex information was explained by the mediation of stimulus–response (S–R) connections through whole chains of covert associations.

B. Cognitive psychology reflects Gestalt psychology's emphasis on organization in memory, rejecting the narrowness of early associationism. New information is assimilated in the context of existing systems of knowledge which can be reorganized in the light of this new information.

C. The term cognitive psychology is used to describe the experimental study of how people acquire, store, manipulate, and use information. One viewpoint within this larger perspective has drawn an analogy between human memory and the electronic computer. It stresses that both people and machines acquire, store, and retrieve considerable amounts of information at great speeds. Information processing refers to attempts to specify the sequence of mental operations involved in retention and how these operations interrelate. It distinguishes between the structural components of memory (sensory memory, short-term, and long-term memory) and the control processes which guide how they are used.

5. *The Search for Memory*

A. The variety of approaches to memory have had their greatest impact on the ways in which they have directed research in the attempt to answer different kinds of questions. These theories are different in how they conceptualize the memory process, and in their notions of what must be explained. All of these theories, however, share the common goal of understanding human memory capacities and how they are exercised.

B. Our development of memory theory will follow the early attempts to study memory associations under controlled experimental conditions, the later analyses of distinct memory structures, and current alternatives to these views. We end with some practical uses to which our understanding of memory theory can be put.

LONG-TERM MEMORY AND THE EBBINGHAUS TRADITION

CHAPTER OUTLINE

TOPIC QUESTIONS

1. Historical Background.
What theoretical ideas formed the basis for the earliest studies of memory? Who made the major contributions to the experimental development of these ideas?

2. Procedures in Verbal Learning.
What kinds of experiments were used to study how associations are acquired? What methods were used to measure the retention of associations? How are differences in the measurement of retention important to our understanding of memory?

3. Interference in Memory.
What were the two major theories first used to explain forgetting? How were studies of forgetting during sleep used to decide between these theories? Can a firm conclusion be drawn on the basis of forgetting during sleep?

4. Varieties of Interference.
What are the major kinds of interference among associations? How does the setting in which associations are learned affect the amount of interference observed?

5. Acquisition and Interference.
What are the stages involved in learning an association? What is *transfer,* and how is it involved in associative learning? What major factors determine the amount of transfer in learning an association?

Learning is a cumulative process in which future acquisitions are based on knowledge and skills acquired in the past. Learning to read and write builds on our prior mastery of language as a communicative medium, just as learning algebra presumes some knowledge of arithmetic. In this sense we rarely learn anything completely new. But how does the acquisition of one piece of information affect our retention of another? One goal of an adequate theory of memory must be to specify how memories interact.

There are three logically distinct stages in the learning process when memory interaction might occur: (1) during initial acquisition of the information, (2) during storage and retention of the information over time, and (3) during retrieval when the information is reactivated to produce some appropriate response.

Over the years, numerous investigators developed a series of standard tasks and a sophisticated methodology to disentangle the various components of the memory process in an attempt to understand this interaction. The subject of remembering and forgetting is so vast that one can only hope to touch on the landmarks of this very large literature. The beginnings of this literature can be traced to the development of the "associationist" tradition of British philosophy and its adaptation into the first systematic studies of memory. These studies were conducted by the German psychologist Hermann Ebbinghaus (1850–1909).

HISTORICAL BACKGROUND
The British Associationists

The group of philosophers usually classified as associationists (e.g., Locke, Berkeley, Hume, James Mill, and John Stuart Mill) differed considerably among themselves both in some particulars and in many of their basic assumptions. We can, however, attempt to broadly sketch those major aspects of their views which had important collective influence on the later study of learning and memory.

First, the majority of these philosophers argued for a theory of knowledge called "empiricism." The content and organization of mental life was thought to be derived entirely from experience and one's reflection on that experience. The structural element of mental life was the sensation. Sensations were linked together by the laws of association of which the most important was contiguity. Sensations which were experienced close together in time, or contiguously, would become associated. For example, the "idea" of an apple might be composed of the sensations of "redness" and "roundness" that became associated as a result of their contiguous occurrence.

While contiguity in time would determine which sensations would become associated, two additional factors would determine the strength of these associations: (1) the frequency with which the sensations occurred together; and (2) the vividness of these sensations. The complexity of any idea was simply the result of the addition of elements to form larger numbers of interconnected associations.

While this use of the terms "idea" and "sensation" may seem alien to the modern reader, the impact of the associationists' strategy of explanation had a lasting effect on psychology. The doctrine of empiricism led to the elevation of learning and memory to one of the major topics of interest in the newly developing science of mental life. The elementalism of their theories had its counterpart in later theories in which the elements were stimuli and responses (S and R). The association of sensations gave way to the association of S and R. The variables of practice and stimulus intensity (or salience) replaced frequency and vividness. This tradition seemed to dictate both the problems and the mode of solution for theories of memory for almost a century. The full history of the associationist movement is a long and interesting one and the interested reader can find excellent accounts in Boring (1950) or in Anderson and Bower (1973). The earliest experimental fruits of their thinking were the investigations of Hermann Ebbinghaus, to which we now turn.

Ebbinghaus and the Nonsense Syllable

Ebbinghaus, working in the latter part of the nineteenth century, had the opportunity to study the associationist movement during his postdoctoral studies in England. It seemed to him that the time was right to explore these notions of memory with the exact methods of experimental science. Ebbinghaus intentionally chose to concentrate on memory in its "pure" form. Since memory, in the associationists' view, was simply a complex web of associations, Ebbinghaus sought to objectify and measure that basic unit, the single association, in an experimental situation. Using himself as his only subject, he attempted to chart the course of the acquisition of associations and their loss through normal forgetting.

In order to achieve his goal, Ebbinghaus required experimental materials ("ideas") which were not already associated to other ideas or to each other. To this end, he created the so-called *nonsense syllable*, a meaningless consonant–vowel–consonant (CVC) combination, such as DAX, NEB, or ZIL. A description of how associations among these items were acquired would then be a description of the most elementary form of learning from which all other memory phenomena might be derived.

In Ebbinghaus' original experiments, he would read aloud to himself a list of a dozen or so CVCs (to the beat of a metronome), and then try to recall as much of the list as he could. He measured ease of learning by the number of times he had to repeat this process until the complete list could be recalled without error. He measured the degree of retention by the savings in the number of trials needed to relearn the materials at a later time.

From these studies Ebbinghaus was able to produce his classic "forgetting curve" showing the progressive loss of retention over a period ranging from 20 minutes to 31 days. Figure 2-1 shows his results for learning lists of 13 CVCs, with retention measured by the "savings"

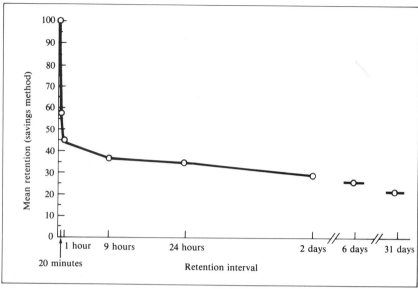

FIGURE 2-1　Rate of forgetting of lists of nonsense syllables over a 31 day period as obtained by Ebbinghaus (1885). Retention score determined by the savings method, which bases degree of retention on the number of trials required to relearn the lists after various intervals.

method: the number of trials required for relearning as a percentage of the number required to learn them initially.

What causes this forgetting? How does the learning and retention of nonsense syllables relate to learning and retention of conceptually meaningful materials, such as pictures or stories? Ebbinghaus intentionally chose to concentrate on meaningless material with the dual motives of studying retention in its ''pure'' form, and in showing that at least some forms of memory could be made amenable to objective test and controlled experiment.

While it is not correct to assume that all CVC nonsense syllables are uniformly unrelated, either to each other or to our everyday language patterns, Ebbinghaus was nevertheless successful in producing results and methods that continued to occupy the attention of psychologists for decades to come (Ebbinghaus, 1885). His studies of rates of learning and rates of forgetting and the way he formulated theoretical and empirical issues left an indelible imprint on how these problems were posed and studied for the next 75 years. In particular, verbal learning research after Ebbinghaus enthusiastically adopted the analytical notion that our study of associations should begin with the most elemental of memories.

PROCEDURES IN VERBAL LEARNING

The fledgling science of memory of the 1930s and 1940s saw in Ebbinghaus' approach a promising way to explore human learning and memory. It was not long before countless experiments were being performed to study rote memorization of words, nonsense syllables, strings of digits, and often, whole sentences or prose passages. The approach, following this tradition, continued to be associative in nature. What came to be called the field of *verbal learning* concentrated almost exclusively on learned associations between small sets of verbal elements.

Methods of Learning

Studies of verbal learning began to concentrate on two general learning tasks as prototypes of the acquisition and retention of verbal associations. While admittedly artificial, the hope was that they would apply in principle to real-world learning. These two learning tasks were *serial learning* and *paired-associate learning*. Both these tasks, as techniques for the study of associations, were introduced at the turn of the century; serial learning by Ebbinghaus (1885) and paired-associate learning by Calkins (1894). It is true that the specific procedures used and the methods of testing have gone through a variety of changes since that time. But the data from these two tasks remain the central phenomena for verbal learning almost 100 years after their study was begun.

Serial Learning. The method used by Ebbinghaus, which was described earlier, is called the method of *serial reproduction* or *serial recall*. An entire sequence of items was read at a constant rate in time to the beat of a metronome. Once he thought the list had been mastered, Ebbinghaus would attempt to reproduce all the items in the series in their correct order. If an error occurred in this reproduction, he returned to the controlled study of the original items and repeated this cycle of study and test until the list could be accurately recited. The measure of learning used most often for this method was the total time necessary to learn a list in the correct order to a criterion of one perfect reproduction.

Over the years, the serial reproduction method was largely replaced in the study of verbal learning by the *serial anticipation method*. In this paradigm, each item in a serial list is presented successively for a controlled duration. As each item is presented, the subject is required to anticipate the next list item. In this case, learning is measured by the number of trials necessary before the list is mastered, or the number of errors of anticipation that occur for each item in the list before mastery is attained.

The most familiar and often studied phenomenon of serial learning is the *serial position effect* illustrated in Figure 2-2. This graph, taken from Hovland (1938), shows the distribution of errors of anticipation across different parts of a serial list. Notice, first of all, that the serial position curve of errors is bowed. In the course of learning a list by the anticipation method, more errors are made in the middle of the list than at either the beginning or the end. The advantage for items in the beginning of the list is called a *primacy effect*, while the advantage for terminal items is called a *recency effect*. Second, the curve is asymmetrical; more errors are made at the end of the list than at the beginning.

While our illustration is of serial position effects obtained with the serial anticipation method, the phenomenon is quite general and occurs in the serial recall of lists as well. The same error distribution, in fact,

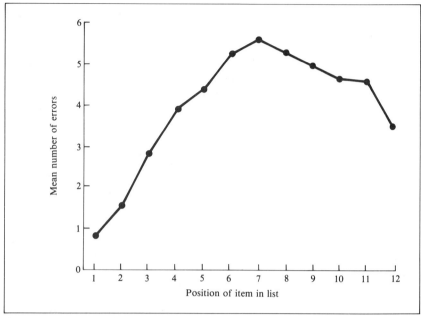

FIGURE 2-2   The Serial Position Effect: The average number of errors across serial positions for 12 nonsense syllables presented at a rate of one every two seconds, and learned to a criterion of seven correct ''anticipations'' on a single trial. (Adapted from Hovland, 1938.)

often occurs in spelling mistakes (Jensen, 1962), and in the retention of information from lectures (Holen & Oaster, 1976). Errors of spelling are more frequent for letters from the middle of a word, while errors on examinations following a lecture are more frequent for material from the middle of the presentation than on information presented at the beginning or the end.

The occurrence of serial position effects in all situations involving serial learning and the stability of this pattern across types of material and modes of presentation has made the explanation of this phenomenon one of the important theoretical problems in verbal learning. In addition, serial position effects, generated by the serial recall method, have been central to the arguments of information processing theorists. We will have several occasions to return to this phenomenon of serial learning in our discussion of memory and forgetting.

Paired-Associate Learning.   The second major learning task investigated by students of verbal learning involved learning an association between pairs of items, usually words, nonsense syllables, or numbers. In the associative tradition, the first member of the pair was referred to as the *stimulus* and the second member as the *response*. The two most common procedures used in paired-associate learning were the *study–test method* and the *method of anticipation*.

In the anticipation method, as each stimulus term is presented, the subject must try to remember, or "anticipate," the correct response term before it appears. In these studies the stimulus terms may occur in any order since only the individual associations between members of a pair are of interest. In the study–test method, subjects are exposed to all the pairs in the stimulus–response sets. After a study interval, retention of the association is tested by presenting the stimulus terms alone and requiring recall or recognition of the response. Again, stimulus terms are presented in random order during testing.

The early students of paired-associate (both study–test and anticipation) and of serial learning tasks assumed that subjects learned similar associations in the two situations. That is, learning of a serial list consisted of forming an association between the first and the second item, between the second and the third item, and so forth, just as individual associations were formed in paired-associate learning. If this were true, we would expect that learning a paired-associate list would be relatively easy after learning a serial list of the same items in the same order. For example, assume that a subject learns a serial list of the items PENCIL-TOOTH-BOOK-TYPE-GLASS. . . , and then learns a paired-associate list consisting of the pairs PENCIL-TOOTH, BOOK-TYPE, and so forth. If these tasks in fact represent the same types of learning, then the associations to be acquired in the paired-associate learning would be the identical associations that had already been formed during the serial learning task. Serial learning of these items in this particular order should, then, make paired-associate learning easier than would serial learning of a list unrelated to these pairs.

Although this parallel between serial and paired-associate learning is appealing, it is apparently wrong. Investigations of the effects of serial learning on later paired-associate learning have failed to find the facilitating effects we just described (Young, 1968). The associative strategies involved in these two tasks are apparently sufficiently dissimilar so that little of what is learned involves common associations. Thus there seems to be something very special about the circumstances under which a stimulus is learned to the way it will be retained. This issue reappears in a variety of guises and forms throughout the history of the experimental study of memory.

Measures of Retention

The retention of a list or an association may be measured in a variety of ways. Three basic measures, each of which have many variations, have been most commonly used. These measures are *recall*, *savings*, and *recognition*.

Recall.   As in the *serial recall* method first described by Ebbinghaus, a subject may be asked to recall in order the items of a list learned some time previous to the test. Here the subject must provide not only the items, but the correct temporal relationships between them. Alternatively, we might ask for *free recall* in which the order of the items in recall is unrestricted. Finally, we may use some variation of *cued recall* in which the subject is given some clue and is asked to respond with the appropriate information. In one variant of this method, *probed recall*, the subject is given an item from a serial list and is required to give the next item that occurred in that list. Each of these methods, as we shall see, is useful for asking different kinds of questions and can be informative about different aspects of memory acquisition, storage, and retrieval.

Savings.   An alternative test of retention is to ask the subject to relearn a list after some time has elapsed. Memory that is insufficient to permit recall may, nonetheless, permit the same material to be learned more easily the second time around. You may recall that this was, in fact, the measure of retention used by Ebbinghaus.

This method, called the *savings measure*, is usually expressed as a *savings score* based on the difference between the time or trials required for initial learning and the time, or trials required to relearn the same material on a later occasion. The savings score is calculated from the formula:

$$\text{SAVINGS} = \frac{\text{(trials for original learning)} - \text{(trials for relearning)}}{\text{(trials for original learning)}} \times 100$$

Consider, for example, a subject who required 12 trials to initially learn a list of several paired-associates. Some 3 weeks later the same subject required only three trials to relearn the same list. The subject's savings score would be $\frac{(12 - 3)}{12} \times 100$, or 75%, of the original 12 trials. In other words, the savings score is simply the advantage in number of trials expressed as a percentage of the number of original learning trials.

Recognition.   A final method of measuring retention, *recognition* testing, resembles the familiar multiple-choice examination. It is often our experience that we can fail to produce a correct answer when required to recall some information, but we nevertheless have little difficulty in recognizing the correct answer when we see it.

Two basic recognition procedures have been commonly used. In the first, the subject is presented with a series of items one at a time and is asked to indicate, for each item, whether it is "old" (from the previously learned item set) or "new" (items not in the previously learned set). The second recognition procedure requires that the subject be presented with several alternatives at once. The correct items, those which appeared in the learning set, must be distinguished from the "foils," or "distractors," which did not occur in this set. Each of these methods, again, is useful for asking particular kinds of questions about memory performance. For example, the multiple-choice recognition method permits us to ask questions about how well the subject can discriminate previously learned items from similar looking distractors which are not correct.

The object of all of these procedures, whether serial or paired-associate learning using savings, recall, or recognition testing, was, of course, the same. The goal was to detect and measure the residue in memory of prior learning and to determine how this prior learning is represented. Much of the data and many of the issues dealing with serial and paired-associate learning became classic in the study of verbal learning, and many are still being researched. Kausler (1974), among others, offers a scholarly and exhaustive survey of this enormous literature.

For example, in addition to asking questions about the subject's memory for order, items, and the relationships among them, we can also ask for judgements about the *recency* of an item (how long ago did this item occur?), the *frequency* of its occurrence (how often did this item appear in the list?), the *spacing* between previous occurrences of an item, or the *modality* of presentation (was the item printed in green or blue?). In each case we obtain different information about the amount and quality of information that resides in memory as a result of prior learning.

Considerable research reinforces our own experience that not all retention measures are equally sensitive in detecting the effects of past experience. We have already mentioned that the savings score may reflect an effect of previous learning where recall scores may show none. Recognition procedures are also more sensitive than recall under most conditions. Students of memory were quick to recognize that the differences among these measures were important to our understanding of how the memory system works.

Recall versus Recognition

How many times have you walked into a party, a supermarket, or a public library and have seen someone you clearly recognize? You know you have seen them before, but where, when, and who they are totally eludes you. You just cannot recall. This has happened to all of us, and we all know how foolish we feel when they remind us who they are and how we met. As we have said, not all tests of memory are equally effective.

Figure 2-3 shows an idealized graph of the comparative results typically obtained when all three measures of retention are used to chart the time course of forgetting for meaningless material. Such results, originally reported by Luh (1922) and verified many times since (Postman & Rau, 1957), illustrate the generalization that recognition memory produces the highest retention scores, free recall the lowest, and relearning somewhere in between.

While this "law of retention" became treated as common knowledge in textbooks over the decades, it is not without important qualification. First, the raw data of such retention scores are in fact quite difficult to compare. Can one, as Crowder (1976, p. 371) asks, actually compare a 50% savings score in relearning with, for example, a score of 6 out of 10

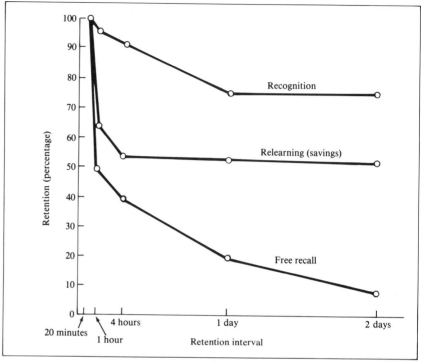

FIGURE 2-3   Retention curves for nonsense syllables over a two-day period as measured by the methods of recognition, savings, and free recall. (From Luh, 1922.)

items correct in free recall? The absolute comparison is in fact difficult to make.

A second qualification is the finding that learning strategies are important to the relative effectiveness of recognition and recall tests. Subjects who know that they will be tested later either by recall or by recognition will do significantly better if actually tested with the expected method than if surprised by testing with the other method. A subject expecting recognition, but tested by the recall method could, in principle, do poorer than a subject expecting a test in free recall and actually tested by that mode (Tversky, 1973).

The Superiority of Recognition Memory.   Under certain circumstances, recognition memory can often produce phenomenal results. In one well-known case, Shepard (1967) gave subjects 540 words in rapid sequence and later presented them for recognition along with a set of distractor items not present in the original list. Each recognition test presented only two words at a time. One of the words had been present in the original list and the other had not. The subject's task was to indicate which of the two was the ''old'' item.

Shepard recorded an astonishing average of 88% correct, or 475 words correctly recognized after a single exposure! Using the same procedure for a list of 612 sentences also produced recognition scores as high as 89% correct. Two subjects who had been presented with a list of 1224 sentences were able to attain recognition scores of no less than 88% correct. This would be equivalent in free recall to recalling some 1077 sentences.

To understand these dramatic results it is important to note that Shepard's testing procedure was specifically designed to produce maximum performance. The features of the design that produced maximum performance also illuminate several features of recognition memory in general.

1. Recognition usually produces higher scores than recall because it restricts the size of the set of alternatives from which the correct response must be drawn. That is, reducing the number of possible incorrect alternatives automatically increases the likelihood of a correct response. If you have to guess on a multiple-choice exam, your chances are better if there are few alternatives. The greater the number of alternatives the more likely you will be to guess wrong. Davis, Sutherland, and Judd (1961) illustrated this point by showing that when a set of alternatives is limited (e.g., only the digits 0 to 9) recognition and recall can be equal. Only when the range of possible alternatives is large (e.g., all two digit numbers) does one obtain the usual superiority of recognition over recall scores.

2. The recognition procedure allows for correct judgements on the basis of partial recall. You may not remember enough on an exam question to recall the answer, but you may remember enough to distinguish incorrect alternatives from correct ones (see Hollingsworth, 1913, and McNulty, 1965, for corroborative evidence).

3. A final factor influencing performance in the recognition task is the similarity between the learned stimulus and the other members of the test set. If the incorrect items are very different from the correct alternatives, one can easily produce high recognition scores. On the other hand, making all of the incorrect alternatives very similar to the test items can actually reverse the usual superiority of recognition over recall. Such results can be found in studies where the similarity between stimuli and distractor items are systematically varied (Bahrick & Bahrick, 1964; Underwood, 1965; Anisfeld & Knapp, 1968). On a multiple-choice test in which the student is asked to discriminate among very fine nuances of meaning, choosing the correct alternative can be very difficult indeed.

Threshold versus Two-Stage Processes.   Many theorists saw recognition and recall as nothing more or less than two ways of measuring the same process. Recognition, for the reasons described, is simply "easier." This interpretation can be called a *threshold* explanation of recall versus recognition. This model assumes that different memories have different strengths and that only stronger memories will exceed a certain threshold and thus be accessible for free recall. Weaker memories may still be present in the memory trace, but they are below this threshold of accessibility. Recognition is a low threshold process (it is capable of detecting even the weakest of memories), while free recall is a high threshold process.

Other theorists have proposed that recognition and recall tests may in fact tap two different processes. In free recall, subjects must first mentally generate a list of potential responses. Once this is done they then scan this mental representation to determine which of these potential responses are the appropriate ones for the particular task. This can be referred to as a *two-stage model* of recall. It argues that since the recognition test already supplies the possible alternatives to the subject, the initial step of generating them is eliminated. Hence, recognition scores are typically higher than recall scores because recognition requires one process while recall requires two.

It may at first seem that it would be impossible to distinguish between these two very reasonable possibilities. Both nicely predict the superiority of recognition tests over recall as usually obtained. Crowder (1976, p. 378), however, points to a critical distinction. A threshold explanation of recognition versus recall would logically imply that anything which influences recognition scores should also influence recall in a similar way since both are presumed to be measures of the same process. Sufficient experimental data bearing on this issue are available for Crowder to argue that while the two-stage model still has its critics, the original threshold explanation has been almost totally discredited. Two separate lines of evidence should make this clear.

Numerous studies of verbal learning have shown a fairly consistent effect of *word-frequency* on recall performance. Using a common word count, such as that prepared by Thorndike and Lorge (1944), it is possible to give subjects lists of words whose relative frequency of occurrence in the language is known. Recall for common words is typically superior to recall for rare ones (Bousfield & Cohen, 1955; Deese, 1961; Hall, 1954). The effect of word-frequency on recognition performance, however, is just the opposite. When Shepard (1967) examined the effect of word-frequency in the study we previously cited, he found better recognition scores for rare words than for common ones. These separate findings have been verified within a single experiment by Kinsbourne and George (1974).

The second example of a differential effect of a single factor on recognition versus recall performance comes from studies of *incidental learning*. Incidental learning is defined as learning which occurs without any conscious intention on the part of the subject under circumstances where he or she does not expect to be later tested for retention. It is generally known that subjects will do better in recall when they know they will be tested than when they do not.

Eagle and Leiter (1964) gave three groups of subjects a 36-word list. One group, the intentional learning group, was given the word list and told to remember it for subsequent testing. A second group, the incidental learning group, was simply asked to classify the 36 words as parts of speech. No mention was made of the fact that they would later be tested on their memory for the words. (The third group was a control group which was required to both classify the words and to remember them for later testing.) All three groups were later tested for free recall of the lists and then given a four-choice recognition test. In this latter case the subjects were simply to say which of the four words had been in the previous list.

Of main interest are the results for the two experimental groups. On the recall test the intentional group performed better than the incidental group. On the recognition test, however, the incidental group was actually superior to the intentional learning group. While these results are quite fascinating in themselves, the important point in the present context is the clear reversal of the effects of intention on recognition versus recall. These results could be consistent with a two-stage process since one could, in principle, influence one stage or the other independently. This lack of correlation between retention measures, however, is not consistent with the single-process threshold model.

Again, we find that any single method used alone seemed to yield a different picture of how memory works. As you have seen from our examples, recognition testing led to extraordinarily good performance, while recall seemed to show relatively rapid forgetting. Recall of familiar words was easier than recall of unfamiliar words, while recognition scores showed the opposite. Recognition yielded evidence for learning without conscious intention, while recall was more dependent on a conscious effort to memorize.

Recall and recognition, then, came to be regarded by many as not being equivalent methods for answering the same questions. In fact, the differences between the two measures of retention remain a central focus of contention among memory theorists (Anderson & Bower, 1972, 1974; Tulving, 1968a; Watkins & Tulving, 1975). We will return to this difference in our discussions of associative theories of forgetting and in our treatment of information processing views of memory retrieval. It is important at this point, however, to be aware that the methods used to examine memory may determine one's views of what memory is and one's ideas of what must be explained.

INTERFERENCE IN MEMORY

In Figure 2-1 we got our first look at Ebbinghaus' classic memory decay curve which shows a progressive memory loss over a period ranging from 20 minutes to 31 days. Very simply, memory for nonconceptual material (or unconnected facts or rote-memorized formulas) appears to steadily decay with the passage of time. One of the oldest questions in memory theory has addressed just this issue. What is it that causes this loss of information over time: is it the spontaneous erosion of our memories over time, or is it interference from other experiences which

Interference in Memory: A famous ichthyologist who claimed that every time he learned the name of a new student he forgot the name of a fish.

occur during this passage of time? That is, do memories simply decay autonomously, or does the new displace the old?

In this connection, we are reminded of Ceraso's (1967) anecdote about a professor of ichthyology who claimed that every time he learned the name of a new student, he forgot the name of a fish. Ceraso's point, of course, is that forgetting occurs over the passage of time because of new memories which displace or *interfere* with the earlier ones.

Decay versus Interference

The notion that memories fade with the passage of time is as old as the scientific study of learning itself. Thorndike (1911), for example, formulated the principle in a way consistent with his associationist views. Briefly, Thorndike saw all learning as the formation and strengthening of stimulus–response bonds through practice (the "law of exercise"). The more the bond is practiced, the stronger it becomes, and the greater its resistance to weakening with time will be. His "law of disuse" was equally simple. If a bond is not practiced it will gradually decrease in strength and finally be lost completely.

The notion of memory "fading" with the passage of time has sufficient intuitive appeal to have kept the idea alive in the literature in various forms (cf. Brown, 1958; Broadbent, 1958). We must be clear, however, that none of these theorists would propose that it is the passage of time itself that has an effect. This would be no more true than to say that "time" causes our bodies to age. There are known (and some unknown) biological processes which cause the body to age and to produce the effects we observe. In theory, as well as in science fiction, arresting these bodily processes would keep us young forever.

As research on aging must specify those processes which operate over the course of time, so psychological theory must determine the nature of the events during a retention interval which produce forgetting. There are two major alternatives.

Spontaneous Memory Decay. One possibility is that there are processes in the nervous system which cause unrehearsed memory representations to passively deteriorate over time, independent of the type of information stored, or the effects of other learning. Such memories would gradually fade, much as the page of a newspaper would gradually fade if left for a long period in the bright sun. The newsprint becomes less and less distinct as the result of chemical decomposition produced by the sun's energy. The amount of fading—the rate of deterioration—will of course be independent of what is written on the newspaper. In a similar way, the *spontaneous decay* theory sees memory loss as the result of an autonomous time-dependent process which runs its course independent of the nature of the information acquired, and independent of other experience.

Interference Theory. The major alternative to spontaneous decay theory, and the one currently given the most credibility, can be referred to as an *interference theory* of memory: forgetting is the direct result of the negative influence of other learning. Time is relevant only to the extent that it allows the opportunity for new (interfering) learning to occur, or time for interference from old learning to take its full effect. The anecdote about the forgetful ichthyologist is essentially a parable of interference theory.

According to the interference hypothesis, forgetting is not independent of what has been learned. What you learn prior to and after any given piece of information will determine how you will remember that information. Without other learning, no forgetting would occur.

And So to Sleep

While the distinction between the hypotheses of interference versus decay may seem clear in principle, in practice they prove very hard to separate. Short of placing a person in suspended animation there is really no way to prevent an individual from having experiences that might interfere with retention. That is, we cannot directly observe the predicted effects of decay in the absence of all possible interfering effects. The longer the retention interval between learning and testing, the more likely it will be for the person to encounter potentially interfering events. It would not be possible to determine whether the forgetting over the retention interval was due to decay processes or interference processes because we cannot selectively eliminate one and leave the other.

Lower Animal Research.   Although people cannot be put into suspended animation to test these two hypotheses, numerous attempts were made to approach the problem of interference-free time with lower animals. Some studies used drugs to anesthetize creatures such as bees and rats between learning and testing (Plath, 1924; Russell & Hunter, 1937), while others lowered the ambient temperature of cold-blooded creatures such as ants (Hoagland, 1931) or goldfish (French, 1942). Both attempts were intended to reduce activity (interference) during the retention interval to see the effects on forgetting.

Unfortunately, the results of these and other studies remained ambiguous and were hardly a triumph for either theory. One interpretive problem, of course, was the unknown effect such fundamental changes in the animals' biological states might have had on their performance. An animal who has forgotten a response will fail to respond, but so too will a poor creature who is half-dead.

Tenacity was finally rewarded when Minimi and Dallenbach (1946) conditioned photophobic cockroaches to avoid a dark area in their cage by shocking them whenever they approached it. Following this training, the roaches were either allowed normal activity for various retention intervals, or else were immobilized by confining them in a tiny, tissue-paper lined box. Thus immobilized, it was argued, they would be protected from the "interference" of normal activity. Figure 2-4 (A) shows

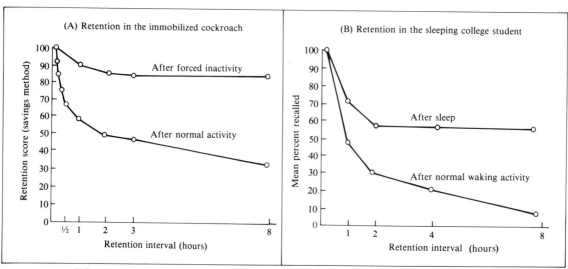

FIGURE 2-4   The interference theory of forgetting. Left-hand panel (A) shows data taken from Minimi and Dallenbach (1946) who compared retention of an avoidance task over an 8-hour period for cockroaches either allowed normal activity or physically immobilized for similar retention intervals. Right-hand panel (B) shows data based on Jenkins and Dallenbach (1924) who measured retention of CVCs for college students over an 8-hour period of either sleep or normal waking activity.

their results. For intervals of up to 8 hours, the immobilized insects showed greater retention of the avoidance response than the group allowed normal activity during the same period. The interference hypothesis, at least for cockroaches, seemed favored by the results.

The Jenkins and Dallenbach Experiment.   Forgetting in cockroaches, of course, may be quite different than forgetting in human beings. While we cannot put people into tissue lined boxes to prevent interference, we might provide a comparable situation by presenting the learning material just before the human subject goes to sleep. On the assumption that sleeping represents minimal possibilities for interfering experience, a subject who slept during the retention interval should remember the information more accurately upon waking than another subject who spent the retention interval awake and active.

Figure 2-4 (B) shows retention curves for two college students who had memorized CVCs and were then tested either after 1–8 hours of normal daily activity, or after 1–8 hours of sleep. These results, taken from Jenkins and Dallenbach (1924), were seen as a direct test of the interference hypothesis. The time period involved was the same. The difference, they argued, was in the likelihood of external interference from new learning.

The results demonstrate what one would expect from an interference hypothesis. While the waking (interference) group shows a progressive decrease in ability to recall the materials, the sleep group shows only a small loss over the first 2 hours of the sleep period, followed by virtually no additional loss from that point on. Indeed, it might be argued that the subjects were not fully asleep during this first 2-hour period, and that interfering events during this time period produced this slight degree of loss. Seeing these results, Jenkins and Dallenbach (1924) concluded:

> Forgetting is not so much a matter of decay of old impressions and associations as it is a matter of the interference, inhibition, or obliteration of the old by the new. (p. 612)

Jenkins and Dallenbach's finding that retention is better following an interval of sleep than following an equivalent interval of waking activity is well established. These basic results have been replicated by many other studies (Ekstrand, 1967; Barrett & Ekstrand, 1972; Dillon, 1970). Several points require emphasis, however. First, we must recognize that the nature of mental activity during sleep remains a relatively unknown topic. The available evidence suggests that little, if any, learning takes place during deep to light sleep (Simon & Emmons, 1956). This is consistent with the notion that sleep would represent retention uncomplicated by interfering events. On the other hand, sleeping subjects are not in a state of mental "suspended animation." For example, dream activity might introduce interference (although the good recall after sleep suggests that this is not the case), or, alternatively, dream activity might include rehearsal of the material which kept the trace alive. This feature of the problem has yet to be resolved, but several experiments have begun to ask the relevant questions regarding the potential role of dream activity during the retention intervals in sleep studies (e.g., Empson & Clarke, 1970; Ekstrand, 1972).

A second qualification concerns another possible explanation of the "sleep effect." While sleep does appear to represent a period of minimal external interference, it also represents a particular time of day; that is, a particular point in our cycle of activity. We know that the nervous system varies regularly in its *state of arousal* or responsiveness over a day, and that changes in this state of arousal affect a variety of mental processes (e.g., the speed of reaction in a simple perceptual task). Therefore, the memory preserving effects observed by Jenkins and Dallenbach and others may have been due to the characteristics of the nervous system during this part of the arousal cycle (at night) rather than to sleep itself. Of course this can be checked by having subjects sleep during a retention interval positioned at different times of the day.

Hockey, Davis, and Gray (1972) performed just this kind of study. They had subjects memorize a set of materials in the evening and then tested them for retention 5 hours later. One group of subjects slept during this retention interval, another group remained awake. Two other groups learned the materials in the morning and were also tested 5 hours later. One of these slept during this daytime retention interval while the other remained awake. Hockey, Davis, and Gray found that less was forgotten during the nightime retention interval whether or not subjects were awake. That is, the time of day of the retention interval seemed to be more important in determining the rate of forgetting than was sleep.

The issue, however, is still not closed, even at the time of this writing. Many other investigators would still be unwilling to attribute Jenkins and Dallenbach's findings solely to time-of-day effects (cf., Benson & Feinberg, 1977). As we shall see in more detail in Chapter 9, time of day, level of arousal, and memory performance do relate in interesting ways. The point we wish to make here is that the Jenkins and Dallenbach study, though it certainly discouraged interest in the concept of decay, is not unambiguous evidence for a simple interference theory of forgetting. Their study, followed by its contemporary ramifications, does add another layer of complexity to our theories of remembering.

A third feature is no less important. This is not so much a criticism of the early sleep studies, as a reminder that they represent a very limited type of learning. That is, the results of Jenkins and Dallenbach relate to simple associative learning for meaningless CVCs, in the Ebbinghaus tradition. They may have limited applicability to memory for conceptually meaningful material. Indeed, the results one gets depend heavily on the type of learning materials employed. Meaningful materials generally show much less loss, whether the retention interval is occupied by sleep or by normal waking activity (Newman, 1939). One of the complicating factors preventing an easy resolution to the question of dream activity during the retention interval is the suggestion that dream activity may favor retention of meaningful material but not rote learning of nonsense material (Stones, 1974, cited by Baddeley, 1976, p. 62).

The Status of Decay Theory

The forgetting curves for cockroaches learning a shock avoidance task and humans learning CVC associations should emphasize the limited ground on which the decay versus interference question has been asked. As we shall see in a later chapter, conceptual memory presents an entirely different picture. For example, we may forget the details of a story or a film over an 8-hour period of interference, but we will be less likely to forget the general plot line or its semantic content. Similarly, forgetting that the word "cloud" was on a word list learned in an experiment does not imply that we have forgotten what a cloud is.

Within this limited framework, however, decay theory was dealt a resounding blow by the Jenkins and Dallenbach study, and one from which it was never able to fully recover. The fact that time is important to forgetting cannot be denied. McGeoch (1932), one of the earliest proponents of modern interference theory, likened the role of time in forgetting to the role of time in "causing" rust on a steel girder. Rust is caused by an active chemical process (oxidation) that simply requires time to occur. The passage of time itself, however, is not the cause. In a similar way, the interference theory saw forgetting as an active process in which other learning activity interferes with information storage over time. Time is involved, but not as a causal factor.

With the notion of autonomous decay processes generally discredited as an explanation for forgetting from long-term memory, interference theory in one form or another became the dominant view guiding research on forgetting. Psychologists were to attack the question on two fronts. First, they wished to determine the conditions under which interference occurred and to examine the influence of the learning materials themselves on the forgetting process. Second, they made a direct attempt to understand *how* interference operated in the forgetting process. It is to the first of these two questions that we now turn.

VARIETIES OF INTERFERENCE

The essence of interference is the presumed detrimental effect of learning similar or related material. Our anecdote about the forgetful ichthyologist illustrates one type of interference. This is the detrimental effect of new learning on the recall of older learning. This is called *retroactive interference* (RI). The second type of interference is the detrimental effect of previous learning on retention of more recently learned material. This is called *proactive interference* (PI).

The RI Paradigm

Early studies of interference emphasized the RI effect because it is the most obvious and easily measured form of interference. All of us are familiar with the detrimental effects of RI. The first few lectures in a history course, for example, may seem crystal clear, and their content easily retained in memory. As the lectures and readings progress, however, the number of characters, dates, countries, and events begin to increase. As these associations enlarge, so the recall of that earlier material seems to become nearly impossible.

Controlled laboratory studies using verbal learning techniques have confirmed what may be your own intuitions about RI. First, the more similar the new materials are to those previously learned, the greater will be the RI effect when we attempt to recall the earlier material. Second, the more practice the new material receives relative to the old, the greater will be the RI effect. Finally, the effects of RI will be diminished the more rehearsal given to the original material (Slamecka, 1960).

Real-life forgetting is seldom simple, and the ability to study RI effects in everyday forgetting is difficult. We ordinarily have little control over the previously mentioned variables of how much new material has been acquired since the original material was learned, or the relative amounts of practice given to the old versus the new learning. Let us examine how the previously described verbal learning techniques can be used in this study.

Here is a typical experiment to study the effects of RI. First, the subject learns a list of ten paired-associate terms, through the anticipation method. The paired-associate sets might be CVC-word pairs, such as DAX–quickly, ZIL–happy, YOV–trouble, etc. By convention, the first such list is called an A–B list; the subject must learn to associate each stimulus term A with its paired-associate response B. This A–B list will represent the ''old'' learning in this paradigm. The A–B list would ordinarily be practiced to the point where the subject is able to give the appropriate response as each of the stimulus items is presented alone.

To represent the ''new'' learning, the same subject is later required to study a second list of paired-associates composed of the same stimulus terms, but different response items. If the first three paired-associates of the A–B list were, as above, DAX–quickly, ZIL–happy, YOV–trouble, the second list of pairs might begin with DAX–soldier, ZIL–traffic, YOV–heavy. By convention, the second list is referred to as the A–C list, denoting the same stimulus terms as the first list, but with new response terms.

A typical RI experiment requires two groups of subjects as illustrated in Table 2-1 (top). The Experimental (RI) group learns the A–B list, and then the A–C list. After a predetermined retention interval, this group is then asked to recall the A–B list. Typically, the A terms are supplied, and the subject must give the associated B terms.

The performance of the experimental (RI) group is compared with that of a control group of subjects who learn the A–B list only. Instead of learning the A–C list, this group simply waits, or engages in some irrelevant activity for the same duration, and then attempts to recall the A–B list. The scores of the control group in recalling the A–B list tells us

TABLE 2-1 Diagram of procedures for the study of retroactive interference (top panel) and proactive interference (lower panel). The paradigms are illustrated for paired-associate learning.

Retroactive Interference (RI)				
Experimental (RI) Group	Learn List 1 (A–B)	Learn List 2 (A–C)	Retention Interval	Recall List 1
Control Group	Learn List 1 (A–B)	— —	Retention Interval	Recall List 1
Proactive Interference (PI)				
Experimental (PI) Group	Learn List 1 (A–B)	Learn List 2 (A–B)	Retention Interval	Recall List 2
Control Group	— —	Learn List 2 (A–C)	Retention Interval	Recall List 2

the level of performance expected in the absence of directly related interfering material.

The degree of RI produced by the second list is measured by comparing performance of the experimental group with performance of the control group during the test stage of the experiment. This would be calculated as:

$$RI = \frac{\% \text{ correct for control group} - \% \text{ correct for experimental group}}{\% \text{ correct for control group}}$$

For example, if the control group recalled 80% of the A–B items after the retention interval, while the experimental group recalled only 60%, the calculated degree of RI would be RI = (80 − 60) / 80, or 25%. Note, in this case, that there was some retention loss also suffered by the control group. The RI paradigm does not eliminate all potential sources of interference. Rather, it merely guarantees that any loss suffered by the control group was not due to RI produced by the A–C list.

We will later see examples of this paradigm used in actual experiments, and specific results obtained. Remember at this point that we should expect to see significantly poorer performance in the experimental (RI) group than in a comparable control group.

The PI Paradigm

In our previous example we saw that there was some retention loss even for the control group, however small this loss was in relation to the experimental (RI) group. This is not unusual in RI experiments. To what can we attribute this loss? We might suggest that the control group was subject to hidden RI effects due to other experience during the retention interval. To reduce this possibility, however, special steps are always taken to ensure that any intervening activity between A–B learning and recall for the control group is as different from CVC learning as possible. We should only expect major interference from the learning of similar materials. Must we therefore fall back on autonomous time decay?

Underwood (1957) argued a resounding ''no.'' He argued that even in the classical RI paradigm, there may be hidden effects of proactive interference (PI) on the retention scores. Underwood's suspicions became aroused when he observed that Ebbinghaus (who was his own subject in several years of CVC work), showed as much as 65% loss for CVCs over 24 hours. This was true even though there was never any intervening learning of additional CVCs during the retention interval. This seemed like an implausibly large amount of forgetting to be caused by experiences in the interval between learning and recall. It occurred to Underwood that Ebbinghaus may have been suffering PI effects for CVCs after years of working with those highly confusable materials.

As Underwood began to review the literature of retention studies, he verified the fact that subjects in such experiments typically learn large numbers of CVC lists prior to the trials for which we see the reported data. The RI experiments were often repeated several times on each subject to ensure reliability of the data. Often the subjects were given prior practice with CVCs to familiarize them with the task. Finally, it was common to have the subjects serve in several conditions of a single experiment so that each subject's data could be compared with his or her own level of learning ability. While ordinarily desirable precautions, these procedures might have accidentally allowed PI effects from the previous CVC learning to contaminate the supposedly pure RI findings. The effects would occur for both the experimental and for the control group; the former would suffer RI plus PI while the latter would suffer the effects of PI alone.

Underwood capped the issue by plotting the graph reproduced in Figure 2-5. This figure shows data from 14 separate experiments conducted in different laboratories in which recall was tested following a 24-hour retention interval. Underwood plotted these data on the single dimension of the number of lists subjects in these various experiments had already had to memorize prior to the reported learning–recall tests. The more lists learned prior to the main experiment, the poorer were the retention scores. The importance of PI was clearly established.

From observations such as these there developed a standard paradigm for the study of PI, i.e., the detrimental effects of prior learning on the acquisition and retention of new materials. A typical PI experiment would begin by having the subjects in the experimental group learn a first list (A–B) to a certain criterion, and then learn a second list (A–C) consisting of the same stimulus terms but new response terms. Unlike the RI paradigm, the subjects must now recall the second (A–C) list in the test stage. The control group learns only the second list prior to the same retention interval. The stages of the PI experiment are illustrated at the bottom of Table 2-1. The performance difference between the

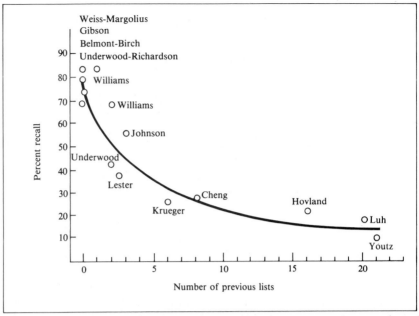

FIGURE 2-5   A demonstration of proactive interference: Recall as a function of the number of previous lists learned by subjects as determined by analysis of a number of different experiments.
(From Underwood, 1957. Copyright © 1957 by the American Psychological Association. Reprinted by permission.)

experimental and control groups will reflect the amount of forgetting attributable to the PI caused by prior learning of the A–B list. The degree of PI is calculated as:

$$PI = \frac{\% \text{ correct for control group} - \% \text{ correct for experimental group}}{\% \text{ correct for control group}}$$

Using such a paradigm, one can reliably observe poorer performance for an experimental (PI) group as compared to a control group. Typically, the degree of PI increases with the number of similar lists learned prior to the test stage and is dependent on the relative amounts of practice given to the old versus the new learning (Slamecka, 1961; Underwood, 1957).

Context-Dependent Memory

A major criticism of the rote learning approach to memory was its willingness to accept a degree of sterility in order to gain tight experimental control of the learning material. As we shall see later, the effects of RI and PI tend to be exaggerated when the learning materials consist of meaningless CVCs or lists of unrelated words. Conceptually organized material, experiences which can be quickly processed to a "deep" or semantic level, show considerably less memory loss.

Interestingly, we can find a hint to these limits on any simple idea of interference even within the rarified atmosphere of rote learning studies. One source of this complexity is the importance of the context in which learning takes place, to the level of recall performance. For example, assume you are taking three courses in history. Your memory for the material you learn in these three courses will be subject to the effects of RI and PI we have described. There are, however, cues in the environment that might permit you to distinguish what was learned in one course from what was learned in another. The instructors are different, and the information was discussed in different rooms using different textbooks. All these cues, though not explicitly related to the materials themselves, are relevant to distinguishing one body of material from another. It has, in fact, been demonstrated that recall can be better when testing is conducted in the same environment in which learning originally took place (Dallett & Wilcox, 1968). Information, then, in the form of contextual cues relevant to distinguishing one set of materials from another can reduce and limit the degree of interference among these sets.

One of the more striking examples of context effects on retention comes from a study by Godden and Baddeley (1975). This experiment was conducted with 16 members of an underwater diving club who learned lists of 36 unrelated words either on shore, or at a depth of 20 feet underwater. Retention tests were then conducted with the divers either in the same or a different environment from the one in which the lists were originally learned.

Table 2-2 shows the average recall scores for the four experimental conditions. Those subjects who learned on shore ("dry") did better when tested on shore, and those who learned underwater ("wet") did better underwater.

Earlier we said that dissimilar learning materials cause less interference in retention than similar learning materials. We now see that this concept of similarity may apply also to the contexts in which the materials are learned. In this final section we examine the question of similarity and interference.

TABLE 2–2. Average recall scores for word-lists learned by divers as a function of learning and recall environment. Lists were either learned or recalled in either a "dry" (on shore) or "wet" (20 feet under water) environment. (Adapted from Godden & Baddeley, 1975.)

Learning Environment	Recall Environment		
	Dry	Wet	Total
Dry	13.5	8.6	22.1
Wet	8.4	11.4	19.8
Total	21.9	20.0	

ACQUISITION AND INTERFERENCE

Similarity between sets of learning materials is probably the single most obvious and troublesome source of interference in remembering. The variety of effects obtained present a very complex picture, but the results are somewhat more intelligible in the context of a *stage analysis* of associative learning (Underwood & Schulz, 1960).

Stage Analysis of Interference Tasks

The notion of stage analysis begins with the realization that learning a list of paired-associates involves at least three logically distinct steps. First, the subject must learn to recognize the stimulus terms of the pairs, discriminating them from the other stimulus terms in the list. If the stimulus terms are meaningful words this process will be far easier than if they are highly confusable, difficult to pronounce CVCs. Second, the subject must learn about the response terms. If we are again dealing with CVCs, the three letters that make up the response term may not initially form a perceptual "unit" for the subject. The letters making up the response must be *integrated* by the subject to the point where the person can recall that item as a single response when presented with the appropriate stimulus terms. Until one has served as a subject in such experiments and faced CVCs such as KIJ, XAD, XYF, and NIJ, it is hard to appreciate how difficult this task can be. The third stage, and the one which most preoccupied the early workers in verbal learning, is the *association* or *hook up stage,* where the subject learns to connect each stimulus term with its appropriate response.

Separating the independent effects of these three operations is difficult since they need not occur in sequence but could be carried on simultaneously or overlapping in time. In spite of this difficulty, it is possible to illustrate how one can arrange the conditions of an experiment to differentially emphasize the effects of each stage relative to the others.

The stimuli in Figure 2-6 serve as such an example. This illustration comes from Crowder (1976, p. 22) and is based on an experiment by McGuire (1961). The left-hand panel gives an example of Stage 1 difficulty (difficult stimulus learning) by using stimulus items consisting

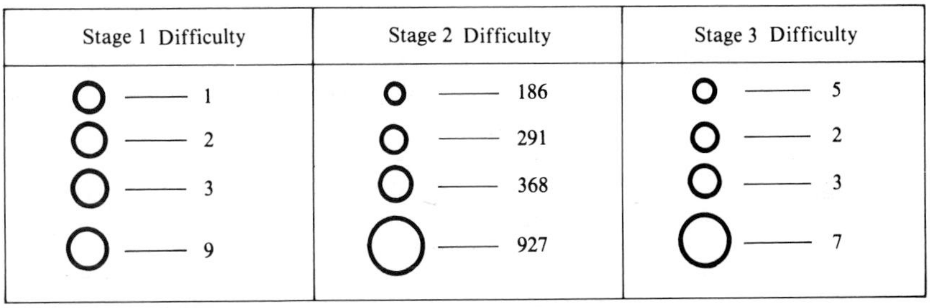

Stage 1 Difficulty	Stage 2 Difficulty	Stage 3 Difficulty
⚬ —— 1	⚬ —— 186	⚬ —— 5
⚬ —— 2	⚬ —— 291	⚬ —— 2
⚬ —— 3	⚬ —— 368	⚬ —— 3
⚪ —— 9	⚪ —— 927	⚪ —— 7

FIGURE 2-6   Examples of paired-associate materials used by McGuire (1961) to illustrate the independent effects of difficulties in stimulus learning (Stage 1), response learning (Stage 2), or associative "hook up" learning (Stage 3). (Adapted from Crowder, 1976.)

of circles which differed only slightly in size. While discriminating the stimuli from each other may be difficult, note that the response terms are simple one-digit numbers which increase numerically with the size of the circles. These last two factors should produce rapid response learning (Stage 2) and rapid establishment of the associations (Stage 3) once the circle sizes have been discriminated.

The middle panel illustrates Stage 2 (response learning) difficulty by using more complex sets of three-digit numbers as response terms. Once the numbers have been learned, however, the other two stages are relatively easy. The circle sizes are easy to discriminate (Stage 1), and the response numbers increase with increasing circle size, making for an easy association (Stage 3).

The right-hand panel shows relatively easy discrimination (Stage 1), and the use of simple, one-digit numbers as response terms (Stage 2). The association stage (Stage 3), however, has been made purposely difficult by using numbers whose size does not correspond with the relative sizes of the stimuli.

One can see the essence of these three stages in an infant's increasingly appropriate use of the words "daddy" and "mommy." The same three stages must be accomplished by the child for these words to be used correctly. First (Stage 1), the child must learn to distinguish these two individuals from each other, and from all other people. The baby must learn to distinguish between his or her father, and all other men. The mother must become distinct from other women. Second (Stage 2), the child must learn the words themselves, putting together the separate movements of the lips, tongue, and vocal apparatus in order to pronounce these words as separate responses. Finally (Stage 3), the child must "hook up" the stimulus with the response; to call his or her parents "mommy" and "daddy" and verbally respond in some other way to other people.

It is of course difficult to observe these three stages by themselves, but most parents are familiar with aspects of a child's behavior that seem to emphasize one or the other of these stages. The child can sometimes be heard repeating a particular word or name over and over again in the absence of the stimulus named by that word. However, even once the words are acquired, they can be applied without much specificity. The family friend may be called "daddy," as well as any male stranger who may happen by. Although the child can recognize his or her own parents and be capable of producing the word, its use is not yet restricted (associated) to these particular people.

Transfer Experiments and Similarity

The experimental study of similarity effects often takes the form of a *transfer task* (Osgood, 1949). For example, the subject may learn a list of paired-associate items (an A–B list), followed by learning a second list consisting of the same stimulus terms with different response terms (an A–C list). Our interest in this case would be to vary the similarity between the response terms of the first list (B set) and the response terms of the second list (C set) to determine how the degree of similarity influences acquisition of the second list. One could study these effects by measuring the relative difficulty of learning the second list as a function of the similarity of stimuli and responses in the two lists.

The transfer task differs in several respects from the PI and RI paradigms previously described. In those experiments the focus was on interference with retention of a set of associations. In the transfer experiments, on the other hand, the focus is on interference with the acquisition of a set of associations. In the PI and RI tasks, the *memory performance* of an experimental group (A–B, A–C), is compared to the memory performance of a control group (A–B for the RI paradigm, or A–C for the PI paradigm) that did not learn the interfering list. Testing takes place after the elapse of some retention interval. In the transfer task, on the other hand, *learning performance* of the second list by an experimental group (e.g., A–B, A–C) is compared to the second list learning of a control group that learns two unrelated lists (A–B, C–D). In the first case, we measure interference by the effect of the interfering list on accuracy of recall after a retention interval. In the latter case, we measure transfer by the effect of first list learning on second list learning.

Thus, while the transfer task is procedurally different from the RI and PI paradigms, these experiments can embody aspects of the same underlying memory mechanisms. It is often difficult in both types of experiment to determine whether differences among conditions in performance are due to differences in acquisition, storage, or retrieval of the information. We can nevertheless learn a great deal about interference effects by observing the conditions under which they occur. It is necessary to have a good understanding of these effects in transfer of learning if we wish to determine how prior experience relates to current memory performance. Such an understanding is necessary, as we suggested earlier, as one requisite for an adequate theory of memory.

Conditions of Transfer. Any transfer study can have three possible outcomes: *positive transfer, negative transfer,* or *no transfer.* Positive transfer refers to cases where learning a prior list facilitates performance on a second list. Negative transfer refers to cases where a previously learned list creates difficulties for second-list learning. Finally, we speak of "no transfer" when first-list learning produces no effect at all on the learning of a second list.

We must, in these studies, be able to distinguish between the specific transfer effects of interest, versus generalized, or *nonspecific transfer* which can occur independent of the characteristics of the learning materials. Consider, for example, one group of subjects who learns a single list with another group who learns two totally unrelated lists. In spite of possible PI effects, the second group might in fact show some advantage over the first group. This could be due to nonspecific transfer. Subjects unfamiliar with nonsense syllables may take some time to acquire general strategies and know-how about the best way to learn these unusual items. These general learning strategies can then be brought to bear on the second list, giving an advantage not available to the group learning only the single list. Sometimes referred to as *warm-up effects* or *learning-to-learn,* numerous studies have shown how first-list learning can facilitate second list learning with initially inexperienced subjects (e.g., Thune, 1951; Ward, 1937).

This is the reason most transfer studies compare groups of subjects who both learn two lists with a difference only in the character of the two lists to be learned. Since both groups have learned a previous set of nonsense syllables, both groups have benefited equally from nonspecific transfer. The difference can thus be directly related to the similarity characteristics of the two lists.

Examples of Specific Transfer.   Let us assume that all subjects learn the same set of paired-associates as a first list (A–B list). It is now possible to compare the interference or facilitation when different groups of these subjects are required to learn a second list consisting of new stimuli to the old responses (C–B) or new responses to the old stimuli (A–C). Furthermore, we can vary the similarity of the new terms to the terms in the first list.

From our discussion of stage analysis we should be alert to the fact that the interference produced will be a consequence of relative contributions represented by the stimulus, response, or associative learning stages involved in the two learning sets of the transfer task. This point was given special emphasis in the context of transfer experiments by Martin (1965). Consider a case, for example, where the stimuli are well-integrated prior to the experiment (e.g., familiar words) and the responses are equally well learned (e.g., single digits). An A–B, C–B paradigm (the same response terms must be connected to new stimulus terms) might produce little, if any, specific transfer. On the other hand, if the response terms are unfamiliar, such as each response consisting of a string of four unrelated consonants, we might expect some positive transfer. That is, the difficult stage of response learning would have already occurred during the first list, A–B phase of the experiment. Positive transfer would occur due to a carryover from the response learning stage of the A–B learning to the response stage of the C–B learning.

Let us take a final example. In this case, both the first and second lists have the same stimulus and response terms, but in the second list the particular pairings of A and B terms have been rearranged. This is conventionally symbolized as an A–B, A–B$_r$ paradigm. The r subscript stands for "rearranged," or "re-paired." In this case the result will be strong negative transfer. Here, the associative stage of learning must be responsible for the interference, since response and stimulus learning had already been accomplished during the learning of the first list.

An example of results frequently obtained with CVC-CVC pairs is shown in Table 2-3. In all cases in these examples, subjects learn the same CVC–CVC pairs on the first list (e.g., BEC–LIM, CUZ–RAD, and so forth). The difference lies in the characteristics of the stimulus or response terms on the second list. In all cases the determination of positive or negative transfer would be against a baseline derived from subjects learning two unrelated lists, each consisting of totally different stimulus and response terms. This control condition would be conventionally symbolized as A–B, C–D. The conventional symbols for the experimental conditions illustrated are also shown in the table.

Similarity of stimuli and responses, then, can produce either positive or negative transfer depending on how this similarity contributes to the three components of the task. For example, if stimulus learning is difficult, a similarity in the stimuli for the two lists will facilitate learning the stimulus for List 2 (positive transfer of stimulus learning). The same effect would be expected where response terms are identical in the two lists (positive transfer of response learning). However, similarity of stimuli in the two lists will also produce associative interference; learning a new response in List 2 conflicts with a different response previously acquired for a similar stimulus (negative transfer of associative learning). Stage analysis, then, sees the transfer effects produced by a particular paradigm as the sum of the transfer effects for each stage of paired-associate learning. The maximum positive transfer, of course, would be the relearning of the same list where all three components contribute positive transfer to learning List 2.

TABLE 2-3. Examples of transfer conditions producing either positive transfer (facilitation), or negative transfer (interference). In all cases the control condition would involve learning two lists, each consisting of totally different stimulus and response terms (A–B, C–D).

Transfer Paradigm	List 1	List 2	Expected Transfer Effects
A–B, C–B (Different stimuli, same responses)	BEC–LIM CUZ–RAD	DAX–LIM HOV–RAD	Slight positive transfer
A–B, A–B (Same stimuli, similar responses)	BEC–LIM CUZ–RAD	BEC–LIN CUZ–RAF	Slight positive transfer
A–B, A–C (Same stimuli, different responses)	BEC–LIM CUZ–RAD	BEC–MOT CUZ–NEB	Negative transfer
A–B, A–B$_r$ (Same stimuli, responses re-paired)	BEC–LIM CUZ–RAD	BEC–RAD CUZ–LIM	Strong negative transfer

Interference and Ordinary Forgetting

Are the paradigms discussed to this point too simple to provide us with information relevant to everyday forgetting? First, the materials used are relatively meaningless. Unlike the knowlege we acquire in the course of everday experience, the materials in the verbal learning laboratory are not easy to relate to prior knowledge. Second, the learning tasks used typically involve rote learning through simple repetition. Finally, the separation of PI, RI, and transfer effects as attempted in the laboratory ordinarily co-occur with considerable complexity in everyday forgetting.

The simplicity of these experiments was purposeful. For these investigators, their simplicity was their advantage, and their objectives were clearly articulated. In order to make and test hypotheses about forgetting, we must first be able to specify, and then to isolate, the factors involved. We must be able to observe and measure the influence of each factor independent of the influence of the others. The goal was to analyze the phenomenon of forgetting into separate components; to take the complex phenomenon apart and see how it works.

The usefulness of this analytic strategy can only be demonstrated if we can put these parts back together again and make successful predictions about more complex cases. This is a question of the adequacy or sufficiency of a particular approach to learning and memory. At this point, you must keep in mind that the particular approach under discussion makes certain assumptions regarding the elements appropriate to the analysis. The approach assumes that the most complex cases can be decomposed into the acquisition, storage, and retrieval of associations between discrete stimuli and responses. Other equally analytic approaches may reject these assumptions, while still others might modify and complicate them. Nevertheless, the so-called verbal learning approach is central to our understanding of memory, either as it served as the focus of criticism from its detractors, or as the basis of elaboration by its supporters.

The techniques described to this point provide the groundwork for our further discussion of interference theories of forgetting in the following chapter. The reader should have them firmly in mind before proceeding.

CHAPTER SUMMARY

1. *Historical Background*

    A. One of the earliest views of memory can be traced to the British Associationists, who stressed associations between stimuli as a consequence of their contiguous occurrence close together in time.

    B. In order to bring experimental control and objectivity to the study of verbal learning and memory, Hermann Ebbinghaus introduced the use of nonsense syllables; pronounceable but meaningless consonant–vowel–consonant (CVC) combinations.

2. *Procedures in Verbal Learning*

A. Contemporary studies of verbal learning frequently employ either serial or paired-associate learning tasks. Serial learning involves the presentation of a list of items which must be memorized in the order in which they were presented. Subjects either have to report the full list or, in the anticipation method, they must give the following item as each item is presented, one at a time. Paired-associate learning requires the acquisition of an association between verbal items, usually through the anticipation method. As each stimulus is presented, the subject must anticipate the appropriate response term.

B. Retention can be measured through the method of recall, in which the subject must recall the items in the learning list, either in order (serial recall), without regard to order (free recall), or in response to some clue (cued recall). Other methods include the savings method, in which retention is gauged by a reduction in the time necessary to relearn a set of items, and the recognition method, in which the subject must select the correct item from a small set of alternatives.

C. As a general rule, recognition memory is the most sensitive measure of retention, in the sense that it will often show evidence of retention not apparent using the method of recall (least sensitive) or savings (intermediate). A two-stage view of the recall process proposes first that items must be generated from memory, and second, the correct responses must be selected from this generated list. Recognition involves only the stage of response selection.

3. *Interference in Memory*

A. The autonomous, or spontaneous decay, theory of forgetting, saw memory loss solely as a time-dependent process, in which all memories, regardless of their character, passively decay with time. The primary alternative is the interference theory which proposes that forgetting is directly due to interference from other learning.

B. The decay theory was dealt a severe blow by Jenkins and Dallenbach's demonstration that recall for nonsense material declines rapidly over an 8-hour period of normal waking activity, while retention over a similar period of sleep showed virtually no retention loss.

C. While Jenkins and Dallenbach's study did not constitute final disproof of the decay theory of memory, their results sufficiently discredited this view to shift the emphasis in theory and research to investigations of the conditions of interference.

4. *Varieties of Interference*

  A. Retroactive interference (RI) refers to the detrimental effect of new learning on the retention of older learning. Proactive interference (PI) refers to the detrimental effect of previous learning on the retention of more recently learned material.

  B. An example of the limits on the effects of proactive and retroactive interference is seen in the effects of context on memory. Recall is typically better when materials learned in one context are tested in that context, than when they are learned in one environment and tested in another.

5. *Acquisition and Interference*

  A. The learning of paired-associate terms can be divided into three logically distinct stages: (1) learning, or discrimination, of the stimulus terms; (2) learning, or integration, of the response terms; and (3) the association, or "hook up," of the stimulus and response terms. Each of these stages can contribute independently, or together, to the degree of difficulty in paired-associate learning.

  B. Transfer tasks examine the effects of learning one set of materials on the acquisition of other materials. Positive transfer refers to cases where prior learning facilitates new learning. Negative transfer refers to cases where prior learning interferes with new learning.

  C. The degree of similarity between items in two learning tasks is a major factor leading to transfer effects, whether positive or negative. Two examples of cases producing strong negative transfer (interference) in paired-associate learning occur when a second list contains the same stimulus terms as the first list, but now requires the attachment of different responses (A–B, A–C), and when a second list contains the same stimulus terms and response terms but now repaired in different combinations (A–B, A–B$_r$).

ASSOCIATIONS AND FORGETTING IN LONG-TERM MEMORY

TOPIC QUESTIONS

1. Interference Theories of Forgetting.
How did the idea of a *competition* among responses explain the forgetting of associations? How did the hypothesis that associations could be *unlearned* supplement the response competition theory of forgetting?

2. Testing the Two-Factor Theory.
Why was a direct measurement of "unlearning" important for this theory of forgetting? What were the procedures used to measure unlearning?

3. Elaborations and Amendments to Interference Theory.
What was the *response set interference* hypothesis, and how did it change earlier interference theory? How was the notion that we may pay attention to different aspects of a stimulus at different times incorporated into interference theory (*stimulus encoding variability*)?

4. The Concept of Mediation.
What are *mediated associations,* and how was the concept of *mediation* used to explain rapid learning and good retention of meaningful materials? How do verbal mediators, imagery, and mnemonics function to improve recall?

5. Organization in Free Recall.
How does the *organization* of learning materials based on associations or category membership affect the way we recall information? Does the organization of learning materials help in learning the information, or does it aid us in retrieving this information when we later try to remember? What is the principle of *encoding specificity,* and how does it relate to this question? What is the distinction between *semantic memory* and *episodic memory,* and what does it say about the generality of verbal learning research?

Associationism, the notion that ideas and experiences get "hooked up" somehow in our minds, seems to be a big part of how everyone thinks about memory. This viewpoint is not new. It is as old as the ancient Greeks. It still determines, to a large extent, our notions of what memory is and how one might investigate it. Our purpose in this chapter is to examine two aspects of association theory. First, we will look in greater detail at the interference theory of forgetting and at several major views of how associations both become established and become lost. Second, we will look at how the basic principles of associationism were used as a beginning attempt to explain memory organization.

Let us set the stage for this discussion by reviewing the elements of association theory and its rise to predominance in the experimental analyses of memory. The basic unit of analysis was the individual association between a stimulus and response or, more abstractly, between distinct ideas or memory traces. Knowledge and meaning were viewed as nothing more (or less) than the building of increasingly complex networks of individual associations. This ambitious view held that a description and explanation of changes in the strengths of individual associations could culminate in a general theory of memory and learning, and perhaps, even in an explanation of knowledge and thought. As we indicated at the close of the previous chapter, this was a way of talking about memory, one which drew a particular picture of what memory might be like. It was a picture that led to particular kinds of experiments and particular ways of explaining natural phenomena.

INTERFERENCE THEORIES OF FORGETTING

As we saw previously, Thorndike's (1911) view that memories fade with disuse was largely discredited by the studies of retention after sleep. Relatively little forgetting occurred during 8 hours of sleep as compared with the very large losses that occurred during a similar 8-hour period of normal waking activity. With interference thus established as the major cause of memory loss, the problem of explaining forgetting became the problem of explaining interference: an explanation of how interference produces its effects would also be an explanation of why we forget.

What we described in the previous chapter as "interference theory" turns out to be not really a single theory but several different hypotheses of how interference works. Some of these hypotheses are compatible with one another. There is no reason why interference could not operate in more than one way. More often, however, each hypothesis was set in direct opposition to the others. The early workers seemed to be unwilling to admit compromise so long as there was any chance that one theory was right and the others wrong.

These interference hypotheses ranged from relatively simple notions of competition among associations to more elaborate ideas regarding the direction of attention and the utilization of complex learning strategies. As the alternative theories called for new, crucial experiments, the data to be explained grew more complex. One of our goals in this chapter will be to describe the more conspicuous turning points in the continual adjustment of interference theory in the light of new data and developing ideas.

Research Strategy

To understand the approach to be described in these pages, recall that the steep forgetting curves described in the previous chapter were based on the retention of meaningless materials such as CVCs. We are equally aware that meaningful material, such as the plot of a favorite book or film, and very well-rehearsed material, such as your address or telephone number, may be retained for indefinitely long periods. In the extreme case of semantic memory, such as our knowledge of the meaning of words, or how to pluralize the word "cat," the memories may never be lost.

Associationism, however, did not begin with the unique human capabilities of language and conceptual memory. Associationism was identified with the development of animal conditioning theory and with studies of rote verbal learning in the Ebbinghaus tradition. The experiments were thought to be measuring the strength of associations that connected a stimulus with a response, and the later associationist writers represented a merger of early work on nonsense syllables with theories developed originally in the animal laboratory.

Human beings were seen as more complicated than animals in the sense that they had language and consequently a greater capacity for higher order associations. But the basic principles, the connecting of distinct elements, were the same. Recall, for example, that the forgetting curves of the cockroach and of the human were virtually indistinguishable. Ignoring the fact that retention of CVCs is hardly representative of our human predispositions, such similarities led associationists to believe that a picture of memory and how it works should be the same whether applied to a dog learning to salivate or to a college student learning to associate DAC with ZIR.

An animal could presumably learn any association so long as it could discriminate between the stimuli. Since acquiring an association was seen as a general process, what one found out about one association should apply to the formation of any other association. In the study of verbal learning, what was discovered about paired-associate learning was thought to generalize to how one acquired associations outside the laboratory. In these latter studies, the paired-associate method became the method of choice. Serial learning is deceptively more complex, since each word must serve as both a response to the previous word and as a stimulus for the next one. Paired-associates also seemed to best parallel the animal laboratory procedures of acquiring a particular response to a particular stimulus.

Over the years, the development of verbal learning research began to separate itself more and more from its animal laboratory connections. In this later research, paired-associate CVCs and word lists were seen simply as a convenient vehicle for memory studies. In the Ebbinghaus tradition, they continued to see a virtue in the study of memory "uncontaminated" by the uncertainties of prior language habits and linguistic competence. These views and this picture of memory motivated the kinds of studies and theories used to explain forgetting.

Response Competition

If forgetting is the result of interference from other learning, how is this interference produced? The earliest answer was that different responses must surely compete with each other (McGeoch, 1932). According to the original version of this hypothesis, individual associations are acquired independently. If this view is correct, learning two different responses for a single stimulus, as in the RI paradigm (A-B, A-C), occurs without any interaction at the time of acquisition. During the retention interval both associations reside in memory at the same time. When the experimenter presents the A term in the retention test and the subject is instructed to report either the B term or the C term (the RI or PI paradigm, respectively), one's ability to do so is the result of a competition between the alternative possible responses to the A stimulus.

According to this theory, both responses remain present in memory, but one dominates and hence blocks the occurrence of the other. This hypothesis not only attributed forgetting to such competition, but it located the interference effect as occurring at the moment of recall. Which response wins, and blocks out the other, would depend on the relative strengths of the competing responses. The most important variable determining strength would be the amount of practice given to each list: the A-B list versus the A-C list. The more practice the subject receives on the interfering list, the more likely it will be that the interfering response will dominate and prevent recall of the appropriate CVC. The blocked response has not been eliminated from memory. It still exists at exactly the same strength it had at the end of the acquisition trials. It is only temporarily (or permanently) suppressed. This view, in other words, implies that once associations are formed, they are permanent.

Tulving and Pearlstone (1966) have made a useful distinction which can be helpful in understanding McGeoch's competition idea. We could say that the association that is blocked is still *available,* in the sense that it remains in storage. It is, however, no longer *accessible;* it cannot be retrieved. This distinction has important implications for research methodology. We cannot infer that an association has been erased from memory simply on the grounds that the subject cannot produce it at any particular moment. This was the essence of McGeoch's position.

There were two additional details to the response competition theory as it was first presented. It was the details, rather than the general notion of competition, that gave the theory its greatest difficulty. The first of

A desired response, like a desired book, may be available but not accessible.

these could be called an *independence hypothesis*. It claimed that the learning of later associations has no effect on the strength or availability of associations acquired earlier. Interference does not affect the storage of associations, nor are the earlier memories lost or distorted by new learning. All acquired associations continue to exist in their original form at their original strength.

The second detail was the claim that interference is the result of *specific competition* between responses at the time of recall. That is, competition is not simply a matter of confusing the two lists. The specific responses, those that have been associated with a particular stimulus, compete, and the stronger one directly blocks the weaker one, preventing its retrieval even when it is the appropriate response.

Most of us have experienced a kind of persisting error that seems to actively prevent the recall of what we are trying to remember. We know of a young student who was asked some years ago to appear on a local TV quiz show. Our student was clever enough to watch a number of the shows to get some idea of the sorts of questions typically asked. Thus armed, he devoted several days prior to the show to the rote memorization of assorted facts, among these, the names of each of the states and their capital cities. Sure enough, the moment the audience lights dimmed in the TV studio, the first question began, "The State of Illinois has a number of well-known cities … Give the name of its *largest city.*"

The student's mind, alas, did not go blank, nor could he think of Illinois' largest city. All that came to mind was the recently rehearsed response "Springfield." He knew this was not the answer required, but so strong was the recently practiced "Springfield" response, that the student sat in agonized silence, the word "Chicago" totally out of reach. This episode is as good an example of response competition as it was a frustrating experience for a student who lost the game because he knew the rules too well.

Unlearning

The first major challenge to the competition theory began by questioning the independence hypothesis, and ended with a rejection of the entire independence assumption itself. Is it the case, as McGeoch (1932) seemed to imply, that all associations are acquired independently? That is, in the RI paradigm, is it the case that the learning of A-C has no effect on the strength or availability (in Tulving's sense) of the A-B association?

Melton and Irwin (1940) tested the implications of the response competition hypothesis and found it insufficient to account for forgetting in the typical paired-associate RI study. Melton and Irwin's study is a classic, and its results are reproduced in virtually every graduate or undergraduate textbook on memory written since 1940. To see why, it is necessary to examine the implications of response competition in more detail.

First, recall the typical RI paradigm as described in the previous chapter. The experiment begins with the subject learning List 1, consisting of a number of paired-associates (A-B pairs). After some interval, the subject then learns List 2, consisting of the same stimulus terms now paired with new responses (A-C pairs). Our next step, of course, is to wait some period (the retention interval) and then retest the subject's memory for the first list learned (A-B). As each A term is presented, the subject must try to produce the appropriate B term. The amount of RI is measured by comparing this recall performance with recall by a control group who learned only the first list and not the second.

If you think about the response competition argument you will see that it implies two specific predictions. First, we would expect that the greater the amount of practice on List 2 responses, the less able the subject will be to recall the List 1 responses. That is, RI will increase with the strength of the List 2 learning. If the theory is correct, however, the strength of A-B will always remain the same regardless of the amount of practice on the second list. The practice on A-C will result in greater strength of the C responses, but this will mean only that the C responses will dominate at the moment of recall. This brings us to the second prediction made by the theory. Response competition implies that the errors the subject makes in trying to recall List 1 will invariably be in the form of intrusions from List 2. Let us give an example to make the situation clear.

Suppose one of the pairs on List 1 is DAX-QUICKLY. The corresponding pair on List 2 might be DAX-SOLDIER. Given the A term DAX after the retention interval, the subject's attempt to recall the B term QUICKLY will be inhibited by a competition between this old response and the more recently learned response, SOLDIER. One or the other of these responses should occur in recall. The one which does not occur is presumed to be blocked by the dominance of the stronger one. If the subject makes an error, says the response competition hypothesis, the error will be the result of the dominance of the first list responses by the more recently learned second list responses. The majority of erroneous responses, then, should be substitutions of responses from the wrong list.

Melton and Irwin's (1940) study tested these predictions. Their experiment used recall of nonsense syllable lists rather than paired-associates, but the logic of their argument is the same as that described above. Each list consisted of 18 nonsense syllables. List 1 items were practiced for five trials. The subjects were then divided into four groups. Each group received a different amount of practice on List 2, either 5, 10, 20, or 40 trials. The retention test consisted of relearning the original lists to a criterion of two perfect reproductions. The number of practice trials required to relearn List 1 would be the measure of the amount of RI produced by having had to learn List 2.

The results supported the notion that RI increases as practice on the interfering list increases. Groups with more practice on List 2 experience more forgetting than groups that had fewer trials on the interpolated learning. Intrusion errors did occur when subjects tried to recall List 1. However, these intrusions made up the majority of errors only for those groups with relatively little practice on List 2. The total amount of RI, on the other hand, continued to increase up to a maximum for 20 trials on the interfering list.

Figure 3-1 shows these results as they were first reported by Melton and Irwin. The top curve represents the total amount of retroactive interference based on the difference between the number of trials required to relearn List 1 for the experimental groups versus a control group that did not have to learn the second list. Each point on this curve represents the amount of RI for the groups having different amounts of practice on the interfering list. It is clear that total RI does build up progressively as subjects receive more practice on List 2. There is, in other words, decreasing retention of List 1 items. The question, of course, is whether this decreasing retention is due to competition from List 2 responses preventing List 1 recall.

The lowest curve (dotted line) was intended to represent the proportion of errors which were erroneous intrusions from the second list. This

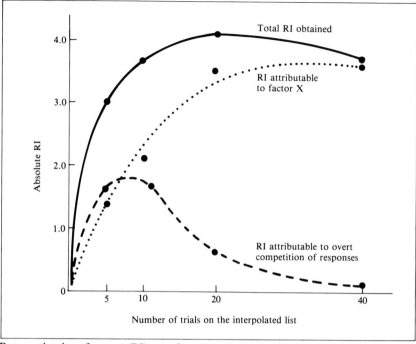

FIGURE 3-1 Retroactive interference (RI) as a function of the number of trials of interpolated learning. The top curve shows the total amount of obtained RI and the lowest dashed curve shows the interference attributable to overt intrusions at recall. The middle dashed curve shows the amount of interference attributable to factor X.
(From Melton & Irwin, 1940.)

would be the response competition component of the total amount of obtained RI. As you can see, the number of intrusions increases at first, but then declines. By the time a subject has had 40 practice trials on the second list there is, by this definition, no response competition at all.

Melton and Irwin concluded that there must be a second factor at work in addition to response competition which contributes to the total retroactive effect. They plotted this second function by subtracting the amount of RI due to competition from the total amount of obtained RI. They added some drama to their findings by labeling this unknown contributor "factor X." It may be, they argued, that initially there is competition between the two lists. There is evidence of this competition in the increase in intrusion errors for the early stages of practice on the interpolated list. But even when intrusion errors disappear, a substantial amount of RI remains. This is the effect due to factor X.

The most likely candidate for the identity of factor X, according to Melton and Irwin, was what they termed *unlearning*. The acccquisition of the two sets of associations, they argued, does not take place independently. As the second list responses are acquired, the first list associations become weakened, "inhibited," or "unlearned." The strengthening of one response directly affects the strength, and hence availability, of the other. This explanation also places the locus of the unlearning effect at the time the second list is being learned not, as the response competition theory argued, at the moment of recall.

Following the Melton and Irwin (1940) study, the focus of attention for students of verbal learning shifted to the measurement and description of this new factor and its presumed contribution to forgetting.

Unlearning as Extinction

As we indicated earlier, the antecedents of associationism in verbal learning lay in the animal laboratory and studies of animal conditioning. It should come as no surprise, therefore, that one of the earliest attempts to explain unlearning occurred when Underwood (1945) compared unlearning with experimental extinction in the animal laboratory.

The reader with some knowledge of animal learning procedures may recall that a conditioned response in a lower animal (or human) can result from repeated pairings of a neutral stimulus (CS) with an unconditioned stimulus (UCS). For example, if a tone is consistently followed by a shock to your finger, you will soon begin to withdraw your finger in response to the tone itself, even when it is no longer followed by the shock.

Underwood proposed that learning a verbal association between, for example, DAX and QUICKLY might be directly analogous. The word QUICKLY would serve as an unconditioned stimulus for saying the word "quickly," just as a shock is an unconditioned stimulus for reflexively withdrawing your finger. If we repeatedly pair DAX and QUICKLY, an association will be built up between the two items. The syllable DAX is now analogous to a conditioned stimulus: seeing the word DAX will result in your responding with the word QUICKLY. People, in other words, may learn the responses in paired-associate tasks the same way that Pavlov used the taste of food to condition his dogs to salivate at the sound of a bell, or, in our example, the same way you may learn to withdraw your finger at the sound of a tone.

What happens when the tone (CS) is no longer followed by the reinforcing shock (UCS)? Precisely the same thing that happened to Pavlov's dogs when the sound of a bell was no longer followed by the taste of food. The tendency to produce the conditioned response systematically decreases. In conditioning experiments, we would describe this as an *extinction procedure*. To Underwood, the "unlearning" that occurs when the DAX-QUICKLY association is no longer reinforced could be described as nothing more or less than extinction, as originally described by Pavlov.

If this analogy held, Underwood argued, one should also expect to occasionally see *spontaneous recovery;* the reemergence of a conditioned response some time after it had apparently been extinguished. That is, one should expect to see some recovery of the A-B response after a long enough retention interval. Specifically, the longer the retention interval, the greater should be the chances of seeing the A-B associations recover, and the more likely it will be that the A stimulus will elicit a B rather than a C response. This is in fact exactly what Underwood (1948a, 1948b) reported finding when he conducted the appropriate experiments.

The analogy between animal conditioning and paired-associate learning became more and more strained in the years after it was originally proposed by Underwood. Indeed, the RI procedure would more properly be called "counter conditioning" since another association is being formed (e.g., DAX-SOLDIER) as the first one is being extinguished. We will have more to say about the reported incidence of spontaneous recovery in verbal learning experiments later, as some doubt has been expressed about its reliability. The analogy between unlearning and extinction, however, was a provocative one because it linked the experimental work with animals to the literature of verbal learning in an explicit way. It conceptualized the process as essentially the same in animals and humans. It was only the identity of the stimuli and responses that were different.

TESTING THE TWO-FACTOR THEORY

Melton and Irwin's explanation of interference effects has been called a *two-factor theory of interference* since they had no doubt that the factor of response competition might play some role in forgetting, at least in the initial stages of practice on List 2. Their contention was that the second factor, unlearning, accounted for the greater effects of interference on retention. The full picture, however, was far from clear.

In his original formulation of the response competition hypothesis, McGeoch (1932) recognized that overt intrusions were only a small proportion of the total errors subjects typically produce in RI experiments. Some errors, he suggested, could be recognized as mistakes by subjects and simply be withheld rather than being said aloud. Overt, spoken intrusions, therefore, would always underestimate the total effects of response competition. Indeed, two competing responses of the same strength might block each other and produce neither an intrusion nor any conscious inhibition of the response.

Melton and Irwin's point was that even if there is more response competition than is suggested by intrusion errors, one should still expect to see their number steadily increase as subjects receive more practice on the interfering list. As the A-C associations become stronger, so there should be a greater opportunity for intrusions to occur. The fact that Melton and Irwin found just the opposite, that intrusion errors actually decreased with A-C practice, was their major reason for invoking factor X. The evidence in both cases was thus indirect. Both sides drew inferences about the fate of first-list associations, rather than having direct evidence.

Some Problems for Factor X

Underwood (1945), who likened unlearning to extinction, also proposed a way that McGeoch's response competition theory might be rescued. This was the notion of *list differentiation*. If the competition argument were correct, overt intrusions might be maximum when the strength of the first and second list associations were the same. This would represent the point during practice with the second list at which subjects have the most difficulty in distinguishing which responses belong to which lists (somewhere between 5 and 10 trials of practice on List 2 in Figure 3-1). With practice beyond this point it becomes easier and easier to tell the two sets of responses apart. When this happens, subjects can easily recognize and suppress the C responses when the B responses are being tested and hence the number of overt intrusions should decline. This is exactly what we see in Figure 3-1 taken from Melton and Irwin's data.

The idea that subjects get better at differentiating between two lists with practice has been confirmed more directly by Winograd (1968). Such results could thus permit one to account for the data of Figure 3-1 entirely in terms of response competition without the addition of factor X. (List differentiation is not itself a factor in forgetting, but only an explanation of the relative proportions of overt versus presumed covert errors.) The decline in the number of intrusions with increasing A-C practice, in other words, does not necessarily demand the invention of notions like unlearning or extinction.

Proponents of the two-factor theory were not defeated by this line of argument and soon brought other evidence to bear on the issue. They looked closely at the two-factor theory, and at one of its implications. Forgetting was presumed to be the result of two distinct processes: (1) the response competition that occurred at the time an association was tested, and (2) an unlearning process that takes place during the course of second-list learning. Notice that this is a theory about retroactive interference only.

In a proactive interference paradigm, we would test retention for the second, A-C, list. The prior, A-B, list would produce response competition and hence interfere with A-C recall. On the other hand, since no new learning has followed the A-C list, the unlearning found in the RI paradigm should not occur. Following this logic, the two-factor theory would predict that RI effects will invariably be stronger than PI effects for equal amounts of practice on the respective interfering lists. This was in fact found by Melton and von Lackum (1941) and is consistent with what one would expect if PI is due to response competition alone, while RI is due to both response competition and unlearning.

The comparison between RI and PI effects remains a relatively indirect source of evidence for unlearning. Most investigators realized that a more direct measure of unlearning would be required; a means of actually charting the course of the presumed unlearning of A-B as A-C is practiced. If associations are unlearned, we should theoretically be able to observe this change in strength. To do this required the invention of several variations on the traditional paired-associate task.

Measuring Unlearning

The goal of numerous experiments since Melton and Irwin published their results has been the attempt to determine, in a more direct way, the relative change in strength of A-B associations during the course of A-C learning. Of the many such experiments, we will describe only two in this section. Both are well-known studies, and both represent the flavor of the various studies we cannot mention. The first was an experiment by Briggs (1954), and the second a study by Barnes and Underwood (1959). Both added support to the unlearning hypothesis.

Modified Free Recall (MFR). It occurred to Briggs (1954) that one method of observing the changes in strength of the two sets of associations would be to ask subjects neither specifically for List 1 responses nor List 2 responses in the test phase of the RI experiment. Rather, the A terms would be presented and subjects would be asked to give either the B or C response, whichever came to mind first. Let us consider in advance what we might expect to see according to the unlearning hypothesis.

At the beginning of List 1 practice, the stimulus A term will of course produce no response at all, unless perhaps some free association the subject might bring to the experiment from previous experience. A subject might, for example, spontaneously respond with the word "duck" the first time he or she sees the syllable DAX. As practice continues, the repeated exposure of the B term (e.g., QUICKLY) following A, should strengthen the correct A-B association and produce this B response with increasing frequency. Eventually, the correct B response should be the first thing that comes to mind whenever the subject sees the stimulus syllable. During the second stage of the experiment, List 2 learning, we should now begin to observe a decline in the B responses as the A-B association becomes extinguished and the A-C association becomes strengthened.

Figure 3-2 shows the results of the three phases of the Briggs experiment. First, we see in the extreme left-hand panel the expected rise in the number of List 1 B responses with continued A-B practice. Pre-experimental responses (like "duck") progressively decrease. At the beginning of A-C learning in the middle panel, List 1 responses continue to dominate in the free recall. At this point they are still the first ones that come to mind when the A stimulus is presented. With continued practice with the new list, however, we see a decline in List 1 B responses, and an increase in the List 2 C responses. List 2 responses clearly dominate at the end of this second phase of the experiment.

The final panel gives the results of testing after various retention intervals during which there was no new learning. The subject was again asked to give the first response that came to mind, whether B or C. With short retention intervals, the most recent C associations continue to dominate in recall. With longer retention intervals, however, we begin to see the recovery of the first list responses. By the end of a 24-hour

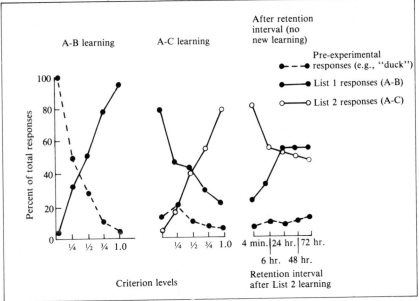

FIGURE 3-2 Percentage of responses for preexperimental, List 1, and List 2 responses during original learning (A-B learning), interpolated learning (A-C learning), and over various retention intervals using the MFR technique.
(From Briggs, 1954. Copyright © 1954 by the American Psychological Association. Reprinted by permission.)

retention interval, the frequency of the subject producing either of the two responses was almost equal. This is exactly the *spontaneous recovery* the extinction analogy for unlearning predicts: the reappearance of first-list associations apparently extinguished by the interfering learning.

Modified Modified Free Recall (MMFR). Briggs' technique, called *Modified Free Recall* (MFR), was clearly successful in demonstrating systematic changes in the dominance of one association over another. On the other hand, it was possible that some responses were not given simply because only one response was required in testing. Thus, we do not have direct evidence that the original associations were unlearned, but only that (1) they came to be dominated by the more recent associations, and (2) they recovered somewhat over time. While consistent with the unlearning-extinction hypothesis, more evidence was needed.

In a terminological escalation, Barnes and Underwood (1959) invented another version of the Briggs task which they called *Modified Modified Free Recall* (MMFR). It was a further attempt to discover the "fate" of first-list associations. In MMFR, the subject would again be required to learn the first list of A-B paired-associates, followed by learning a second list of A-C associates. This time, however, a single retention test would be given in which the subject would be asked to give, if possible, both the B and C responses when A was presented. They would also be allowed as much time as they needed to do so.

The availability of unlimited time for the responses was the key to the Barnes and Underwood experiment. They assumed that the MMFR technique would eliminate response competition. That is, the hypothetical blocking of one response by another was presumed to be a temporary phenomenon, such that providing unlimited time for the responses should permit the subject to recover from this initial inhibition. If a response was available, it should, after a time, reappear. If not, they could assume that the first-list responses had indeed faded completely from memory.

In fact, later writers were to argue that this assumption regarding the temporary nature of response competition may not be valid. As we shall see in a moment, there is some evidence to suggest that the conditions of MMFR may not be entirely free from response competition. But for the time being, let us accept Barnes and Underwood's assumption and examine their results.

Figure 3-3 shows the MMFR results, and they do appear to be in support of Briggs' findings and Melton and Irwin's unlearning hypothesis. After first learning List 1, consisting of A-B associates such as

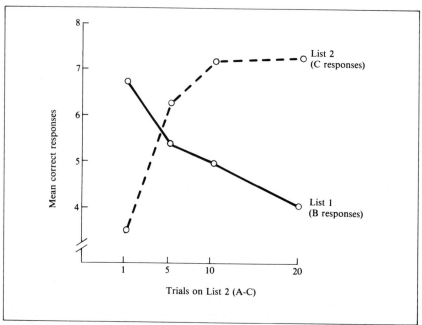

FIGURE 3-3   The ability to recall List 1 and List 2 responses as a function of the amount of practice on List 2 using the MMFR technique.
(From Barnes & Underwood, 1959. Copyright © 1959 by the American Psychological Association. Reprinted by permission.)

DAX-QUICKLY, subjects were then given various amounts of practice on List 2 consisting of A-C terms such as DAX-SOLDIER. When, after each set of practice trials on List 2 subjects were asked to give both responses, we see both a progressive increase in the ability to give List 2 responses and a progressive inability to give List 1 responses.

Barnes and Underwood saw these results as clear evidence that A-B associations actually do lose availability during the course of A-C learning. We could further argue that list differentiation could not account for these results. This would be the case at least if we accept both the idea that list differentiation occcurs with response competition and that response competition was eliminated by the unlimited response time of the MMFR technique. We are thus left with unlearning (extinction) as the primary cause of the decline in the ability to give first list responses.

Evaluation of the Two-Factor Theory

These results may leave the impression that the die is cast and two-factor theory must be accepted as the valid explanation of how interference operates in forgetting. As with many of the issues in memory research, however, things are far from settled. The experiments we described are classic ones, those that mark the beginnings of programs of research rather than their conclusion. In the course of this research, each working assumption and each interpretation of these studies has been meticulously analyzed. Little turns out to be as clear as it once seemed.

First, as we hinted earlier, the assumption that MMFR eliminates response competition may not be supportable. For example, we have seen the argument that proactive interference is thought to be entirely dependent on response competition only. It can be shown, however, that there are significant PI effects in MMFR (e.g., Ceraso & Henderson, 1965). In other words, subjects who learn two paired-associate lists and give both sets of responses under MMFR, are unable to recall second-list responses as well as a control group who learn only the second list. If PI is present, the MMFR results may in fact have been influenced by response competition. What then of the conclusion that MMFR demonstrated only the influence of unlearning effects?

Second, let us return to the unlearning-extinction analogy with its emphasis on spontaneous recovery. While it is true that spontaneous recovery of first-list associations does occur (Postman & Underwood, 1973), it occurs as a reliable phenomenon only over surprisingly brief periods (30 minutes). Other derivations of the extinction analogy have fared even less well. For example, if extinction is caused by the nonreinforced occurrence of the CS for a particular association (the A term of List 1 no longer followed by the original B term), then the amount of extinction should depend on the number of extinction trials. Attempts have been made to test this by manipulating the ease of second-list learning (see, for example, Figure 2-5 in Chapter 2). If the second list is a relatively easy one, and therefore learned rapidly, it would require fewer learning trials and hence would result in fewer extinction trials for List 1. Sometimes these procedures are successful in producing different amounts of unlearning, but sometimes they are not. The exact conditions which determine which result occurs have yet to be determined (Postman & Underwood, 1973).

The evidence for two-factor theory, taken as a whole, has weak spots and inconsistencies. Melton and Irwin (1940) argued that the response competition hypothesis was not adequate to account for the pattern of performance observed when a subject forgets. Now we find that even two factors do not seem sufficient to reliably predict our observations. Other determinants in addition to, or instead of, these two factors must play a part in a subject's inability to remember.

Association theories had to become more complicated by adding further processes to explain what response competition and unlearning failed to handle. Some of these amendments remained in the spirit of the view of memory described in Chapter 2: fundamental elements, connections between these elements, and the building up of chains of connections. Other additions, however, began to substantially change the picture of what memory might be like. These latter changes began to portray memory organization as a hierarchy rather than as an interlacing network of functionally identical units. In this altered picture of memory operations, descriptions began to be cast in terms of control over "categories," "sets," or "levels," rather than in terms of the accessibility and availability of specific associative links.

ELABORATIONS AND AMENDMENTS TO INTERFERENCE THEORY

In the latter part of the previous chapter we saw that paired-associate learning can be divided into at least three separate components: learning to discriminate or recognize the stimuli, learning the response terms, and finally, learning the associations between them. While the relative importance of stimulus and response factors remains a matter of considerable controversy within association theories (Postman & Underwood, 1973), such a componential analysis can be applied to interference paradigms to determine the possible independent contribution of each to the amount of interference produced (McGovern, 1964).

As we consider this analysis, it becomes clear that our discussion of interference theory to this point concentrated almost entirely on the final, associative, factor in paired-associate learning. Two extensions of interference theory will be discussed. The first, referred to as *response set interference,* and proposed by Postman, Stark, and Fraser (1968), concentrates primarily on the nature of the responses in paired-associate learning (see also, Newton & Wickens, 1956). It postulates that competition and dominance may operate not at the level of individual associations, but on a more general level of whole sets of responses. The second position, attributed to Martin (1971, 1974), is discussed under the heading of *stimulus encoding variability.* As the name implies, it looks for the source of interference in the stimulus learning component of the paired-associate task.

Response Set Interference

The *response set suppression hypothesis,* proposed by Postman, Stark, and Fraser (1968), is in some ways similar to McGeoch's response competition hypothesis. It is, however, a more complex level of explanation which introduces several new notions. Essentially, response set suppression suggests that the entire set of response items belonging to a particular list are either inhibited or made available as a single unit.

This theory's shift from single associations to response set availability was made necessary by the observation that different kinds of retention tests produce very different estimates of interference effects. As we have frequently noted, retroactive interference is a very powerful source of forgetting when recall tests are used, that is, when the subject sees A and must give the first list response B. However, when recognition testing was used, Postman and his colleagues found that there was in fact little or no RI. For example, if a subject is given the A term and several alternatives from which B is to be chosen, such a "multiple-choice" recognition test shows generally good performance. This is true even if the test is given immediately after second-list learning.

The results of recognition testing were interpreted as implying that the associations formed during learning the first lists are still present in memory. They have not been unlearned. If you recall the argument in Chapter 2 that recognition and recall involve different processes it then follows that recall tests might show such large amounts of retroactive interference because subjects have trouble in coming up with the appropriate set of responses from which to choose the correct syllable. If alternatives are provided, as in recognition testing, the subject does not have the problem of retrieving the response set, and hence, there is no evidence of interference. RI could thus be attributed entirely to selection and retrieval of the response set.

The simpler two-factor theory would be unable to account for the differences observed between recognition and recall. Response set suppression accounts for these data in terms of the switching of a *response set selector* and the "inertia" involved in this switching.

Let us consider for a moment the standard RI paradigm, and how this scheme would account for the typical results obtained. As the subject learns the first list (A-B), the postulated response selector mechanism activates the whole list of B responses and suppresses any extraexperimental associations to the stimulus terms (e.g., an initial association between DAX and "duck"). During A-C learning, it is the B responses that become suppressed, as a group, and the list of C responses which become activated.

This hypothetical selector is unable to switch instantaneously between response sets, such that a test of first list retention immediately after second-list learning will find the selector still activating the most recent response set. All other sets will remain inhibited. This would account for the fact that retroactive interference is greatest immediately after learning List 2. Longer retention intervals would provide time during which the selector mechanism has the opportunity to switch to the earlier response set. The result, of course, would be the now familiar spontaneous recovery of responses often observed as retention intervals are increased. Interference, then, is a result of the "sluggishness" of this response selector, combined with a persisting bias to select responses from the most recently learned list.

Notice that this hypothesis says nothing about the loss or unlearning of individual associations. Response set suppression in some ways thus parallels the response competition hypothesis, but in this case it is a whole response set that becomes temporarily unavailable. Trials on the interfering list shift dominance to a new set of responses. Little or no associative unlearning need take place to account for the observed results.

Although associative unlearning plays no major role in this theory, the response set suppression idea is not necessarily incompatible with the notion that individual associations may be unlearned, nor with the notion that there is response competition at the level of the individual association. It is possible that all three factors could occur and the summation of their combined effects produce the total RI observed. The weight of the Postman, Stark, and Fraser explanation, however, falls at the level of selection of response sets rather than at the level of individual associations.

Stimulus Encoding Variability   In our three part analysis of paired-associate learning, we distinguished between stimulus discrimination, response learning, and the "hook up," or association stage. We have concentrated so far on explanations which have emphasized the role of the association and response learning stages in forgetting. Martin (1971) has proposed that the greater part of retroactive interference can be traced to the process of stimulus learning, variations in what the subject notices and codes when initially observing the stimuli.

In paired-associate learning, there are several things a subject can attend to in learning about a nonsense syllable. For example, if there is only one stimulus item that begins with the letter "G," the subject may attend only to this letter and associate it with the appropriate response. The remaining letters in the nonsense syllable may not enter into the association at all. Similarly, in learning the second list (A-C), the subject may attend to some other aspect of the A stimulus; perhaps the second letter. Thus, while we refer to the A-B, A-C paradigm as learning different responses to the same stimuli, it is possible that the associations learned for Lists 1 and 2 may not in fact be associations to the "same" stimulus. The *nominal stimulus,* the one the experimenter presents, is not necessarily the stimulus the subject actually uses. The aspect of the stimulus the subject encodes for use in the association can be called the *functional stimulus*.

Interference, Martin suggests, may result from a subject's tendency to encode the stimuli in different ways and to have a bias toward the functional stimulus used on the most recent trial. If, in the RI paradigm, the subject attends to one cue in learning the A stimulus in List 1 and to another cue in learning the A stimulus for List 2, the subject may persist in attending to the List 2 cue when attempting to recall the B term of the first list. Should this occur, the result would be production of the second-list responses which are inappropriate to this RI test. This is the essence of the *encoding variability hypothesis;* the subject shifts from trial to trial and list to list the particular aspect of the stimulus that is associated to the response.

The response set suppression hypothesis involves a persistence of a tendency to select from the most recently learned response set. Encoding variability explains interference effects by appealing to a tendency to persist in attending to the most recently learned stimulus cues.

Stimulus cues, according to Martin, have different probabilities of selection. If one of the words were in red ink, for example, its "redness" would have a high probability of being selected as the functional stimulus for this item. Unfamiliar, or complex stimuli may lead to greater variability from trial to trial in which cue is selected as the functional stimulus. This inconsistency will make learning more difficult. If a different cue is learned on every trial, there will be little transfer from one trial to the next. To master the list, the subject must develop a plan or strategy that will ensure that the same cue is consistently selected. The strategy of selecting the same cues that were used in learning List 2 persisting when the subject tries to recall List 1, would produce retroactive interference. The stimulus encoding view, like response suppression, places very little emphasis on associative unlearning. Martin (1974), in fact, is skeptical as to the very existence of associative unlearning.

Each of these hypotheses has departed from the simple connectionist picture of memory. The response set suppression hypothesis alters the original picture by referring to a new level of analysis in which lists of responses become "units" to be operated on by mechanisms of interference. Stimulus encoding introduces the idea of attentional selection and a distinction between the nominal stimulus and the functional stimulus. These ideas represent significant modifications in the single association elemental view we first encountered as associationism.

Interference and Forgetting: Conclusions

We began this discussion of associative theory with the simple observation that forgetting is caused by interference. Other learning somehow prevents appropriate remembering. It is this "somehow" that the associationist's theories tried to specify and to explain. We found that no single mechanism or factor is sufficient to account for interference effects. Several processes and mechanisms were proposed, each of which may contribute to the total interference effects observed in any particular case. Some of these proposals had more experimental support than others; some still have the status of provocative speculation.

First, the original hypothesis of McGeoch (1932) proposed that interference effects were due to an item specific response competition that was triggered by the stimulus at the time of testing. Associations remained intact but one dominated and suppressed the other. Second, item specific associative unlearning was suggested by Melton and Irwin (1940) to account for the fact that mistakes seldom take the form of response substitution. The principle of unlearning supposes that practice on interfering items extinguishes prior associations to the same stimulus. The temporal locus of this factor, then, is during second-list learning.

List differentiation was a third factor proposed to play some role in the forgetting effects observed in paired-associate tasks. Learning to identify which items belonged to which lists permits a subject to withhold responses that might otherwise occur as overt intrusions. If the subject is unable to identify the list membership of a response, no "editing" of the performance can take place.

A fourth factor proposed was that of response set suppression. This factor is assumed to operate on the whole set of list responses as a unit. The response set belonging to a particular list may be either activated or suppressed as a group by a selector mechanism. This mechanism is "tuned" to the response set during acquisition of a particular list. Because the mechanism cannot be switched from one set to another instantaneously, a particular response set may be temporarily unavailable until the selector mechanism has time to reactivate this set.

Finally, stimulus encoding mechanisms, based on attentional factors at the time of learning, may play some role in determining the amount of interference produced by other learning. What the subject attends to and encodes will determine what is learned. If the subject develops strategies or plans to attend to certain cues, these persisting strategies may prevent attending to what was learned for the previous list.

Few theorists of forgetting accept all five of these processes as equally important to interference effects. Stimulus encoding variability, for example, is proposed as a fundamental alternative to associative unlearning and response set suppression (Martin, 1974). The controversy concerns both conceptual and methodological issues (Postman & Underwood, 1973). All these notions, however, grew from a basic picture of what memory is like: a structure of elements interconnected by associative bonds. The idea of response set suppression and the mechanism of attention are outside this conception. They are, however, additions to, rather than serious revisions of, this picture. Interference theories account for a great deal of the data obtained in studying forgetting of paired-associate materials, and this was a major accomplishment of the associationist tradition.

The interference theory and its several offspring have dominated the study of verbal learning for several decades. The studies described in this section have concerned themselves primarily with the phenomenon of forgetting of relatively isolated verbal materials acquired through rote practice. As we all know, however, not all associations are equally difficult to learn or as quickly forgotten. Differences in the elements to be associated and the subject's prior knowledge seem to produce these substantial differences in ease of learning and good retention. We know, for example, that many associations are more resistant to the effects of RI and PI than others, and also, that subjects often give responses as associations to stimuli with which they have never been paired. The answer, according to association theory, lies in the concept of *mediation*.

THE CONCEPT OF MEDIATION

In any experimental study of memory we can expect our subjects to do their best to impart some coherence or meaning to the material. They may, for example, use logical categories. If a list consists of the words blue, doctor, Mary, carpenter, Jill, green, Catherine, red, plumber, we can expect subjects to reorganize the list as blue, green, red; Mary, Jill, Catherine; doctor, carpenter, plumber. Should no convenient structure be available, subjects may group words that rhyme, or words which begin with the same letter. In short, subjects use what they already know about language and about the world to invest meaning and structure into the task.

In discussing this effort of typical experimental subjects, Bower (1972) defines structure and organization as all the possible relations among a set of elements. A group of elements is a set connected by a common relation, or a common property. Some of these relations may be supplied by the conditions of the experiment itself. For example, if the items are grouped in time by the experimenter (53-78-24), the subject will reproduce this grouped pattern in recall.

Other types of organization will require that the subject use information already known in order to transform the materials into meaningful form. It is this latter kind of organization that concerns us in this section. A relationship in these cases is thought to be mediated by associations acquired prior to the experiment. Long-term memory serves to link or *mediate* between the to-be-remembered materials and the structure of recall. It is this mediation from long-term memory that can serve to facilitate both acquisition and retention.

Natural Language Mediation

Ebbinghaus invented the nonsense syllable to minimize the effects of prior experience on his observations of associative learning. He was aware that the invention was not totally successful, and that some syllables were easier to learn than others. It was left to other investigators to examine specifically how this comes about.

However "meaningless" CVCs may appear to be, subjects' past language habits can impose meaning on them. Some CVCs quickly elicit associations to common English words. The syllable FAM may suggest "family," "famine," "familiar," and so forth. Such syllables that easily produce associations may be contrasted with other syllables that produce fewer associations, such as the CVCs CIJ or GUQ. Noble and McNeely (1957) defined a syllable's "meaningfulness" as the number of English words that could be given in free association within a given time limit. They suggested that different degrees of meaningfulness in this sense explained why some syllables were more easily learned than others. These associations, they said, mediated the recall of the more "meaningful" items.

The awareness that prior associations have substantial effects on current learning led research workers to measure the association values of their stimulus materials and to establish norms that could be used to control for these effects in experiments. At the same time, other students of verbal learning turned their attention to the study of the mediation process itself and the ways in which it can facilitate learning and recall.

The facilitation of learning and retention by prior learning is called *positive transfer* (see Chapter 2). In a typical study of positive transfer Jenkins (1963) had subjects learn a list of paired-associates containing pairs such as DAX-*hammer* and WUG-*king*. Once this set was learned, the subjects were given a second set containing the items DAX-*nail* and WUG-*queen*. In such cases, the second set will be learned with fewer trials than would be required by a group learning only this list. We assume that the subject used preexisting associations between *hammer* and *nail,* and between *king* and *queen* to make a connection. Once the DAX-*hammer* association has been acquired, the DAX-*nail* association can be linked through an association the subject already has between *hammer* and *nail*. Diagrammatically, the mediations for this example would be: DAX→*(hammer)→nail* and WUG→*(king)→queen*.

Linking items through associations which exist as part of one's knowledge of language is called *natural language mediation (NLM)*. Russell and Storms (1965) have shown how NLMs can be extended into whole chains of associations. This can occur when subjects are given a list containing such pairs as ZUG-*soldier,* followed by a second list containing ZUG-*navy*. Since most subjects already have a strong association between *soldier* and *sailor,* and *sailor* and *navy,* the second list is learned as ZUG→*(soldier)→(sailor)→navy*. Without supplemental questioning, all we may observe in such an experiment is the relatively rapid acquisition of the correct response. Our intuitions about what goes on in these situations are supported by extensive studies in which the subjects are asked to report the mediators that they used (e.g., Underwood & Schultz, 1960; Bugelski, 1962; Martin, Boersma & Cox, 1965).

These examples are typical of those specially constructed to encourage the use of mediators. This is possible because potential mediators can be inferred from studies of the association norms of ordinary English words (e.g., Postman & Keppel, 1970). Even without such structured lists, however, subjects will frequently employ NLMs to facilitate learning.

Montague, Adams, and Kiess (1966) gave subjects lists of paired-associates for retention, requiring them to write down any associates that occurred to them in the course of learning. These associations were based on a variety of different relations between the CVC and potential mediators. There were associations of sound, similarities in letter groups, acronyms, etc. Twenty-four hours later a retention test was administered. Subjects were asked to produce both the response member of the pair and the associations they had generated at the time of learning.

For some pairs, subjects reported the use of an NLM both at the time of acquisition and at the time of the retention test. The response terms for these pairs were correctly reproduced 72.6% of the time. If the subjects reported using an NLM during learning, but could not produce the NLM at recall, the accuracy of performance fell to 1.8%. Finally, if the subjects reported no use of NLMs during initial learning, later retention of the response term was also quite low (5.8%).

The main point of this experiment is the superior performance of the group who used the same appropriate NLM both during learning and at the time of retrieval. We cannot avoid noticing, however, that the final group who reported no use of NLMs at all did slightly better than subjects who reported using NLMs during learning but not at recall. These results imply that the use of an unretrievable memory code can be more detrimental to performance than no code at all. We have already seen a hint of this possibility in Martin's (1971) work on stimulus encoding variability. We will later see the other side of this coin when we discuss stimulus encoding specificity (Tulving & Thomson, 1973). At this point, however, let us look more closely at the use of strategies in determination and later utilization of NLMs in paired-associate tasks.

The Montague, Adams, and Kiess (1966) study clearly shows that the use of natural language mediators is correlated with a facilitation of learning and a higher level of retention. It also suggests that some effort may be required on the part of the subject to find appropriate NLMs. For example, in studies such as these, subjects who are able to report the kind of strategies or techniques they used in forming NLMs typically show significantly higher recall scores than those who report not using any particular strategy (Martin, Boersma & Cox, 1965; Martin, Cox & Boersma, 1965). This notion of effort in the selection of appropriate NLMs can also be seen in studies which show more use of mediation when the rate of presentation of the learning materials is slow (over two seconds per pair) than when it is faster (Montague et al., 1966).

Prytulak (1971) has argued that effective use of mediation involves two stages. The first stage involves formulation of an NLM after seeing the stimulus (encoding). The second stage occurs at the time of the retention test and involves retrieval of the correct NLM and using this in turn to retrieve the original stimulus (decoding). In Prytulak's words, encoding into a mediator involves a "transformation" on the learning material. This transformation may consist of adding a letter to a CVC to make a meaningful word, substitution of letters, deletion of letters, or supplying some semantic association.

Anyone who has ever thought of an ingenious mediator but later forgot what it was supposed to mediate will appreciate that a good NLM must be one which unambiguously arouses the correct original associat-tion. In the terms used here, some transformations are easier to decode than others. For example, using JAZZ as a mediator for remembering JYZ involves the substitution of A for Y and the addition of Z. Using the mediator LOVE to remember LOV involves only the addition of the letter E. Both mediators may come to mind when recall is tested, but LOVE may be easier to translate back to LOV than JAZZ back to JYZ.

Prytulak (1971) considered a variety of stimuli and mediators and found it quite possible to order the various transformations in terms of their effectiveness. He developed what he called a *T-Stack model* to describe how subjects may use mediators. He called it a "T-Stack," envisaging a list ("stack") of transformations ("T-Stack"), ordered in terms of their ease of decoding. He assumed that in initial encoding one will begin with the easiest possible transformation in attempting to convert a stimulus into a mediator. If the first attempt does not work, the process continues on down the stack until an appropriate mediator is produced. The farther down the stack the subject must go to find the mediator, the lower will be the probability that the mediator will be correctly decoded back to the original stimulus at the time of the retention test.

The nature of the stimulus material will determine what kind of mediator is the most likely to be produced. The higher the association value of the stimulus, the more likely it will be that the subject will produce an NLM. In general, we can conclude that subjects actively try to make sense out of isolated words or syllables presented in these studies. Their strategy in conferring meaning on these materials is to associate this information to other strong associations possessed as the result of natural language habits.

Image Mediation and Mnemonics

The use of visual imagery as a form of mediation has attracted increasing attention in recent years with the studies of Paivio and his colleagues (see Paivio, 1971). It has been shown that lists of visualizable nouns, such as *cup* or *chair,* are more accurately retained than lists of more abstract nouns such as *happiness* or *truth.* Sets of words are also more easily recalled if the subject is instructed to incorporate the named objects into a single visual image. Bower (1972), for example, gave two groups of subjects different instructions on how to learn paired-associate word lists. One group was instructed to form a visual image that united the two words of a pair. If a pair consisted of DOG-BICYCLE, the subject might try to imagine a dog riding a bicycle. (Generally, the more unique the association, the more effective it will be.) A control group was given no special imagery instructions. The subjects instructed to use visual imagery did substantially better than the control subjects when later tested for retention of the paired-associates.

We will have occasion to return to the question of imagery later, as the concept of imagery remains a controversial one in memory research (see Chapter 8). Arguments have centered chiefly on whether the information is stored as a literal visual representation, or whether the representation may in fact be in some more abstract form. Introspection may not be a reliable guide here since the process of constructing an image does not seem to be available to conscious awareness. As just one example, a person's feelings of the vividness of an image seems to correlate little with recall accuracy. This is a surprising finding for the notion of a literal visual representation of the stimuli in memory (Neisser, 1970; Sheehan & Neisser, 1969).

Whether or not a subject's performance is based on visual information (Paivio, 1971) or some more abstract derivative representation (Anderson & Bower, 1973; Potter & Faulconer, 1975; Pylyshyn, 1973), instructions to use these representations do serve to facilitate retention. A visual scene, or at least an attempt to form one, provides an organization on which to map the to-be-remembered associations. Plans which provide a ready made organization for information to be remembered are called *mnemonics*.

Imagery and rhyme are both common forms of mnemonics. A striking example of the use of both is offered by Hunter (1964). Subjects were given ten number-object combinations such as ONE-SUGAR, TWO-DAFFODIL, THREE-BOAT, FOUR-TIGER, and so fourth. One group was given a well known rhyming mnemonic:

> One is a Bun, Two is a Shoe,
> Three is a Tree, Four is a Door,
> Five is a Hive, Six is Sticks,
> Seven is Heaven, Eight is a Gate,
> Nine is Wine, Ten is a Hen.

The mnemonic group first memorized the rhyme, then were instructed to picture each object as vividly as possible in the context of the rhyme. For the ONE-SUGAR pair the subject might imagine a bun (One is a bun) coated with sugar, for TWO-DAFFODIL they might imagine a shoe (Two is a shoe) with a daffodil in it, and so forth. This group using the mnemonic scored much higher on a retention test than a control group without the rhyme and imagery instructions. While this particular mnemonic combines both rhyme and imagery, rhyming alone is also a common technique. Common examples are the "Thirty days hath September ..." rhyme for remembering the number of days in the months, and the spelling mnemonic, "i before e, except after c."

Mnemonics are presumed to work by supplying an effective organization for otherwise unrelated materials. The relation in the mnemonic thus becomes the relation between the elements to be remembered. Mnemonics differ from the organization of memory in ordinary experience only in that they are especially invented mediators, a special purpose tool for learning. In the following section we will look at organization in free recall which makes use of preexisting associations and conceptual knowledge.

ORGANI- ZATION IN FREE RECALL

The reader who is impressed by the potency of RI and PI effects may wonder at this point why we do not forget more than we do. Mediators may help in formal paired-associate learning, but what of ordinary memory in more everyday situations? The answer to the question of why we remember as much as we do lies in the natural organization we give to experience. Such organization is usually more than a match for the RI and PI effects which work so powerfully on unrelated materials (CVCs or word pairs).

Our memories, in other words, do not seem to be a helter-skelter of elements and isolated associations, but an organized network of relationships which can help stored information to withstand the effects of interference. Mediators, of the types described in the previous section, rely upon this structure to facilitate acquisition and retention. Natural language mediators, imagery, and mnemonics, are all mediating uses of memory organization.

Since this organization plays a crucial role in how we interpret and remember our experience, students of memory have devoted considerable effort to attempts at describing the structure of this organization and in measuring its effects. This study of memory organization, however, requires us to shift our emphasis away from our examination of the acquisition and retention of individual associations. One way to do this is to examine the structure of recall performance in relatively unconstrained memory tasks. The technique of choice from the very beginning was that of *free recall.*

In this final section we will look at two attempts to understand organization in memory. The first, *associative clustering,* derives from the traditional studies of mediated association. The second, *category clustering,* begins the shift from elemental associationism to organization through conceptual knowledge. It serves as a bridge between the associative view described in this and the previous chapter and the exciting contemporary work to be described in Chapter 4 under the heading of semantic memory.

Associative Clustering

In the section on natural language mediation, we saw how existing word associations can facilitate retention scores in paired-associate learning. An even more dramatic effect can be observed when subjects are given whole sets of associated words for recall. In a typical experiment, subjects might be given 24 word pairs from free association norms. These would be sets of stimulus words known to be strong associates for most people (e.g., mother–father, hammer–nail, hot–cold, king–queen). The members of a pair are not presented together, but are scrambled to appear as a random arrangement of 48 words. Care is taken to ensure that none of the associated words occur together in the list, and no mention is made of the associations "buried" in the full set.

On recall testing, not only do the associated words tend to be grouped together in recall, but the higher the association values between the words, the more likely they are to be recalled together (Jenkins, Mink & Russell, 1958; Jenkins & Russell, 1952). Deese (1959, 1961) and his associates extended these findings to situations in which all the words in a list are associated together. Of special interest was the interitem association strength of these lists.

Interitem association strength is defined by the frequency with which one item elicits another item as a free associate. A list with high interitem associative strength would be one in which each word has a high probability of eliciting each of the others as free associates. A list containing moth, insect, fly, and bird would be a good example of high interitem associative strength. An intermediate list, one composed of items less strongly related to each other, might be garden, sky, flutter, chase, sunshine, and nature. Finally, a zero association list might be book, moon, government, ceiling, and winter.

Deese and others have shown overall recall performance for such lists to be directly related to their association strength. Highest scores are obtained for lists that are highly associated, the poorest scores for lists that have association values of zero. Scores for intermediate associations lie somewhere in between.

While intrusions of strong associates which were not in a list sometimes occur as errors in recall, intrusions of this kind are relatively rare. Subjects clearly have the ability to use associations to facilitate recall, but at the same time they can edit their performance so as to inhibit responses which did not occur in the list.

As reliable as these studies were, it was possible that the associations observed were in fact a consequence of underlying conceptual categories, rather than of associations between the words, per se. That is, table and chair may be given together in memory experiments not because the words themselves are associated, but because both are members of a category we would call "furniture." Let us take a closer at recall clustering in terms of such categories.

Category Clustering

The study of clustering in recall by conceptual category was begun by Bousfield and Sedgewick (1944) who devised a simple technique for examining spontaneous organization in free recall. Their procedure was to ask subjects to list from memory as many items from a specific category as they could. They used simple well-known categories such as names of birds, animals, or cities in the United States. As a general rule, the initial responses were produced in rapid succession, with the rate of output gradually decreasing as the category became exhausted. The exception to this rule was that some sequences would be produced in rapid succession as a cluster of responses. For example, if the category were birds, the instances *hawk, eagle, vulture* might be rapidly recalled as one group, and *chicken, turkey, duck, goose* as another.

These initial demonstrations of *category clustering* in free recall led to other experiments in which the category members were explicitly manipulated. Bousfield (1953) constructed a list of 60 nouns made up of 15 items each drawn from four categories: *animals* (e.g., giraffe, zebra, weasel); *names* (e.g., Bernard, Sherman Howard); *professions* (e.g., chemist, dentist, plumber) and *vegetables* (e.g., melon, spinach, carrot). The 60 names were then scrambled in a random order so that members of the same category did not occur together in the list. The entire list was then read aloud to a group of subjects at a rate of one word every 3 seconds. Although the words were presented in random order, recall showed clear evidence of clustering by category. Words from the same category occurred together and in rapid succession.

A closer look at this timing of responses can be found in an experiment by Pollio, Richards, and Lucas (1969). Subjects were given a scrambled list in which each word fell into one of five categories. Figure 3-4 shows an idealized record of the timing patterns they obtained during free recall. The first four vertical marks on the time dimension represent the rapid rate of output of four members of one category cluster (e.g., animals). This is followed by a noticeable delay before the production of the four words of the next category (e.g., vegetables). This pattern is repeated throughout recall: a rapid production of the category clusters separated by noticeable pauses as the subject seems to shift from one category to another (Pollio, 1974; Pollio et al., 1969).

The results of studies such as these suggested a highly organized, content-addressable memory store, in which items are accessible through active search. By content-addressable, we mean that the store is organized and accessed on the basis of category membership, rather than, for example, the order in which the specific items were heard. At

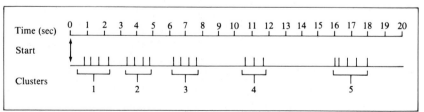

FIGURE 3-4   Idealized time record of a subject's production of categorized word lists in free recall.

(Adapted from Pollio, 1974.)

recall, the subject scans memory until a relevant category is encountered and produced. This is followed by a delay as the subject resumes scanning for the next category cluster. This process of scanning, production, and scanning continues until the full set of relevant categories has been exhausted.

Could we not, however, also suggest that these delays represent the time taken to organize each category for response during the retention test itself? That is, categorical organization is clearly present in the response but it is not immediately clear whether these words were organized during the course of their initial acquisition or whether they were organized during the act of recall itself. We will return to this important question in a moment.

Whatever the answer to this question, categorical clustering looks similar to clustering by association, as we discussed it in the previous section. Because words of the same conceptual category frequently do produce each other in free association, the question was raised whether associative clustering could serve as the explanation for category clustering. Bousfield and Puff (1964) and Wood and Underwood (1967) answered this question by showing that category clustering occurs even when the words within a category have been specially chosen for their low interitem association strengths. Other studies have verified the continued occurrence of categorical clustering even when word associations have been controlled (Cofer, 1965; Marshall & Cofer, 1963). Associative clustering and categorical clustering are thus independent kinds of organization. Indeed, subjects can make use of both when both types of retention are available in the structure of the lists (Cofer, 1965).

Subjective Organization. It is clear from numerous studies that organization plays a key role in memory performance even when we do not supply lists easily amenable to ready organization (Tulving, 1962, 1964, 1968b). In a typical experiment to illustrate this point, Tulving gave subjects a list of 16 unrelated words with the instructions to recall as many words as possible, in any order they wished, after each of a series of practice presentations. The order of words within the list were changed from presentation to presentation to prevent simple associations based solely on consecutive words.

In spite of these precautions, most subjects supplied their own subjective organization to the words; certain words were invariably recalled together after each presentation. Further, for most subjects, the incidence of this clustering increased systematically from trial to trial. The effect of this subjective organization on recall was dramatic. At the end of 16 practice trials, the correlation between the degree of organization and recall performance was an almost perfect .96. In other words, the more the subjective organization, the better the recall.

These results prompt us to ask whether one's own subjective organization might be even more effective for recall performance than organization supplied by the experimenter. Mandler and Pearlstone (1966) gave subjects a set of 52 words, each printed on a separate card. Instructions were to sort the cards into categories using any number of categories from 2 to 7. One group was told to sort the cards on any basis they wished, while a second group of subjects was required to use categories given them by the experimenter. (These categories were taken from those chosen by the first group.)

As your own intuition might have suggested, the group that was allowed to sort into their own categories required fewer trials for consistent sorting than did subjects who had been told how the cards were to be sorted. The difference lay between creating an organization on the one hand, and learning one on the other. On a retention test for the individual items, however, both groups did equally well once the organization had been learned. This suggests that it is the presence, not necessarily the origin of the organization, that is important to recall. For both groups, subjects tended to recall an average of five words per category regardless of how many categories were used. That is, the more categories used, the better the recall score.

Organization: Storage or Recall?

Just as we saw a debate over the locus of interference effects, there was also a spirited controversy over where, in the acquisition–recall sequence, organization had its primary facilitating effects. As we indicated earlier in discussing the Pollio et al. clustering study, the division of opinion has been between those who emphasize the contribution of organization to the storage of materials during initial acquisition versus those who emphasize its contribution to the process of retrieval.

Briefly, the storage view asks questions about how organization affects the information coded or placed in memory. It is concerned with the *availability of information* in memory. As we noted when discussing encoding variability, there is not only a variety of ways in which a stimulus may be stored, there is also a variety of potential aspects of this stimulus which may or may not form a part of the stored information. How the aspects are organized, the way in which relations among the stimuli are coded, may reasonably be expected to affect selection of information at the time of recall.

The emphasis in the retrieval view is on how organization could facilitate selective activation of appropriate responses. Hypotheses here are typically in terms of plans or strategies the subject may develop in order to best gain access to particular information in memory. This view concerns the *accessibility of information* in memory. You may recognize the parallel between this controversy and our discussion of unlearning versus response competition. In both cases, one hypothesis emphasizes effects on storage and the other emphasizes factors that control access to the stored information.

The evidence most relevant to these issues comes from studies of *cuing*. Pollio and Gerow (1968), for example, presented subjects with a 25-item list consisting of five categories of five items each. As in most other studies, the individual items were presented in scrambled order with respect to their category. At the start of the learning trials, one group of subjects was told that each item belonged to one of five categories and each category was named. This procedure was assumed to directly affect how the information would be encoded and stored. A second group received no cuing (information about the categories) during presentation, but were provided with this information just prior to the retention test. Any effect here would be presumed to reflect benefits of organization on retrieval. A final group received no cuing at all.

The results of the Pollio and Gerow study were clear in showing both of the cued groups to have much better recall of the materials than the no-cue group. Within this, however, there was no significant difference between recall accuracy of the two cued groups. Since the cue-at-test group had already stored the materials at the time the cue was given, cuing could not have affected the way in which the items were initially stored. Therefore, the lack of a difference between the two groups seems to suggest that cuing by categories has its most positive effect on the process of retrieval.

Encoding Specificity.   While one can apparently facilitate recall by providing efficient retrieval cues, other studies have clearly shown that presenting cues both at learning and at testing is ordinarily more effective than presenting cues at only one of these points (Tulving & Osler, 1968; Thomson & Tulving, 1970). These studies have led to a current emphasis on the importance of a congruity between encoding and retrieval cues, an emphasis which represents organization effects as a complex interaction between encoding, storage, and retrieval processes.

This emphasis, often referred to as the *encoding specificity principle,* has three postulates: (1) items are stored in memory the way they are first perceived, (2) the particular manner of encoding determines the kind of retrieval cues that will permit access to the stored information, and (3) the closer coding and retrieval cues match each other, the better we can expect the recall to be (Tulving & Thomson, 1973; Wiseman & Tulving, 1976).

The encoding specificity principle thus implies that in order to be an effective retrieval cue, the information used in retrieval must be stored with the to-be-remembered information at the time of learning. Effective organization does just this. The principle also implies that the precision of encoding, the uniqueness of the link between retrieval cues and the encoded information, will play a critical role in recall ability (Craik, 1977a; Stein, 1978).

Many of us are familiar with one example of this principle, the way in which we encode information when preparing for a multiple-choice versus an essay examination. The kinds of information encoded, and the way they are encoded, may be less efficient in preparing for one kind of examination than for another. Encoding specificity is important to successful memory performance and so too is the appropriateness of the later test to the initial manner of encoding (Stein, 1978). The encoding specificity principle is an important component of current views of memory and we will have more to say on this subject in Chapter 8.

Mediation and Organization: Conclusions

The studies of mediation and clustering provide evidence about the way organization in memory can be influenced by the preexisting structure of our vocabularies. When a subject encounters new material, he or she attempts to incorporate this new material into the existing structure, to use the preexisting structure to facilitate the acquisition of the new information. The association theorists saw this organization as a vast network of interlocking associations (Postman, 1972; Wallace, 1970).

The origin of structure, to the association theorists, was in the contiguity, or occurrence together in time, of the to-be-related events. It was not strictly necessary that these contiguities be between the overt stimuli and responses as actually presented by the experimenter. The concept of mediation proposed that contiguity between covert associations and experimenter presented stimuli could facilitate the rapid learning of associated responses. The important point was that association theory saw all of these phenomena as basically dependent on the formation of associations through contiguity, whether this contiguity was direct (S-R associations) or indirect (mediated associations).

The contrary position can be seen in Tulving's (1972) distinction between *semantic* and *episodic memory*. Contiguity between associations is not necessary for the results we observe. The results obtained in studies of associative and category clustering could be derived from the organization provided by semantic memory.

Semantic memory, according to Tulving, contains the storehouse of organized knowledge about words, their meanings, and their relations. Episodic memory, on the other hand, records the perceptual experiences of the individual, those which can be dated autobiographically in terms of time and place. When you had breakfast and what you ate today is typical of episodic memory. Your knowledge of what an egg is, and where it comes from, is something stored in semantic memory. The notions of association and contiguity, in other words, may have utility for understanding limited aspects of episodic memory. But they have little utility for the understanding of semantic memory and they systematically underrate the contribution of semantic memory to the formation of these associations.

This distinction between semantic and episodic memory attempts to do justice to our intuitions that there is something fundamentally different about these kinds of memories. Your knowledge of what an egg is and its relationship with chickens is not information to which you attach any personal context. Nor are you likely to remember when, where, or from whom you acquired this information. In this sense, it is not a memory of something which happened in the past, such as the events surrounding your morning's breakfast. This latter kind of memory is in the domain of episodic memory.

A number of important theorists have attempted to build on Tulving's distinction in order to describe alternative models of organization among meaningful concepts. We will examine Tulving's distinction and the alternatives this distinction engendered in our next chapter.

CHAPTER SUMMARY

1. *Interference Theories of Forgetting*

   A. The research strategies used in the development of interference theory were based on the Ebbinghaus tradition of examining memory for unrelated, meaningless materials such as CVCs. Typically using the paired-associate paradigm, the goal was a study of memory uncontaminated by past knowledge and experience. Response competition theory held that failures of recall in an RI paradigm were due to a competition between old and new associations. More recent, well-learned associations will tend to dominate and block the retrieval of the earlier ones. This blocking occurs at the time of attempted recall. The strength of first list associations remains unaffected by the new learning.

   B. The unlearning hypothesis proposed that earlier associations became unlearned, or extinguished, in the course of learning new associations. This hypothesis was sometimes called the two-factor theory since it accepted the possibility of some response competition early in second list learning. The greater effects of RI than PI were attributed to both competition and unlearning operating in RI but competition alone operating in PI.

2. *Testing the Two-Factor Theory*

   A. The evidence used to support the unlearning hypothesis could also be explained by list differentiation. An initial confusion between old and new associations followed by more effective differentiation could account for the rise and fall in intrusions from the new list as found by Melton and Irwin. The confirmation of unlearning as the major factor in producing interference required that the loss of strength of an association be directly measured.

   B. The methods of Modified Free Recall (MFR) and Modified Modified Free Recall (MMFR) were intended to tap the continued presence of first list associations. Both methods indicated a progressive loss of first list associations during the course of second list learning as predicted by the unlearning hypothesis.

3. *Elaborations and Amendments to Interference Theory*

   A. Response set suppression was a modification to the response competition hypothesis. It proposed a response selection mechanism which must be shifted from one entire set of responses to another. A "sluggishness" in shifting selection, together with a bias toward the most recently learned set, could yield the RI effects and spontaneous recovery observations which had been used to support the unlearning-extinction analogy.

B. Stimulus encoding variability could be an additional factor affecting RI in paired-associate learning. Different features of the stimuli may be encoded on different occasions such that attempts to retrieve first list associations are hindered by the use of cues appropriate to second list learning but inappropriate to first list retrieval.

4. *The Concept of Mediation*

A. The concept of mediation was intended to relate the study of isolated associations in the typical paired-associate task to the rapid learning of more meaningful materials. Mediated associations are associations whose stimulus and response terms are related already by preexisting links established from prior learning. The learning and retention of meaningful materials is more efficient than nonsense materials because nonsense provides less opportunity for the use of memory organization to link the elements.

B. Natural Language Mediation (NLM) refers to the use of existing associations to form a new connection between previously unrelated stimuli. Visual imagery represents another form of mediation in which learning and retention of associations are facilitated by forming a mental "picture" of the connection. Mnemonics are a special case of mediated learning. They are special purpose tools for creating relations between previously unrelated items.

5. *Organization in Free Recall*

A. In free recall, words with strong associations to each other in past experience tend to cluster together, and lists in which all members have a high interitem association strength tend to be recalled better than lists of low interitem strength. Words belonging to the same conceptual category also tend to cluster together in free recall. Categorically related items cluster together in free recall, and are produced in rapid succession. Studies of subjective organization demonstrate the effectiveness with which people exercise their own organizing strategies when attempting to learn otherwise unrelated materials.

B. Organizing cues given either during learning (storage) or at recall (retrieval) will facilitate performance, but the best performance occurs when similar organizing principles are present on both occasions.

C. The encoding specificity principle states that recall will be best when the retrieval cues used most closely match the encoding cues used in initial acquisition.

D. Semantic memory refers to conceptual knowledge unrelated to the time, place, or context in which it was acquired. Episodic memory refers to memory for specific events and the context in which they were learned. Many feel that association theories relate most closely to limited aspects of episodic memory only and have underrated the importance of semantic memory to the retention process.

MEANING AND KNOWLEDGE: STUDIES OF SEMANTIC MEMORY

CHAPTER OUTLINE

TOPIC QUESTIONS

1. The Bartlett Tradition.

What was Bartlett's concept of *schemata*, and how did he use this concept to explain ordinary memory? What are the major characteristics of *constructive memory*? What is the effect of supplying a thematic context on the learning of a set of verbal materials?

2. Inference in Memory.

How does understanding, or comprehension of a set of materials affect the ability to recall these materials? What is *semantic integration*, and what does it suggest about the learning of meaningful materials? How is *inference* used in the process of recall?

3. Memory Organization.

What does the *tip-of-the-tongue phenomenon* tell us about the organization of concepts in memory? What is meant by referring to recall as a *search process*?

4. Models of Semantic Memory.

What were the major characteristics of *network models* of memory organization? What special notions were added by the *HAM model* of memory organization? What aspects of memory were emphasized by *semantic feature models* of memory organization? Can these models of memory organization be incorporated into a single theory?

5. The Intelligent Computer.

How are *decision processes* involved in remembering? How may logical inference be incorporated into the process of recall? How do descriptions of *script* and *text processing* improve upon Bartlett's notion of schemata in memory?

We have examined in these last two chapters the associationist picture of memory and its consequences for memory theory and research. As we saw, the associationists sought to analyze memory into essential atoms of associative elements. The associative bond, derived from a subject's experience with stimuli, represented such a basic atomic element.

For classical association theory there was only one kind of relationship between units, a one-to-one connection. The connections could vary in strength but not in kind. To these elemental theorists, all human memory and its uses were built up from this single type of relationship between individual units.

Whether we examine the everyday uses of memory, or indeed, even its more esoteric uses in the verbal learning laboratory, one-to-one relationships of a single type do not seem to be a sufficient explanation of the behavior we observe. We not only remember specific information about events in our experience, we also remember more general, or context-free, information such as how to do multiplication, or how to spell the word "obscene."

Our understanding of events and of the meanings of concepts is made up of relationships to other events and other concepts. Even more important, we seem also to have some awareness of our own states of knowledge and the processes that act on memory. Asked to give the mathematical formula for the normal curve, for example, most people would simply say "I don't know." They would not begin to generate a variety of associations to the question. One the other hand, if asked to recall where they sat in the first grade, most people would try to search for the answer, knowing, however, that this will require some work. They might even tell you of some particular strategy they used in trying to come up with that piece of information. Through experience we not only acquire knowledge, but also some awareness about what we know and how to go about remembering.

One of the tests of a psychological theory is what has been called *sufficiency conditions* (Anderson & Bower, 1973). That is, it is not enough to account for the isolated results of a particular laboratory procedure. To be adequate, a theory must deal with the full complexity of human behavior as it occurs "naturally." Associationist theories sought to build up to such explanations by starting with simple situations and simple stimulus materials. Another approach to sufficiency begins with the more ordinary kinds of remembering. This approach is usually credited to the several studies described by Sir Frederic Bartlett in his book, *Remembering* (1932).

THE BARTLETT TRADITION: RECON- STRUCTIVE MEMORY

Bartlett began his most famous studies from an interest in how people transmitted and remembered simple stories. The themes and phrasing of the stories he used were alien to the subjects' own cultural experience. His subjects were English undergraduates; the stories were drawn from legends and folk tales of other cultures. Bartlett (1932) described his motivation for undertaking these studies:

1. I . . . had in mind the general problem of what actually happens when a popular story travels from one social group to another, and thought that . . . this (study) might shed some light upon the general conditions of transformation under such circumstances.

2. The incidents described in some of the cases had no manifest interconnection, and I wished particularly to see how educated and rather sophisticated students would deal with this lack of obvious rational order.

3. The dramatic character of some of the events . . . seemed likely to arouse some fairly vivid imagery in suitable subjects, and I thought perhaps further light might be thrown on some of the suggestions regarding the conditions and functions of imagery. (p. 64)

Bartlett used two methods in his investigations. The first he called *serial reproduction*. In this method the subject reads a story and then retells it from memory to another student. This second person tells it to a third person, the third person tells it to a fourth person, and so on. The process ends with a comparison between the final version of the story as passed from person to person, and the original, as it was first presented.

At first glance this seems more a study of gossip than of memory. The results from the method of serial reproduction become meaningful, however, when contrasted with those obtained with the second method, *repeated reproduction*. In this method a single person reads the story, and then must retell it from memory on several subsequent occasions. In repeated retelling of the story, Bartlett observed exactly the same performance characteristics as were observed in serial reproduction. The picture of memory painted by these data was that of an active process of *reconstruction* based on an incomplete memory of the story. The fragments of retention were fleshed out by other knowledge and experience to make these fragments into a coherent narrative. These observations seemed to involve a qualitative distortion in memory rather than simply a loss of associations.

Figure 4-1 shows one of the stories used in this study. As you compare the original version with typical reproductions, you can see the transformations and changes that sometimes characterize long-term retention. There is a loss of some detail which is inconsistent or unnecessary to the subject's version of the theme of the story. One sees *normalization* represented by the addition and/or reordering of events to make the narrative fit better with this new version of the story. This, according to Bartlett, is produced by *assimilation* in memory. The

FIGURE 4-1 Typical recall of an unusual story from memory after a period of 20 hours and after 2 years and 6 months. (From Bartlett, 1932.)

The original story ("The War of the Ghosts")

One night two young men from Egulac went down to the river to hunt seals, and while they were there it became foggy and calm. Then they heard war-cries, and they thought: "Maybe this is a war-party". They escaped to the shore, and hid behind a log. Now canoes came up, and they heard the noise of paddles, and saw one canoe coming up to them. There were five men in the canoe, and they said:

"What do you think? We wish to take you along. We are going up the river to make war on the people".

One of the young men said: "I have no arrows".

"Arrows are in the canoe", they said.

"I will not go along. I might be killed. My relatives do not know where I have gone. But you", he said, turning to the other, "may go with them."

So one of the young men went, but the other returned home.

And the warriors went on up the river to a town on the other side of Kalama. The people came down to the water, and they began to fight, and many were killed. But presently the young man heard one of the warriors say: "Quick, let us go home: that Indian has been hit". Now he thought: "Oh, they are ghosts". He did not feel sick, but they said he had been shot.

So the canoes went back to Egulac, and the young man went ashore to his house, and made a fire. And he told everybody and said: "Behold I accompanied the ghosts, and we went to fight. Many of our fellows were killed, and many of those who attacked us were killed. They said I was hit, and I did not feel sick".

He told it all, and then he became quiet. When the sun rose he fell down. Something black came out of his mouth. His face became contorted. The people jumped up and cried.

He was dead.

Recall from memory after 20 hours

Two men from Edulac went fishing. While thus occupied by the river they heard a noise in the distance.

"It sounds like a cry", said one, and presently there appeared some men in canoes who invited them to join the party on their adventure. One of the young men refused to go, on the ground of family ties, but the other offered to go.

"But there are no arrows", he said.

"The arrows are in the boat", was the reply.

He thereupon took his place, while his friend returned home. The party paddled up the river to Kaloma, and began to land on the banks of the river. The enemy came rushing upon them, and some sharp fighting ensued. Presently some one was injured, and the cry was raised that the enemy were ghosts.

The party returned down the stream, and the young man arrived home feeling none the worse for his experience. The next morning at dawn he endeavoured to recount his adventures. While he was talking something black issued from his mouth. Suddenly he uttered a cry and fell down. His friends gathered round him.

But he was dead.

Recall from memory after 2 years, 6 months

Some warriors went to wage war against the ghosts. They fought all day and one of their number was wounded.

They returned home in the evening, bearing their sick comrade. As the day drew to a close, he became rapidly worse and the villagers came round him. At sunset he sighed: something black came out of his mouth. He was dead.

---

events in the story are organized in terms of the subject's own system of knowledge and beliefs.

We can summarize Bartlett's studies in the following way. (1) Memory for even simple stories seems to be surprisingly inaccurate. Many details are either lost or distorted, with the missing information replaced to make the narrative consistent. By consistency, Bartlett meant both logically consistent and consistent with the subject's existing beliefs and attitudes. (2) In some cases, only isolated detail is remembered. When this happens, a reasonable story is created in recall to rationalize this detail. In other cases, only the general theme or outline of the story is remembered. On retelling, detail is supplied to give the story coherence and credibility. (3) In repeated recall, proper names and titles become lost, while the outline becomes progressively more abbreviated and stereotyped. Much of the subtlety of the original is lost. Again, however, even when memory was noticeably distorted from the original, the recall was always coherent. This was true, even when it required the addition of connecting information not actually present in the original story.

As you can see, the story given in Figure 4-1 has several novel aspects. The thematic perspective of the story is foreign to traditional European culture and the special significance of the events in the story are not clear. This can be compared with a similar study done by Paul (1959). The same stories were used but they were accompanied by a clear explanation of the significance of each of the incidents to the Indian culture from which they came. Recall accuracy for these subjects was significantly better than that observed by Bartlett. Even better performance was obtained when subjects received a story of the same length, but drawn from the subjects' own culture.

Bartlett used the term *schemata* to describe the organization of memory materials into meaningful relations. New information is organized in terms of these schemata, or conceptual "frameworks." Individuals do not behave as if they passively store associations between elements. Rather, they seem to organize experience into their preexisting systems of knowledge and belief. The attempt to make the experience fit these schemata sometimes leads to distortion, or, in other cases, the schemata themselves may change. Bartlett emphasized the creative aspect of memory. He argued that remembering seems ordinarily to be more a reconstructive process than simply one of reproduction.

Memory and Meaning: Another Look at Interference

The inaccuracies observed by Bartlett (1932) in the recall of prose are only one side of the coin of retention of meaningful material. Just as often, what we already know will actively assist us in the retention of facts and events of everyday life. Retention of meaningful prose is much better than the retention of nonsense syllables or of random word strings, and we have already noted the facilitating effects of structure in our discussion of organization in recall. Thus, the differences between literal verbatim memory and memory for the meaning or sense of a passage are quite dramatic.

So dramatic are these differences, that some have claimed that the same rules do not apply to the two situations. This claim is essentially one about sufficiency conditions; verbal learning theory cannot account for learning of natural language materials. As just one example, Ausubel, Stager, and Gaite (1968) have shown that learning two consecutive passages often does not produce the retroactive interference that would be predicted from our earlier description of the RI paradigm.

Ausubel et al., had two groups of subjects read a short passage about Zen Buddhism. One group of subjects was then given a second passage to read on the same topic but which contained slightly different information. Since the two passages were similar, one would expect a considerable amount of RI when recall of the first passage was later required. The second group of subjects also read a second passage, but this one was on an entirely different topic (drug addiction).

Contrary to what one might expect from our knowledge of interference theory, the group who read the similar passages were no worse in their accuracy of recall of the first passage than the group who read entirely different passages. In fact, they were somewhat better! The authors concluded that meaningful learning was not simply a more complex version of associative learning. The learning of meaningful language materials represents a completely different set of problems from those studied with paired-associates.

In one sense, however, their rejection of interference theory might have been premature. Since both of the passages for the first group in the Ausubel et al. (1968) study were on the same topic, there were many points of coincidence as well as of conflict. We would expect that the points of coincidence would facilitate retention, while the points of conflict would produce interference. Thus, it could have been that the areas of agreement in the two passages operated to inflate the overall recall performance of this group and to obscure the detrimental effects of interference.

This interpretation was examined by Anderson and Myrow (1971). Subjects read two stories about a fictional tribe. Some aspects of the lives of these two tribes (religion, agriculture, government, etc.) coincided, some aspects did not. The facts that coincided were remembered better by the group who had read about both tribes than they were by a control group who had read only about one of the tribes. The experimental subjects, however, did do worse than the controls on inconsistent items. Indeed, when Anderson and Myrow applied this same analysis to the original study by Ausubel et al. (1968), it yielded the same results. Interference effects can be observed in meaningful material.

The point of this illustration is not to convince you that associationism is the theory of choice for all phenomena; quite the contrary. On the other hand, we do want to express the caution that the study of language and meaning is not a new world completely separate from the one discussed in the earlier chapters of this book. Any complete theory must contend with the full range of phenomena we find in human memory. Interference is certainly a factor, even when we are discussing memory for the meaning, or sense, of a prose passage.

Memory for Themes Memory for the sense of a passage is usually much better than memory for its verbatim contents. Sachs (1967) presented subjects with a series of taperecorded, paragraph length stories, each containing a critical test sentence. One such story related to the invention of the telescope and contained the test sentence, "He sent a letter about it to Galileo, the great Italian scientist." Later, the subjects were shown a number of sentences and were asked to say which ones were identical to those they had previously encountered in the stories. Of primary interest was whether the subjects would notice any changes from the original, and if so, whether they would be more sensitive to changes in wording or changes in the meanings of the sentences.

In the course of the recognition testing, subjects saw either the identical sentence or sentences with one of the following types of changes: *active/passive change* (sentence changed to passive form but preserving the original meaning: "A letter about it was sent to Galileo, the great Italian scientist"); *formal change* (change in style of wording but preserving the original meaning: "He sent Galileo, the great Italian scientist, a letter about it"); or a *semantic change* (similar wording but a change in the meaning of the sentence: "Galileo, the great Italian scientist, sent him a letter about it").

Sachs' results are shown in Figure 4-2 which gives the subjects' accuracy in detecting changes, as a function of the position of the test sentence in the story. When tested immediately after hearing the sentence, any change from the original was readily detected. However, when the retention interval was longer, and filled with greater amounts of interpolated material, some changes were more difficult to detect than others. While semantic changes, changes in meaning, remained fairly easy to recognize after long intervals, subjects became less able to determine whether they were seeing the identical, original sentences, or ones which changed the wording while preserving the original meaning. In short, changes in meaning, and meaning only, remained relatively easy to spot after retention intervals filled with interpolated material.

As Bartlett originally found, subjects do not ordinarily remember the individual words of a sentence very well. They use the words to determine the theme of the sentence, then record this theme in memory.

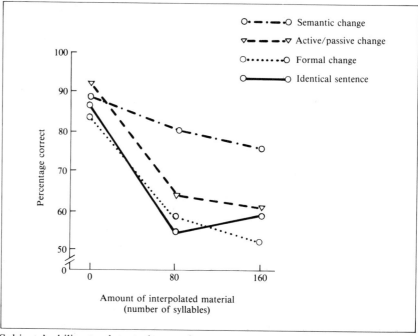

FIGURE 4-2   Subjects' ability to detect changes in a test sentence which involves either a change in wording only (active/passive, formal) or a change in meaning (semantic change). Accuracy is shown as a function of the amount of interpolated material received prior to recognition testing.
(From Sachs, 1967.)

Memory for the theme, or the "idea" of the sentence, is quite accurate. It is certainly the case that subjects can remember the specific wording of a sentence under certain conditions (Anderson & Bower, 1973). However, thematic coding seems to represent the more common form of memory storage. We are seldom required, outside of the elementary school classroom, to literally reproduce what we have heard or seen. Meanings are usually more important to any communication than the actual words used.

Intriguingly, subjects who actually do try to memorize linguistic materials in rote fashion often do not remember these materials as well as subjects who simply hear them and think about their meanings. Hyde and Jenkins (1969, 1973) had subjects perform different tasks on lists of words. Some had to check the words for the letter "E," some subjects had to count the letters in each word, and some were required to rate the words for their "pleasantness." The last task, we assume, requires some "understanding" of the meanings of the words, while the other two tasks do not. Half of the subjects in each group were prewarned that they would later be asked to recall the words, while the other half were told nothing about a later recall test. A final, control group, simply were told to memorize the list of words for later testing.

TABLE 4-1 Recall performance for subjects performing various incidental tasks with, and without, prewarning that retention for the stimuli would later be tested. Final column shows performance of a control group who simply received the list for later memory testing.
(Adapted from Hyde & Jenkins, 1969 Copyright © 1969 by the American Psychological Association. Reprinted by permission.)

	Incidental Tasks Only	Incidental Tasks Plus Prewarning	Control Condition (Memory Instructions Only)
Pleasantness Rating	16.3	16.6	16.1
E Checking	9.4	10.4	
Number of Letters	9.9	12.4	

As we can see from Table 4-1, which shows the results of this experiment, those subjects who were required to give meanings to the words (pleasantness ratings) without any conscious intention of learning them, did as well as the subjects who were specifically told to memorize the words for later testing. Furthermore, subjects who did not attend to the meanings of the words, did worse than the "meaning" group even when they were aware they would later be tested for recall. Similar results have been obtained in a number of studies in which subjects have been induced to attend to the meanings of the memory material (Bobrow & Bower, 1969; Rosenberg & Schiller, 1971; Schulman, 1971).

As we noted previously, subjects can often remember specific wordings, at least over short intervals, or when the wording fits well with other knowledge in long-term memory (Anderson & Paulson, 1977; Cofer, Chmielewski & Brockway, 1976). The point to remember, however, is that memory for wording invariably fades long before retention of the meaning conveyed (Dooling & Christiaansen, 1977; Dooling & Lachman, 1971; McKoon, 1977).

INFERENCE IN MEMORY

To this point we have perhaps paid sufficient tribute to Bartlett's general proposition that everyday memory is best described as the storage of experience "in our own words." The studies cited above suggest that thematic memory is more effective, or at least more usual, than verbatim storage of information. There is also ample evidence for the integration of information from separate experiences into organized, meaningful representations, or schemata.

Studies of Semantic Integration

An experiment devised by Bransford and Franks (1971) offers an excellent illustration of this point. To understand this experiment, consider a single sentence consisting of four clauses which, together, represent a single complex schema. Such a sentence might be: "The ants in the kitchen ate the sweet jelly that was on the table." The four simple ideas represented by this sentence are:

1. "The ants were in the kitchen."

2. "The jelly was sweet."

3. "The jelly was on the table."

4. "The ants ate the jelly."

Several complex ideas like the one above were used in the Bransford and Franks experiment. In all cases, there were four elementary propositions making up each complex idea, and each of these propositions could be combined to yield six different sentences, each with two propositions (called twos). For example, the sentence, "The ants in the kitchen ate the jelly," contains two of the propositions from the complete, complex idea. In the same way, the simple propositions could be combined to form threes: "The ants in the kitchen ate the sweet jelly."

In the actual experiment, subjects were never shown the complete complex sentence containing all four propositions (the four). Rather, they were shown some ones, some twos, and some threes. Notice that the subjects eventually receive all of the information contained in the complex schema even though they never hear this information expressed within a single sentence.

Like some of the subjects in the Hyde and Jenkins experiment, subjects were not told to memorize the sentences. They were induced to simply think about the sentences and to understand them. This was accomplished by following each presentation with a question such as, "Where did the ants eat?" In order to answer these questions it was necessary to attend to the meaning of the sentence. This acquisition phase of the experiment was followed by a surprise recognition test. The subjects were given a whole series of sentences and were asked to say whether these specific sentences had been presented earlier (old sentences), or whether they were being heard for the first time (new sentences).

As we might have expected from the earlier study by Sachs (1967), the subjects showed very accurate retention for the themes represented by the sentences, but very poor memory for the specific forms of the sentences that were actually presented. Bransford and Franks suggested that their subjects must have built up a single complex idea, or structure, from the presented sentences by integrating each of these separate experiences. Once this had occurred, subjects could not distinguish between sentences heard before and sentences not previously encountered. This was true, of course, so long as these new sentences still fit the total semantic theme. Specifically, the subjects' judgements seemed to be based on how closely any given test sentence matched this overall theme. For example, subjects judged that the majority of the fours were old sentences, even though no complete four sentences had ever appeared in the acquisition set.

This finding can be readily understood if we assume that the fours are in fact the closest match to the complete idea from which the original sentences were derived. Figure 4-3 shows data taken from a later

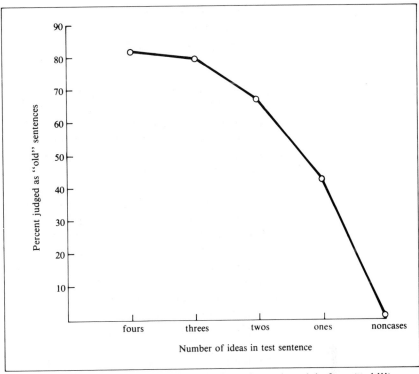

FIGURE 4-3   The percentage of sentences judged to have been heard before ("old") as a function of the number of ideas in the test sentence. Noncases were sentences that combined propositions from two or more different themes.
(Data from Singer & Rosenberg, 1973.)

experiment by Singer and Rosenberg (1973) who used similar procedures to that of Bransford and Franks. Their results show clearly that the more simple propositions included in a particular test sentence, the more likely subjects are to respond "old." That is, the more likely they are to believe they had seen that sentence before. The subjects' judgements of whether sentences were old or new, were directly proportional to how closely they approximated the complete, complex sentence. However, subjects were able to easily reject as new sentences, those that either introduced new information, or violated the meanings of the acquisition set (noncases).

The idea that a semantic schema can be built up from a combination of several simpler ideas is consistent with Bartlett's notions of constructive memory. As we learn that cats drink milk, that cats have whiskers, and that cats go "meow," we store, not these isolated propositions, but a general idea, abstraction, or *prototype* of cats. This representation stores the typical values of the properties that make up the concept "cat." The specific contribution of these integration experiments is that they provide us with a method to study this phenomenon. The general findings of these experiments have been replicated a number of times (Bransford & Franks, 1972; Cofer, 1973; Flagg, Potts & Reynolds, 1975).

Other strategies are possible in remembering sentences. The way in which a sentence is remembered will, not surprisingly, depend in part on the "set" with which the person encounters the information: "What will be required?", or "How will this experience be useful for some later task?" For example, Graesser and Mandler (1975) performed a similar experiment but asked their subjects to judge grammaticalness of the sentences as they were presented. In this case, the subjects might have attended more to the specific words of the sentences than to their overall themes. In fact, in this case, a later recognition test showed considerably better retention for the specific words of the sentences than found when subjects are given a set to attend primarily to the meaning (Bransford & Franks, 1971; Singer & Rosenberg, 1973).

All investigators do not agree on the specifics of the interpretations of these experiments (Reitman & Bower, 1973; Anderson & Bower, 1973; Griggs & Keen, 1977). Baddeley (1978), for example, takes strong exception to the small weight these studies appear to give to the importance of rehearsal and intention to learn. Nevertheless, few would object to the general proposition that memory for semantic abstractions of events is ordinarily the most important form of memory encoding.

Bransford, Barclay, and Franks (1972) took these ideas one step further. They questioned whether one may not indeed often recall information which was not part of a learning experience. Rather, subjects' recall can be based on inferences which can be drawn from that experience. The evidence and arguments to this point seem to suggest that the answer will be in the affirmative.

Bransford et al. compared recall for two types of sentences, such as:

1. Three turtles rested *beside* a floating log and a fish swam beneath them.

2. Three turtles rested *on* a floating log and a fish swam beneath them.

In a recognition test, subjects might be presented with, "Three turtles rested on a floating log and a fish swam beneath *it*." This sentence conveys the same semantic interpretation as sentence 2. As might be expected, subjects who had originally received sentence 2 accepted this test sentence as the one they had encountered before. Sentence 1, on the other hand, does not convey the same semantic interpretation as the test sentence. It is clearly possible for the fish to swim under the turtles and not the log. Indeed, when tested, subjects who had been given sentence 1 showed no tendency to confuse the two sentences. They invariably reported that the test sentence was NEW. Subjects, in other words, seem to confuse test and acquisition sentences only when the test sentence could be considered a reasonable inference from their semantic interpretations of the original sentence.

Imagery and Inference

Begg and Paivio (1969) wondered whether the appeara
inference in recall might not be a partial consequence of sub
a visual image of the sort described in the context of imag
in the previous chapter. Specifically, they offered the h
experimental outcomes such as those illustrated by Bransford et al.
(1972) could be the result of a "dual coding" of the sentences. Information presented to the subject in verbal form may produce two distinctly
different kinds of memory. One of these would be the memory of the
verbal material itself, and the other, the formation of a visual image of
the scene or action as depicted by the verbal material. When the subject
performs a recognition test, judgements may be based on the match
between information in the test sentence and the information coded in
the stored image. Those test sentences which can be derived from
information in the image will be judged to be old sentences; that is, they
will believe they were presented before, even though the wording was in
fact different.

Begg and Paivio (1969) tested their hypothesis by examining sentences
which they felt were easy to image and sentences which seemed more
difficult to image. The distinction they drew was between "concrete"
and "abstract" ideas represented by the sentences. For example, subjects might hear a sentence like, "The vicious hound chased a wild
animal," followed either by a test sentence which changes the wording
but leaves the meaning intact ("A vicious dog chased the wild animal"),
or a test sentence which uses the same words but changes the meaning
("A vicious animal chased a wild hound."). These were considered to be
concrete sentences, since it is relatively easy to imagine a visual scene
containing these elements and actions. The same type of manipulations
were performed for abstract sentences. An example might be, "The
absolute faith aroused an enduring interest."

As they expected, Begg and Paivio found that, for concrete sentences,
test sentences which changed the wording but preserved the meaning
went relatively unnoticed, while test sentences which contained the
same words but had a different meaning were very quickly spotted. Just
the opposite was true for abstract sentences. Changes in wording were
far more noticeable than changes in meaning.

While this and other studies (Paivio, 1975) seem to be consistent with
a dual coding view, not everyone sees the issue in terms of "imagery,"
if this is meant to specifically imply a literal visualization of the scene.
Abstract and concrete sentences as described above could also be seen
to differ in the ease with which we understand their meanings (Bransford
& McCarrell, 1975).

This question refers back to our earlier note that there is currently a
very lively theoretical controversy regarding the general notion of visual
imagery in memory. If imagery were to play a major role in these
experimental examples, it would still be necessary to posit some knowledge structures which could be used to interpret these images. This

structure would appear to be necessary in order to answer questions about them. That is, one must make a provision for a subject's ability to translate, for example, the visual image of a hound, into the more generic concept "dog" in order to explain the results of the Begg and Paivio (1969) study. Regardless of the outcome of the imagery controversy, these examples of the use of inference in memory have a single point. In remembering, people often cannot discriminate between what was actually experienced and interpretations derived from that experience.

As we shall see in detail in Chapter 9, this point is of considerable importance in practical situations that require good memory. It suggests that the processes of remembering can introduce unintended distortion and misleading information into the recall of witnessed events (Loftus, Miller, & Burns, 1978). Advertising may lead us to remember certain assertions about a product even though such claims were never actually made (Harris & Monaco, 1978). Remembering is not simply a process of reactivating traces of prior experience. It involves the exercise of our intelligence on what we know about the world.

The Role of Context in Thematic Memory

We have been exploring the notion that the retention of meaningful material is directly tied to how we understand the material and its relation to what we know. The studies of verbal learning failed to tap this dimension of ordinary memory. They neglected it precisely because they sought to eliminate context and prior knowledge from their experiments. Within the reconstructive approach to memory, what is remembered will depend on the experience itself, on the context in which the experience takes place, and on the knowledge that the person brings to the situation (Royer, Hambleton, & Cadorette, 1978).

The verbal learning approach tried with some success to minimize the effects of these last two factors. Memory performance was measured primarily as a function of manipulating the training experience. If we want to understand how context affects remembering, however, we might create experimental situations allowing for alternative interpretations of a learning experience.

Bransford and Johnson (1972) offer two illustrations of what we mean. In their first experiment, Bransford and Johnson gave subjects the following passage to remember:

If the balloons popped, the sound wouldn't be able to carry since everything would be too far away from the correct floor. A closed window would also prevent the sound from carrying, since most buildings tend to be well insulated. Since the whole operation depends on the steady flow of electricity, a break in the middle of the wire would also cause problems. Of course, the fellow could shout, but the human voice is not loud enough to carry that far.

An additional problem is that the string could break on the instrument. Then there would be no accompaniment to the message. It is clear that the best situation would involve less distance. Then there would be fewer potential problems. With face to face contact, the least number of things could go wrong. (p. 719)

While one group of subjects simply heard the passage for recall with no context, a second group were shown the picture in Figure 4-4 before hearing the passage. This second group recalled on the average twice as much of the passage as the "no context" group. We could say that the picture gave the subjects the appropriate schema for understanding the passage. Once provided with the framework supplied by the schema, the information in the passage was more easily assimilated into what the subject already knew about buildings, amplifiers, and balloons.

As dramatic as this demonstration may be, we might wonder whether the context permitted better retention of the information, or whether the picture permitted the subjects to introduce their knowledge into sophisticated guesses about material they had actually forgotten. To address this question, Bransford and Johnson (1972) performed a second experiment. Three groups of subjects were involved. One group, the topic before, heard the passage below preceded by the instructions, "The paragraph you will hear will be about washing clothes." A second group, the topic after, received the paragraph without this information, but just

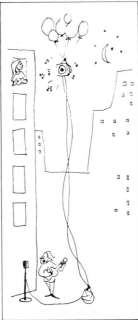

FIGURE 4-4 The Effects of Context on Memory. Memory performance was compared when subjects had to memorize a passage either with or without the aid of a picture which gave meaning to the test passage.
(From Bransford & Johnson, 1972.)

prior to recall testing were told, "It may help you to know that the paragraph was about washing clothes." The final group, no topic, received no information at all about the nature of the topic.

Washing Clothes

The procedure is actually quite simple. First you arrange things into different groups depending on their makeup. Of course, one pile may be sufficient depending on how much there is to do. If you have to go somewhere else due to lack of facilities that is the next step, otherwise you are pretty well set. It is important not to overdo any particular endeavor. That is, it is better to do too few things at once than too many. In the short run this may not seem important, but complications from doing too many can easily arise. A mistake can be expensive as well. The manipulation of the appropriate mechanisms should be self-explanatory, and we need not dwell on it here. At first the whole procedure will seem complicated. Soon, however, it will become just another facet of life. It is difficult to foresee any end to the necessity for this task in the immediate future, but then one never can tell. (Bransford & Johnson, 1972, p. 722)

Table 4-2 shows a summary of the results for the three groups. Not surprisingly, both the no topic and the topic after groups found the passage unintelligible. The topic before group, when scored on the number of ideas recalled from the passage, were able to remember 5.83 ideas out of a possible 18 present in the original passage. The topic after group, however, performed no better than the no topic group. At least in this case, the context appears to facilitate retention of the material rather than simply allowing for effective guessing at the time of recall.

These results do not deny the frequent tendency to introduce existing knowledge at the time of recall. Such an effect was obtained by Sulin and Dooling (1974). These investigators had subjects read short passages about famous people such as Helen Keller or Adolph Hitler. The subjects in this study frequently recalled information that was biographically true but which had not actually been presented in the sketches they read. Further, the greater the time interval between reading the passage and recall testing, the greater was the tendency to add information.

The motive for these studies on meanings, implications, and context can be seen in Bartlett's theorizing about the reconstructive nature of

TABLE 4-2 Mean comprehension ratings and number of ideas recalled for the "Washing Clothes" paragraph when no topic was given and when the topic was given either before or after the paragraph was heard.
(Adapted from Bransford & Johnson, 1972.)

	No Topic	Topic After	Topic Before	Maximum Score
Comprehension	2.29	2.12	4.50	7
Recall	2.82	2.65	5.83	18

remembering. These studies illustrate how people ordinarily code the meaningful theme of a message and construct their recall through inference and interpretation of this meaning. We can contrast this point of view with the Ebbinghaus tradition which led to studies of the conditions that promote or prevent access to some memory trace of the original experience.

Bartlett's views did not have a great impact on research at the time they were first presented (1932). However, the last few years have produced a burgeoning literature (see, for example, Anderson, Spiro, & Montague, 1977; Shaw & Bransford, 1977; Weiner & Palermo, 1975). These experiments move closer to the study of memory in everyday life. These findings do not make the results of verbal learning studies irrelevant. They do, however, add complexity and perspective to our interpretation of those studies. We will not have a satisfactory theory of memory if we exclude the contexts and knowledge that provide the grounds for our ordinary use of these capacities.

ORGANI-ZATION IN MEMORY

Bartlett's views of memory alert us to the influence of prior knowledge and context on remembering. But how are we to characterize that knowledge and how do we describe the effects produced by context? Memory is organized. We observed the effects of organization both in Chapter 3 and in our discussion of knowledge structures in the previous section. When we think of organization in memory, we might draw a rough analogy with a modern library. To be useful, a library needs not only a place to store a great many books, it also needs an indexing system and card catalog to give the user the "addresses" of each of these books. Seen through this analogy, a theory of memory must contemplate at least three elements: (1) the storage of information; (2) an adequate system for indexing this information; and (3) some specification of how to use this indexing system to find the information. We have already encountered some alternative views of storage. The associationists viewed memory as the repository for one-to-one connections between events; memory as a library of associations. On the other hand, we have seen Bartlett's notion that memory is organized in terms of structures, or schemata.

Our goal is to move from these earlier ideas to the development of specific models of how the memory system might work. We need to describe how meanings are represented in memory, how these representations can be combined to yield new meanings, and how these psychological representations can be related to the real world (Smith, 1978). In developing these models, investigators attempt to define some formal system, much in the manner of a computer program, and to specify the correspondence between performance of people in real situations and the operations of this formal system. The development of models of this kind is a problem in designing a memory system that "works." Bobrow (1975) described this invention process as one of finding solutions to problems that must be faced in order to accomplish certain ends. In this case, the end to be accomplished is the imitation of human memory performance. Before examining a sample of these models, we will discuss some of the characteristics which must be reflected in any successful model.

The TOT Phenomenon

We have all experienced that feeling of being sure we know something, such as a person's name, and yet seem totally unable to find that information when we need it. When this happens, we often use the anatomically inaccurate expression "tip-of-the-tongue." Brown and McNeil (1966) described being in this tip-of-the-tongue (TOT) state as analogous to being on the brink of a sneeze. We are seized by a state of mild torment, followed by considerable relief when the act (recall or sneezing) is finally accomplished.

Brown and McNeil (1966) used a simple technique for producing the TOT state in their subjects. The technique was simply to give dictionary definitions of objects and to ask for the name of the defined object. One of their definitions was the following:

> A navigational instrument used in measuring angular distances, especially the altitude of the sun, moon and stars at sea.

Attempts to recall this name will produce a TOT state in a fair number of people. While they may be unable to recall the correct name (a sextant), they may nevertheless feel that the answer is "on the tip-of-the-tongue." Brown and McNeil were not interested in people who knew and could immediately recall the correct name. Neither were they interested in cases in which the subject clearly did not know the correct name. Brown and McNeil's interest was to analyze those recall attempts which manifested this particular and disturbing state, the TOT phenomenon.

The responses the subjects made in trying to recall the names of the objects suggested attempts to retrieve words both by their sounds and by their meaning. While the word itself might be elusive, the subjects seemed to know how many syllables it had, or its general sound pattern ("something like 'secant,' or 'sexton' "), and its semantic or functional relationships ("astrolabe," "compass," "protractor"). No less important, the subjects usually knew these related words were not the ones they were looking for.

Brown and McNeil's analysis suggests a picture of memory for concepts that is composed of collections of features connected through a variety of pathways which can be used to get from one address to another within an organized memory store. A memory for a concept or word seems not to be a single unitary element but a complex of interrelated information that includes physical characteristics of the word, functional relationships, and relationships to other concepts.

A Case of Impaired Memory Search

An especially dramatic way to get a feeling for memory organization is to observe its breakdown in cases of brain damage. Such damage can lead to *aphasia,* a general language impairment, one form of which can be a selective difficulty in the simple act of recalling names for objects, especially when presented in the absence of context.

Figure 4-5 shows the results of a particular patient trying to name a picture of an anchor. The patient was a 54-year-old man of good education who had suffered damage to parts of the left hemisphere of his brain as a result of a war injury. Although his general health and intellectual functions remained intact, naming a simple object was a singularly difficult task (Wingfield, 1979).

When shown the picture, he had no trouble recognizing it. He looked at it briefly, put the picture down, and then spent several minutes in what can be called a "search" for the object's name. His actual

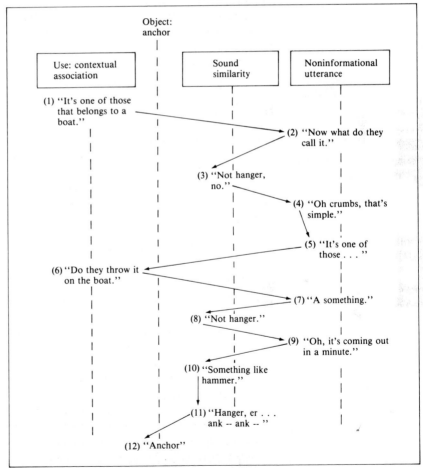

FIGURE 4-5 Complete record of an aphasic patient's attempt to name a picture of an anchor. Responses are categorized by the search strategies employed. (From Wingfield, 1979.)

responses, in the order in which they were given, are shown in Figure 4-5 along with an attempt to classify them in terms of the search strategies he seemed to be using. He first approached the problem by giving its use (". . . belongs to a boat"). Since this appeared to offer little help, he changed to a phonetic approach by trying a word of similar sound (". . . hanger"). Then he returned to the use strategy (". . . throw it on a boat"), and so on.

We seem to be observing a man in the process of a search; first one pathway is tried and then another, until the final pathway leads to the target word. Like any frustrating search, it is punctuated with annoyed, noninformational utterances, such as, "It's got to be here somewhere!"

If the difficulties described here were encountered exclusively by aphasic patients, this phenomenon would have little interest outside its clinical applications. However, numerous studies of normal subjects in the TOT state, and related studies of retrieval cues in recall, suggest that the aphasic example is merely an especially dramatic illustration of a common phenomenon.

MODELS OF SEMANTIC MEMORY

While the earliest memory theories reflected the associationism of the 1940s, the surge in research on semantic memory began to appear in the 1960s. By this time another analogy was available to theorists, the storage and retrieval of information in the electronic computer.

Computers had first made their appearance at the close of World War II. It was not until 1960s, however, that their size and relatively low cost made them familiar in many psychological laboratories and universities. The temptation to draw analogies from the logic of computer programs to the strategies and plans of human memory was a natural one. The computer was a machine for storing and using information. Solving the problem of how to use stored information in a particular way for a computer might thus provide some insight into the problems of using information as described in the earlier parts of this chapter. Through this analogy, man came to be viewed as an information processor, a complicated device that receives, transforms, and transmits information.

A Network Model of Semantic Memory

One of the earliest offshoots of this view was that long-term memory could be represented as a "network" of countless associations between verbal entries (and/or their conceptual counterparts). Memory retrieval would be seen as a search through this maze of pathways formed as the result of past experience. These models could be called "neo-associationist" (Anderson & Bower, 1973) because they incorporated the concept of the association as the mental glue that held their structures together. They differed fundamentally from the associationists in the sense that they used logical relations between elements, hierarchical structures of organization, and the elevation of strategies and programs to a position of primary importance.

An early attempt at modeling memory in this way was the work of Collins and Quillian (1969). Their idea was to develop a computer program to simulate the organization of long-term memory. Based on an original theory by Quillian (1967), their ultimate goal in this work was to design a program that could be used to understand natural language and employ it in the answering of questions and making inferences. In fact, they call one of their papers, "How to Make a Language User" (Collins & Quillian, 1972).

Figure 4-6 illustrates the basic components of their network model. The basic elements of the network are *units* (corresponding to concepts), *pointers* (patterns of interconnections between components), and *properties* (representing features of the units). In Figure 4-6, the units are entries like animal, bird, fish, canary, ostrich, shark, and salmon. Note that these units are *hierarchically* organized. That is, canary and ostrich are listed under their superordinate category, bird; shark and salmon are organized under their superordinate, fish. Both fish and bird are under their superordinate, animal.

Stored along with each unit are its properties. Note that the storage of properties is as economical as possible. The property, "has feathers," would not be stored separately with each type of bird. Rather, this property would be stored with the more general concept bird. The properties stored with a particular concept are the "typical values" of this property; that is, the ones shared by most of the examples, or subordinates of this concept. If a particular example of the concept does not possess these typical values represented in the superordinate cate-

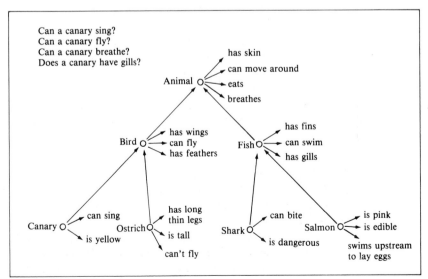

FIGURE 4-6   A Network Model of Semantic Memory. Illustration of a hypothetical memory structure for a three-level hierarchy. Processing time is presumed to be a function of an item's position in the semantic hierarchy.
(From Collins & Quillian, 1969.)

gory, then its unique values would be stored directly with that example. A case in point would be that birds typically can fly, but penguins, which are birds, do not. The concept penguin would have the property "can't fly" stored with it directly. Access to the units and properties within the network is through activation of these pointer pathways between the elements.

We can illustrate how the model works by entering the network with a question like, "Is a canary an animal?" The model verifies sentences like this by a technique called *intersection search*. This begins with an activation of the pointers which lead from each of the concepts represented in the sentence. The search proceeds upward and outward through the network activating more and more pointers. As each node or concept is encountered, it is marked or tagged indicating how it was reached. For example, the search upward from canary encounters the concept bird. This concept is marked as found in the search from the unit canary. At some point, the search originating from one concept will cross a concept that has already been marked by a search from some other concept. This represents an intersection of the two search paths. These two paths, taken together, represent the semantic relation found in the network between the two terms. The model then matches the semantic relation found in the search with the semantic relation between the concepts in the question. If these two match, the sentence is confirmed; if they do not, the sentence is false.

While all the information is retrievable, the relationships between terms like canary and fish cannot be obtained directly. The interconnection between the two is derivable from the hierarchy only after passing through a number of levels. The number of levels that must be crossed determines, in part, the semantic distance between the concepts. If this model were to have validity as a representation of how human beings verify sentences, one would have to predict that the time actually required for people to find a particular relationship should correspond fairly closely with the distance between the concepts represented by the sentence.

Collins and Quillian (1969) report results of experiments in which subjects were given true/false questions such as "A canary can sing," "A canary can fly," "A canary can breathe," or "A canary has gills." Note that these four sample questions represent an increasing distance between canary and particular properties within the network. Thus, the number of pointers that must be crossed should directly affect the relative time required by a subject to confirm or deny each of these propositions. The results of these experiments have shown, for example, that it will in fact take less time to verify that a canary can sing than it will to verify that a canary can fly, or that a canary can breathe. The first proposition requires access to a property stored directly with canaries. The second requires access to a property stored with birds at the next higher level. The third question requires access to a property typical of the animal concept. This requires transit across two pointers.

Figure 4-7 shows data taken from one of Collins and Quillian's (1969) experiments, which shows the average reaction time to answering true/false sentences of this type. As the model predicts, the closer the entries are to each other, the faster the question can be answered. Since the "zero" entry for "A canary can sing" reflects a direct property of canaries, it is on the same level of the hierarchy, and is thus the fastest possible response.

There are other variables which determine the relative speed of sentence verification. Oldfield and Wingfield (1965; Oldfield, 1966; Wingfield, 1967, 1968) found that word retrieval is based in part on the frequency and/or recency with which a word has been used before. Collins and Quillian (1970), for example, examined performance on true/false questions in which previously used words were repeatedly involved in a series of different questions. In a typical case, a subject might have to give a true or false answer to the statement "A canary is a bird." Some time after this first statement is verified, the subject now receives "A canary has wings."

Their thought was that this first question might "prime" the pathway leading from canary to bird, and make this pathway easier and faster to activate when the second question occurs. If this were the case, the second question should be answered faster than it would be without this prime. Collins and Quillian (1970) have found, in fact, shorter reaction times for cases like this. In their model, priming would increase the speed of activation along the primed pathway (Collins & Quillian, 1972; Collins & Loftus, 1975).

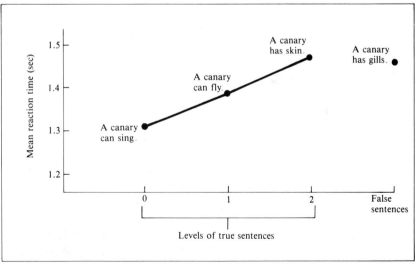

FIGURE 4-7 Average reaction times to saying whether a statement is true or false as a function of the hypothetical distance (levels) between the properties in a semantic network hierarchy.
(From Collins & Quillian, 1969.)

This hierarchical model also accounts for the finding that the size of the category, its number of members, influences verification time. It takes longer, for example, to verify that "A canary is an animal," than it does to verify that "A canary is a bird." The category animal is much larger than the category bird. But the more members a category has, the higher it will be in the hierarchy; that is, all birds will be members of the category animal. This means that more levels must be crossed and so more time will be taken to verify these sentences from lower points on the hierarchy.

The results we have discussed describe mainly the verification of true sentences. The time necessary to respond to false sentences is much more variable and does not fit quite so neatly into a hierarchical theory of semantic memory. "False" responses are generally slower than "true" responses and cannot be ordered in terms of the hierarchy as clearly as can be done for true sentences. This inconsistency was a major problem for this model and the point of attack for some alternative views of retrieval. We will return to this problem in the discussion of these alternatives.

Before leaving this network model, however, we must again call attention to its associative nature. We can nevertheless distinguish it from the associationism of Chapter 3 by its imposition of a logical organization. That is, it contemplates not a complex of individual S-R associations (e.g., birds-wings, canary-sings, etc.,) but organization by semantic category. Certain associations can only be accessed through their categorical relationships.

In spite of its strengths, however, there are some weaknesses of this approach:

1. It overlooks important interactions between episodic and semantic memory. We may not only know that sharks bite, but our memory of the movie "Jaws" may be very much a part of this concept.

2. A strictly hierarchical scheme is based too closely on logical relations and *a priori* intuitions. The structure of memory may be more idiosyncratic and fortuitous than this model can describe.

3. The type of model we have described emphasizes the structure of the memory store, neglecting the dynamics of possible retrieval strategies.

4. Finally, there is more emphasis on verifying specific propositions than on drawing inferences from potential relationships in the network.

Quillian's (1967) theory was originally intended to describe how one might put human semantic structure into the design of a computer program. The version of this theory presented by Collins and Quillian (1969) was simplified in order to test some specific assumptions by the theory about memory structure. Several of the assumptions we have noted as weaknesses in this model are problems with this simplified model. Network models can, in fact, overcome some of these problems as we shall see in discussing later extensions and elaborations of Quillian's notions (Collins & Loftus, 1975; Estes, 1976). Historically, the version of the theory presented by Collins and Quillian was very important in stimulating attempts to model semantic memory and to solve the theoretical problems this model helped to clarify.

Human Associative Memory (HAM)

The Collins and Quillian model can be called a model of semantic memory in the sense that Tulving used the term (see Chapter 3). That is, we know that wings, feathers, and the ability to fly are typical properties of birds. We know this independent of any particular birds we may have observed. There is no particular context associated to these facts. It would be quite unusual to remember exactly where and when we learned this information. Models of semantic memory are concerned chiefly with the retrieval of general propositions from memory. There is less emphasis placed on how this information was originally acquired and integrated into our general knowledge.

However, there are obviously interactions between episodic and semantic memory. If you recall that some years ago you hit a lamp post on the turnpike, the particulars of when, where, and how this occurred are as important as your general knowledge about cars, lamp posts and turnpikes. The memory of this event is composed of both temporally coded, autobiographical memory, combined with your more general semantic knowledge. A variant of the network model which addresses this interaction was called Human Associative Memory (HAM) and was created by Anderson and Bower (1973).

HAM divides memory performance into influences from two separate components. The first component is composed of all the plans and strategies we might use to perform any task. The second component is the long-term memory structure which would be the same from task to task. For this model, there is always a fixed way of encoding the input into memory. What can change from task to task, or from trial to trial in an experiment, is how other cognitive processes might make use of the long-term memory structure. This kind of theory has the potential advantage of enabling investigation of each of these two components separately, and thus determining how the two might interact in everyday memory. Recall, recognition, and answering factual questions, all represent alternative ways of making use of the same structure.

The most important structural element in HAM is the *proposition*. Figure 4-8 illustrates in a schematic way how the HAM model would store the information that a car hit a lamp post on the turnpike. Incoming information would be analyzed into this form by a device called a *parser*. Initially analyzed input is held in temporary memory before it is matched with the structure of long-term memory. Each intersection of arrows in

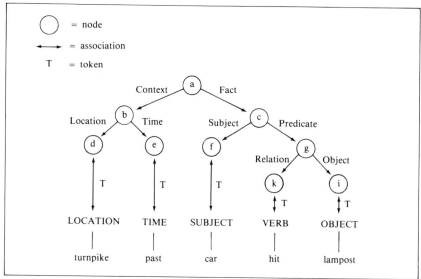

FIGURE 4-8   Representation of a context and event in Anderson and Bower's human associative memory (HAM) model of structure in semantic memory.
(Adapted from Anderson & Bower, 1973).

the figure (the small circles) are called *nodes*. The uppermost node represents the full proposition. The arrows represent types of semantic associations between nodes. The proposition, for example, is the abstract idea that a particular *fact* holds true in a certain *context*. Node b which represents the context as a whole, is composed of an association between a *location* and a *time*.

This scheme describes an input sentence or a question in terms of four types of associations: (1) context-fact, (2) location-time, (3) subject-predicate, and (4) relation-object. A final type of association links the concept, representing all our knowledge about lamp posts, for example, to the words (tokens) used to express this idea.

The proposition described by these relationships is intended to be the meaning or content of the sentence rather than simply the relations between a particular set of words. A given proposition, or meaning, might be expressed by several different sentences. The proposition is intended to be nonlinguistic in the sense that we are representing relationships among concepts or ideas rather than particular words. The structure of HAM was in fact intended to be general enough to encode information about visual scenes as well as linguistic information. The fact that we have drawn the scheme as an English sentence is simply to aid in communicating the structure. The information in the structure is assumed to be conceptual and abstract without any necessary relationship to words and language.

When presented with verbal information, or a verbal episode, the HAM system analyzes this information and represents the result of its analysis in a tree structure like that of Figure 4-8. This structure is

HAM's way of describing the relationship among concepts. This structure is stored in temporary memory while a check is made to see if this same information had been stored previously. If so, the information need not be stored again and will not be. If the proposition describing the input was not already stored in memory, the associations between concepts which make up the proposition will be transferred to the long-term store and become part of this memory structure.

Once the proposition is stored in long-term memory, the model can answer questions about it; for example, "What hit the lamppost on the turnpike?" A propositional representation of the question would be formed leaving one of the final nodes blank (node f in Figure 4-8). All the other concepts in the question would be matched to concepts in long-term memory. The model then searches upward through the tree structure for associative pathways that link the concepts in long-term memory in the same way that they are linked in the question.

Although our example only represents one proposition built on the concept nodes, you probably know a great deal more about lampposts and turnpikes. All this information would be represented by different trees associated with the concept nodes. Once pathways are found that link the concepts in our question, the subject relation can, for example, be used to retrieve the concept "car."

A complete theory of memory organization must reflect relationships between events and the context in which they occurred.

The HAM model can also be used to answer true-false questions of the kind posed by Collins and Quillian (1969). Anderson and Reder (1974) had subjects respond to sentences like "A collie is a cat." The time to respond "false" to this sentence was correlated with verification times for the sentences: "A collie is a dog," and "A dog is not a cat." Anderson and Reder suggested that these separate propositions were first retrieved, and then used, to make the judgment about the original sentence.

HAM is also an associative model and so could be described as a descendant of the views we discussed earlier. There are, however, several important differences between this model and simple associationism. First, the model explicitly claims that there are different kinds of associations (the labeled arrows in Figure 4-8). The associationist theorists used only one type of bond between elements. Second, like the Collins and Quillian model, HAM is hierarchical in structure. The use of this structure and a propositional base permits a linguistic feature called *embedding*. The proposition in Figure 4-8 could be used, for example, as the context of a larger proposition, such as, "When the car hit the lamp post on the turnpike, the driver lost his glasses." Within this model, each proposition can be embedded in another tree.

These differences afford HAM and other network models a flexibility not available to the elemental connectionist theories. This particular model, however, has not been without critics. In particular, like Collins and Quillan's model, HAM has been criticized on the grounds that we store more than a representation of the input. There is evidence that we make inferences and deductions and store these as well (Potts, 1972, 1974). Nevertheless, HAM represents an important and influential step toward adequately representing the awesome complexities of human memory and knowledge. For further developments in the basic HAM model, interested readers are referred to Anderson (1976).

A Semantic Features Model

Much of our discussion of semantic memory has been based on notions about concepts and conceptual categories. How concepts are represented and retrieved is a major issue for cognitive psychology (Rosch, Mervis, Gray, Johnson & Boyes-Braem, 1976). Collins and Quillian, for example, specified the logical relations among concepts as the basis of their model. These logical relations of subordinate and superordinate was one of the central contributions of their theory.

As we have noted, however, the storage of concepts in semantic memory may be more idiosyncratic than this logical scheme implies. We may, for example, have a structure of conceptual categories based on the frequency of encountering specific properties, or specific examples of the concept. Many people would judge a turkey to be less a "bird," than, say, a robin. Or, that a dolphin is less a "mammal" than a horse. Logically, of course, a turkey is or is not a bird, and a dolphin is or is not a mammal. There are no "degrees" of classification in a formal system of logic. However, the frequency with which we encounter instances of a concept does vary widely across the members of a conceptual category. A robin is a more familiar bird than a turkey, and a horse is a more familiar mammal than a dolphin. This characteristic may have a powerful effect on how our semantic memory is structured.

Recent research has concentrated considerable effort to exploring the premise that category membership in human memory is a matter of degree rather than all or none (e.g., McCloskey & Glucksberg, 1978; Rosch & Mervis, 1975). Some concepts may be clearly seen as members of a given category while others are clearly nonmembers. There are, in addition, concepts whose category membership is ambiguous with re- spect to a particular category. For example, bass and trout are clearly fish, and cows and horses are clearly not fish. But what about a whale or a dolphin? These are certainly fishlike in many ways. Semantic feature models improve upon Collins and Quillian's network model and Ander- son and Bower's HAM in attempting to account for some of these ambiguities in real memory performances (see Glass & Holyoak, 1974, for a further discussion and another point of view of the comparison between semantic features and network models).

In a semantic feature model, the meaning of a concept is represented by a list of its properties and descriptions, or *features*. In taking this view, Rips, Shoben, and Smith (1973; Smith, Shoben, & Rips, 1974) see the list of features as ordered from those very important in identifying the concept to those having little importance. For example, the concept "pen" requires as an essential aspect of its meaning that it fulfill a certain function "you write with it"). The exact shape of a pen is less essential to its definition, although most pens have similar shapes. As in this case, the exact dividing line between an essential or *defining* feature and features that are only *characteristic* of the concept is difficult to draw. The model assumes that the person approaches this problem empirically. That is, the person bases judgements on knowledge and experience gained with a particular concept.

We can demonstrate this difference between judgements and formal logic by asking subjects to rate a number of stimuli such as horse, dog, mouse, and so forth, on how closely they are related to each other, and hence, their semantic distance within the single "mammal" category. By taking ratings from a large number of people, appropriate mathematical treatments allow us to "plot" this information on a two-dimensional graph indicating how far apart these stimuli are in semantic memory.

Such a plot, taken from Rips et al. (1973) is shown in Figure 4-9. You can see, for example, that "sheep" and "goats" are close together, while "sheep" and "lion" are more distant. Similarly, when birds are rated, "duck" was somehow less birdlike to most of their subjects than "robin." In this model, the distances are taken to represent *semantic relatedness*. The closer together two words are on this scale, the more similar they are in meaning.

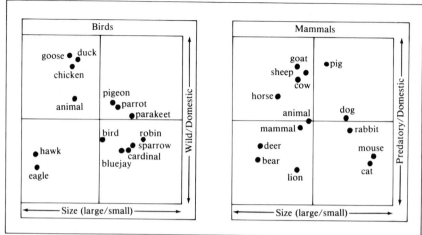

FIGURE 4-9 Two-dimensional spaces representing semantic relatedness of birds and of mammals based on subject ratings.
(From Rips, Shoben, & Smith, 1973.)

We can use such plots to infer the features used in supplying these ratings. Rips et al. (1973) took a start at this by defining the horizontal axis as a large/small dimension and the vertical dimension as a predatory/domestic dimension. We could, in the case of birds, call this second dimension a wild/domestic dimension. The distances, at least in these examples, seem to fit. The subjects' judgements can be understood, at least in part, as grouping the concepts on the basis of similarity on these two sets of dimensions. In principle, we could go beyond the two sets of dimensions illustrated here, into a multidimensional space having as many dimensions as there may be features on which the subjects can order their judgements.

In the feature model, the verification of sentences like "A canary is a bird" takes the form of comparing feature lists belonging to the two concepts. If a great many features are shared, similarity will be high. If few, or no features are shared, the comparison will turn up low or zero similarity. This idea, and the kind of ratings we just described, permits the model to make some predictions about the relative time which would be taken to make true/false judgments. For example, if subjects are asked to verify the sentence, "A cow is a mammal," they do so much more rapidly than they can verify the sentence, "A whale is a mammal" (Rips et al. 1973). When asked to rate these word pairs on meaning, "cow" is closer to "mammal" than is "whale." The reaction time difference in the above example cannot be predicted from the Collins and Quillian model since the distance traveled to verify the two sentences would hypothetically be the same. Both cows and whales are mammals. In this case the differences would be predicted by the semantic distance.

In general, verification times for true sentences are fastest when the concepts are close together. False sentences are easier when the concepts are far apart (Rips et al. 1973). When the subject compares the feature lists of the two concepts, lists that share a great many features can lead to an immediate positive answer. The comparison yields high similarity. When the concepts are very far apart, a rapid ''false'' may be given because the similarity is so low. It is in intermediate cases that responses will be slowest. Therefore, the dimension of semantic relatedness enables us to explain one of the glaring problems of the hierarchical model, why verification of false sentences differ from the verification of true ones. As we can see, the semantic relationships illustrated in these studies often differ from logical relationships and overrule these relationships in their effects on verification times.

Spreading Activation Within a Network Model

Collins and Loftus (1975) have presented a network model that proposes to incorporate the results of investigations of semantic distance, and to provide an explanation of some of the inference processes noted earlier. In this new extension of Quillian's (1967) original theory, they have altered substantially the assumptions we described as the simplified version of this model in earlier pages.

Figure 4-10 presents a sample of a semantic network described by this model. Although the diagram appears to take a different form from the network we illustrated in Figure 4-6, if you look closely, you will see that the subordinate-superordinate structure still remains. For example, we see that roses and violets are connected to the flowers category, and that, for example, red is shown as a property of roses. This remains the case in this new version of the model, even though this particular diagram has omitted the labeling of the particular kinds of associations.

In contrast to our previous description, all pathways are not of the same length. When a concept is processed in this model, activation moves out along the network of pathways connecting the concept with others. The amount of activation received by other concepts decreases with the semantic distance from the original concept. The more properties any two concepts have in common, the more closely related they will be. As you may recall, the semantic feature model represented this as a similarity in the feature lists of the two concepts. The notions of semantic relatedness and the differences among typical and less typical members of a category can thus be handled in a network model by varying the accessibility of one concept from another.

In the original model we described, and in Collins and Loftus' development of it, verification of a sentence or a conceptual judgment, requires an *intersection search*. Concepts involved in the judgement are activated and this activation spreads out along the network depicted in Figure 4-10. When the activation from different nodes intersects, the subject then makes a decision or evaluates the relationship. You can compare this operation with our earlier description of Collins and

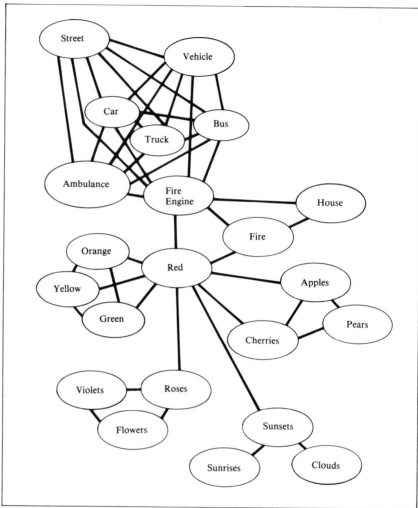

FIGURE 4-10   A schematic representation of concept relatedness within a network model. The shorter lines represent greater relatedness between concepts.
(From Collins & Loftus, 1975. Copyright © 1975 by the American Psychological Association. Reprinted by permission.)

Quillian's network model, where the one decision procedure was an evaluation of whether one of the concepts encountered in the search was a superordinate of the other (e.g., whether a canary is a bird).

Another kind of decision procedure suggested by Collins and Loftus (1975) involves evaluating the common properties or links shared by the concepts. For example, in deciding whether a tent is a home, one might compare the number of property nodes shared by these concepts. A high proportion of shared properties (walls, doors, shelter, etc.) would be evidence in favor of a positive decision, while a high proportion of mismatched properties (permanent versus temporary, many rooms versus single room, etc.) would be evidence for a negative decision. Thus, the essential elements of the feature comparison of Rips et al. (1973) is directly incorporated into the decision procedures of this network model.

The notion of activation spreading from activated concepts can also explain the "priming" phenomenon mentioned earlier. Priming is most clearly illustrated in what are called *lexical decision tasks*. The subject, for example, may be asked to decide whether a series of letters form an English word or not. The string of letters p-a-t-e-l do not form a word, while the string p-a-s-t-e does. In this task, when two associatively related words are presented on successive trials (e.g., "bread" followed on a subsequent trial by "butter"), the decision for the second word is ordinarily faster than it would be if it were preceded by an unrelated word. That is, presentation of a semantically related word facilitates or primes the second judgment (Meyer & Schvaneveldt, 1971).

The Collins and Loftus spreading activation notion accounts for this effect in that activation of a conceptual node will radiate out from that concept to others. Activation is presumed to be additive so that if the concept "butter" has received some indirect effects from having heard "bread," it will require less additional evidence to become active itself. The theory also implies that more distant concepts will produce less priming than closer relationships.

There are many other implications regarding the duration of the priming effects and their automaticity, but we wish to show here, with the few examples mentioned, that network theories are potentially powerful models of human semantic processing. In order to adequately reflect this processing, however, the models must increase their complexity and incorporate the flexibility we know to be a criterial feature of human cognition. The network model of Collins and Loftus (1975) is a step in this direction.

Episodic and Semantic Memory Revisited

At the close of Chapter 3, we mentioned Tulving's (1972) distinction between episodic and semantic memory. Tulving listed several criteria that he thought distinguished episodic from semantic memory. First of all, the memories differ in the nature of the information stored. The events stored in episodic memory can be characterized in terms of their perceptual descriptions and their relationships to each other in time and space. Semantic memory does not have this reference. The relationships in semantic memory are many and varied. Some of the relationships of subordination, superordination, and semantic relatedness have been described in this chapter. Unlike episodic memory, semantic memory is not organized by the time and space coordinates of ordinary experience. The organization is abstract and conceptual.

Since semantic memory is the repository of conceptual relationships and rules, it is possible to combine the contents of this memory in ways that produce new knowledge. In this sense, we can retrieve information from semantic memory that was not originally in store. You may, to use Tulving's example, reorganize the months of the year in alphabetical order. This may represent "new" information for you (e.g., that April is the first month in alphabetical order), even though you received no new information. However, information can be retrieved from episodic memory only if this information had been encoded there. Inferences from episodes must necessarily be based on some logical interpretation of these "facts," on what can be implied from the existence of one event about the existence of other events. This requires the intervention of semantic memory and conceptual structure to the stored episodic material. In addition, if you retrieve information from episodic memory, you are, in a sense, adding to the content of that memory. You remember that you remembered. Retrieval, on the other hand, leaves the content of semantic memory unaffected.

Finally, Tulving (1972) suggests that the two memories show different kinds of forgetting. Episodic memory, as we saw in Chapter 3, is highly susceptible to interference. Semantic memory is less likely to suffer loss from the introduction of new information.

Intuitively, this distinction between two forms of memory appeals to our sense of a difference in the kinds of tasks memory must perform. That is, there seems to be a fundamental difference between remembering the meaning of a word and remembering that you heard that word in a memory experiment. General information, like the meanings of words, has been used countless times in countless situations. We would expect these many contexts in which the general information was used to interfere with one another and thus be lost or irretrievable.

The distinction between semantic and episodic memory was of considerable importance in drawing the attention of psychologists to the more familiar uses of memory, knowledge, and their organization. This attention led to the development and elaboration of the kinds of models described in this chapter. It would be unlikely that such work would be stimulated by the studies of paired-associate or serial learning. On the other hand, it seems premature to conclude that semantic and episodic memories represent separate and different kinds of storage. Rather, they may represent different ends of a continuum on which unique temporal and personal references are gradually forgotten through their frequent use in a variety of different contexts. The more promising models of memory have tried to combine these features into a single system.

THE INTELLIGENT COMPUTER

Modern computers have reached a technological level at which it seems they can hold too much information. Imagine, for example, a computer that holds in its memory the names of all the people in the United States, or indeed, simply all the names of students at a large university. If you should ask the computer a simple question like, "Do you know someone named John?,'' the answer you get will be too complete: the names of countless Johns will come spilling out.

Contrast this with the effect of asking one of your friends the same question. You do not get in reply a list of all the Johns that person knows. The human computer has more intelligence than that. The first step any person will make is to draw some inferences about your question. If you are holding a recently received note in your hand and ask if he or she knows John, he or she will assume you are referring to someone living who might write to you, and might be known to both of you. The response might simply be, ''no,'' which translates as: ''I know many persons named John, but I do not believe any of them who can write are known to you.'' The human information processor has used knowledge of context and his or her knowledge of you to specify more completely what is being requested. A memory system approaching human capability, in other words, must be more intelligent than the interrogations it frequently receives.

Constructive Memory: A Model that Reasons

So far, we have considered a number of models which simulate some of the critical features of human memory. One important feature on which all of these models appear weak is the creative aspect of memory. That is, they do a creditable job of modeling the retrieval of specific information, but are less satisfactory in drawing inferences about facts not actually presented. For example, we can all draw some inferences about the word ''understander'' if someone should happen to use it, even though that word appears in no dictionary, and has never occurred before in our experience. We need a model that can draw inferences and implications from events and their contexts. With this quest, we leave behind the image of the memory system as a storehouse, or library of information, and demand something approximating ''thinking.''

One particular model of memory (Lindsay & Norman, 1977; Norman, 1973; Norman & Rumelhart, 1975) attempts to deal with this problem. One of the first questions we have to ask is one so basic that it may not immediately occur to us. That is, how do we know whether or not we know something? Lindsay and Norman (1977) offer the following examples:

1. What was Beethoven's telephone number?
2. What is the telephone number of the White House?
3. What is your best friend's telephone number?
4. What is your telephone number?

These questions are graded in a very important way. Your own telephone number probably pops to mind with no conscious effort. The telephone number of your friend is probably known, but you may require a moment's pause before it occurs to you. The telephone number of the White House is also likely to produce a slight pause. Assuming you do not know the number (202-456-1414), it may take you a moment to realize this before you reply that you do not know. You may even start to search for the number before you realize that it isn't there. Beethoven's telephone number, presumably, does not initiate a search at all.

All this is to say that all memory queries do not send us rushing off to search memory. We seem first to make a decision about the memory's availability, and perhaps, its location, before a search is begun. These decisions, as Lindsay and Norman (1977) point out, are not invariably good ones. Many unsuccessful test takers are familiar with the frustrating realization that they had terminated their search prematurely. Thrown by the wording of a particular question, or temporarily panicked when the answer did not leap to mind, these students had decided "I don't know," when more reflection might have brought the answer.

One's decisions about more general information are usually accurate however. For example, Hart (1965) asked subjects general questions and, when they were unable to give the correct answer, asked them to state whether they "felt" they knew. This resembles the tip-of-the-tongue procedure, but here we are asking the subject to make a judgement about their state of knowledge. On a later recognition test of the items, subjects correctly identified 76% of the words they felt they knew, as compared with only 43% of the items they felt they did not know.

Ordinary retrieval is not always simply obtaining some information from storage. As we have illustrated several times, it is frequently an active reconstruction. If, for example, you were asked where you were last Monday morning at 10 o'clock, you might recall that you have a class at that hour and, therefore, that must have been where you were. Sometimes inference lets you down, and it is only then that we clearly see the inference process at work. For example, if you were asked to draw a floor plan of your home or apartment right now, you would not have to rely totally on specific detail in memory. If you live on the second floor, you know that there must be stairs, that windows are on the outside walls only, and that there are doors or openings between rooms. Figure 4-11 shows the standard floor plan of married students' housing at the University of California, San Diego, together with a typical attempt to draw it from memory (Norman, 1973).

Note how details are missing (two storage rooms at the top of the stairs, and the bedroom closets), and some details are added (the balcony has been made flush with the bedroom wall). All of these changes and omissions are logical and reasonable. In fact, 47% of the people tested drew this same reasonable, if incorrect, placement of the balcony. What they drew represented reasonable features one might expect in an apartment of this kind. (The solid walls on each side of the balcony would prevent the occupant from being aware that the balcony protrudes from the side of the apartment.)

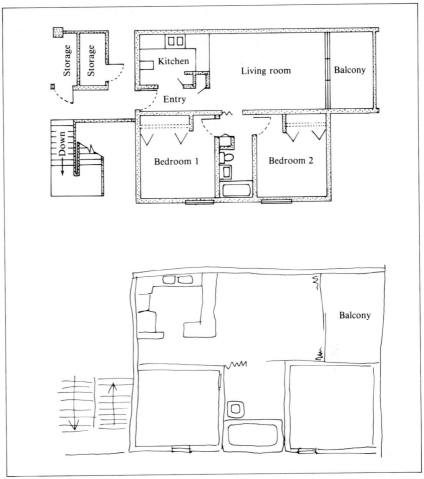

FIGURE 4-11 Floor plan of married students' apartment at the University of California, San Diego (top) and one long-term resident's attempt to draw it from memory (bottom). Balcony has brick walls on both sides, which may explain the resident's failure to show it correctly protruding from the building. Forty-seven percent of those tested made this error.
(From *Explorations in Cognition* by Donald A. Norman, David E. Rumelhart and the LNR Research Group. W. H. Freeman and Company. Copyright © 1975.)

Morton and Byrne (1975) asked English housewives to list the kinds of things necessary to equip a house. They found that the responses were organized in easily discernable ways. For example, the responses might be grouped by the category of item (furniture, dishes, etc.) or they might be grouped in terms of the places in the house these things belonged (bedroom, living room, etc.). They also found that recall of the ingredients of recipes followed the order in which these ingredients were typically handled. To relate this to our example of recalling the layout of an apartment, note that recall of events can ordinarily proceed from a plan. The plan can be derived from our general knowledge about the way things are. We know in trying to recall the layout of an apartment, that there is a kitchen, a bath, and so forth, and we know the likely contents of these areas. If we are missing some particular piece of information, it is easy to fill it in. The stored facts and relations outlined in the previous section on semantic models can be called the *data base*. In addition, we need an *interpretive process* that operates on the data base as part of the constructive or reconstructive act of recall.

The Talking Computer

Winograd (1972) made an ambitious effort to construct an intelligent artificial system that engages in the types of inference that we described above. Its attempt was to represent a computer data base and interpretive processes that employ a memory system and reasoning processes in a way not unlike human problem solving. Note especially its intelligent handling of inadequately worded questions put to it. While only a beginning, we can see in the dialogue most of the characteristics the semantic models presented in the previous sections have tried to address.

The following is a partial reproduction of a dialogue between a person (in italics) and the computer (in capital letters). The parenthetic comments describe and explain the program's responses.

1. *Pick up a big red block.*

   OK.

   (The system answers "OK" when it carries out a command. In order to pick up the red block, it had to clear it off by finding a space for a green one and moving the green one away.)

2. *Grasp the Pyramid.*

   I DON'T UNDERSTAND WHICH PYRAMID YOU MEAN.

   (There are three pyramids in the scene, so the program does nothing.)

3. *Find a block which is taller than the one you are holding and put it into the box.*

   BY "IT" I ASSUME YOU MEAN THE BLOCK WHICH IS TALLER THAN THE ONE I AM HOLDING.

   (The system has to figure out what is meant by "one" and "it," as well as using deduction to decide which block it is holding.) OK.

4. *What does the box contain?*

   THE BLUE PYRAMID AND THE BLUE BLOCK.

   (Winograd, 1972, pp. 8-9)

Winograd's program is obviously a limited one; we do not go through life picking up blue pyramids and deciding how many blocks there are in a container. More important, the invention of even the most sophisticated and ingenious computer program to mirror human capability within a narrow world does not necessarily mean that humans operate under the same principles. Dresher and Hornstein (1976) make this point with great care in specific reference to Winograd's program.

On the other hand, the success of this program, even in this limited domain, illustrates how computer simulation can help us define the properties of a semantic system and the cognitive operations necessary to its functioning. Computer simulations of cognitive functioning may not give us all the answers, but they can be very helpful in suggesting fruitful questions and lines of enquiry. The design problems faced by the model builder are the same problems we must solve in trying to determine how the human mind copes with similar tasks. If this program does nothing else, it reinforces in a very dramatic way our intuitive notions that inference must play a critical role in any complete theory of memory operations.

Another Look at Inference: Script and Text Processing

Memory for meaningful events, whether the layout of an apartment, the ingredients of a recipe, or how a house is furnished, seems to reflect organization; not simply associations among the experienced stimuli, but conceptual organization of our understanding of apartments, recipes, and home furnishings. Contemporary theorists have revived Bartlett's (1932) notion of schemata to describe this kind of conceptual organization. Bartlett's contribution, as we noted earlier, was principally to point out that memory possesses structure beyond what could be described as clusters of associations. His theory viewed the processes of comprehension as the key to this structure. Interpretation of what was experienced served both to determine how information was stored in memory (encoded) and to guide remembering (retrieval). Remembering an experience, according to Bartlett, involved using one's conceptual understanding of a previous experience (the schema) to reconstruct the event. He was, however, admittedly vague about the nature of schemata and the processes that used these schemata to aid comprehension and recall.

Modern versions of schema theory (e.g., Bobrow & Norman, 1975; Rumelhart & Ortony, 1977; Schank & Abelson, 1976; van Dijk & Kintsch, 1977) have used the computer as an analogy to human information processing and have employed some modern notions of linguistic analysis to add specificity to Bartlett's concepts. The schemata described by many of these theorists take the form of computer programs which intend to take into account not only associations among the elements in learned materials, but also the learner's intentions, beliefs, and the conventions of culture. These ideas, of course, are not new. Much of what we will describe is really a formalization of many earlier notions and common intuitions of how we understand meaningful verbal materials. However, these formalizations permit the testing of particular hypotheses about memory representations, and provide a more explicit way of talking about how these representations may be used.

One of the clearest examples of this form of theorizing is the schemata notions developed by Schank and Abelson (1977) to describe our knowledge structures for everyday activities. These authors describe the schemata for such activities as *scripts*. As we shall see in a moment, these "scripts," or "schemata," serve as the conceptual frameworks we will use to perform, encode, and later, to remember, our activities.

The script for "going to a restaurant" is listed in Figure 4-12. It is a simplified version of Schank and Abelson's script given by Bower, Black, and Turner (1979). The parts of a script like this one include the reasons for entering into the activity and the conditions necessary to begin, the objects or "props" used in the activity, the typical roles in such a script, and the consequences of completing the script. The script itself describes the major actions or scenes one would ordinarily go through in performing this activity.

Schank and Abelson suggest that our knowledge of activities like going to a restaurant, riding buses, attending lectures, and so forth, is organized around such scripts. They further argue that schemata of this kind serve at least three functions: (1) They set up expectations, or predictions about what we are likely to encounter in these activities. These expectations, in turn, are used in planning and carrying out what we wish to do. (2) They function to structure our comprehension when such activities are described to us by someone else. Such scripts can provide a framework that organizes the information in what we hear or read. (3) Finally, the script can be used to guide our recall of the events we have experienced, or information we have heard. In the example shown in Figure 4-12, the various parts of the script and the order of the script events can be used to structure retrieval of information about what was eaten in a restaurant, whether there was a waiter or a waitress, how the bill was paid, and so forth. Each of these elements is part of going to a restaurant and should be represented in the particulars of any restaurant-going experience.

In short, schemata, in the sense used by Bartlett, or scripts, in the sense used by Schank and Abelson (1976), refer to an organized representation of a person's conceptual knowledge of an idea, event, or action. They provide a structure within which the various elements are related to each other. A schema, or script, then, organizes the major features of a knowledge "unit," and includes rules for when and how this knowledge unit should be applied.

Modern schema notions possess several advantages as a way of conceptualizing memory representations. First, schemata represent relationships among concepts rather than among words. This has an important implication: while an enactment of a script might be verbally described in many different ways, the relationships among the script elements (e.g., waiters, customers, food, ordering, paying the bill) would remain the same in any narrative description. As we saw before in the

Name: Restaurant

Props: Tables   **Roles:** Customer
     Menu   Waiter
     Food   Cook
     Bill   Cashier
     Money   Owner
     Tip

Entry Conditions: Customer is hungry.   **Results:** Customer has less money.
     Customer has money.   Owner has more money.
                                            Customer is not hungry.

Scene 1: *Entering*
    Customer enters restaurant.
    Customer looks for table.
    Customer decides where to sit.
    Customer goes to table.
    Customer sits down.

Scene 2: *Ordering*
    Customer picks up menu.
    Customer looks at menu.
    Customer decides on food.
    Customer signals waitress.
    Waitress comes to table.
    Customer orders food.
    Waitress goes to cook.
    Waitress gives food order to cook.
    Cook prepares food.

Scene 3: *Eating*
    Cook gives food to waitress.
    Waitress brings food to customer.
    Customer eats food.

Scene 4: *Exiting*
    Waitress writes bill.
    Waitress goes over to customer.
    Waitress gives bill to customer.
    Customer gives tip to waitress.
    Customer goes to cashier.
    Customer gives money to cashier.
    Customer leaves restaurant.

FIGURE 4-12   A simplified version of Schank and Abelson's (1976) schematic representation of our organized knowledge of activities involved in going to a restaurant. (From: Bower, Black, & Turner, 1979.)

studies of Sachs (1967), Bransford and Franks (1971), and others, subjects invariably retain the meaning of an episode rather than the specific words used to describe that episode.

The second characteristic of schemata also relates to their generality. Each of the script elements can be viewed as a *variable* which takes on different values as a function of the concrete situation. The *value* of "waiter" for a particular enactment of the restaurant script, for example, might be a bearded fellow in a tuxedo. In another case the "waiter" variable might be a middle-aged woman in a sarong.

Script theorists often call the particular value taken on by a variable in a script the *instantiation* of that variable. Instantiation implies that each value represents a possible instance or exemplar of a script variable that might possibly be encountered. Consider another example, our schema for the ordinary activity of eating. In a typical enactment of eating there is some edible object, an agent that does the eating, some consummatory activities, and the consequences of the activity (tastes, satiety, heartburn, or whatever). When someone tells us about a meal they had eaten, this generalized schema will become activated, leading us to think about the presence of certain elements and the relationships among them. As we match our friend's description of the meal against our schema, or script, we may notice that certain expected variables were not mentioned, or were not given values in their story. This will lead us to ask questions about what was eaten, who ate the steak, or where the eating took place. These particulars are the instantiations of the variables related to the schema.

Without general schemata of this kind some narrative information might be unintelligible. Think of, for example, Bransford and Johnson's (1972) story of washing clothes mentioned earlier in this chapter. The paragraph describing clothes washing is difficult to understand without the accompanying title. The function of the title, for schema theory, is the selection of the appropriate script in memory which contains the elements of this activity and relates them to each other. Bransford and Johnson were particularly clever in writing this narrative to avoid explicitly naming any element that might have resulted in the retrieval of the washing clothes schema (e.g., detergent, washing machine, laundry). In fact, the success of their experiment rested on the assumption that their paragraph was insufficient to arouse the schema appropriate to its interpretation.

The eating and restaurant examples illustrate a third characteristic of schemata. Schemata can represent several different levels of generality. The eating schema is embedded in the more general restaurant script. There may be an even more general schema, such as "going out," which could include both restaurant and eating. Intuitively, our own experience seems to be organized in this way with subgoals being planned and organized within the context of more inclusive plans and goals.

Bower, Black, and Turner (1979) have demonstrated that there is a wide agreement among people about the standard constituents of common scripts. They gave their subjects lists of common situations (visiting a doctor, shopping at a grocery store, and so forth), and asked them to describe "what people generally do" in these situations. There was substantial overlap across subjects in what actions were mentioned, and those events mentioned most often were also rated as the most important elements in the descriptions. Some of the activities and events rated as most important in grocery shopping were: "Getting a cart," "picking out items," "waiting in line," "paying cashier." Other actions and events less essential to the script were organized around these central events which could be described as occupying the central positions in the script.

In addition to representing the organization of our knowledge about everyday activities, the concept of schemata has also been applied to our understanding of the structure of narratives or stories. These studies are sometimes called studies of *text processing* (Mandler & Johnson, 1977; Meyer, 1977; Rumelhart, 1975; Thorndyke, 1977).

Studies of Text Processing.   People have certain expectations about how a story should be structured. They have no difficulty in distinguishing major themes from minor themes in a story, or in paraphrasing the story once they have heard it. Rumelhart (1975), among others, has suggested that the schema or organization underlying comprehension and paraphrasing of a simple story can be represented as a *story grammar*. The term "grammar" is drawn from analogy to modern linguistic theory which defines a sentence grammar as the rules used to organize, order, and structure the elements of a sentence in a meaningful way. In text processing, the "grammar" represents rules for structuring and organizing conceptual elements within a whole narrative.

Figure 4-13 is the Rumelhart grammar as adapted by Thorndyke (1977) to study simple stories. Each rule of the grammar indicates how the story might be broken down from its major constituents into instantiations of its elements. Rule (1), for example, indicates that the story is composed of four major constituents: its setting, its theme, its plot, and its resolution. Rule (4) indicates that the plot is composed of a series of episodes, while Rule (5) defines an episode as consisting of a subgoal, attempts to achieve the subgoal, and the outcome of these attempts.

Figure 4-14 shows a concrete example of how Thorndyke used this grammar to diagram the structure of a simple story, the story of "Circle Island." As you can see from the diagram, the story is organized as a hierarchy of increasingly specific elements as we move down the "tree" until, at the bottom of the tree, the elements of this particular story are instantiated by the numbered sentences that appear in the text.

This mode of representing stories assumes that we possess some very abstract conceptualizations of what stories in general are like. Stories, in this view, share a common set of constituents and relationships among

Rule number	Rule
(1)	Story → Setting + Theme + Plot + Resolution
(2)	Setting → Characters + Location + Time
(3)	Theme → (Event) + Goal
(4)	Plot → Episode
(5)	Episode → Subgoal + Attempt + Outcome
(6)	Attempt → Event / Episode
(7)	Outcome → Event / State
(8)	Resolution → Event / State
(9)	Subgoal / Goal → Desired state
(10)	Characters / Location / Time → State

FIGURE 4-13   The study of text processing: Structural rules for a simple story. (From Thorndyke, 1977.)

constituents. When listening to, or reading a story, we automatically organize the information into this schema, instantiating the general components with specific information.

Thinking about memory organization in this way provides us with relatively specific ways of predicting what kinds of distortions might be introduced in remembering and how inference processes might facilitate or cause intrusions in the recall of a story. Do we in fact remember stories in this way? This is a hard question to answer, but Thorndyke's experiments suggest that this may be so. In one case, for example, Thorndyke (1977) found that comprehension of a story and memory of story events were best when the structure of the presented story conformed to the structure described in Figure 4-14. When the same semantic content was presented in a different order, comprehension was rated as more difficult and memory was less accurate.

In theorizing about the forgetting of narrative information or of accounts of everyday activities, we can treat the schema as an entire memory "unit." As Thorndyke and Hayes-Roth (1979) have pointed out, many of the principles you have already encountered in this book fit nicely with the notion of a schema unit in which the entire schema or script is used as a whole in encoding and retrieving memory elements. That is, in encoding or retrieval of meaningful information, the schema itself must be retrieved or activated. The accessibility of a schema may further be thought of as a function of the same variables that we previously described as affecting the accessibility of an association. The ease of activation of a particular schema, for example, should depend on how well the information in the input matches information in the schema (encoding specificity), and the frequency and recency with which the schema has been activated in the past. In addition, we might also assume that on each occasion that the schema is used, concrete instantiations are connected associatively to the general concepts of the schema. This would imply that these associations would compete with one another in a way similar to that encountered in the studies of paired-associate

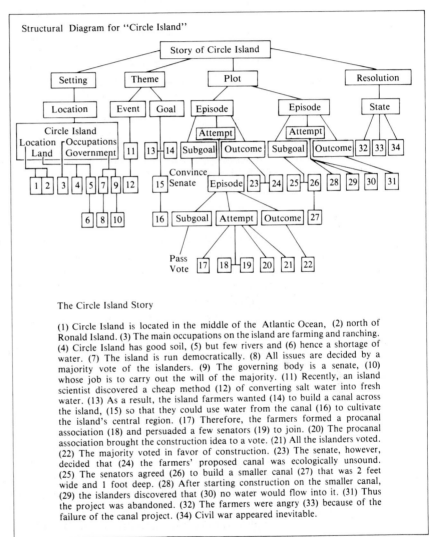

The Circle Island Story

(1) Circle Island is located in the middle of the Atlantic Ocean, (2) north of Ronald Island. (3) The main occupations on the island are farming and ranching. (4) Circle Island has good soil, (5) but few rivers and (6) hence a shortage of water. (7) The island is run democratically. (8) All issues are decided by a majority vote of the islanders. (9) The governing body is a senate, (10) whose job is to carry out the will of the majority. (11) Recently, an island scientist discovered a cheap method (12) of converting salt water into fresh water. (13) As a result, the island farmers wanted (14) to build a canal across the island, (15) so that they could use water from the canal (16) to cultivate the island's central region. (17) Therefore, the farmers formed a procanal association (18) and persuaded a few senators (19) to join. (20) The procanal association brought the construction idea to a vote. (21) All the islanders voted. (22) The majority voted in favor of construction. (23) The senate, however, decided that (24) the farmers' proposed canal was ecologically unsound. (25) The senators agreed (26) to build a smaller canal (27) that was 2 feet wide and 1 foot deep. (28) After starting construction on the smaller canal, (29) the islanders discovered that (30) no water would flow into it. (31) Thus the project was abandoned. (32) The farmers were angry (33) because of the failure of the canal project. (34) Civil war appeared inevitable.

FIGURE 4-14 A structural diagram for the "Circle Island" story. The numbered elements in the diagram represent the instantiations of the structural elements derived from the numbered sentences in the story.
(From Thorndyke, 1977.)

learning. This approach, in other words, might help to explain those studies, such as that of Ausubel, Stager, and Gaite (1968) and of Anderson and Myrow (1971) mentioned at the beginning of this chapter. The question was, you will recall, whether learning different, but conceptually related, information will cause interference or facilitation in later recall of this information.

Thorndyke and Hayes-Roth (1979) showed, in fact, that memory for passages about a conceptual category (e.g., constellations of stars) could be predicted from assumptions about the accessibility of a schema and about interference among the various instantiations of variables within a schema. They had their subjects read passages about one constellation and then tested their acquisition and retention of information of a second passage describing similar information about another constellation. For example, the subject might read a passage about Pisces, Aries, or Orion. In the first passage would be a sentence such as, "This constellation was originally charted at the Palomar Observatory." In the second passage, about another constellation, the subject would read that, "This constellation was originally charted at the Mount Wilson Observatory."

According to the arguments made above, as the subject learns about the first constellation a schema would begin to be formed within which one might organize information about other constellations. The formation of this schema should lead to positive transfer when information about a new constellation is presented. That is, there should be the beginning of a conceptual structure that can aid in the organization of all new, related information. On the one hand, we would expect this schema to become better formed and generally more accessible with repeated use. On the other hand, many different instantiations of the same concepts within the same schema might produce associative interference and forgetting. It would thus follow that specific items of information should become more and more difficult to remember as the subject learns about a greater number of constellations.

Thorndyke and Hayes-Roth (1979) confirmed these predictions. If subjects had heard only a few passages, there was facilitation, or positive transfer, in learning a new passage. Here, the positive effects of increased schema accessibility outweighed the effects of associative interference among a few instantiations of the concepts in the schema. As more passages were read, the accuracy of recall declined indicating that associative interference within the schema now outweighed the organizational advantages of schema accessibility. Bower, Black, and Turner (1979) found similar effects when studying the scripts mentioned earlier.

These notions of schema, then, do not sweep aside all the data and principles we were at such pains to describe in earlier chapters. The ideas of interference and how it works may still be applied to memory for ordinary discourse and meaningful learning. These ideas, however, might have to be assimilated into the more comprehensive notions of schemata. When a schema is used to comprehend several similar events, the different instantiations of variables within the schema compete and produce forgetting. Schemata themselves may compete with one another as possible interpretations of a single experience.

Associations and Schemata.   The concepts of schema theory do provide us with a more effective theoretical tool for describing meaningful learning than is possible when we treat individual associations as the unit of memory. Indeed, considerable work is now being devoted almost entirely to the exploration of the applicability of schema theory to meaningful learning in education (cf., Anderson, Spiro, & Montague, 1977). As you might have anticipated, the authors of this work see education as communicating to the student the structure of a particular body of knowledge. Examples in instruction serve the function of building up the schemata and providing instantiations of variables which, in turn, demonstrate the range of possible values the variables can assume. An example of this latter point is the student of learning theory who encounters many specific examples of stimuli which can function as ''reinforcement'' in operant conditioning. From these specific instantiations can come the derivation of boundary conditions for a concept and from this, in turn, can come the development of a full schema. This general idea of using boundary conditions was encountered earlier when we spoke of the asking of intelligent questions prior to beginning a memory search (e.g., ''What was Beethoven's telephone number?''). We now see how such limiting questions relate to the boundary conditions of a concept.

An equally useful contrast to this ''bottom-up'' approach to learning is a ''top-down'' approach typified by the use of metaphors and analogies. In this case, metaphors and analogies, such as, ''The brain is like a computer,'' can function to facilitate the formation of a new schema by utilizing the structure of another schema already in memory. Both examples and analogies should demonstrate the conceptual structure of the subject matter, illustrate a set of concepts and the relationships among them, rather than list facts or provide a sequence of associations.

An amusing example of constructing a new schema through an analogy is provided by what Norman, Gentner, and Stevens (1976) call, the ''Mayonnaise Problem.'' The two sets of dialogues in Figure 4-15 are between one of these experimenters and two subjects, one an 8-year-old child and the other an adult colleague. The level of sophistication of the two respondents may be very different (we hesitate to say which is more sophisticated). But both nevertheless appear to solve the problem by analogy. Norman, Gentner, and Stevens (1976) describe the process of solving the problem like this:

1. No knowledge of the components of mayonnaise existed.

2. It is known that mayonnaise is smooth, creamy, off-white in color. Its taste is known (and it is somewhat acidic).

3. General schema:

Blends of foods blend their properties.

Texture: sour cream or whipped cream yields a color that is too white and a taste that is not right.

Correction: Add yellow-spicy-acidic mustard.

Schema theory, then, can provide us with several possible sources of forgetting and distortion in memory performance and a basis for the inference and problem solving processes that seem to work when someone tries to remember. (1) The input information may be misinterpreted; that is, an inappropriate schema may be applied in encoding events. This would be

---

Protocol of the experimenter (DAN) and an 8-year-old female (CN)

DAN: How do you make mayonnaise?

  CN: How you make mayonnaise is you look at a cookbook.

DAN: OK, but without looking at a cookbook, can you guess what it is that's inside of mayonnaise?

  CN: Uh.

DAN: How you would make it?

  CN: Uh Butter—uh let me think (5-sec pause) hmm (10-sec pause) whipped cream very very very fine—ly whipped so it's smooth. That's probably how you make it, just with whipped cream, very very very very fine and smooth.

DAN: Anything else?

  CN: You might add a little taste to it.

DAN: Taste of what?

  CN: (10-sec pause) Sort of a vanilla taste.

DAN: Suppose I said that mayonnaise is made from egg yolk—and oil. What would you say?

  CN: I would say it's very very—wrong.

DAN: Why?

  CN: You can't just make mayonnaise out of egg yolks and water—I mean and oil.

DAN: Why not?

  CN: Because of taste and smoothness and stuff like that.

Protocol of the experimenter (DAN) and an adult male psychology Professor (GB)

DAN: How would you make something like mayonnaise?

  GB: Mayonnaise? How do you make mayonnaise? You can't make mayonnaise, it has to be bought in jars. Mayonnaise. Um. You mix whipped cream with, umm some mustard.

FIGURE 4-15   An example of attempts to construct a new schema through analogy: protocols for the ''Mayonnaise Problem.''
(From Norman, Gentner, & Stevens, 1976.)

an error in acquisition of the information. (2) A subject may be unable to access or activate the appropriate schema when trying to remember. Without the retrieval cues provided by the schema organization, the subject may not recall the associated information. (3) There may be interference among the various instantiations of a concept within a schema. As you look back over your college career, for example, it may be difficult for you to remember which class you shared with a particular friend. There are many instantiations of the role of "fellow student" in your attending-a-lecture script, and these undoubtedly interfere with one another when you try to recall. (4) Finally, in remembering, we may fill in values of variables in the schema which were not actually present in the original experience. We may, after some time has past, be unable to discriminate which variables were instantiated and which were not. The result produces intrusions in recall of the experience. Similar effects often come into play when recall of meaningful prose becomes distorted in the direction of conventional cultural stereotypes, as was the case with Bartlett's "War of the Ghosts." If forgetting has occurred, the values of the forgotten variables in the schema may be replaced by instantiations that are more typical in the subject's experience.

The formalization of the notion of schemata through the studies of script and text processing is a potentially powerful theoretical tool for describing the learning and remembering of meaningful materials. However, this development is still in its infancy. We continue to attempt to specify the nature of schemata and the processes that operate on them. While the theories may eventually succeed in describing "what" we know and how to use it, their present status remains exploratory in nature and one must await further verification and development. What they do give us is yet another way of talking about memory phenomena, another schema around which we might organize our knowledge of the activity of remembering.

CHAPTER SUMMARY

1. *The Bartlett Tradition: Reconstructive Memory*

   A. One of the earliest critics of the associationsts' verbal learning tradition was F.C. Bartlett, who argued that memory was often more reconstructive than reproductive. He argued that memory for meaningful material and events is ordinarily organized around a conceptual framework or schema. In recall, subjects use these schemata to retrieve details and fill in gaps in the memory data.

   B. Comparing the results of serial reproduction and repeated reproduction of themes and stories, Bartlett noted qualitative distortion in recall. This distortion could be viewed as another aspect of interference effects in memory. In this case, the notion of constructive recall implies that memory of, for example, a story, will retain the meaning of the narrative rather than its literal form.

C. Contemporary studies of memory for themes show the importance of external context in giving meaning to learning materials. Typically, supplying a context results in better recall than when materials are presented context-free. The context appears to supply a framework which can be used to interpret, and later to retrieve, the presented information.

2. *Inference in Memory*

A. Understanding or comprehension of potentially meaningful materials typically yields higher recall scores than for materials that are not analyzed for meaning. This frequently occurs when there is no intention to learn the materials.

B. Separate items of information presented independently over a period of time can be used to build a semantic prototype, or generalized schemata representing a unified, complex idea. Subjects tend to remember the results of this semantic integration rather than the specific words or sentence forms in which the information was presented.

C. Once the semantic component of a sentence has been encoded, subjects will show recognition errors indicating that they used inference to go beyond the specifics of the original information. The results of this inference process are often not distinguished from the original event in memory performance.

3. *Memory Organization*

A. Giving a subject dictionary definitions of uncommon words, such as "sextant," will frequently produce a TOT state in subjects. Responses made in attempting to recall the correct word suggest that concepts are stored in memory as complexes of associated attributes which include the general sound pattern and its functional and semantic relationships to other concepts.

B. Memory can be viewed as an active search process in which subjects explore an organized memory store, using external or internal retrieval cues to aid the search.

4. *Models of Semantic Memory*

A. Models of semantic memory attempt to describe how items might be organized in memory and how semantic relationships might be represented in such a system. Collins and Quillian's network model consisted of units, corresponding to concepts, pointers, representing patterns of association between the units, and properties, representing descriptions and attributes of the units. Reaction time experiments were used to explore how one might hypothetically move from one unit to another within the network in order to answer simple true/false questions.

B. Anderson and Bower offered a model of human associative memory (HAM) which operated within an associative network similar to Collins and Quillian's. HAM added episodic information to the model allowing one to analyze propositions, or relations between facts, and the context in which they were acquired.

C. The semantic feature model of Rips, Shoben, and Smith depicts concept storage as lists of features which exhaustively describe the properties and relations of the concepts. Sentence verification in this model proceeds by comparing the list of features for the concepts involved and deriving a similarity index. Mathematical techniques have been used to determine semantic distance between concepts from subjects' judgements. This distance represents the similarity among concepts and can be used to infer the dimensions on which concepts are evaluated.

D. Collins and Loftus have described a network model which incorporates the notions of feature comparisons and semantic distance. This is accomplished in the model through variations in the accessibility of one concept from another and by variations in the possible decision strategies used to evaluate judgments.

5. *The Intelligent Computer*

A. One feature of human memory absent from most information retrieval programs is the human ability to interpret questions so as to limit the range of possible responses. In an attempt to portray this ability, Lindsay, Norman, and Rumelhart distinguish between the data base, which represents the memory store itself, and interpretive processes which operate on the data base as part of the constructive process in remembering.

B. A special attempt to model the use of logical inference in memory and decision processes was made by Winograd who developed a computer program which can hold an interactive dialog with the questioner. An important feature of the program is its ability to determine inadequacies in the form of questions put to it and to draw logical inferences in the absence of this specificity.

C. Recent work on script and text processing has served to formalize the general notion of schemata through the development of computer programs that model a conceptual structure as a relationship among knowledge elements. The scripts and story grammars that are the result of this formalization permit us to make relatively specific predictions about what elements are most likely to be forgotten, the kinds of intrusions that are likely to be introduced, and the inferences that are likely to be made in the course of a memory performance.

CODING PROCESSES: I. SENSORY MEMORY

TOPIC QUESTIONS

1. A Memory System: Structure versus Process.
How did theorists analyze the total memory system into separate components of memory or *memory structures?* How does a theory which emphasizes *memory processes* differ from one which emphasizes memory structures?

2. The First Stage: Sensory Memory.
What are the three characteristics that distinguish *sensory memory* from other memory structures?

3. Visual Sensory Memory.
What experimental procedures were used to study visual sensory memory *(iconic memory),* how long can such sensory information be retained, and what are the characteristics of this retention? What are the major controversial issues in interpreting these studies?

4. Auditory Sensory Memory.
Why does it appear logically necessary to have a sensory memory for auditory events *(echoic memory)?* How have the characteristics of auditory sensory memory been studied?

5. Sensory Memory and a Process Model.
How do theories which emphasize memory processes interpret studies of sensory memory?

In the opening pages of this book we described memory as the ability to retain information, to recall it when needed, and to recognize its familiarity when seen or heard again. We noted that a failure of recall or recognition may often be the result of initial inattention, or a failure to effectively code the material when it was first experienced.

From our own experiences in looking, listening, and learning, we know that there are clearly limitations in our normal capacity to rapidly acquire information. There are some things we cannot effectively do at one time, such as trying to simultaneously listen to two separate conversations and hope to follow both in detail. A list of four or five numbers spoken aloud can be "taken in" after hearing them just once, and a written list of similar length can be acquired with a single glance. We also know that we cannot take in a list of 10, 12, or 14 digits. Not only does such a list require conscious rehearsal, but we ordinarily cannot even hold the full set in memory in order to give it this practice. We have to learn such a list in parts, returning to the original from time to time to take in yet another segment for rehearsal.

While there seems to be a limited capacity in the *amount* of information we can easily code at any one time, there also seems to be a limit on the *rate* at which it can be coded. We often wish a rapid-fire speaker would slow down or just occasionally pause while speaking. In everyday terms we say we need time for what has just been heard to "sink in" before we are bombarded by the arrival of yet more information.

In more technical terms, we would say that the perceptual-memory system has an upper limit on the amount of information which can be coded per unit time. We can handle fairly simple stimulus inputs that arrive rapidly, or fairly complex inputs that arrive slowly. What we cannot handle effectively is complex material arriving at a rapid rate.

Some have referred to this limitation as a "bottleneck" in the memory system. The information flow, no matter how large the ultimate capacity, is limited by the narrow neck of this metaphorical bottle, and it is only once past this neck that the capacity again becomes large.

Our goal in this chapter and the subsequent two will be to examine research and theory as psychologists have attempted to understand the nature of these input limitations on the amount and rate of coding information. Before doing this, however, let us take a brief look at two pictures of human information processing current in psychological theory.

A MEMORY SYSTEM: STRUCTURE VERSUS PROCESS

When an engineer attempts to design or to understand the functioning of some system, the first step is often to draw a picture of the system, its components, and the order in which each component must operate for the system to work. A case in point is the electronic computer whose system requires first that the data punched on cards or paper tape be "read into" the system. This process involves the conversion of the data, whether numbers, letters, or both, into electronic signals that are used in running the program. Finally, these electronic representations must be stored in a fairly permanent way before they are put to use.

How does one draw a "picture" of the analogous mental activity involved in human memory? We cannot gain much by drawing a picture of the actual neurons and blood vessels of the brain. This would be no more helpful to most of us than if we tried to understand the functions of a computer by seeing a diagram of its wires, relays, and solid-state components.

A Structural Model of Memory

Beginning in the 1950s with theorists such as Broadbent (1958) and culminating in the work of Atkinson and Shiffrin (1968), psychologists tried to draw such a "picture" of the memory system. Their goal was not to draw a picture of the blood vessels and neurons of the brain, but to specify those component operations which must logically be involved in memory processing. No less important, they attempted to specify the *order* in which these components must come into play for the system to function as it does.

This approach typically emphasized several structures in the information processing system depicted as a flow diagram of the sort shown in Figure 5-1 (A). Let us look briefly at each of these components and why this particular order was thought to be logically necessary.

The recognition of any stimulus, whether the letter "A" or the spoken word "hello," does not occur instantaneously. For such recognition to take place, we must analyze the visual pattern of the letter, or the sound pattern of the word, and then compare these patterns with other information about visual or sound patterns stored from past experience. From this match we will form a tentative perceptual identification of the stimulus.

While sometimes this process may seem automatic, there are occasions when we realize that it is not; that the stimulus may need several "looks" before it can be recognized. Consider, for example, our attempts to recognize a letter written in poor handwriting, or to understand a word spoken in a foreign accent or muffled by extraneous noise.

Many theorists argued that if the identification of a stimulus is not instantaneous, then logically there must be some structure early in the system to temporarily hold this new sensory input just long enough for it to be recognized, or "read in" to the higher levels of memory. This structure has been referred to as a *sensory memory*.

This sensory memory, with a potential counterpart for each sense modality, was conceived as lasting for only a very brief duration, less than a second for visual sensation, and several seconds for auditory sensation. These were called "sensory" memories not because of their brief duration, but because the information was thought to be stored in almost exactly the way in which it arrived, as "raw" sensory patterns.

Within sensory memory, no meaning would be given to the material. The A is not the alphabetic "A," the first letter of the alphabet or the start of the word "apple." It is simply a visual pattern of two angled

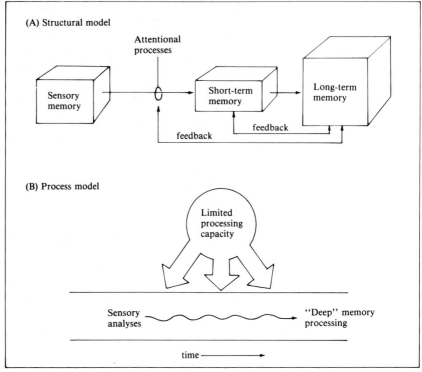

FIGURE 5-1   A comparison of a discrete, linear, structural model of memory common throughout the 1960s (A) with a conception of memory processing as a continuous "shallow" to "deep" level of analysis without discrete stages (B).

verticals crossed by a horizontal. The word "hello" is not stored as a meaningful greeting, but as an acoustic contour of a certain frequency and intensity pattern.

Not all information temporarily stored in sensory memory is attended to, analyzed, and thought about. We are not ordinarily aware of the sound of a ticking clock (until it stops), nor can we concentrate on two separate speakers, both talking at the same time. Thus, an important requirement of the system was an *attentional process* which would select those elements to be read out from the sensory "buffer" memory for further processing.

Thus, those stimuli that have been selected were seen as now entering a second structure in the memory system which also had a limiting effect on information flow. This structure, *short-term memory*, served as a second temporary holding store for newly arrived information. In this case, however, the stimuli were now coded as meaningful symbols whose names could be rehearsed and thought about. Through this process of rehearsal, the information could now be transferred for relatively permanent storage in *long-term memory*, the third and final structure in the system. In long-term memory the information would, for the first time, acquire full access to, and become part of, the complete semantic system as previously described.

Anywhere along the line from sensory memory through short-term memory, material not selected, coded, and transferred to the next level might be lost. These mechanisms ensured the storage of only significant information by protecting the system from overload. Without these limiting features, too much information might well arrive too quickly to be effectively coded into the semantic system.

Sensory memory, short-term memory, and long-term memory were all seen as fixed structures in information processing. Each was a stage in the flow of information, having a particular capacity, a typical duration of holding stimuli, and a specific and necessary function.

In addition to these structures, there were also what could be called "control processes" (Atkinson & Shiffrin, 1968). One of these was the attentional process with its flexibility in selecting some aspects of the sensory memory for further processing while rejecting others. Two additional control processes are indicated by lines in Figure 5-1 (A). One of these runs "backward" from long-term memory to short-term memory, and the other from long-term memory to the attentional process. While information is seen as flowing from left to right in the diagram, long-term knowledge must be used both to aid in stimulus selection and to identify those stimuli as linguistic elements for rehearsal in short-term memory.

This sytem may strike you as very much like a machine, a human "computer," transferring information from one memory structure to the next with almost mechanical precision. There was a certain intuitive appeal to this approach, however, and it became increasingly popular throughout the 1950s and 1960s. More important, considerable evidence came to light during this period which seemed to support its viability and usefulness.

A Process Model of Memory

This sequential, linear model of memory had a long and impressive development over the 20 or so years it served as the dominant view of information processing in human memory. Interested readers can find an excellent review of this development in Lachman, Mistler-Lachman, and Butterfield (1979).

It has been said that a good theory in psychology, or in any other science, is one which both helps to organize an otherwise confusing mass of data in a coherent way, and one which suggests fruitful lines for research. In this sense, the structural model of memory was a "good" theory indeed. For this reason we will devote some energy to its description in subsequent pages.

Beginning in the 1970s, however, many began to question the picture this model painted of the memory system. It was to some perhaps too simple. But more important, it was leading us to ask the wrong experimental questions. For example, we will review evidence suggesting that the clear-cut divisions between the stages are in fact more blurred than this conception would imply. These writers, led by such investigators as Craik and Lockhart (1972), saw a continuity in memory processing, together with a functional overlap not allowed for by the structural approach.

Figure 5-1 (B) shows a very much simpler picture of a memory system. Its simplicity in fact belies its complexity. We see information undergoing sensory analyses and "deep" memory processing, with overall capacity limited by finite attentional and processing resources. Essentially, these theorists argued that stimuli, from the moment of their arrival, undergo continual processing and elaboration as their sensory patterns are analyzed, given lexical classification, and connected with past associations for assimilation into the semantic system. Retention, they argued, was not so much a consequence of transferring information from sensory memory to short-term memory to long-term memory, as it was a function of the depth of processing given to the materials over the first few seconds or minutes following its arrival.

"Memory," in this view, should not be identified with the contents of a particular memory structure. There are, in fact, no explicit stages or structures in this system. Instead, the presentation of a stimulus initiates processes of analysis beginning with analysis of the physical form and characteristics of the object (e.g., color, lines, angles) and continues through categorization of the object and its relationships with other objects. The processing is continuous from the extraction of sensory features to the extraction of meaning. There is no particular point in this continuum that we can label *the* sensory memory, or *the* short-term memory. Rather, different kinds of information becomes available as processing proceeds to deeper and deeper levels of analysis. The nature of the information we have available, then, is not dependent on the contents of a particular store but on the level to which the stimulus has been processed.

The "bottleneck" was seen as a limit on total processing resources which must be allocated among various stimuli, their maintenance in memory, and their deep processing. "Attention" is thus not an isolated operation within a linear sequential system, but a process sharing the same limited pool of resources.

This, however, is getting ahead of our story. Let us look more closely at the phenomena to be explained, how they fit into a structural model, and as we go along, to examine the weaknesses we perceive in this explanation. In this chapter we will look at the first stage of the memory processing system, so-called "sensory memory."

THE FIRST STAGE: SENSORY MEMORY

The processes that produce perception and recognition take time. The data from the senses must be "matched up" with our knowledge of the world, how things look, and how they sound and feel. If sensory experience terminated before these processes were completed, we would be unable to identify what was "out there." Some amount of time, however brief, is necessary to allow for the processing of incoming information. Sensory memory guarantees a minimum processing time by temporarily preserving the stimulation.

Sensory memory has traditionally been seen as having several characteristics which distinguish it from ordinary memory, as we usually use the term. First, its content is solely a record of the sensory effects of the stimulus. The information preserved in sensory memory is no more or less than a representation of the physical characteristics of the stimulus. Visual experience, for example, is first analyzed in terms of size, color, and brightness. While this "raw" sensory data may represent a patterned form in the sensory store, this initial stage contains no reference to the meaning of the stimulus, its relationship to other things we know, or its associations with other stimuli. Sensory memory holds a representation prior to those structures and processes that make up our knowledge of the world.

A second characteristic of sensory memory is its relatively large capacity. We take in much more information in a single glance than we could ever use. From this initial stimulation only some small portion produces any lasting effect on later memory or thought. Most of what occurs goes unnoticed, forming merely the background for meaningful, memorable events. The capacity of sensory storage would appear to be limited only by the physical conditions and the sensitivity of our receptors. We cannot, of course, see in the dark, nor are we sensitive to infrared light. No sensory memory would be formed under these conditions. But, under normal viewing conditions, more registers in the sensory system then ever reaches the level of memory or awareness.

The third characteristic distinguishing sensory memory from other forms of storage is its brief duration. Under most conditions, visual sensory memory persists for much less than a second. Although there is less agreement on its duration, auditory sensory memory seems to persist for only a few seconds. The loss of information in sensory memory, whether visual or auditory, is thus quite rapid.

Sensory memory, then, represents a persistence of the stimulus in the nervous system for some period after its objective termination. Its function is to preserve this information long enough for further processing by later, more limited capacity mechanisms. Sensory memory thus differs from other forms of storage in its content, capacity, and duration. Let us now consider the evidence for these conclusions, looking first at the visual modality, and then at audition.

VISUAL SENSORY MEMORY

In scanning a visual scene, or in reading, the eyes fixate for a fraction of a second and then move to fixate on a new location. Normally, the eyes change fixations three to five times per second. We are largely unaware of these periodic shifts in fixation, nor are we aware that we take in no new information during this movement of the eyes. The latency of an eye movement, the time it takes the eye to move to a new fixation, is approximately 200 milliseconds (msec), or $\frac{1}{5}$ second (sec) (Rayner, 1978).

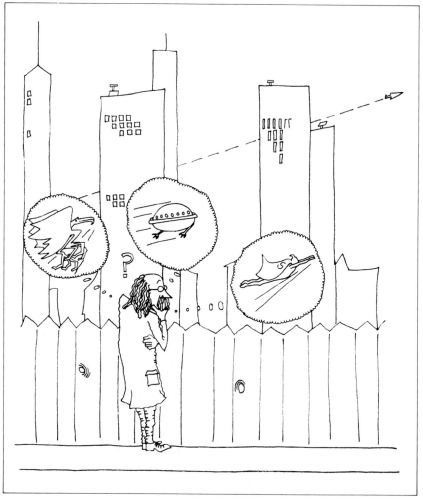

It is sometimes the case that stimuli are seen for too brief a duration for correct identification. A sensory mechanism that could prolong our perceptual experience—even for a brief instant—might be an advantage.

How Much Can We See in a Glance?

From these two facts, the frequency and latency of eye movements, we know that visual information must be taken in, or "extracted from the environment," in a succession of rapid but discrete fixations. An important limitation to the operation to our system of visual intake, therefore, is the amount of information we can derive from a single glance.

Some of the most important techniques used to study these questions were originated by George Sperling (1960, 1963, 1967) as part of his doctoral dissertation at Harvard University. Sperling wanted to measure what he called the "span of apprehension," the number of items a person could remember from a single brief exposure. To do this, he presented observers with a matrix of printed letters such as those shown below. These letters were seen in a tachistoscope, and were illuminated by a single 50-msec flash of light. (One millisecond equals one thousandth of a second; i.e., 50 msec = .05 sec.) This duration was especially chosen as it is much shorter than the average duration of a fixation, and too brief for the occurrence of any eye movements during the single presentation.

T D R

S R N

F Z G

Sperling found that if the number of letters presented were less than four, observers could easily report the whole matrix without error. When more than four letters were exposed at any one time, however, performance was no better. In fact, subjects could never report more than four or five letters correctly regardless of the total number of items presented. There appeared to be a fixed limit on the amount of information that could be obtained from a single glance.

Although observers could not recall more than four or five letters from Sperling's displays, they frequently did say that they had "seen" more letters than they could report. They claimed, however, that they could no longer remember them the instant later when they were asked to say what they had seen. These admittedly subjective impressions suggested to Sperling that the apparent limit on the span of apprehension may in fact occur at a stage of processing *after* the visual analysis of the stimulus has been completed. That is, the visual characteristics of the stimulus may have been taken in and stored, but the process of classifying and identifying these stimuli had not yet been completed before this representation was lost. This suggestion involved a clear hypothesis about the locus of the limitations on performance for this particular task. Here is how Sperling went about exploring this hypothesis.

Whole versus Partial Report.   In the initial study we described, subjects were simply instructed to report all the items they could after the brief flash. This procedure is called *whole report*. In this procedure, according to Sperling's hypothesis, information originally available from the visual analysis of the stimulus may have been lost during the course of the subjects' attempted recall. The problem was to devise some technique to allow him to measure how much information was actually present immediately after the display went off, and for the brief instant before that visual information decayed.

The technique Sperling used was to *sample* the information present in this hypothetical "visual memory," rather than to require the subjects to attempt a complete report of its entire contents. When an instructor gives an examination, not all of the possible questions relating to the material are asked. Only some sample of the total course material is actually tested. If you answer all, or a certain proportion of the questions accurately, it is assumed that you know the same proportion of the information that was not asked. By the same logic, if a subject in Sperling's experiment is required only to recall a part of the total information presented in the display, we could use this to estimate how much of the total display was still in storage at the moment of testing. The advantage of this sampling technique, called *partial report*, is its ability to tap the content of the visual trace without the necessity of the time consuming process of total recall.

In one version of this procedure, subjects were again presented with a 50-msec exposure of an array of nine letters in three rows as previously illustrated. In the whole report procedure, subjects were again simply asked to recall as many of the letters they had seen as possible. In the partial report procedure, however, subjects were told to expect one of three tones immediately following the flash. A high-pitched tone would be the signal to report just the top row of letters, a tone of medium pitch would signal recall of just the middle row, and a low tone would signal recall of just the bottom row. The particular letter array would differ from trial to trial. On any particular trial the subject knew only that one of the tones would occur, but not which one.

Figure 5-2 shows the results of this comparison (Sperling, 1960). Looking first at the data for whole report performance, we can see that as the number of letters in the visual arrays were increased from 3 to 12 letters, recall performance continued to remain between 4 or 5 letters. Average recall accuracy, lying just below the horizontal dotted line, never exceeded 4.3 letters. We can also see how quickly this ceiling on performance was reached as we compare this level with the diagonal dotted line representing maximum possible performance.

The picture for partial report, however, is quite different. Using the proportion of letters in any one requested row given correctly as the basis of his estimate, Sperling found that the number of letters available immediately after a presentation increased steadily with the total number presented. While the level of accuracy does not quite reach 100%, the partial report function lies parallel with, and close to, the line of maximum possible performance.

On the basis of these data, Sperling thus inferred that when the tone arrived immediately after, for example, a nine-letter array, subjects must still have had available to them some 90% of the visual information. Indeed, Sperling's subjects often reported that when the tone occurred the letters were still clear and "readable," even though, obviously, the actual stimulus display had since terminated.

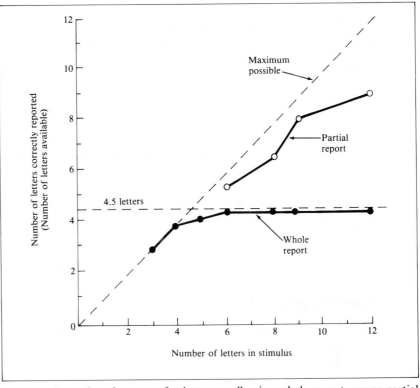

FIGURE 5-2   A comparison of performance for letter recall using whole report versus partial report techniques. The lower curve shows actual recall performance level (number of letters correct) using whole report. The upper curve shows an estimate of number of letters available, based on the proportion of letters correct in the requested sample.
(Adapted from Sperling, 1960. Copyright © 1960 by the American Psychological Association. Reprinted by permission.)

　•We can interpret this difference between whole and partial report in the context of the hypothesis of a limited capacity system. When whole report is required, the subject must transform or code all the visual information present into some form that can be stored and used for later recall. Such a code might be the names of the stimuli. The process of "reading out" visual information to enable the formation of the code takes time, time over which the initial sensory representation begins to decay. There may be a further limitation imposed by the memory systems that follow which cannot hold all of the information necessary to make a complete whole report.

　The limit of four or five letters subjects ordinarily recall in whole report is therefore not a limit on what is "seen"; the amount of visual information in a single glance. As we have seen, partial report seems to indicate that immediately after the stimulus is terminated, and the tone occurs, 90% of the visual information is still available. Instead, the limitation appears to be in the rate of information transfer and storage of this information in later parts of the memory system. The visual image apparently becomes lost before these slower processes are completed.

This is the advantage of partial report. The subject may code the information from the visual store selectively. Only a portion of the total stimulus matrix needs to be transformed into a recallable representation. The process of coding could thus be completed more rapidly simply because there is less total information to be coded. Since the limitations of later storage are not exceeded with the smaller amount, all of this information achieves a more permanent form in memory.

These results, taken together, permitted Sperling to infer that there is a sensory representation of the stimulus which is stored for a very brief period of time but has a capacity much larger than the later parts of the system. The short life of this sensory memory and the limited capacity of later stages explains why we can see more than we can say.

Sperling first called this visual sensory memory a "visual image," a term which quickly became confused with two other kinds of images. One of these is the so-called "afterimage," the continual firing of retinal receptors after a bright flash, such as the spots you see before your eyes after a camera flashbulb has gone off close to your face. It also became confused with the mental "images" we are able to form of past events in the absence of any new visual stimulation. As these confusions began to appear, Neisser (1967) coined a new, hopefully neutral, term for Sperling's discovery. Neisser dubbed the visual sensory memory as *iconic memory*.

The Duration of Iconic Memory

If there were not some upper limit on the duration of this sensory, or "iconic" memory, the continued persistence of visual images would lead to an overlap and hence confusion of the information contained in successive images. Obviously this does not happen in ordinary vision. It would therefore seem unlikely that the iconic image of a stimulus would outlast the usual interval between successive eye fixations. Three general procedures have been used in order to gain a more precise estimate of the usable duration of iconic memory: *partial report with cue delay,* the use of *successive stimuli,* and a technique called *backward masking.*

Partial Report: Cue Delay.   The first systematic estimate of the duration of visual persistence was supplied by Sperling (1960) who used a slight variation of his original partial report procedure. In this case, Sperling gave his subjects the instructional cue either immediately before presenting the letter array, immediately after the letter array terminated (zero delay), or at .15, .30, or 1.0 sec (150, 300, and 1000 msec) after the display had terminated.

Figure 5-3 shows his results for 12-letter arrays. The arrows indicate the onset and offset of the visual display. The distance between the arrows represents the 50-msec duration of the stimulus exposure. As we

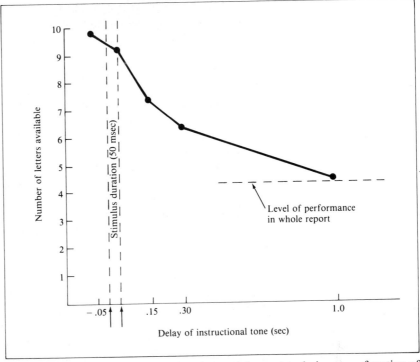

FIGURE 5-3 Decay of available information using the partial report technique as a function of the time delay of the instruction tone telling the subject which row of letters to report. Small arrows and vertical lines indicate the actual duration of the visual display. Level of performance using the whole report technique is shown by the horizontal dotted line.
(Adapted from Sperling, 1960. Copyright © 1960 by the American Psychological Association. Reprinted by permission.)

study the graph, we can see that a zero delay yields almost the same level of performance as when the tone was presented before the letter array. As the delay interval was increased, however, there was a progressive decline in accuracy. In fact, at a delay of one second, performance was no better than the level obtained with whole report. Other studies have shown that partial report continues to run at about the same level as whole report with cue delays well beyond the 1 sec tested here (e.g., Averbach & Coriell, 1961).

The subjects' use of the partial report cue might be described as follows. With zero delay, when the tone immediately followed the visual display, the subject selected the cued row from the iconic image that was still fairly complete. These items were then processed for identification and recall. As the cue was delayed, less and less information remained in the visual image by the time the cue occurred. The delayed cue was thus less helpful because there was less information remaining in the iconic store to be selected.

Accuracy with even very long delays, however, was not zero. If any of the information was retained, the subjects began coding the information before the cue occurred. This nonselective readout would have begun immediately when the stimulus occurred. As we have seen, the subject has time before the image is lost to process four or five items. Sometimes these will be the "correct" items (the ones later cued by the experimenter), and sometimes they will not. On the average, the subjects will code the correct items about 50% of the time. This explains why performance does not fall to zero with very long cue delays even when the iconic image is presumably totally lost.

The duration of sensory memory inferred from this task is the longest cue delay for which the tone cue is still useful; the longest cue delay for which partial report is still superior to whole report. From Figure 5–3 we can see that the cue has no advantage over whole report if it is delayed for 1 sec or longer. The image that permits the selective readout of information, then, must persist for something less than 1 sec.

Successive Stimuli: Estimation and Combination. A second technique used to estimate iconic duration involves repeated presentation of a single stimulus (Haber & Standing, 1969). A visual pattern is flashed very briefly (50 msec), there is a blank field, then the stimulus is flashed again. This cycle occurs repeatedly. The subject is asked to adjust the size of the blank interval until the image of the stimulus appears to be continuous rather than going on and off. If we assume that the first flash establishes a sensory memory, and if the second flash occurs before the first one has decayed, the first image would be reinforced. Rather than seeing a stimulus flash on and off, the subject should see one continuous image. Thus, the maximum interval between flashes that still produces this continuity can be used as an estimate of sensory storage for this task. Using this technique, Haber and Standing found the average interflash interval used by subjects in this study was 250 msec ($\frac{1}{4}$ sec).

A related technique for measuring sensory persistence is called the successive field paradigm (Eriksen & Collins, 1967). Here, two stimuli are presented with some interval between them. The subject's task is to make a response that requires combining the information from the two brief presentations. Eriksen and Collins used random dot patterns of the sort shown in Figure 5-4. Each stimulus by itself was quite meaningless, but if the two patterns are superimposed, the letters VOH can be seen against a background of the other dots.

The rationale for this study is similar to that of the previous experiment. In order to combine information from two flashes that follow each other, information from the first flash must be stored. If the interval between the two flashes is increased until the three letters can no longer be seen, we assume that this is the limit to the useful duration of sensory memory for this task. This is the point at which most of the information from the earlier stimulus has decayed and is no longer available for combination with the second stimulus.

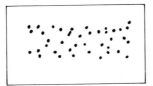

Pattern 1

Pattern 2

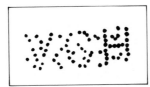

Patterns 1 and 2
combined

FIGURE 5-4 Two sets of random dot patterns used to estimate the duration of sensory persistence. When patterns 1 and 2 are superimposed they reveal the three-letter nonsense syllable VOH.
(From Eriksen & Collins, 1967. Copyright © 1967 by the American Psychological Association. Reprinted by permission.)

Erikson and Collins also found the critical interval in the successive field paradigm to be less than 1 sec. We should note, however, that subjects did not perform at chance levels even with very long interflash intervals. Since each separate stimulus does contain some information about what letters will occur, this information can aid the subjects' guessing in this task. However, with delays longer than 1 sec, subjects do not "see" these letters in the sense discussed earlier.

Stromeyer and Psotka (1970) have reported dramatic results using the successive field paradigm in the study of a truly unique person. The stimuli in their experiment were Julesz stereograms (Julesz, 1964), a pair of visual patterns consisting of a random distribution of dots. The distribution of dots in one stimulus is identical to the distribution in the other stimulus except for a small area. Within this area, the dots are shifted slightly to one side in one stimulus relative to the other. When these two patterns are viewed together in a stereoscope (one stimulus to the right eye, the other to the left), the region having the displaced dots is seen as a shape in depth.

To study sensory memory, the two stimuli are presented successively; the two patterns are never present at the same time. In order to obtain the stereoscopic effect (i.e., to see the object in depth), information from the two patterns must be combined. The interval between presentation of the first and second patterns can be varied until the figure is no longer visible. We would assume that this interval represents the point in time at which sensory memory of the first stimulus has decayed and is no longer available for fusion with the second stimulus. Stromeyer and Psotka, however, found a subject who accurately reported the stereoscopic figure even with delays of a day or longer between the two images. The young woman who performed these feats reported that the task was "ridiculously easy." We will discuss the puzzle of such enduring images further in Chapter 9. Here, we wish to point out simply that sensory information can apparently be represented for considerable durations by rare individuals, and that our understanding of the nature of sensory representation is far from complete.

Successive Stimuli: Backward Masking.   The estimates of duration obtained in the studies above depend very much on the precise conditions used to obtain them. In the partial report experiment, delay of the probe produces different effects depending on how the visual stimuli are presented. If the visual field following the flash is dark, the duration of the usable sensory image is longer than if the postexposure field is bright (Mackworth, 1963). The sensitivity of the visual storage to physical variables like brightness fits our notion of what kind of representations form the content of this memory; a record of the stimulus events prior to any contact with our knowledge or classification system.

The responsiveness of sensory memory to physical characteristics of the stimulus distinguishes this form of storage from others. We can contrast these studies with the learning of lists of words or paired-associates as discussed in earlier chapters. In those cases, recall of these materials is relatively unaffected by the physical conditions of their presentation. It did not matter how bright the letters were, their color, or their size. Recall of these materials was based on verbal or other codes more permanent than the form of storage available from sensory memory. The effect of visual variables on partial report from iconic memory permits us to infer that performance must be based primarily on a visual representation of the physical stimulus.

The sensory content of early storage is also indicated by the phenomenon of *erasure*. Under certain circumstances a second stimulus can effectively eliminate or erase another stimulus that precedes it. This phenomenon has had a considerable history in the study of perception (Weisstein, 1972) where it is called *backward masking* or *metacontrast*. Averbach and Coriell (1961) encountered this phenomenon when they used a visually presented circle as a recall cue for partial report. The sequence of events are illustrated in Figure 5-5. A visual display of letters was presented in a 50-msec flash, followed at a variable time

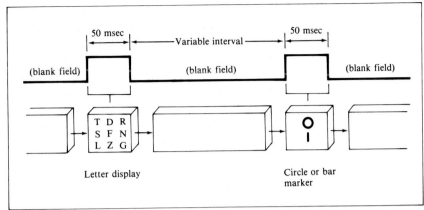

FIGURE 5-5 The sequence of stimulus events in Averbach and Coriell's use of circle and bar markers to estimate the duration of visual persistence. When the second field appeared it would contain either a circle or a bar indicating the position of a single letter to be reported. The blank field was matched to the other stimuli in brightness.

interval by another 50-msec flash which displayed a circle in one of the letter positions of the previous display.

The circle was drawn to be slightly larger than the letter in the first flash such that if the two were superimposed the subject would see the letter surrounded by the circle. As you can see from the diagram in Figure 5-5, of course, they were never actually superimposed. The subject would first see the letter array and only later see the circle marker. The subject's task would be to report the single letter from the position marked by the circle. The presumption was that if the circle indicator occurred before the sensory image of the letters had decayed, this marker should permit the selective readout of this letter and lead to accurate performance. Averbach and Coriell also used an alternative indicator which we would expect in principle to yield the same results. This was a simple bar marker which would appear slightly above the position of the letter to be reported.

The graph in the upper part of Figure 5-6 shows a summary of their results. The conditions using the bar marker give the sort of results we would expect from a partial report technique with a delayed instructional cue. We see a gradual decline in report accuracy as the marker is delayed, with accuracy reaching its lowest point and leveling out somewhere between 200 and 300 msec. This procedure, quite analogous to partial report, fits nicely with the 250 msec duration estimated for iconic storage found by other studies.

The results for the circle marker, however, are quite different. While at zero delay and at longer delays of 300 to 400 msec the circle marker shows the same results as the bar marker, at the intermediate delays the circle marker actually seemed to interfere with performance rather than to aid it.

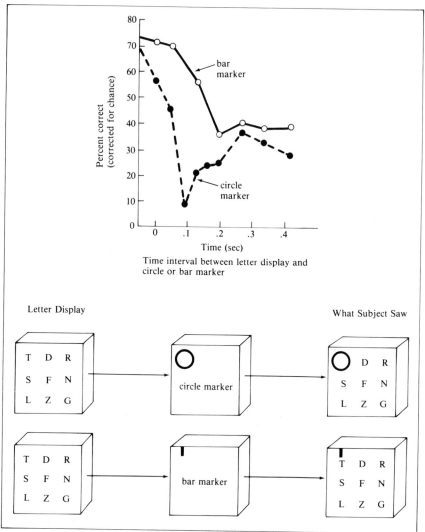

FIGURE 5-6   Accuracy of recall of letters when indicated either by a circle or bar marker appearing at various intervals after termination of the letter display. Lower diagram shows the different perceptual experiences reported by subjects in these two cases.

(Adapted from Averbach & Coriell, 1961. Copyright © 1961, American Telephone and Telegraph Company. Reprinted by permission.)

These rather intriguing results for the circle marker suggest the following interpretation. When the circle marker occurred at zero delay, subjects saw the letter *in* the circle as we previously described it. Here, the sensory memory treats the two stimuli as a single image and no interference is produced. The two displays are registered as one image: a letter surrounded by a circle. At this point we get the same partial report advantage as the bar marker, or Sperling's use of an instructional tone.

At the intermediate delays, between 0 and 300 msec, the circle seems to *mask* or *erase* the letter from the sensory image. We have tried to indicate how this might actually look to a subject in the lower portion of Figure 5–6. If the circle erased the letter, the subject would see the circle alone, thus explaining the poor performance. This effect is sometimes called *backward masking*, since the second stimulus seems to operate backward in time to interfere with the image of the first stimulus. No such effect is obtained for the bar marker which, as we have shown in our illustration, is spaced sufficiently far from the letter to cause no interference.

The degree to which this erasure occurs depends on the visual similarity between the marker and the letter. Not only does a bar marker produce less interference than a circle, but the letter "C" is more affected by a circle than the letter "X."

The final area of the circle marker curve, the longer delays at which circle and bar marker performance produce equivalent results, is also consistent with this interpretation. At these longer delays beyond 250 msec the image is almost gone. In other words, the circle can no longer interfere with coding because there is not much left to code. At this point on the curve the subject's performance is based primarily on the product of the nonselective readout that had begun to take place before the cue, whether bar or a circle, had occurred.

A variety of investigators using a variety of methods have also offered estimates of the duration of sensory memory as considerably less than 1 sec, the estimates varying somewhat with the precise physical conditions of measurement (e.g., Briggs & Kinsbourne, 1972; Efron, 1973; Haber & Nathanson, 1968; Haber & Standing, 1970; McCloskey & Watkins, 1978). Although not without controversy, these studies have all appeared to demonstrate an early stage of visual processing which produces a representation of the stimulus with a life of something less than 1 sec. This form of storage has a capacity much larger than the forms of storage that follow it.

We have devoted a great deal of space to describing these attempts to measure the duration of the icon. For a stage approach to memory, the duration of each component is a fundamental question. Sensory memory, in this conception, is analogous to a storage container that is quickly filled by the processes of sensory analysis, and then, once the stimulus terminates, is rapidly drained of its contents. If this conception were appropriate, we might expect all our estimates to converge on the same duration for the icon reflecting a common rate of decay of information regardless of the method used to measure this decay.

DiLollo (1977, 1980) represents those who have questioned the whole structural approach to visual memory. Specifically, DiLollo has proposed that visual persistence reflects ongoing pattern analyses that are initiated with the onset of the stimulus and continue to completion whether the stimulus is present or not. Our estimates of iconic duration do not represent the decay of an iconic store, but instead, the duration of processes that continue for a fixed duration following stimulus onset. This would explain the finding that stimuli having longer durations seem to produce shorter icons (e.g., DiLollo, 1977, 1980; Haber, 1971). Since perceptual processes would begin with stimulus onset, more processing would be completed during the longer presentations and, therefore, less processing would remain to be performed after stimulus termination.

This is clearly a process view of visual persistence. There is no single kind of information or duration estimate that is characteristic of a single kind of memory. Instead, later levels of processing act on the products of earlier levels in the continuum. It is the products of this processing that become available as sensory information. Questions generated by the process orientation, then, concern not the duration of a hypothetical stage, but the nature of the processes which produce this information and how these processes may affect one another. We will pick up these questions again at a later point in this chapter. Next, however, we must discuss the distinctive characteristics of sensory information as contrasted with the products of later processing.

The Content of Iconic Memory

The occurrence of masking reinforces the distinction between sensory memory and other forms of storage. The retention of lists of paired associates is relatively unaffected by the occurrence of irrelevant stimuli. Later storage systems are thus not erasable in this way.

The uniqueness of visual sensory memory has also been inferred from the kinds of cues that are effective in partial report studies. In most of the studies we described (Sperling, 1960; Averbach & Coriell, 1961), the subject's selective coding of the display was directed to a location. It has also been shown that subjects can select information from the image on the basis of shape (Turvey & Kravetz, 1970) and color (von Wright, 1970; Banks & Barber, 1977). However, nonphysical cues cannot be used effectively, i.e., they do not produce an advantage over whole report. For example, if told to recall only the numbers from a brief flash consisting of both numbers and letters, subjects typically do no better than if asked to report all of the items (Sperling, 1960).

In order to use a categorical cue like "numbers," it would be necessary to have the visual information classified in this way, as numbers and letters. The fact that categorical cues are not effective supports the hypothesis that the information used in the partial report task is precategorical, prior to processes which identify items and assign them some classification.

We have discussed the effects of practice on remembering in earlier chapters. If visual sensory memory is precategorical, we would not expect repetition of unselected items on a series of trials to have any effect on recall performance. This would be so if this store does not participate in the associative and organizing processes that characterize later memories. This does seem to be the case. When parts of the display are repeated in a partial report experiment, repetition of unselected rows of the display seems to have no effect on later performance. If these items are cued after having been repeated in previous trials, there is no improvement over a condition in which the cued items have never appeared before (Turvey, 1967; Merluzzi & Johnson, 1974). The presentation of associated elements in the display in a similar fashion also does little to improve performance over the level of nonassociated elements (Wickelgren & Whitman, 1970).

Finally, the registration of the stimulus into visual storage seems to take place automatically without requiring attention or effort. When transferred to short-term memory, the maintenance of information seems to require effort on our part. If some other activity is demanded at the same time, memory performance deteriorates. However, several investigators (Chow & Murdock, 1975; Doost & Turvey, 1971) have shown that requiring some irrelevant task does not affect the rate of decay of visual storage as indicated by the effect of delaying the cue in partial report. The registration and availability of sensory information, then, appears to be independent of shifts in attention.

Interpretations of Iconic Memory

Our discussion so far has focused on the characteristics of sensory memory for visual information. These characteristics include its large capacity, brief duration, and sensory content. There is fair agreement on these characteristics, but there is less consensus on explaining how this system works.

One point of contention concerns the processes that transform visual information into a more enduring form of storage. Sperling (1963; 1967) tried to estimate the rate at which information was extracted from this store by varying the interval between a display of letters and the onset of a random pattern that masked the visual image. He found that for each 10 msec that he increased this blank interval, the subject could report one more letter. He concluded that one could read out this information at a rate of 10 msec per item. However, it has been demonstrated that subjects cannot rehearse or repeat items to themselves at anywhere near this rate (Landauer, 1962). The average rate of rehearsal is closer to 100 msec per item. This would mean that the code used for the next stage of storage could not be a "name" code. The rate of readout was too fast.

Sperling (1967) reasoned, however, that readout from visual sensory memory merely set up "articulatory programs," that is, instructions for saying names. The rate of setting up these programs might be very much faster than the rate of executing them (actually saying the names). On the other hand, Turvey (1978) argues from other evidence, that while the form of storage following sensory memory must involve a more complete and thoroughly coded description of the visual stimulus, the later code is still, in some sense, a visual representation.

A second and related controversy concerns the contrast between two hypotheses suggested to explain the phenomenon of erasure, or backward masking (Kahneman, 1968). The first hypothesis assumes that the effects of erasure are on the image itself. This view, the *integration hypothesis* (e.g., Eriksen & Collins, 1965), supposes that two visual stimuli occurring close together in time are combined into a single image. The image in this case is an integration of the two stimuli. The effect of this integration will be to degrade the information in the image making it more difficult for later processes to analyze the information and correctly classify the stimulus events. The effect is analogous to making several exposures of the same piece of film creating a blurred and indecipherable picture.

The second hypothesis explaining backward masking suggests that the effect of the second stimulus is to interfere with the readout or later processing of the first stimulus. Kolers (1968) has suggested that this *interruption hypothesis* is analogous to a situation in which a store clerk's service to one customer is interrupted by the arrival of an especially insistent second customer. The second stimulus interferes with the ability to report the first stimulus because it interrupts the necessary processing of this information.

The first hypothesis (integration) locates the effect of masking peripherally. That is, the effects occur quite early in the processing of the visual signal. The second hypothesis (interruption) is a more "central" notion of where these effects occur since it claims that erasure is due to interference with the processes of decision and analysis that take place after the image is formed.

In a very systematic analysis of masking effects, Turvey (1973) has in fact shown that no single hypothesis can account for the effects observed. He has demonstrated that both peripheral and central masking effects occur and that these processes probably overlap with one another. In addition, he suggested that the U-shaped erasure function shown in Figure 5-6 (Averbach & Coriell, 1961) reflected a shift from one type of effect (integration) to the other (interruption). We will not detail the complex analyses presented in Turvey's paper but we urge you to consult his work as an excellent example of how one may experimentally analyze the processing of information into its component operations.

Researchers have also attempted to determine the locus of visual persistence in the nervous system. Sakitt and others (Sakitt, 1975, 1976; Sakitt & Long, 1978, 1979) have suggested that iconic memory is a "retinal phenomenon." A retinal locus for iconic memory would mean that visual persistence is the result of biochemical processes in the retina that are initiated by the stimulus and continue after the termination of the stimulus. If the icon were "located" at this level of analysis, we would expect iconic duration to depend on the duration and nature of these retinal processes. Sakitt and her colleagues have demonstrated that, under some conditions, the receptors in the eye that permit our sensation of color (cones) produce extremely brief icons (100 msec). The other kind of receptors on the retina (rods), which permit only brightness discrimination, can register longer (400 msec), and more stable images. Thus, a difference in processes at the retinal level can produce a difference in the duration of iconic memory.

This conclusion was based on the fact that it is possible to construct stimuli that appear identical to the rod system (equal brightness) but are discriminable for the cone system (different colors). In one of their experiments, Sakitt and Long (1979) had subjects judge whether two red dots, presented one after the other, were aligned horizontally or vertically as illustrated in the lower portion of Figure 5-7.

In one condition, the dots were matched in brightness to the background and so were invisible to the rod system, those receptors on the retina of the eye which are insensitive to color and react only to brightness differences. This condition would presumably reflect the function of the color-detecting cones only. Under these conditions, performance dropped to chance (50% correct) when the two dots were separated by any more than 100 msec.

When the two sets of stimuli were not matched for brightness with the background so that the rod system would now be participating in the formation of the sensory image, there was a gradual decline in correct performance which nevertheless remained relatively high up to the maximum tested delay of 400 msec. These findings suggested that the image formed from information detected by the cones of the eye was lost after only 100 msec, while information from the rods remained available considerably longer.

There is, however, considerable experimental evidence challenging the notion that iconic memory is due solely to the persistence of processing in the rods. Adelson (1978), using a partial report task rather than successive stimuli, failed to replicate Sakitt's finding that cones yielded short icons, and rods yielded longer icons. Banks and Barber (1977) found that information could be selected throughout the duration of a longer icon on the basis of color cues. Since only cones can produce information for color discriminations, this indicates that cones participate in formation of the icon.

In addition, there are other variables which produce effects on icon duration which are unlikely to affect the duration of biochemical processes on the retina. For example, several experiments have shown that the number of stripes *(spatial frequency)* in a simple pattern of black-and-white stripes (such a pattern is called a *visual grating*) affects the duration of the icon. A greater number of stripes (higher spatial frequencies) produced longer icons (Meyer & Maguire, 1977; Bowling, Lovegrove & Mapperson, 1979). If subjects were *adapted* to a particular pattern, i.e., exposed to the same pattern repeatedly, the ability of the visual system to maintain an iconic representation of this pattern temporarily decreased. The duration of the icon for these patterns was shorter than the iconic persistence for unadapted patterns (Meyer, Lawson, & Cohen, 1975). These effects also were transferred between

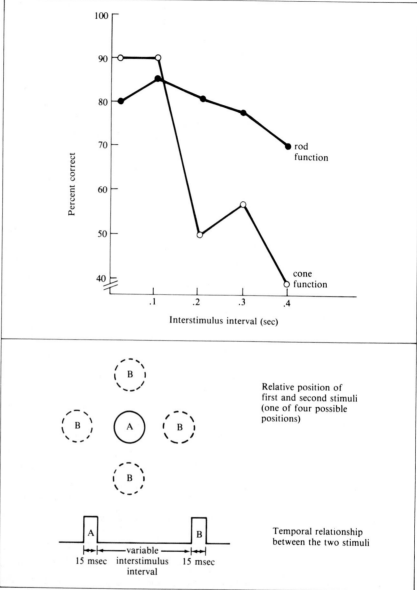

FIGURE 5-7   The two curves in the upper panel show the presumed rod and cone functions in visual persistence. These curves are based on accuracy of detecting the spatial position of a second dot relative to the position of an earlier one as a function of the time interval between the two. The two dots were matched to brightness of the background such that they would be visible either only to the cones or to both the rods and cones. The lower panel illustrates relative spatial positions of the first and second stimuli (one of four possible positions) and temporal relationships between the two.

(Adapted from Sakitt & Long, 1979. Copyright © 1979 by the American Psychological Association. Reprinted by permission.)

eyes. If one eye was adapted to a pattern, the same pattern presented to the other eye produced a shorter icon than was the case for patterns that had not been seen repeatedly (Meyer, et al., 1975; Meyer, Jackson, & Yang, 1979). It is unlikely that any of these effects could be produced at the level of the retina. The mechanisms responsible for pattern analysis and adaptation effects are located more centrally in the nervous system (see also McCloskey & Watkins, 1978).

Breitmeyer and Ganz (1976) have suggested that there may be two icons: an image representing the analyses carried out by the retinal receptor cells and the early visual system (a peripheral icon) and a more fully processed image that has undergone a thorough pattern analysis (a central icon). The results of Sakitt, therefore, would relate primarily to the duration of such a peripheral icon. Adaptation and pattern variables would affect the central icon.

It is perhaps the case that further discussion of these data and arguments would lead us too far afield into considerations of the neurophysiology of perception. However, we recommend the paper by Breitmeyer and Ganz (1976) as an excellent example of the fertile interaction between concepts of information processing and concepts of how the nervous system functions.

A final issue of interpretation concerns what many consider to be a dramatic role played by iconic memory in an extremely important aspect of visual perception. This is the question of the function of iconic memory in maintaining an image during eye movements.

We noted earlier that visual persistence permits processing of brief stimuli to continue after the stimulus is no longer present. Under normal conditions, vision is interrupted several times per second by the occurrence of eye movements, called *saccades,* in which the eyes move from one fixation point to another. In the course of these eye movements we ordinarily do not pick up any visual information. You will realize this intuitively if you think about what a picture would look like if you held the lens of a camera open as you moved it across a visual scene. The resulting photograph would be blurred and smeared. This same physical effect is produced on the retina of the eye but we do not ordinarily perceive this "smearing." The lack of perception during eye movements also becomes apparent if you try to observe your own eye movements in a mirror. You cannot see your own eyes in motion, but see them only while stationary at the end and the beginning of successive fixations. The "smearing" of the visual image during eye movements, then, has no counterpart in visual experience.

In studying this phenomenon, Campbell and Wurz (1978) have shown experimentally that the capacity of the eye to register information is not reduced by eye movements themselves. When the visual scene was illuminated only during an eye movement and not before or after the movement, subjects did report the smearing of visual information that should occur as the scene is moved across the retina. Their subjects sat in the dark and, through electronic means, the experimenters triggered a brief flash of light just after the eye movement began. The flash ended just before the eyes assumed a new fixation point. Under these conditions, subjects saw the blurring and smearing that we noted would occur on a picture if a camera was moved across a visual scene. However, if the beginning of the flash preceded the eye movement, or followed the eye movement by a brief interval, the perception of blur was eliminated. In other words, when information from the fixation preceding or following the eye movement was included, this information eliminated experience of the visual changes occurring during the saccade.

Corfield, Frosdick, and Campbell (1978) suggested that the blurred image during a saccade is treated by the visual system as a zero-input stimulus and that during the saccade the visual information from the preceding fixation is stored and replaced only by information from the next fixation. These experimenters found that the ability of an image to eliminate the perception of blur depended on spatial frequency. Again, it would appear that the role of the icon in suppressing vision during eye movements does not involve retinal processes.

We are thus left to wonder whether the icon, as described by Sperling and other early investigators, represents persistence of information originating in rod function, cone function, or some further analyzed derivative of this retinal information. The studies and speculations mentioned above also raise the possibility that different combinations of separate processes may be involved in the previous studies of iconic memory. They further suggest that some of the effects we discussed may have reflected later processes which are no longer sensory in nature. That is, different tasks may tap different levels of processing.

We will have more to say on this issue at the conclusion of this chapter. At this point, however, we can sympathize with the reader whose "limited capacity system" may have become overloaded by these controversies. What exactly is "true" about iconic memory?

The first step is to appreciate those areas in which controversies exist, and those that are generally accepted. Since the time of the initial work by Sperling in 1960 there has been, and still is, general agreement that there is a sensory memory for visual stimuli that exists for a very brief duration of about 250 msec. This is accepted as a "sensory" store in that it holds the physical characteristics of the stimulus in an unanalyzed, "precategorical" form, as yet uncoded with the associations in ordinary memory that will later give them meaning. This can occur only as the content of this rapid decay store is "read out" for higher levels of analysis.

The controversies we have described deal primarily with the details of this sytem: the details of this readout procedure (Turvey, 1978), the detailed question of how backward masking operates to terminate the icon or its processing (Kolers, 1968; Turvey, 1973), and the physiological basis of the visual persistence (Sakitt & Long, 1979).

The question of the interaction between the iconic store and deeper levels of processing is very important to the position we hope to develop in subsequent chapters. Before we continue with this development, however, we are bound to ask whether there exists a counterpart sensory memory for other input modalities. For example, there is some tentative evidence for a counterpart sensory memory for tactile stimulation (e.g., Gilson & Baddeley, 1969; Millar, 1974; Shiffrin, Craig, & Cohen, 1973). Next to the study of visual persistence, however, by far the greatest amount of work has been devoted to the question of a parallel sensory store for auditory information. It is to this question that we now turn.

AUDITORY SENSORY MEMORY

Throughout our discussion of iconic memory we emphasized its precategorical, sensory character. This transient store was called a "sensory" store because of the evidence that it maintained a perceptual image aligned directly with the sensory modality of its arrival. By the same reasoning that led to the study of visual sensory memory, we are bound to ask whether there may exist an analogous counterpart for the transient sensory storage of auditory information.

Such an auditory counterpart to iconic memory has indeed been proposed. It is sometimes called *echoic memory*, after Neisser (1967), who saw this store as a very brief, transient "echo" of recently received auditory information. Although the comparable study of echoic memory began much later than the study of its visual counterpart, the argument for the necessity of its existence is no less compelling.

While both visual and auditory events occur over time, auditory experiences such as the recognition of speech would be impossible without the ability to retain sensory impressions for periods longer than their actual physical duration. The average duration of a spoken syllable, such as "ga" or "be," typically takes between 200 to 300 msec (.2 to .3 sec) to produce. Although this is not a very long span of time, the recognition of such a syllable depends on the analysis of what is a constantly changing acoustic pattern over this 200- to 300-msec period. Unless we could maintain some auditory memory for at least this long, we would have lost the beginning of a syllable before the speaker had a chance to finish the end of it!

Let us carry this line of reasoning one step farther. Detailed studies of speech recognition have shown that how an individual sound within a syllable is perceived will be different, depending on the nature of the sounds which immediately preceed or follow it. In this sense, the recognition of these elemental sounds, or *phonemes*, is heavily "context dependent" (Liberman, Cooper, Shankweiler, & Studdert-Kennedy, 1967; Cole & Scott, 1974). We can demonstrate this experimentally using artificial speech synthesized by a computer, or by splicing together different combinations of sounds on a tape recording. In one such study,

Liberman, Delattre, and Cooper (1952) presented subjects with a very brief, 15 msec burst of noise followed by one of several different vowel sounds. This same noise burst was heard as a /p/ before an /i/, a /k/ before an /a/, and again as a /p/ before a /u/. Again, such an effect of acoustic context could not occur unless a listener could perceive the entire pattern based on some brief auditory "echo" of a duration longer than each of these speech elements. Such an echo would have to last for at least the 200- to 300-msec duration of the full syllable for its individual subelements to be analyzed as a whole.

If 200 msec represents the minimum necessary duration of echoic memory, other examples from our everyday experience suggest that it might in fact be considerably longer. Most people have had the experience of hearing a person say a word with a foreign accent, or trying to follow muffled speech heard over a poor telephone connection. Although the words seem initially unintelligible, we can nevertheless often seem to "play it over" to ourselves as we consider different hypotheses of what the speaker had said. We seem, in other words, to be able to maintain some brief, but fairly accurate sensory record of the auditory event that can be checked again to make sure of what we heard. In this case, the echoic trace would seem to last in the order of several full seconds, rather than hundreds of milliseconds.

As we shall see in the following section, some form of echoic memory does seem to exist. Further, the evidence for its existence was first demonstrated using a partial report technique quite analogous to the one introduced by Sperling (1960) to demonstrate the experimental reality of iconic memory.

The Cocktail Party Problem

The first experimental demonstration of echoic memory derived from one's common, ordinary experience at any noisy party or gathering (Cherry, 1953). At a large party everyone seems to be talking at once, frequently accompanied by loud music playing on a phonograph. Out of this cacaphony, however, we usually seem to notice very little beyond the speech of the person to whom we are listening. For example, if later asked to report the content of the conversations going on around us, we would probably be unable to recall anything at all.

We saw in the previous section that this is equally true of vision. Very little of our total visual sensory experience has any effect on our memory, thought, or action. If we think back to the typical cocktail party, however, we know that if someone across the room were to call our name, there is a high probability that we would hear it and respond. This is an intriguing paradox, since it is not immediately clear how one could possibly hear one's name if the other conversations were being totally ignored. On the other hand, if one were monitoring these other conversations, how is it that one remains totally unaware of their content up to the point where your name is spoken?

This general problem is one of *selective attention,* a topic we will consider in some detail in the following chapter. At this point, however, we can say that many investigators became convinced that there must be some temporary storage of unattended auditory information, and that only a part of this information is selected to "get through" to conscious awareness. The question relevant to our present discussion, however, is what happens to that auditory information which is not selected for further processing.

To explore this question, Moray, Bates, and Barnett (1965) used a partial report technique in an experimental paradigm they referred to as the "four-eared man." In this experiment, each subject sat alone in a room containing four high-fidelity loudspeakers placed in different locations, far enough apart so that the subject could easily discriminate which sounds were coming from which loudspeakers.

During the course of the experiment, the subject would hear four simultaneous lists of spoken letters of the alphabet, one list coming from each of the four loudspeakers. Each list varied in length from one to four letters. The spoken letters, which were prerecorded on good quality tape recorders, were synchronized so that at any one moment four spoken letters would be heard simultaneously. For example, from loudspeaker 1 they might hear the letter "e" at the same instant that loudspeaker 2 produced the letter "k," number 3 produced the letter "i," and loudspeaker number 4 the letter "t."

On some blocks of trials, subjects were asked to try to report all of the information presented from all of the four locations. This *whole report* request produced poor results. Subjects were rarely able to report more than a small proportion of the total number of letters presented. Quite different results were obtained, however, when Moray and his colleagues presented similar materials using a recall procedure directly analogous to Sperling's *partial report.* In this case, immediately following the termination of the four simultaneous messages, subjects were given a visual light cue indicating just one of the four loudspeakers. Their task would be to report only the message from this single location. In this case, recall accuracy was excellent.

Moray et al. interpreted these results using the same line of reasoning previously employed by Sperling. Since the visual cue indicating which message to report occurred only after all of the messages had terminated, there must have been some auditory memory of the information from all four locations at the time the visual cue occurred. There seemed to be, in other words, some brief auditory image, an echoic memory, whose capacity exceeds the more limited capacity of ordinary memory.

The weakness of this study, of course was that while Moray and his colleagues had demonstrated the likely existence of an echoic memory, they could say little about its possible duration. All one knew was that it lasted for the duration of the full stimulus presentation, plus the time required to give the instructional cue.

The Duration of Echoic Memory

As in the case of iconic memory, a number of imaginative techniques were used to measure the duration of persistence of this auditory sensory store. As we shall see, these were to produce a variety of duration estimates, raising the possibility that each may tap something slightly different about auditory information processing. The three methods we will describe can be referred to as *cue delay, backward masking,* and the so-called *suffix effect.*

Partial Report: Cue Delay. Darwin, Turvey, and Crowder (1972) used a direct extension of the Moray experiment, this time taking care to vary the time interval between termination of a list and the instructional cue as to which part of the total set was to be reported.

In this study, subjects heard three simultaneous lists from three different spatial locations. The lists were composed of mixed letters and spoken digits, and spatial locations were simulated by an ingenious use of stereophonic earphones. One list was heard in the left ear, one list was heard in the right ear, and the third list (which had been recorded binaurally to both ears) sounded as if it was coming from the middle of the head. Each list was three items long. Other than these differences, the procedures of Darwin et al. were similar to those in the previous experiment.

Immediately following each presentation, or at delays of 1, 2, or 4 seconds after the termination of the lists, subjects would see a visual display telling them whether to report the message from the left, middle, or right. These results would be compared with a no-cue whole report condition in which subjects would attempt to recall all three lists after they were presented.

Figure 5-8 shows the average number of items correct out of nine possible items, as a function of the time delay between termination of the lists and the onset of the partial report instruction cue. One can also use Sperling's method to estimate the total number of items presumably available to the subject when the instructional cue was presented. That is, if two-thirds of a list can be given correctly when only one list is requested in partial report, we can assume that the subject must have had two-thirds of the full set of nine items available in echoic memory.

The advantage of partial report over whole report is clear from these results, as is the rapid decay of this advantage over the course of time. With a 4-sec cue delay, partial report was only slightly higher than whole report performance, and this difference was not statistically significant. To Darwin et al., their results seemed to "functionally define a store in which material is held for about 2 seconds" (1972, pg. 260).

As we compare this graph to Figure 5-3 which shows Sperling's parallel results for iconic memory, we see first that the advantage of partial report over whole report is not as great when sampling echoic memory as was found for iconic memory. Second, we see that the presumed duration of echoic memory is significantly longer than that of iconic memory. The first of these differences may have been due simply

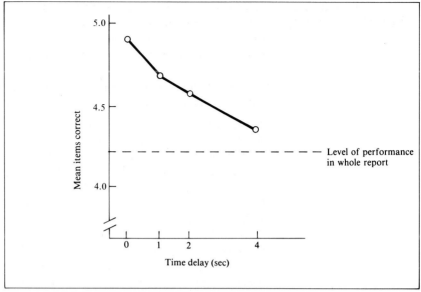

FIGURE 5-8 Mean number of items correctly recalled using the partial report technique as a function of the time delay of instruction cue as to which list to report. Horizontal dotted line shows level of performance for similar materials when whole report was required immediately.
(From Darwin, Turvey, & Crowder, 1972.)

to subjects' ability to discriminate each of the three locations from each other. There were numerous occasions where items from the wrong list would intrude in a partial report response.

The second feature, however, is to be taken more seriously. Just as in Sperling's experiments, the subjects seemed to be able to use a partial report cue to improve performance through selective coding from a large capacity sensory store. In this case, however, this auditory store appears to have a useful life of about 2 sec.

Successive Stimuli: Backward Masking. A second approach to estimating the duration of an echoic image derived directly from the studies of backward masking in vision (e.g., Averbach & Coriell, 1961). In this case the procedure involved the presentation of two successive auditory stimuli close together in time. The first was of a very short duration and was followed either immediately, or after some controlled delay, by a second auditory stimulus.

If we assume that the second stimulus would interfere with, or "mask" the echoic trace of the first one, we could determine exactly how long an interval between the two would be necessary to eliminate the interference effect. This, presumably, would reflect the duration of the echoic trace; the point beyond which the storage is no longer sensory in nature, and hence, no longer affected by a new sensory input.

Using such a paradigm, Elliot (1967) presented subjects with a very brief 10-msec tone followed at various intervals by a 100-msec noise burst. The results were quite surprising. If the noise stimulus occurred within 100 msec of the tone, subjects reported that they did not hear the first stimulus.

We call this result surprising, since an echoic trace of 100-msec duration seems inconsistent with the much longer estimate of Darwin et al., and with the logically necessary time spans required for reliable speech perception. Yet, using a slightly different paradigm, Efron (1970) obtained a similar estimate in apparent support of Elliot's figure.

Efron (1970) required subjects to attempt to adjust the onset of a light to exactly coincide with the offset of a tone. The results suggested that the subjects continued to "hear" the tone for approximately 130 msec, even when the tone was of considerably shorter duration. This finding that apparent duration of a stimulus is fixed regardless of its objective duration is similar to that found for vision by Haber (1971).

We have two clues to these surprisingly short estimates of echoic duration, and both relate to the use of rather simple tone stimuli rather than speech. The first is derived from Turvey's (1978) general observation that experiments involving subjective duration may reflect the time required for processing the image rather than its maximum potential duration. There is evidence that visual stimuli which are less difficult to code (e.g., more familiar stimuli) yield shorter estimates of duration than do stimuli more difficult to code (e.g., less familiar) (Erwin, 1976; Erwin & Hershenson, 1974). The subjects' duration estimates may thus have been based on the rapid completion of processing of rather uncomplicated tone stimuli, rather than on the potential decay rate of an auditory image.

A second, related criticism comes from Massaro (1972) who cautions in general that masking studies requiring only the detection of simple stimuli may tap perceptual operations having little bearing on true auditory persistence. While cautious about the interpretation of *detection masking* studies, Massaro did see a virtue to using simple stimuli such as pure tones for studies of echoic duration. He argued, however, that studies of *recognition masking* should give a more valid estimate.

In a systematic series of studies, Massaro (1972) gave subjects practice at identifying a pair of tones either as "high" or "low." After this training, a single tone would be presented followed by a variable silent interval and then another tone which was neither one of the two previously practiced. This second tone would be considered the masking stimulus. The subject's task would be to identify the first tone by saying whether it was the "high" tone or the "low" one.

Using both tones (masked by other tones) and vowels (masked by other vowels), Massaro found that if a masking stimulus occurs within 250 msec of the first stimulus, recognition is severely impaired and, the shorter the interstimulus interval within this range, the poorer the recognition performance. Once the interval between the two stimuli exceeds 250 msec, however, performance became quite accurate. At this point the occurrence of a second stimulus apparently no longer interfered with the recognition of the first. Massaro thus argued that this 250-msec interval represented the duration of auditory sensory memory.

Although Massaro's figure may represent the lower range of estimates of echoic duration, there are claims that extensive practice can produce substantial effects on this task (e.g., Cudahy & Leshowitz, 1974; Leshowitz & Cudahy, 1973; Loeb & Holding, 1975). With highly practiced subjects, the critical interval for recognition masking can shrink to as little as 50 msec. Presumably, following our previous argument, practice permits the subject to complete the processing of the auditory image more rapidly than with less familiar stimuli. Prior to practice, the "masking" tone interrupts processing, or interferes with the processing in some way. According to this criticism, in other words, the time interval over which recognition occurs is a measure of the time required for processing, and not the potential duration of auditory memory.

If Massaro's studies of recognition masking represent the lower range of the estimates of the duration of echoic memory, so studies involving the so-called *suffix effect* represent the upper range.

Serial Position Effects: The Suffix Effect.   A final approach to estimating the duration of echoic memory begins with one aspect of the well-known serial position effect in memory. When lists of unrelated materials such as nonsense syllables are presented for rote learning, one ordinarily finds best recall for the items at the beginning and end of the list, with those items in the middle showing the highest percentage of errors (McCrary & Hunter, 1953; Murdock, 1962). As it happens, however, the modality of the presentation, whether it is visual or auditory, has a major influence on the effect. This influence, furthermore, seems to have a direct bearing on the existence of echoic memory.

Conrad and Hull (1964) visually presented subjects with lists of random digits. Each list contained seven digits presented one at a time at a rate of 100 msec per digit. Following a brief 400-msec delay, subjects were to attempt to recall as many of the seven digits in that particular list as possible. In one case subjects were told merely to look at each digit as it was presented and to remain silent until the time for recall. In a second condition the subject was instructed to say the name of each digit aloud as it was presented.

Conrad and Hull's results are given in Figure 5-9 and they show a striking effect on the shape of the serial position curves under these two conditions. Although the early items in a list (items 1 through 5) are not affected by either silent or auditory conditions, the final items on the list show a clear disadvantage under visual conditions. Auditory conditions, in this case supplied by the subject's own voice, show a clear advantage in producing fewer errors. This general modality effect of an advantage

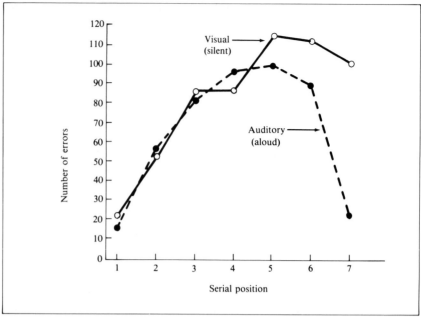

FIGURE 5-9   Effect of visual (silent) or auditory (aloud) presentation mode on number of errors as a function of serial position.
(From Conrad & Hull, 1968.)

to auditory presentation over a visual one is true whether the subject reads the items aloud to himself or herself, or whether they are presented auditorially by the experimenter (Corballis, 1966; Murray, 1966).

One interpretation of these results is the claim that auditory presentation leaves an echoic trace of the final few items from which the subject can continue to "read out" correct responses even after the list has finished. If we add the 400-msec interval prior to recall together with the several hundred milliseconds occupied by the presentation of the last few items in the list, we arrive at a figure well within the 2-sec estimate of echoic duration offered by Darwin and his colleagues. Visual presentation has no such advantage since the much shorter duration of iconic storage would have long since faded prior to the time of recall. There is no particular advantage to auditory presentation for the early items in the list since echoic memory would not be involved over the much longer time span these items represent. These items presumably would have already been identified and stored in short-term memory having gone beyond the precategorical sensory stage.

If superior recall performance for final list items were due to the presence of an echoic trace, anything we could do to eliminate this trace should have an adverse effect on this performance. We can find a hint of this possibility in an early study by Murray (1965) who found that using a loud masking noise to prevent subjects from hearing their own voices while reciting the list will eliminate the advantage usually shown for the final few list items.

Following these early leads, Crowder (1971, 1976; Crowder & Morton, 1969) began an important series of experiments using the serial position effect to analyze the character and duration of echoic memory. These studies allowed for a return to the interference approach previously described, but this time employing the same sort of verbal materials that led to the longer estimates of echoic duration when the partial report cue delay technique was used.

In a typical experiment subjects would hear a list of eight random letters of the alphabet spoken at a fairly rapid rate of two letters per second. After a specified delay they would be required to recall as many of the eight letters as possible in the correct order. These conditions reproduce the same serial position curve as found by Conrad and Hull for auditory presentation. Recall accuracy for the final items are superior to those in the middle of the list (see Figure 5-9).

The question we now ask, however, is what effect an intervening item occurring between the end of the list and recall might have on recall accuracy. Specifically, we wish to know whether such an item would cause the same sort of "backward masking" interference as previously described. Crowder reports just such an effect. Whenever a list is followed by a final verbal item, a "stimulus suffix," recall performance for the last item in the test list is always poorer than in a control condition in which the last item is followed only by silence. This is true even though the suffix is a word subjects are told to expect and to ignore. For example, just hearing the word "zero" after each list is sufficient to interfere with final item retention (Dallett, 1965). Further, only verbal items will produce this effect: a buzzer sound occurring in place of the word "zero" has no more effect than silence (Crowder, 1971).

These results are consistent with the conception of echoic memory as a precategorical sensory store, in which only acoustically similar stimuli will cause interference. Thus, not only will a buzzer fail to produce the "suffix effect" of interference with final item recall, but the effect is considerably reduced if a verbal suffix is spoken in a different voice or is heard from a different location from the rest of the items in the list (Crowder, 1973). Also consistent with the presumed sensory character of the echoic store, there is no demonstrable effect of the meaning, if any, of the suffix word (Crowder & Raeburn, 1970). Physical similarity alone seems to be the key.

You should note here that while physical aspects of the stimuli play the major role in these effects, the nature of the underlying processes are not clear. The early levels of processing segregate and group the perceptual information in ways that will determine what stimuli are "similar" enough to interfere with one another. Neisser, Hoenig, and Goldstein (1969), for example, have shown that interference effects may be based on rhythmic groups. Neisser and Kahneman (Kahneman, 1973) have shown that stimulus suffix effects may be produced with visual stimuli that belong to the same spatial group as the items in a visually presented list. However, it is generally agreed that these processes are "preattentive" and take place prior to assigning meaning to a stimulus.

Figure 5-10 shows one aspect of the results just described. The left-hand panel shows the clear effect of a stimulus suffix, in this case the word "zero," as compared with a control condition in which the suffix was replaced by silence. The right-hand panel shows the absence of any effect when the suffix was replaced by a buzzer sound (Crowder, 1971).

Of immediate interest in Figure 5-10, however, is Crowder's use of various delays prior to the onset of the stimulus suffix. When the spoken word "zero" followed within .5 sec of the end of the list, the suffix effect is very strong: the last item in the list shows little advantage over those immediately preceding it. The suffix has apparently interfered with the usefulness of the echoic trace facilitating the availability of that final item. Less interference, as reflected in fewer errors, is observed when the delay is increased to 2 sec, although there is still some effect as compared with the control condition where there was no suffix at all. The right-hand panel reinforces our previous point. A buzzer has no interfering effect on recall of the final item, regardless of its delay.

Unfortunately for those of us who would like a clear statement of "the" duration of echoic memory, we have to report that estimates using the suffix effect can vary anywhere between 2 to 6.4 sec, depending on

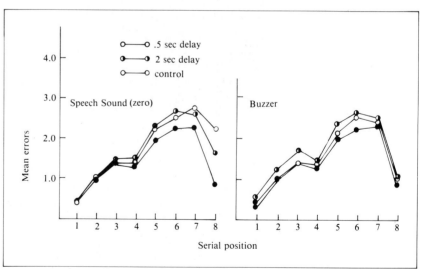

FIGURE 5-10   Mean number of errors as a function of serial position. Left panel shows two suffix conditions with a speech sound delivered at different delays as compared with a no-suffix control. Right panel shows identical conditions except that a buzzer is substituted for the speech suffix.
(From Crowder, 1971.)

the experiment (Crowder & Morton, 1969; Crowder & Prussin, 1971; Crowder & Raeburn, 1970; Morton & Holloway, 1970; Routh & Mayes, 1974).

The stimulus suffix effect, however, does appear to implicate a sensory, precategorical memory for an auditory stimulus of approximately the same time course as other estimates using verbal materials. We are thus forced to raise the question of whether the use of verbal versus nonverbal procedures measure the same form of storage. Obviously, the duration estimates are very different, a few hundred milliseconds for nonverbal stimuli and a few seconds for verbal. This question is more important than the fact that this auditory persistence is called a *preperceptual auditory image* by Massaro (1972) and a *precategorical acoustic store* by Crowder (Crowder & Morton, 1969). These are alternative, but equally accurate descriptions of the character of what we have been calling sensory, or echoic, memory.

The best answer we can offer at this point is that the clear demarcation between the sensory echoic store, and postcategorical short-term memory, may not be as clear-cut as the early structural approaches to memory would have it. That is, any measure of "pure" echoic memory may well suffer from some contamination introduced by processing operations on this trace.

On the other hand, the estimates of Massaro (1972), Efron (1970), and Elliot (1967), using the method of successive stimuli, may have underestimated potential echoic duration. This would be true if the echoic store ceased to show usefulness once its content has been processed beyond this sensory stage. On the other hand, the suffix effect may overestimate its duration through some influence of postcategorical memory which may have inflated the measures obtained. We will, at this point, opt for a figure about 2 sec as the average duration of the echoic store, provided we remember the word ABOUT is heavily capitalized.

The Content of Echoic Memory

The arguments regarding sensory memory have hinged on the idea that information processing by a listener is based on a selective process which is able to transform only some of the sensory information in echoic memory into a more durable and more permanent form of memory. Glucksberg and Cowen (1970) give a striking example of the flavor of this selective coding of available sensory information.

Imagine you are asked the question, "Do you want a beer?" as you are absorbed in listening to the radio. Since you apparently did not hear the question, a part of it is repeated: "Do you?" At this point you can often feel as if you can scan back in time and remember the original question, even though it had not been "heard" when it was first spoken. Even though the question itself is not repeated, the "Do you?" can be sufficient for a "yes" (or maybe "no") answer.

The second utterance, "Do you?," is analogous to the delayed instruction cues used by Sperling and by Darwin and his colleagues in their partial report experiments. A message which has seemed to pass unnoticed can still be recovered if attention is called to it quickly enough. This, in essence, is the nature of echoic memory and the selective coding process.

Several investigators have felt that a good way to accurately determine the characteristics of echoic memory would be to examine the availability of such "unattended" information when attention is suddenly switched to it. The *shadowing task,* originated by Colin Cherry (1953), is a procedure that allows us to monitor the direction and efficiency of attention to a particular input. In shadowing, the subject hears different messages in each ear, or from different speakers. The instructions require him or her to repeat back, or "shadow" one of these messages as rapidly as possible. By varying the difficulty of the material and measuring the accuracy of shadowing, we can monitor the degree of attention devoted to this message.

Treisman (1964d) had subjects shadow one message while, unknown to them, the identical message was being played to the other ear. The unattended message was either a little ahead of the shadowed message, or a little behind it. The subjects were told that the purpose of the experiment was to determine how well they could shadow the attended message. The question of interest to Treisman, however, concerned the time at which the subject would spontaneously notice that the two messages were the same as the amount of asynchrony between the two messages were reduced.

Subjects, on the average, noticed the identity when the ignored message was 1.3 sec or less ahead of the shadowed message. If the ignored message was leading the attended message by more than this, there was no awareness that the two messages were the same. On the other hand, if the ignored message was behind the attended message, the identity was noticed even when the lag was as great as 4 sec.

Treisman (1964d) interpreted the difference in the leading and lagging conditions as reflecting differences in forms of storage of the attended and unattended messages. When the ignored message was ahead of the shadowed message, the ignored information was being registered in the brief duration, sensory store. The information in this memory decayed in a little more than one second. For delays greater than this, a word that occurred on the ignored ear would be lost from the sensory store by the time the same word occurred in the shadowed ear. In order for the recognition of identity to take place it was necessary that identical information be in storage at the same time. With the ignored message leading, this could not occur unless the lead time was one second or less.

The situation was different when the ignored message lagged the attended message. The attended information had been selected and coded into some form that could be maintained for several seconds. This attended information was still in storage when the identical information occurred on the ignored ear up to 4 sec later. The different results obtained under leading and lagging conditions, then, reflect the different characteristics of the relatively short lasting precategorical image of the stimulus and a longer lasting fully coded representation of the same information.

The only problem with Treisman's use of spontaneous reports, of course, is that a subject could only be used once in this experiment. Once the identity had been noticed, subjects would become alerted to this possibility and we would expect them to be constantly switching their attention to the ignored ear to try to pick up any future identical messages.

Glucksberg and Cowan (1970) performed a variation on this experiment which avoided the problem of having to rely on spontaneous reports. In their study, subjects again shadowed one message while a different message was simultaneously played to the other ear. At odd times during the experimental trial, a digit might occur in the ignored prose message. The end of a trial was signaled by a visual cue that instructed the subject to report whether or not a digit had occurred in the ignored message on that trial. The critical measurement was the time that had elapsed between the occurrence of a digit and the occurrence of the report signal. Figure 5-11 shows a summary of their results.

If the signal to report occurred more than 5 sec after a digit had occurred in the ignored message, subjects usually failed to report that they had heard a digit. Indeed, after a 5-sec cue delay, detection accuracy was no better than the rate of spontaneous detection for digits which were presented in trials with no cue at all. This level of performance is shown by the horizontal dotted line in the figure.

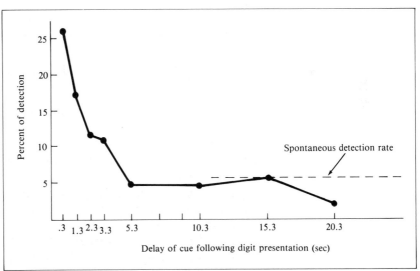

FIGURE 5-11 Probability of reporting a digit presented in an unattended ear shown as a function of the delay between the digit and the cue.
(From Glucksberg & Cowen, 1970.)

On the other hand, at cue delays under 5 sec, detection performance shows considerable improvement. Further, the shorter the cue delay within this range, the better was the level of detection accuracy. Both Treisman's and Glucksberg and Cowan's results are thus consistent with the notion of a precategorical representation of all auditory inputs which is formed automatically, but which fades rapidly if not coded by selective attention to it.

From these studies we might expect that echoic information which is left unselected, and hence uncoded, will have no lasting effect on more permanent memory. There is some evidence that this is so. Moray (1959), for example, used a shadowing experiment to show that a series of digits repeated up to 35 times in an ignored ear will be recognized or recalled no better than if this particular series had not previously occurred at all.

There thus seems to be ample evidence for the existence of a sensory, uncoded form of memory for auditory material, and that this representation is quite brief as compared with more fully processed codes.

SENSORY MEMORY AND A PROCESS MODEL

We have taken a fairly consistent stand to this point, presenting the reader with the weight of evidence favoring the structural reality of an identifiably distinct iconic memory in vision and an echoic store in auditory information processing. Together with the possibility of counterpart "buffer" memories for other modalities, such as tactile stimulation, these were specific forms of sensory persistence commonly described as rapid decay, precategorical, sensory stores.

When discussing iconic memory in an earlier section, we were careful to emphasize that the areas of controversy lie primarily in the specifics of some recent studies which go rather deeply into the interpretation of the iconic phenomenon. The existence of a very short-term visual persistence in an as yet relatively unanalyzed sensory form, however, was not at issue.

Similarly, when we turn to echoic memory, we have seen that the only worrisome results reported have related to the variety of different duration estimates obtained under different experimental procedures. Indeed, as we argued earlier, these differences in duration estimates could reflect nothing more or less than measurement error due to one form or another of "contamination" from other memory processes interacting with the echoic trace. This may be so, and we await further research on this question.

On the other hand, some of these questions have led theorists to wonder whether the structural picture of memory with its distinct, fixed, structural "stores" is the best way to characterize the way in which information is actually processed in the memory system (e.g., Craik & Lockhart, 1972; Schneider & Shiffrin, 1977). We characterized this alternative view as a *process model* of memory in an earlier section. Let us review this position in the context of these studies of sensory memory.

We saw a hint of this alternative in our discussion of interpretations of iconic memory. The possibility was raised that the different experimental techniques, such as backward masking and successive stimuli, may in fact be tapping different levels of processing of visual stimulation. That is, the distinction between sensory memory and postcategorical memory may represent different levels of coding that differ in the degree to which they are formed automatically, or the degree to which they require attentional resources and further processing activity on the part of the subject.

There may in reality be a continual transformation from a literal sensory persistence to more abstract levels of coding which includes perceptual classification and semantic analysis. Such a continuity of processing could appear as structurally isolated stages if we erroneously tap only the two extreme levels along this continuum. According to this conception, we should not be at all surprised to see occasional arguments that one measure or another is "contaminated" by higher level, postcategorical processing.

These experiments may in fact be giving us a very clear, and equally valid, picture of memory processing as each taps a slightly different aspect of a complex of coding operations. In the case of echoic memory, for example, tapping the earliest levels of auditory processing might sometimes reflect the automatic registration of a raw acoustic image. On other occasions, however, our procedures may imply representations in the form of speech elements such as phonemes or sound patterns. Both of these codes are "precategorical," in the sense that they precede identification of the syllable or word. But they are also on different levels, in the sense that one requires more processing to achieve than the other.

This idea implies a progression of coding formats ranging from simple sensory persistence through increasingly abstract representations of the stimulus, rather than simply a transfer from one kind of memory store to another. While the different character of the memory codes at the extremes of this progression are clear to see, at what point do we call a particular representation pre- or postcategorical?

This middle level is a blurred distinction in the studies we have cited. But this need not be seen as a weakness in these studies or in their methodology. Rather, the reality could be that these distinctions *are* blurred, that different experimental procedures tap different levels of a continuous elaborative process. The studies of backward masking which describe a physical representation at 250 msec, and studies of the suffix effect which describe an acoustic representation occurring several seconds beyond this point, may each be tapping different regions of a continuous transformation of the sensory code. To say that the suffix effect reflects an interaction with higher levels of memory, then, should be no cause for theoretical concern.

The concept of *attention*, the notion of a selective coding of some information for deeper processing, can perhaps best be seen as an operation that is necessary in order to form some types of memory codes but not others. How we allocate our attentional resources will determine the kinds of memories and knowledge we will have available from any particular experience.

In the following chapter we will take a close look at the concept of attention and the major hypotheses which have attempted to explain how it is limited, how it is allocated, and how it plays a functional role in the total memory system.

CHAPTER SUMMARY

1. *A Memory System: Structure versus Process*

   A. Structural models of memory see information processing as proceeding through a sequence of functionally distinct memory stores; sensory memory, short-term memory, and long-term memory. Selective attention and feedback from long-term memory were referred to as control processes which operate on these structural stores.

   B. In a process model of memory, stimuli undergo a progression of increasingly abstract representations. This progression runs from "raw" sensory representations to "deep," semantic analyses, with attentional processes sharing the same limited pool of resources.

2. *The First Stage: Sensory Memory*

   A. Sensory memory, whether visual or auditory, can be characterized as having a capacity larger than later memory levels, as being in a precategorical, unanalyzed form, and as having a duration of under one second for visual stimuli and below several seconds for auditory stimuli.

3. *Visual Sensory Memory*

   A. The existence of iconic memory was first demonstrated by Sperling, using a partial report procedure in which subjects were asked only to report a limited part of a larger visual display after the display had terminated. When he delayed the cue as to which part of the display to report, accuracy rapidly declined. This implied a visual representation of the full display which is lost in under a second. A second method involved presenting two stimuli in rapid succession and examining the longest separation in time between the two that still produced a combined image. This method yielded duration estimates of iconic memory as short as 250 msec. A third technique used studies of backward masking. These verified the limited duration of iconic memory and reinforced its precategorical, sensory nature. The more physically similar the masking stimulus to the target stimulus, the greater were the interference effects.

B. Some questions of detail have been raised about the rate of information read-out from the iconic store, whether a masking stimulus operates by perceptually mixing with the iconic image or interrupting its processing, and whether the usual duration measurements reflect a combination of rod and cone functions of the eye, each with a different decay rate.

4. *Auditory Sensory Memory*

A. Auditory experiences such as the recognition of speech would be impossible without the ability to retain sensory impressions for periods longer than their actual physical duration.

B. Echoic memory has been demonstrated using a variation of the partial report technique previously employed in visual experiments. Requesting partial report from a larger set of simultaneous auditory messages demonstrated the persistence of an auditory image which lasts for some time after stimulus termination. Systematically delaying the onset of an instructional cue in a partial report paradigm for several simultaneous messages implied a 2-sec duration of echoic memory. Other techniques, such as successive stimuli for judgements of subjective duration, and studies of backward masking, have yielded duration estimates of echoic memory as short as 100 to 250 msec. Studies of the "suffix effect," on the other hand, yielded estimates as long as 2 to 6 sec. Studies requiring the shadowing of one message while ignoring another message support the notion that unattended auditory information is held briefly in an unanalyzed, precategorical store whose content can still be sampled if attention is switched within a period of about 1 sec.

5. *Sensory Memory and A Process Model*

A. The areas of apparent disagreement in studies of iconic and echoic memory can be reanalyzed within the framework of a process model of memory. This would assume that various experiments tap different levels of processing as stimuli undergo a continuous transformation of coding formats.

CODING PROCESSES: II. ATTENTION AND CAPACITY

TOPIC QUESTIONS

1. Aspects of Attention.
In what contexts has the term *attention* been used? How does one's ordinary experience in handling several conversations at a cocktail party demonstrate the paradox of selective attention? What two general conceptions have been offered to describe selective attention, and what are their basic elements?

2. The Early Experiments.
What are the procedures used in *shadowing* and in *split-span* experiments? What did these experiments say about the process of selective attention?

3. Time-Sharing Models of Attention.
What were the basic elements of the *filter theory* of attention, and how did available evidence appear to support this model? Why was there a need to modify this model with the notion of an *attenuating filter*? What evidence led to the search for alternative theories?

4. Capacity Models of Attention.
What are the basic elements of a *capacity model* of attention, and how did some theorists view the relationship between "attention," "effort," and "performance?" What is a *multiprocessor model* of attention, and what is meant by the term *automaticity*?

5. Flexibility and Task Demands.
How is the effort required to process a stimulus related to the clarity of that stimulus? What is the importance of this relationship to the understanding of selective attention? How flexible are attentional strategies, and how can this flexibility explain the diversity of theory encountered over the years?

The previous chapter gave us our first close look at what Atkinson and Shiffrin (1968) called the *structural components* of a hypothetical memory system. Within this traditional tripartite system, *sensory memory* was seen as the first stage or level of processing, which receives and briefly stores an unanalyzed, sensory representation of the perceptual effects of a stimulus. *Short-term memory* was seen as a second component of the system, one which involves a "deeper" analysis of the stimulus information and which stores this information for a temporary, but longer period of time, as a coherent auditory (or visual) pattern. The final, "deepest" level of processing required that this new experience be related to the context of past experience, thus giving the stimulus true meaning within our existing framework of knowledge. This final stage would, of course, involve the coding of the information within the organized semantic structure of *long-term memory*.

In addition to these three structural components, we also referred to *control processes* which serve to select information for further processing, to direct this processing and, in general, to determine how the information stored at each level will be used. Rehearsal in short-term memory, the preservation of information through overt or covert repetition, or "recirculation," is one type of control process. Without it, material—or at least meaningless material—will quickly be lost. Within long-term memory, control processes include active operations such as search and retrieval within the organized memory store.

Of immediate interest, however, is one very important "control process" we referred to in relation to the use of information stored in sensory memory. As we saw, considerable research suggests that only a limited amount of information stored in echoic and iconic memory can be selected and extracted for further analysis and storage in short-term memory. Unselected information will be quickly lost in the rapid decay of the perceptual trace. This particular control process, the selection and extraction of information from sensory memory, is referred to as *selective attention*.

Although the subject of active research over the past two decades, we have all had first-hand experience with this selective process. We know from our own experience that not everything within our visual field is noticed and remembered, and that many of the sounds and voices within our hearing go unheeded. At the same time, most of us have the sense that we can choose to direct our attention to certain aspects of these sights and sounds and that, as we do so, they seem to become more intense, clearer, or otherwise invade our awareness. Like the pressure of the clothes on our bodies, these sensations were always there. What changes is our awareness of them.

The studies of the capacity of sensory memory showed dramatically that more information does indeed arrive at the senses than can ever be reported or remembered. They also showed how effectively we can direct our attention to one aspect of a display or another, to report a single row of letters or the information from a single loudspeaker. Yet, there is more to the attentional process than conscious selection.

Some years ago when the Chicago transit system discontinued service along one branch of its noisy elevated railway, the Chicago police received a number of worried calls from residents to say that something "strange" or "funny" had occurred during the night. Although this mysterious phenomenon was sufficient to wake them from sleep they could not say exactly what it was. The mystery was solved when the police discovered that the bulk of these calls coincided with the time the train would normally have passed had it not been discontinued (Reynolds & Flagg, 1977, p. 24). In the same way that we can remain unaware of the sound of a ticking clock until it stops, these callers had literally been awakened by the unexpected sound of silence. These people had suddenly become aware that something they had been ignoring was no longer there.

How selective is selective attention? Are apparently ignored events and sensations completely without effect? What are the bases of selection, and can we fully attend to more than one thing at a time? Our goal in this chapter will be to provide some of the answers to these and related questions.

ASPECTS OF ATTENTION

Definitions of Attention

The term "attention" is as difficult to define as any in psychology. This is not so much because the term has no meaning, as it is that "attention" seems to have a variety of different meanings in different contexts. The potential for confusion is only heightened by the fact that these very different meanings are all ultimately rather closely related.

One meaning of the term attention relates to *arousal,* that physical state in which one is alert, excited, and keenly aware of the environment. Closely tied to our levels of motivation and interest in our surroundings, this state of mental alertness heightens our sensitivity to sensation. Our mind and body are "poised to respond to any event, external or internal" (Mackworth, 1970).

In this state of what we might call "alertness," one can observe a variety of physiological correlates, such as dramatic changes in heart and breathing rate, cortical brain wave patterns, differences in skin conductance, and even changes in the diameter of the pupil of the eye—which enlarges in states of high arousal (Kahneman, 1973; Mackworth, 1970). When arousal is high, our senses are alerted and our reactions, both mental and physical, are at their height. It is the sense of alertness we felt on hearing our name called by the teacher in the third grade, or the alertness that comes with the shout of ATTENTION by an army sergeant.

There are, of course, qualifications to the positive relationship between level of physiological arousal, mental alertness, and performance. These are complex variables, and arousal may affect different cognitive processes in different ways (Hamilton, Hockey, & Rejman, 1977). One of the best known examples of an interaction between arousal and performance is called the *Yerkes–Dodson Law* (Yerkes & Dodson, 1908). This law reminds us that for any task there is an optimal level of arousal for peak performance; below this level (boredom, fatigue, indifference) mental performance will be poor, while above this level (anxiety, stress, panic) performance will also markedly deteriorate (Kahneman, 1973). The optimal level of arousal is not the same for all tasks. For example, if the task is fairly easy, a high level of arousal should lead to good performance. If the task is difficult, however, higher levels of arousal could be disruptive, such that a lower level might yield best performance.

Closely related to attention and arousal is the notion of "effort," since ordinarily the more attention we give to a task, the greater the effort we are willing to allocate to its completion. Indeed, to Kahneman and others, attention and effort are terms that can be used almost interchangeably.

Attention, in the sense of one's overall state of alertness, is certainly one common and very legitimate use of the term. Another equally common, and equally legitimate use, was given by Neisser in his contrast between *focal attention* and *preattentive* processes (Neisser, 1967, pp. 87–89). Neisser took the term "focal attention" from Schachtel, a psychoanalytic theorist who referred to focusing one's attention fully on a single object, so as to "perceive it or understand it from many sides, as clearly as possible" (Schachtel, 1959, p. 251). Focal attention, according to Neisser, cannot operate on more than a limited aspect of the visual or auditory world at any one time. Focal attention can be concentrated only after a preliminary operation, a preattentive process, has scanned the environment in a global or holistic way until the object for concentrated attention is found.

We can offer a common analogy for the sense of focal attention versus preattentive processes (Wachtel, 1967). Imagine yourself entering a darkened room in search of a particular object, say, a particular book. Imagine further that you are armed with a very special flashlight which allows you to control the width of the beam. The light can be adjusted either to a bright, narrow focus, or alternatively, to a wider, but dimmer beam. A good strategy would be to enter the room with the flashlight on its widest setting to illuminate the entire contents of the room at once, however indistinct the objects may appear. This "preattentive" operation would be sufficient to quickly reject most of the objects in the room as not being of interest. The objects are identified not so much as being a particular table, a particular chair, or a particular picture, but rather, as all "not books." This broad-beam, global view, would be the most efficient way to quickly isolate a bookcase from among the other contents of the room. It is at this point that we would adjust the beam to its narrowest but brightest setting to serially scan each book title, one at a time, until the desired book is found. This, by analogy, would represent focal attention.

Considerable research by Neisser and his colleagues was devoted to the question of the viability of this distinction. According to this view, preattentive processing of many stimuli could be conducted simultaneously and very quickly (parallel processing), while focal attention represented a slower process which could concentrate on only one stimulus at a time (serial processing). Neisser (1967) provides a good summary of this research, and we will look more closely at this distinction later in this chapter from a slightly different perspective.

In Neisser's terms, one could decide to concentrate "focal attention" on one particular stimulus, whether a visual object or a particular conversation in a noisy room. This brings us to our final use of the term "attention." In this case, attention is used in the context of *selective attention,* our ability to select one stimulus source from among others, and to filter out or ignore potential distractors. It is this selective aspect of attention which is our immediate concern. This represents the "control process" that will ultimately determine what information receives conscious awareness and encoding in memory, and what information will not. As we turn to the research on selective attention, however, it would be good to keep these other senses of attention in mind. We will have occasion to refer to them again.

Some Limits on Attention: Back to the Cocktail Party

That there are upper limits on attention should be apparent to anyone who has ever tried to concentrate on two complex activities at once. On the one hand, we can easily drive a car down the highway at a steady 55 miles per hour listening to the radio, holding a conversation with one or more passengers, and perhaps at the same time thinking about where to stop for lunch. Assuming a wide road with little traffic, and not too engrossing a conversation, all of these activities can be carried on with little apparent strain. While experimental analyses show that car driving behavior requires extraordinarily complex attentional skills (c.f., Senders, 1967), we do it every day. But the moment something unexpected occurs, such as seeing a car stalled in front of us, or a bicycle suddenly appearing from nowhere, all activities other than concentration on the road suddenly cease. The conversation stops in mid-sentence and all thoughts of lunch immediately disappear. Attention, in all meanings of the term, becomes mobilized for the single task of avoiding collision. All potential distractors are just as suddenly tuned out of awareness.

As clear and dramatic as are the upper limits on attentional capacity, the underlying complexities of the process have traditionally brought more anguish than solutions from the ranks of experimental psychology. Titchener (1908) expressed this anguish vividly: "The discovery of attention [by the psychologists] did not result in any triumph of the experimental method. It was something like the discovery of a hornet's nest; the first touch brought out a whole swarm of insistent problems" (p. 173).

As we will try to show, we can be less pessimistic today about understanding the processes of attention than Titchener was so many years ago. While we do not yet have all of the answers, we have nevertheless done much to isolate this particular hornet's nest, and to define its major characteristics. As we shall see, however, this prodding of Titchener's nest of hornets was not accomplished without a few very painful stings.

To begin with, we should recognize that selective attention can, on the one hand, seem quite absolute. Treisman (1966), for example, quotes an early study by Hovey (1928) who gave a group of subjects an IQ test while at the same time trying to distract them with "seven electric bells, four buzzers, two organ pipes, a circular metal saw, a flashlight, and several peculiarly dressed people walking about carrying strange objects" (p. 98). Extraordinarily, these subjects did nearly as well as a control group taking the same test under quiet conditions.

While at times selective attention can seem quite absolute, we are also aware that, like the Chicago residents awakened by the absence of accustomed noise, some events can break through this selective barrier and force themselves on our awareness. In extreme cases, such as frequently found in schizophrenia, the ability to block out extraneous or irrelevant stimuli can be especially difficult (McGhie, 1969; McGhie & Chapman, 1961). Here is a direct quotation from one schizophrenic patient as reported by McGhie and Chapman (1961):

> My concentration is very poor. I jump from one thing to another. If I am talking to someone, they only need to cross their legs or scratch their heads and I am distracted and forget what I was saying. I think I would concentrate better with my eyes shut. (p. 104)

Other patients report similar feelings: "You only hear snatches of conversation and you can't fit them together," or "If it is just one person who is speaking, that's not too bad, but if others join in, then I can't pick it up at all. I just can't get into tune with that conversation." The effects of this difficulty in focusing concentration can be devastating: "It makes me feel open—as if things are closing in on me and I have lost control." It is not surprising that considerable research has been devoted to the study of attentional deficits in schizophrenics (e.g., Chapman & Chapman, 1973; Oltmanns & Neale, 1975).

It is possible to get the feeling for the upper limit on attention and its selective character without either becoming a schizophrenic or subjecting yourself to seven electric bells, four buzzers, two organ pipes, and so forth. The full range of the problem of selective attention can be quickly appreciated by simply entering that same cocktail party we referred to in the previous chapter. As you recall, everyone seemed to be talking at once, and loud music played on a phonograph. Yet, out of this unbelievable cacophony, one could nevertheless concentrate on a single conversation. We effectively block out all of the other sounds and conversations in the room, even becoming unaware of their presence. If later asked about the content of these other conversations, we would probably be unable to give much of a report. We were, after all, not "paying attention."

In a real sense, then, our ability to selectively attend to a single source (or "channel") of information seems quite absolute. There is a limit to the amount of information we can process at any one time, and full attention to one channel can be accomplished only at the expense of others. We referred, however, to a second aspect of our experience at a crowded party, the first sting from Titchener's nest of hornets. While we may be totally unaware of the content of these other conversations, we soon become aware of them if someone happens to speak our name. At this point we find ourselves very definitely switched into this other conversation, while at the same time switching out of the one in which we were previously engaged.

The elements of the paradox are clear. First, our capacity for attention seems sharply limited: We can follow the content of either one channel or another, but concentrating on one means the exclusion of the other. Second, and here is the sting, we can nevertheless detect relevant information in what was apparently a totally ignored conversation. The question, of course, is a simple one. How can we "hear" our name spoken in a conversation we were apparently ignoring, and if we were not ignoring it, why could we not recall anything of its contents before our name was spoken?

One's experience in a noisy party thus contains all of the essential elements of the phenomenon of selective attention. It is for this reason that research on selective attention became almost universally known as simply, "the cocktail party problem" (Cherry, 1953).

Two Concepts of Selective Attention   The recognition that there are upper-bound limits to the amount of information we can take in and analyze has been with us since the writings of William James (1890). The question of how to characterize, or determine the source of, this limited capacity has received much less agreement. It has been seen in terms of limits on perception (Broadbent, 1958, 1971; Welford, 1952), short-term memory (Shiffrin, Pisoni, & Casteneda-Mendez, 1974), or more general notions of limits of resource allocation within a single perceptual-memory system (Kahneman, 1973; Norman & Bobrow, 1975).

Indeed, in the current literature alone, one can find over a dozen identifiably different theoretical models which attempt to explain selective attention. Broadly, however, all of these theories can generally be grouped into one of two categories which we can call either *time-sharing* or *capacity* models of attention. Let us look briefly at these two general classes of explanation before we turn to a detailed examination of each of them. As we do so, bear in mind one very important point. We are dealing here primarily with different ways of conceptualizing the problem, and the impact these conceptualizations have had on the sorts of questions asked and the experiments suggested. This has been a repeated theme throughout this book. Both conceptualizations, however, fully agree on the basic facts of the issue: when two or more simultaneous inputs are fairly simple or redundant and they are delivered slowly, one can usually handle both of them fairly successfully. When these inputs are either complex, or presented rapidly, there is a marked deterioration in performance. Finally, when they are both complex and rapid, simultaneous handling of more than one channel is virtually impossible. The question rests only on why this is so.

The Elements of Time-Sharing.   The essence of time-sharing models of attention is the postulate of a limited system capable of accomodating only one meaningful input at a time (e.g., a single speech message). The only way one can hope to cope with simultaneous inputs (e.g., two speech messages) is to employ a principle of time-sharing. This is analogous to the way a modern computer can switch its "attention" between any number of input terminals so rapidly that one gets the impression that all of them are being simultaneously monitored. In fact, information from only one terminal is ever being processed by the computer at any one time.

According to this time-sharing analogy, we can either continuously process the information from one channel, to the exclusion of all others, or we can rapidly switch back and forth between these channels (or their echoic representation) for brief periods on a sampling basis. Attentional strategies, such as giving priority to one input over another, would be determined by the relative amount of time devoted to the analysis of one channel versus the time devoted to the analysis of the others. Broadbent's (1958, 1971) "filter theory," and its modification by Treisman (1964a, 1969) are the best known examples, along with other so-called "single channel" models such as those of Cherry and Taylor (1954) and Welford (1959, 1968, 1977).

The Elements of Capacity Allocation.   The primary alternative to the time-sharing models of attention are the so-called "capacity" models. These models also assume that we have some upper limits on our capacity to process information, but that all simultaneous inputs can be processed, to one degree or another, in parallel. Faced with simultaneous inputs and limited resources, the subject must allocate relative amounts of "space" or processing capacity to the analysis of one input or another on a priority basis.

In this case, attentional strategies take the form of differential allocation of these limited processing resources among the various inputs, with some receiving deeper, or more complete processing than others. A number of important theorists have offered this type of explanation including Moray (1967), Kahneman (1973), Norman and Bobrow (1975), and Johnston and Heinz (1978).

With this broad outline in mind, let us now turn to a more detailed look at representatives of these two general classes of attentional theory, and the experiments used in their support.

THE EARLY EXPERIMENTS

Unless one is a social psychologist, cocktail parties are hardly the best place to conduct controlled experiments. Luckily, a renewed interest in selective attention in the 1950s coincided with the availability of a new device for home entertainment: the stereophonic tape recorder. In the hands of the experimental psychologist, this now very common instrument became a powerful tool for investigating the full range of the "cocktail party problem." Two types of experiments were typically performed; the so-called "shadowing" and the "split-span" experiments.

Shadowing Experiments

In order to prepare a typical experiment the investigator first records a prose passage (e.g., reading from a newspaper article) on one channel of a stereophonic tape-recorder. The machine is then rewound and the investigator now records a second passage (e.g., reading from a history textbook) on the second channel. When the tape is again rewound and monitored over stereophonic earphones, the subject hears what is called *dichotic* speech: two different simultaneous passages, one heard in each ear.

In the conduct of these early experiments, Cherry (1953; Cherry & Taylor, 1954) employed a technique known as *shadowing,* or "echoing," of one of the two messages. The subject would be told which message to consider the primary one (e.g., the speech in the left ear), and which to consider the secondary message (e.g., the speech in the right ear). Instructed to "shadow" the primary message, the subject would have to speak aloud the message from the left ear on a word-by-word basis as it was heard. Although this process of speaking while listening may sound difficult, subjects can become quite adept after surprisingly little practice (e.g., Broadbent, 1952; Treisman, 1964b).

In his early experiments, Cherry found that the presence of a distracting message in the secondary ear had very little effect on shadowing accuracy for the message in the primary ear. That is, subjects could shadow the primary message as well in the presence of a second, "distracting" message, as when there was no secondary message at all. Of course the subjects were usually aware of the presence of the secondary message, in the sense that they knew when speech was present in that ear and when it was not. The critical point, however, is that they remained totally unaware of what was being said. Subjects could report absolutely none of its content, even in the vaguest terms.

Some information did seem to get through from the secondary ear, or "channel," as it came to be called. For example, if midway through a passage the speaker in the secondary channel was changed from a male to a female, or if a 400 Hz pure tone was presented along with the speech, these would very quickly be noticed. On the other hand, playing speech backward in the secondary channel would go totally unnoticed. Subjects might report that something seemed odd, but they could not tell you that what began as meaningful speech had become speechlike, but meaningless, sounds.

These early findings were later extended by Treisman (1960, 1964a, b, c) who showed convincingly that subjects can totally reject a secondary message in one ear when they are instructed to shadow the message in the other. The literature, in fact, began to use the term "rejected" channel. For example, while the subject might notice that the speaker in the rejected ear had changed from a male to a female, gradually switching the unattended message from English to French would very likely go unnoticed (Treisman, 1964a).

Effects of Physical Characteristics.   A number of early studies using the shadowing technique built up a picture of selective attention as a perceptual filtering of all but a single source, or "channel," with this selection based almost entirely on the physical characteristics of the acoustical signal. Meaning, or the content of a message, seemed to play little or no part in message selection.

Part of this belief came from the fact that subjects are obviously quite good at selecting one message from another on the basis of their physical parameters. This was true whether two messages were presented to different ears, whether they were heard over different loudspeakers some distance apart in a room, or whether two voices heard from a single location were discriminable in terms of voice quality, such as a male and a female speaker (Spieth, Curtis, & Webster, 1954).

The second basis for this belief came from those characteristics of a secondary channel which would usually be noticed by subjects and those which would not. For example, while subjects ordinarily remain unaware of the content of a secondary channel, we have seen that they will notice when the speaker changes from a male to a female, or if a pure tone is unexpectedly inserted into the "rejected" message. These are, of course, changes in the gross acoustic parameters of the signal in the unattended channel. Perhaps, it was thought, subjects fail to notice when speech is run backward in the unattended channel precisely because reversed speech has the same physical characteristics as normal speech (which it does). The fact that its content conveys no meaning had no effect on the subjects' awareness.

Finally, one could also add to this weight of evidence the fact that whether subjects will notice a change from one language to another in the secondary channel depends on the physical similarity of that language to English. For example, bilingual subjects who have greater familiarity with the sound pattern of the second language will be more likely to notice the change than subjects who are not (Treisman, 1964a).

The early emphasis on physical characteristics for message selection was accompanied by other studies which seemed to imply that this selection process was quite absolute. We have already seen that subjects have no conscious recollection of the content of an "ignored" message, and that Cherry was able to show that subjects could shadow a message from one ear just as easily with or without a distracting message in the other ear.

While shadowing is a good way to ensure full concentration on one channel or another, Moray and O'Brien (1967) were to show that shadowing is not necessary to obtain comparable results. Subjects were instructed to listen for the occurrence of digits in a list of spoken letters and simply to press a button when a digit occurred. Even though no shadowing was involved, this detection task was just as easy when a competing message was presented to the other ear as without one. However, even when listeners were trying to hear both messages at once, if a digit occurred on both channels at the same time, the subject usually missed one of these targets. A response to one channel usually meant that a digit on the other channel went unnoticed. The effects we have been describing are thus truly attentional ones, and not merely an artifact of shadowing masking the secondary message to prevent its being heard.

This emphasis on physical characteristics again appeared when investigators asked whether the number of competing messages had any effect on shadowing accuracy. To put it another way, are three howling children in a movie theater more difficult to ignore than one? In one study, stereophonic earphones were used in the way described in the previous chapter to simulate three simultaneous messages, one heard in the left ear, one heard in the right ear, and one heard as if it was coming from the middle of the head. In this case, as you might have expected, shadowing accuracy for one of the three messages was not as good as when only one message had to be ignored instead of two. On the other hand, if the subjects had to shadow speech in one ear while two messages were both presented together in the other ear, two messages were just as easy to ignore as one (Treisman, 1964a). If there are three howling children in a movie theater, we can only hope they are all sitting together, rather than dispersed throughout the audience!

To early attention theory, these results were a dramatic demonstration that it is not the number of messages which matters in selective listening, but the number of sources or "channels" which must be ignored. A channel, as we have seen, was to be defined not by its content, but by its physical parameters. In this case, selection was based on spatial localization, a physical dimension of the stimulus, with all information from that source treated as a single channel to be rejected.

Effects of Meaning. To this point we have been discussing the efficiency of selection, and the early conclusions about the physical basis of this selection. Is it the case, however, that all unselected information fades automatically from sensory memory without any chance of further analysis or effect? It would obviously not be very adaptive if this were the case. If all of the content of ignored channels were rejected too efficiently, being engaged in a conversation would be sufficient to prevent us from ever hearing the warning, FIRE, or to come when our name was called. In vision, for example, we could never notice a STOP sign out of the corner of our eye while intent on watching the road in front of us.

There must be some monitoring of unattended channels, since we obviously can detect information of critical importance or personal significance when it occurs from these sources. In a single experiment, Moray (1959) demonstrated both that such monitoring does occur, and at the same time, reinforced the validity of laboratory shadowing experiments for the study of everyday, ''cocktail party,'' listening experience.

First, Moray replicated the finding that when subjects are told to shadow one of two speech messages presented dichotically, they seem to have no recollection of the material presented in the other ear. He found, for example, that in a later recognition task, subjects' recognition scores for words which had occurred in that ear were no better than chance. On the other hand, when Moray had unexpectedly prerecorded the subjects' own names in the unattended channel, followed by instructions to stop shadowing, or to switch shadowing to this ear, the subjects often did react almost immediately. As in our own experience at a noisy party when we do hear our name, 30% of Moray's subjects did indeed ''switch over'' and become aware of the content of that previously unattended channel.

Although Treisman, Cherry, and their colleagues devoted most of their effort to the study of selective listening, Neisser (Neisser, 1969; Neisser & Becklen, 1975) reported quite analogous results for vision. In one rather ingenious experiment, for example, subjects saw two separate videotaped activities (two hands clapping and three people passing a basketball) which appeared as one superimposed over the other on a single TV screen. As in the case of selective listening, subjects had no trouble following the action in one scene or the other, but they could not simultaneously follow the action in both (Neisser & Becklen, 1975). In vision, as in hearing, we seem to organize our perception of events to follow a particular flow of information, or action, ignoring with apparent ease the potential distraction of other stimuli deemed to be irrelevant. As Neisser and Becklen argue, selective perception is determined by one's expectations. Indeed, in their experiment even when something unexpected occurred in the unattended action, it frequently went unnoticed.

As Neisser has also shown, we can even find a parallel to Moray's name detection results in vision. In this case, Neisser (1969) designed an experiment in which subjects saw two lines of print, one in black ink which they were to read aloud, and one just below it in red ink which they were to ignore. The subjects apparently followed their instructions, and in later testing showed absolutely no awareness of, or recall ability for, the content of the to-be-ignored line printed in red. When the subjects' own names appeared in this ignored message, however, over half of the subjects (66%) did immediately notice this fact.

The full paradox of Cherry's cocktail party problem is thus apparent for both auditory and visual modalities. The subjects in the Moray (1959) and Neisser (1969) experiments were apparently not attending to the secondary channels as they had no awareness of their content, nor could they recall any of the words presented. On the other hand, the subjects must have been attending to them in some sense, since they could detect their names when they occurred.

Hearing (or seeing) one's name turns out not to be the only case where selection on the basis of importance or significance can override selection based on physical parameters. In one well-known experiment, Treisman (1960) again had subjects shadow one of two prose passages presented simultaneously to the two ears. Halfway through the course of a particular trial, however, the message in the primary channel (the one being shadowed) was suddenly switched to the secondary channel (the ignored ear) and vice versa. For example, the subject might be shadowing I LAID THE BOOK ON THE MAHOGANY. . . . heard in the left ear, while ignoring the message THE LION'S SHARE OF STOCK MARKET PROFITS . . . which was simultaneously being presented in the right ear. At this point, however, the messages were switched. In the primary ear the subject now heard GO TO THE LARGE INSTITU-TIONAL INVESTOR . . . while the ignored ear now contained TABLE AND WALKED OUT OF THE LIBRARY.

If the subjects were accurately following their instructions, their shadowing report should have been: "I LAID THE BOOK ON THE MAHOGANY GO TO THE LARGE INSTITUTIONAL INVESTOR." As it turned out, however, subjects' shadowing tended to cross ears to follow the semantic content. That is, they tended to report: "I LAID THE BOOK ON THE MAHOGANY <u>TABLE AND WALKED OUT OF THE LIBRARY</u>." Indeed, a large proportion of the subjects did this without even realizing that they had switched channels until it was pointed out to them. These results could again only be possible if there were some monitoring of the apparently ignored channel.

This nagging paradox appeared in a variety of forms in the early shadowing studies. We mentioned, for example, that subjects will often remain unaware that speech in the ignored ear has been gradually changed from English to another language. We also mentioned that this was less true for bilingual subjects who knew the other language. When Treisman changed from English to French in the ignored ear, but used English–French bilingual subjects, they often would notice the change in the language. This is not to say that they would necessarily be aware of its specific content as they were kept busy shadowing the primary ear. The content would invariably be noticed, however, if the secondary ear contained a slightly delayed, but exact translation, of the English passage being shadowed in the primary ear (Treisman, 1964d).

These indications of some level of semantic processing of unattended channels in the absence of any conscious awareness was later to become the central focus for the opposing theories of the attentional process. We will have more to say on this subject as we begin to discuss these theories in detail.

Split-Span Experiments

A variation on the shadowing experiments, and one which many felt allowed for tighter experimental control of the listening situation, were the so-called split-span studies first conducted by Broadbent (1954, 1958). These experiments had the virtue of eliminating the shadowing requirement which itself is a rather complex task (c.f., Lackner & Garrett, 1972).

In an ordinary study of memory span, a subject might hear a list of perhaps six spoken digits, $\frac{1}{2}$ second (sec) apart, spoken in a monotone. The subjects' task would simply be to wait until the list had finished, and then to report as many of the digits heard as possible, in the correct order. As we know, six digits ordinarily presents no problem to the average young adult. In Broadbent's case, however, the six digits were not presented as a single list. Rather, they were presented dichotically, as three pairs of digits, one member of each pair presented simultaneously to each of the two ears as illustrated below.

LEFT EAR: 4   9   1

RIGHT EAR: 7   2   6

Broadbent's first discovery was that, if left to their own devices, subjects invariably reported digits such as these on an ear-by-ear basis (e.g., 491, 726), rather than pair-by-pair, as in the order of their arrival (e.g., 47, 92, 16). Even more interesting were the results Broadbent obtained when he required subjects to either report ear-by-ear or pair-by-pair. While ear-by-ear report showed relatively good accuracy, subjects in pair-by-pair recall could often report only one or two pairs of digits correctly, and they were often in the wrong order. When one considers that only six digits were involved, there certainly had to be some "bottleneck" in the subjects' attempts to process the digit pairs when they arrived simultaneously.

Based on these studies, Broadbent (1958) theorized that there must be an attentional mechanism that acted much like a switch, or a filter, that could allow the information from only one source at a time to "pass through" to higher levels of processing. If we assume that this filter takes a certain amount of time to switch from one channel, or ear, to another, we could perhaps explain these results in the following way. In ear-by-ear report, the filter is first switched to the information from one ear and these three digits are reported. The filter then switches to the information in the other ear, still being held in their echoic representation, and these are reported. Only one switching operation is thus involved.

For pair-by-pair report, on the other hand, a number of switches of the filter would have to be involved. Thus, in the example above, the subject might begin with the first digit of the left ear (4). To report the simultaneous digit (7) the subject would switch to the echoic trace from the other ear, then back to the first ear for the first member of the second pair (9), then to the other ear for the second member (2), and so on. Again, if we assume that each switch of attention takes a finite amount of time, the echoic trace of the as yet unreported digits would have faded by the time the first few responses had been given. Estimates of this "switching time" from other experiments were in the order of $\frac{1}{6}$ sec (e.g., Cherry & Taylor, 1954). Some additional support for this notion came from the fact that pair-by-pair report is most difficult at faster rates of presentation (e.g., $\frac{1}{2}$ sec between pairs), but becomes as easy as ear-by-ear report at slower rates (e.g., 1 sec between pairs) (Bryden, 1962). At slower rates there would be time to switch attention and code one pair of digits in memory before the arrival of the next pair.

Effects of Physical Parameters versus Meaning. As we shall see in the following section, Broadbent was to develop this simple notion of a single-channel filter into a model of some complexity which would attempt to explain not only the results of his original split-span experiments, but also the results of the shadowing studies as well. Before we temporarily leave the split-span experiments, however, we should ask whether it is also true, as Treisman found for shadowing speech, that meaning can override the physical source of the message.

The answer, according to Gray and Wedderburn (1960), was that it could. Their procedure was to present split-span stimuli which had a meaningful run of speech alternating between the two ears. Imagine, for example, hearing:

LEFT EAR: Dear   9   Jane

RIGHT EAR: 4   Aunt   7

If source of arrival took priority, one would expect subjects' spontaneous reports to be ear-by-ear as, for example, Dear 9 Jane, 4 Aunt 7. In fact, the subjects invariably switched rapidly between the two ears to report either "Dear Aunt Jane, 497," or "497, Dear Aunt Jane," depending on which ear they preferred to begin with.

This rather simple study, conducted by two experimenters who were at that time undergraduates at Oxford University (Broadbent was at Cambridge), was soon followed by supportive evidence for their general finding (Yntema & Trask, 1963). To be sure, these results were ambiguous (cf., Broadbent & Gregory, 1964). On the other hand, these studies did point out that such factors as linguistic context or meaning can take priority over source of arrival. They also raised the first of many questions concerning explanations based on limits imposed by the switching time of a hypothetical filter.

TIME-SHARING MODELS OF ATTENTION

Broadbent's Filter Theory

Broadbent's *filter theory* of selective attention became the most widely known and respected of the general class of single-channel, time-sharing models of attention. It was a theory that gradually evolved over the years with the arrival of new data and new criticisms, and the reader can find a fascinating picture of this evolution in Broadbent's own writings (Broadbent, 1958, 1971). As the dominant theory throughout the 1960s, Broadbent fundamentally saw selective attention as a control process within a structural view of memory along the lines we described at the beginning of the previous chapter.

Figure 6-1 shows the basic elements of a time-sharing model of attention. This diagram departs in some respects from Broadbent's original formulation, primarily in its attempt to represent the structural components in terms now more familiar to most readers. As we describe this model, we will attempt to explain selective listening in the face of competing speech streams as in the "cocktail party." The general principle of time-sharing, however, could apply equally to divided attention between a variety of tasks and modalities.

(1) *Discrimination and channel separation.* The first element of the model, shown here as *discrimination and channel separation,* represents a logically necessary, preliminary process, which must isolate and sepa-

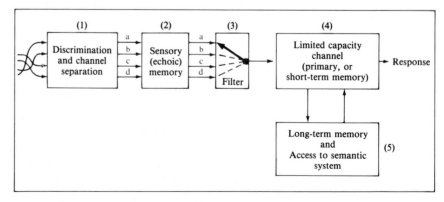

FIGURE 6-1   Basic elements of a time-sharing (filter) model of attention of the sort proposed by Broadbent.
(From Wingfield & Sandoval, 1980.)

rate the conflicting buzz of several voices, music, and so forth, into identifiably different speech streams or *channels*. The use of the term "channel" in this model began with Broadbent and others' early emphasis on the physical characteristics of the speech signals. At a cocktail party, channel separation would be based on the locations of the different voices in the room, their vocal quality, and so forth.

This emphasis on physical characteristics for early discrimination was an important feature of the early time-sharing models, since it was presumed that semantic analysis, analysis for meaning, could not be performed on stimuli not yet passed to higher-levels by the single-channel filter (c.f., Broadbent, 1958; Treisman, 1960, 1964b, c; Treisman & Geffen, 1967). As we hinted, we will have more to say on this point later.

(2) *Sensory (echoic) memory*. The sensory information, now segregated by channels, is held very briefly, in parallel, in the transient form of *sensory (echoic) memory* as described in the previous chapter. Recall that while echoic memory can hold more information than can ever be reported, the form of this storage is sensory in character having yet to receive any analysis for meaning.

We can thus conceptualize echoic memory as holding recent information simultaneously from several channels, with those traces not receiving immediate selection being rapidly lost from the echoic store. The "trick," of course, is to quickly select and code the primary channel for a more durable form of storage before it too fades forever.

(3) *The filter*. The third element, a perceptual *filter*, was the heart of Broadbent's model. Capable of handling only a single channel at a time, the filter could only be switched to pass either one channel or another. We could liken this filter to the channel selector on a TV set which allows the viewer (listener) to see (process) only one channel at a time.

As in the case of TV viewing, one could rapidly switch back and forth between two or more channels to roughly follow what is happening in each. While this periodic sampling might be sufficient if the "programs" were fairly simple in content and slow in rate of delivery, as most TV programs are, the fact that one can only process one channel at a time soon becomes apparent if these conditions are not met.

(4, 5) *Short-term memory and semantic analysis*. To Broadbent, what we have been calling *short-term* or *primary memory* was a "limited capacity channel," in the sense that it could hold only a limited amount of information at a time without becoming overloaded. Indeed, the purpose of the filter in this model was precisely to prevent this potential overload in short-term memory.

Within short-term memory, the information which has been passed by the filter is now categorized as meaningful through access to the semantic system in *long-term memory*. In this form, the material can now either be rehearsed in short-term memory, given as an immediate response (as in shadowing), or be given permanent or relatively permanent storage in long-term memory.

Let us take some representative examples to see how this model would operate in practice. We have already seen in the split-span task how the three digits of each ear would be held simultaneously, as two separate channels, in the sensory echoic store, and how the filter would allow first one channel and then the other to pass into short-term memory for response. Assuming the rapid decay of echoic memory, one would indeed expect channel-by-channel report, with its single switch of the filter, to yield better recall performance than the frequent, and time-consuming, switching between channels for pair-by-pair report. Good performance at slower rates of presentation would be possible since there would be time to switch the hypothetical filter between channels after the presentation of one pair and before the onset of the next pair.

In shadowing experiments, how could a subject detect his or her name if the filter were an absolute one which passed only a single channel? The only possible answer within this theory would be the rapid periodic sampling of the echoic trace of those unattended channels from time to time. For example, if the tape is suddenly stopped in a shadowing experiment, subjects can often report the last few words which had occurred in the unattended ear (Glucksberg & Cowen, 1970; Norman, 1969). This, according to filter theory, would be possible only if the subject is allowed to stop shadowing the primary channel when the recorder is stopped, and to "switch" to the rapidly fading echoic trace of this secondary information.

Thus, our experience of apparently being able to monitor two conversations at one time would have to be the result of periodically switching the filter to the echoic trace of the secondary conversation and then back again to the primary one. Primary and secondary channels are, in this model, a direct consequence of the relative proportions of time the filter dwells on one channel versus the other, a matter which could be under conscious or unconscious control. Since speech is ordinarily quite redundant, the short segments periodically missed from each of the channels could be inferred from our knowledge of linguistic structure and context. Considerable research has shown that speech can in fact be fairly easily followed if small segments are periodically missing from the signal, provided there is sufficient redundancy (e.g., Miller & Licklider, 1950).

Since only the information which gets past the filter can receive any analysis for meaning, the way—the only way—one could "hear" one's name being spoken in a previously ignored channel would be if the filter happened to be sampling that channel at the moment one's name was spoken, or before the immediate echoic trace of that channel had decayed. Does this explanation rely too much on chance? Perhaps so, but remember that in Moray's experiment subjects did not always hear their name when it was spoken in the unattended ear. It was missed some 70% of the time!

This general model is an interesting one, in that it attempts to account for a surprising amount of data, both in the laboratory and outside, within a relatively simple system. One of its implications, of course, is that one can never process two channels simultaneously without some loss of input from both channels. If the two channels contain sufficiently familiar or redundant information, sampling may allow for effective processing of both (e.g., reading a newspaper article in the presence of background music). If both channels have complex information (e.g., reading a textbook while listening to a friend speaking) there will be a dramatic loss of input from one or both, depending on how one chooses to allocate one's processing time.

Before we look more critically at the filter theory, let us take one more experimental example and show how it appears to fit this system. This was a shadowing experiment performed by Treisman (1964a, d), which we mentioned in the previous chapter. As you recall, Treisman began her experiment in the usual way, with two different prose passages, one to each ear, with the subject instructed to shadow the speech from one ear, while ignoring the speech from the other. At a certain point during the shadowing, however, the message in the ignored ear became identical to that in the ear being shadowed. Her subjects had no idea this would happen; they were told that the information in the nonshadowed ear was simply a distractor which should be ignored. Treisman's question was whether, and under what circumstances, her subjects might notice this identity.

Over a series of trials she found that the identical segment could invariably be recognized by the subject if it occurred in the ignored ear within approximately 4.5 sec of its original occurrence in the shadowed ear. When the identical segment began first in the ignored ear, the gap would have to be no greater than 1.4 sec for it to be noticed. As Treisman analyzed these two time spans, it seemed very much as if they represented two different forms of memory.

When the identical segment occurred first in the attended ear, we could assume that it had passed through the filter and was being held in short-term memory just long enough for the shadowing response. Thus, the occurrence of the identical segment in the ignored ear would be noticed so long as it did not exceed the duration of this temporary store (in this case, 4.5 sec). When the identical segment led in the ignored ear, it would presumably be held only in echoic memory and thus, once the time separation exceeded 1.4 sec, the identity would go unnoticed since by that time, the trace would be gone.

We should perhaps have put the word "ignored" in quotations throughout this explanation since logically this information could not have been totally rejected or else the identity could never have been noticed, no matter how small the time separation between the identical segments. (At zero interval, of course, it would have to be noticed as the speech from the shadowed ear would suddenly seem to jump to the middle of the head as the subject would be hearing a single message binaurally.)

How could the subject detect this identity within the filter model? Again, the only way possible within Broadbent's system would be for the filter to periodically sample the ignored message, happening to dwell on the echoic trace of the "rejected" channel when the identical segment occurred.

An Attenuating Filter

For many investigators, especially Anne Treisman at Oxford, the original filter theory seemed to founder precisely on the question of the stage at which stimulus information receives analysis for meaning. As we have seen, both semantic content and linguistic structure can be as effective, or even more effective, in defining a channel than either voice quality or spatial localization (Gray & Wedderburn, 1960; Treisman, 1960). Since, according to filter theory, processing an input for meaning was thought to occur only after it had been selected by the filter for analysis, one is hard pressed to say how meaning could be used as a basis for this initial selection. Clearly, the filter model as it was originally presented needed some drastic modification to be at all viable. At the same time, it would be nice if such a modification could eliminate the necessary coincidence of fortuitous sampling just as one's name, or some other item of interest, occurred in the rejected channel.

At a cocktail party you can easily "tune out" a particular conversation in order to focus full attention on a potentially more important or interesting one.

In order to accommodate these problems, Treisman (1969) offered a major modification to Broadbent's original version of all-or-none analysis on a time-sharing basis. She postulated a similar filter, but one which *attenuated,* rather than completely blocked, all but the relevant channels.

Treisman's notion of "attenuation" involved a very special sense of the term. Many people saw this as a "turning down" of the volume of secondary channels, while allowing the primary channel to be transmitted at full strength. This does convey the general thrust of her proposal, but only if we use it as a rough analogy. The term attenuation was not actually intended to imply that the intensity of unattended channels was reduced. Rather, attenuation in the Treisman modification represented a reduction in the *amount of information* reaching higher levels of analysis from the secondary channels.

Treisman's formulation explains superior performance on the primary channel as due to the passing of its signal through the filter without attenuation. As noted above, some information also passes through the filter from secondary channels, although the amount of information available for further analysis is much less than for the selected channel. The information from secondary channels that reaches the next stage of processing would ordinarily be insufficient to identify more than the gross physical characteristics of the message (e.g., speech versus nonspeech, sex of speaker, location of the sound source). This attenuation of secondary channel information would explain the subject's inability to detect more complex, meaningful information in the ignored ear.

Since the amount of information available from these channels is ordinarily too little to permit identification of content, no memory remains of the message. Occasionally, however, when a word is highly probable in a context, we may respond appropriately even when the information is insufficient to identify that word in isolation. When something is highly probable or significant (e.g., our own name), its recognition threshold would be lower, and we require very little information to specify what was heard. The context of the message or the importance of the word causes a "bias" toward hearing particular items. Thus, very little information may be necessary to produce encodings of these items.

This simple modification to Broadbent's absolute filter would neatly account both for the demonstration that subjects will switch attention between the ears to follow the context of a message (e.g., SITTING AT A MAHOGANY TABLE . . .) and that subjects will recognize that an identical segment is occurring both in the shadowed ear and the ignored ear. This explanation, when applied to her bilingual subjects recognizing a French translation of the shadowed message, would hold that context allowed for recognition even of an attenuated signal.

Treisman's model nevertheless retained much of the spirit of Broadbent's original theory. It was still an explanation based on a perceptual filter, however leaky, and one which switched from one channel to another to follow the subject's interest. That is, once an attenuated message was recognized and determined to be of relevance, the filter would switch to that channel. This channel would now become the primary, unattenuated, channel. Conversely, all of the others, including the originally primary one, would now be attenuated.

Although Broadbent himself came to recognize the utility of her ideas (Broadbent, 1971; Broadbent & Gregory, 1964), the "attenuating filter" did not receive universal acceptance. To put it simply, if all input received some semantic analysis prior to selection, we may be permitted to wonder why one needs the explanatory concept of a filter at all.

Treisman's modification advanced attention theory in a very important way, however. It suggested for the first time that there may be differences in levels of analysis in the processing of simultaneous inputs, and that some analysis for meaning can occur in the absence of conscious attention. It marked the beginnings of a shift away from the simple all-or-none time-sharing schemes to the more dynamic capacity models soon to be discussed.

Further Evidence   While Broadbent's model in its several variations continued to maintain dominance in attention theory for well over a decade, new data and alternative explanations continued to hammer away at the basic notion of a perceptual filter. Some of these alternatives were even radical enough to dismiss the necessity of any perceptual filtering at all, with or without attenuation (c.f., Deutsch & Deutsch, 1963; Yntema & Trask, 1963). While we do not intend to review all of these data, we can cite a few representative examples to give a flavor of these new findings and criticisms. A good place to begin is with Broadbent's own split-span paradigm. Then we will turn to some additional studies of shadowing.

Figure 6-2, taken from a study by Wingfield and Byrnes (1972), shows the essence of Broadbent's split-span results, but this time combined with an additional piece of information not ordinarily associated with split-span experiments. The procedures themselves were quite simple. Subjects heard three pairs of simultaneous digits spoken at a rate of one pair every half-second. In this case a single loudspeaker was used, with the two channels defined by voice quality: One member of each digit pair was spoken by a male speaker and the other by a female. The subjects' task was either to report the three digits spoken by one voice followed by the three digits spoken by the other voice (successive report), or to report the six digits by pairs in their order of arrival (pair-by-pair report).

Figure 6-2 shows results quite similar to those originally obtained by Broadbent (1954), although plotted in a rather unusual way. The height of the bars in the upper panel show average recall performance for successive report to be quite good, with overall accuracy just over 87% correct. The lower panel shows the contrast with pair-by-pair report.

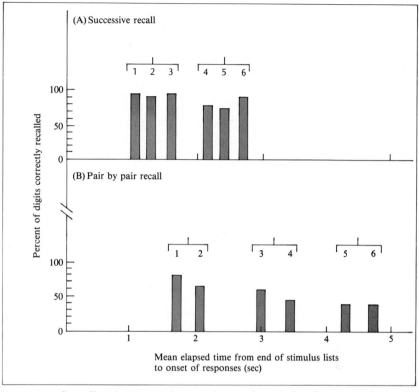

FIGURE 6-2 Accuracy of recall and response latency (mean elapsed time from end of stimulus lists to onset of responses) for each of the six serial positions in successive and in pair-by-pair report.
(From Wingfield & Byrnes, 1972. Copyright © 1972 by the American Association for the Advancement of Science.)

Not only does recall accuracy tend to decrease with the attempt to recall each succeeding pair, but overall performance is generally quite poor, averaging just over 55% correct.

While these results are similar to those usually found in split-span studies, their plotting is unusual in that each of the vertical bars represents the responses in successive and in pair-by-pair report as a function of the average time which elapsed between the end of the lists and the onset of each of the six responses when they were correct. This was made possible through the use of a second tape recorder which, unknown to the subject, would later be used for the measurement of the spontaneous timing of their responses. While the subjects knew they were being recorded, they did not know that their spontaneous timing patterns were of central interest.

With this measure, Figure 6-2 shows not only a difference in level of accuracy, but also a striking difference in the temporal pattern of report under these two conditions. Successive report is characterized by the rapid output of the three digits of one channel, a delay, and then the rapid output of the three digits of the second channel. Pair-by-pair report shows a relatively long initial delay before the report of the first pair of digits, followed by a long delay before the output of the second pair, and then another delay before the output of the third pair. These two patterns were typical for all of the subjects tested.

At first glance, it might appear that alternating between channels on a time-sharing basis could account for these results. The delay between each group of two digits in pair-by-pair report might represent the switching time of our hypothetical filter as it selects two digits from echoic memory for transfer to the output system, while the single longer pause in successive recall would represent the one switch that would be involved between selecting one channel for report and the next.

This explanation, however, would not account for the noticeably longer delay in pair-by-pair report before even the first digit of that pair of responses is produced. It would seem likely that some organization of the response may well be occurring at that point before the first digit in pair-by-pair report is given.

One way to account for these data is suggested by Figure 6-3 which shows the probability of recalling each of the six digits in successive and in pair-by-pair report as a function of the total time each of these six digits actually remained in memory before they were reported. This

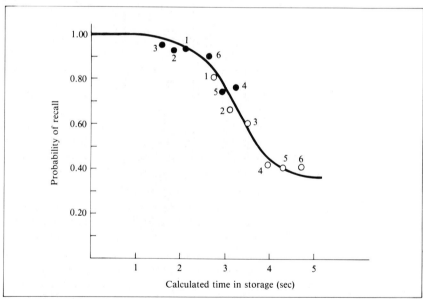

FIGURE 6-3   Probability of recall for successive report (filled circles) and pair-by-pair report (open circles) as a function of calculated time in storage. Numbers along curve indicate actual serial order of responses.
(From Wingfield & Byrnes, 1972. Copyright © 1972 by the American Association for the Advancement of Science.)

information was obtained by carefully measuring the intervals between the instant a subject heard a particular digit and the instant that digit was recalled. You can see that because the output rate in successive recall was so rapid in relation to the original presentation rates of the digits, the third item recalled was actually stored for less time prior to report than the first digit recalled.

Plotting these data on a single time decay curve shows that accuracy of recall for both report strategies seems to be a simple function of how long each item had to remain in memory, regardless of whether recall was successive or pair-by-pair. Note, for example, that when some items in pair-by-pair recall (such as the first and second digits) have remained in memory for about the same time as other items in successive report (such as the fourth and fifth digits), their recall accuracy is roughly equivalent.

To say that pair-by-pair report tends to be less accurate in split-span studies because these responses are on average recalled later than successive report is only part of the answer. There remains the question of why this is so. The beginnings of an answer to this complex question may lie in an earlier study by Savin (1967) who also replicated Broadbent's original experiment with a slight twist. In this case, Savin's subjects heard digit pairs over a single loudspeaker, with both digits spoken by the same voice!

Although, in a sense, all of the items occurred in the same "channel," such that the concept of switching seems inappropriate, Savin's subjects nevertheless still recalled the digits successively. That is, they first recalled one member of each of the three digit pairs in serial order, and then they returned to the beginning of the list to report the remaining three digits of each pair.

While echoic memory has been assumed to store information in parallel, with all simultaneous information registered at the same time, Savin's results imply that the coding, or "readout" from this store into higher levels of analysis is serial: the readout proceeds forward in time. Thus, it might be that entry into, and retrieval from, the higher levels of memory, proceeds most efficiently by grouping items in their serial order of presentation. This postulate would have some ecological validity in that ordinary sound patterns, whether speech or the sound of wind in the trees, are analyzed forward in time and not, as it were, "sideways." Specifically, alternation between simultaneous digit pairs in split-span studies may be difficult not because any switching between perceptual channels is required, but because serially coded information must be drastically reorganized in memory for pair-by-pair report.

Other studies of the split-span task have also offered interpretations in terms of organization and retrieval processes in memory, rather than in terms of perceptual gating (e.g., Byrnes, 1976; Byrnes & Wingfield, 1979; Yntema & Trask, 1963). Other work, such as that of Cherry and Taylor (1954) which originally suggested the notion of a finite switching time in attention, has also yielded to alternative interpretations (e.g., Huggins, 1964; Wingfield, 1977; Wingfield & Wheale, 1975).

Undoubtedly the greatest amount of research, however, has centered on the shadowing task, as numerous investigators produced a variety of imaginative experiments to determine the "fate" of information from an ignored channel. Treisman and Geffen (1967), for example, had subjects shadow speech heard in one ear, while attempting to detect a specific target word that would be embedded in the speech presented to the other ear. Rather than attempting to test retention for any of the words in the ignored ear, subjects merely had to tap a microphone the moment it was heard. Their thought was that this very simple response might be sensitive enough to show some evidence of an analysis of information from the ignored ear.

In fact, Treisman and Geffen found detection rates to be significantly lower when a target word arrived in the unattended ear than in the attended one. To them, and to Broadbent (1971), who later reviewed this work, it seemed that shadowing the primary ear "required the filtering system to close off all inputs from the neglected ear" (p. 151).

Contrary evidence, however, began to arrive from a variety of sources to suggest that information from a secondary channel can receive some level of semantic processing, even though the subject may remain consciously unaware of this information. Lewis (1970), for example, showed that shadowing words in one ear was often delayed when a semantically related word (a synonym) occurred simultaneously in the other ear. Only if the unattended information was receiving some semantic analysis would this have been so.

Similar evidence for some semantic analysis of unattended messages came from McKay (1973) who had subjects shadow ambiguous sentences such as "They threw stones toward the bank yesterday," while the word *money* or the word *river* was simultaneously presented to the other ear. A later recognition test for the meaning for the ambiguous shadowed sentence showed that subjects who had the word *money* presented to the unattended ear were likely to select the sentence, "They threw stones at the savings and loan association yesterday," while those having the word *river* presented to the unattended ear were more likely to choose, "They threw stones toward the side of the river yesterday." The supposedly ignored message, therefore, determined the interpretation of the information in the attended ear.

Other investigators used a verbal conditioning paradigm to explore the fate of the unattended channels. Their first step was to present a particular word followed by a mild electric shock, and to keep pairing presentations of the word and the shock until subjects showed a reliable galvanic skin response (GSR) to the sound of the word alone. When this conditioned word was later presented in an unattended ear during a shadowing experiment, subjects had no conscious awareness of its occurrence. A detectable GSR could nevertheless often be observed. There have also been reports of finding a GSR (of a lesser magnitude) to the occurrence of words meaningfully related to the conditioned word when presented in an unattended ear (Corteen & Wood, 1972; Von-Wright, Anderson, & Stenman, 1975).

To many, it seemed clear that material from an apparently unattended channel can receive some level of semantic analysis, a finding quite inconsistent with the all-or-none notion of a time-sharing filter theory. Could we not argue that rapid attention switching for brief periods to sample from the unattended channel could account for these results? The answer is probably a cautious "yes," however strained an account this might be. What these data seem to illustrate is that semantic analyses can indeed occur without conscious awareness or recollection even moments after the analysis has occurred, a finding as compatible with Broadbent's sampling filter as with any other model.

Interestingly, however, there has seemed to be very little impetus in the field to continue these arguments. Attempts to salvage the filter theory gave way to newer, more novel approaches to the question of attention. This newer look, which we have summarized as "capacity" models of attention, began to ask new questions, and to introduce new experimental paradigms.

CAPACITY MODELS OF ATTENTION

Broadbent's filter theory fit very nicely within the context of a structural stores view of information processing. To highlight the elements of his position, he saw the processing of simultaneous inputs as possible only by rapidly switching attentional focus first to one input and then to another on a time-sharing basis. To Broadbent, selective attention was the consequence of perceptual filtering which would help to reduce the flood of simultaneous inputs all of which would surely overload the cognitive system if each were to receive simultaneous analysis.

It seemed to many only reasonable to postulate this early rejection. It certainly would be uneconomical to expend mental energy on a full analysis of stimuli only to later reject some of them. Early rejection also seemed logical because it was hard to envisage multiple inputs receiving any semantic analysis without conscious awareness of this analysis or of its consequences.

There were, in fact, a number of hints in the early literature that all of these assumptions, as reasonable as they might have seemed, were wrong. Deutsch and Deutsch (1963) and Norman (1968) began to argue for the principle of an automatic, and fairly complete processing of multiple inputs, only some of which would reach the level of conscious awareness. To be sure, there was selectivity in which inputs would reach awareness, but this selection was seen as occurring much later in the information processing sequence than Broadbent's filter theory would ever envisage.

To understand this position, let us consider another analogy with the modern digital computer. Broadbent's analogy, you will recall, concentrated on its time-sharing characteristics. This second analogy concentrates instead on the operations which are performed on this input. In a series of developing arguments, Moray (1967, 1969) suggested the notion of a single pool of processing resources analogous to the capacity or "space" available in a modern digital computer. When we wish to use a computer to solve a problem or to analyze data, two sorts of information must be programmed into the machine. The first represents the instructions given to the computer on the analyses to be performed on our data, and the detailed specification of how these instructions will be carried out. Only then do we program in the second item of information, the data itself.

Although users are often not aware of the fact, even the largest computers have a finite upper limit on the amount of information they can accommodate at any one time. The more complex the instructional program detailing the operations to be performed on the data, the less space there will be available for storing the data itself. Conversely, the more data the computer must store, the less space will be available for the operating routines.

By analogy, Moray suggested that we could view sensory input, and the operations to be performed on this input, as both competing for a limited pool of available resources or "capacity." For example, if the input is of poor quality, or is degraded in some way, a considerable amount of available capacity would have to be allocated for its perceptual analysis. As a direct result of this, little capacity would remain for any operations you might wish to perform on the results of this analysis. Conversely, if the specific operations you want to perform require complex cognitive operations, relatively little capacity would be available for the analysis of new incoming stimuli. In principle, parallel processing, the ability to do two things at one time, could be possible, provided the total capacity is not exceeded by the combined demands of the task requirements and the analysis of the sensory input.

Within this simple framework we have the essence of a capacity model of attention as distinct from the single-channel time-sharing model envisaged by Broadbent. Here in review are its major elements.

1. Simultaneous inputs can sometimes be processed in parallel on what might be termed a "space-sharing" basis. Some processing can be conducted on all information available in sensory memory: there is no perceptual switching out, turning off, or attenuation of one channel or another. One can indeed hear one's name on an unattended channel (Moray, 1959, 1960) or follow semantic context as it crosses channels (Treisman, 1960).

2. There is, however, a single pool of processing resources (capacity) that must be allocated proportionally among all incoming stimuli and the operations to be performed on them. When the number of stimuli requiring analysis exceeds the limits of this capacity, task priorities are set by the individual and the limited processing resources are distributed accordingly. In this way, some stimuli will receive fairly

complete analyses and some will receive only superficial analysis. Only those stimuli receiving the most complete analysis and elaborative operations will be available to conscious memory or awareness.

3. While complex processing of a primary channel might not leave sufficient capacity for complete processing of a secondary channel, the lower level processing it does receive might be sufficient to detect the relevance of one's name, a cry of warning, or to recognize relevance on the basis of preceding context. With this recognition would come a reallocation of the limited resources to the deeper processing of this now relevant channel.

It Takes Attention to Pay Attention

We can give a fairly good feeling for the general idea of a capacity model of attention with a demonstration reported some years ago by Johnston and Heinz (1974). The experiment begins in a now very familiar way: A subject is given stereophonic earphones and is told to shadow speech heard in one ear, and to ignore speech heard in the other.

Johnston and Heinz's experiment, however, added a new dimension to the standard shadowing task. While shadowing one of these two messages, the subjects also had to carefully watch a small light placed within their field of vision. They were told that at random moments this light would suddenly change its intensity, growing brighter or dimmer. The instant this change in intensity occurred, they were to press a response button as quickly as possible. Their reaction times to this detection were carefully recorded. At no time during this reaction time response, however, were they to stop or even to slow their shadowing.

Not surprisingly, most subjects found this task quite difficult, and this difficulty was reflected directly in their reaction times to detecting the intensity change of the stimulus light. Reaction times were significantly longer when subjects had to simultaneously shadow the speech as compared with a control condition where only the light had to be monitored without the presence of accompanying speech.

The speech passages the subjects heard were of course initially unfamiliar to them and thus, in the sense of the capacity notion, their shadowing required considerable resource allocation. The consequence of this heavy draw on processing resources would have been a corresponding reduction in resources available for the reaction time task. Hence, more time was required to perform these responses.

Following this logic one might expect that if subjects were allowed to hear and shadow the same passage a number of times their familiarity would reduce the amount of processing resources required for accurate shadowing. This in turn should be reflected in increasingly more rapid reaction times to the light stimulus as more processing resources became available for that task. Johnston and Heinz (1974) report just this finding, and other studies using analogous procedures have added experimental support for this general capacity principle (Johnston & Heinz, 1978; Wingfield & Sandoval, 1980).

Notice the shift in the kind of experiment we are now describing from those discussed in previous sections. Investigations of filter theory tended to employ paradigms which either explicitly or implicitly emphasized *selective* attention. That is, they contrived tasks, such as the dichotic shadowing paradigm, which would require complete concentration on a single channel. It was the subject's ability to block distracting stimuli that was in fact the primary focus of study. What these studies systematically discouraged was *divided attention,* the use of paradigms which might specifically encourage subjects to try to perform two tasks at once. Thus, the questions that were asked very much determined the kinds of experiments that were performed.

Studies of divided attention, or "dual task interference" studies as they are sometimes called, do not of course unambiguously *prove* the occurrence of simultaneous processing. The possibility of some form of alternation of attention can never be completely dismissed so long as there is any possibility that input rates could allow two tasks to be accomplished by intermittent sampling, or where grouping in response organization could periodically leave a single channel free for alternate processing of the multiple stimuli. Such arguments have been cogently made by, for example, Fisher (1975a, b), and by Welford (1977).

Nevertheless, one begins to see with these studies a subtle change in the meaning of attention. Attention is no longer viewed as an "act," where one "attends" to this stimulus and does "not attend" to another. Rather, one begins to see attention in the sense of a process in which attentional resources may be shared among various inputs and the operations being performed on these inputs. We begin to see the concept of attention as a single pool of limited resources being allocated on a priority basis to stimulus analysis, response decisions, or indeed, simply holding these stimuli in memory for some later response. In this sense, we could indeed say that it takes attention to pay attention (Johnston & Heinz, 1974).

Kahneman's Model of Attentional Allocation.   The general principle of a capacity model of attention was presented in its most complete form by Kahneman (1973), who was also one of the first to emphasize the potential flexibility of resource allocation. To Kahneman (1973), a capacity theory must deal with three essential questions: (1) What makes an activity more or less demanding? (2) What factors control the total amount of capacity available at any one time? (3) What rules govern the allocation policy for distributing these attentional resources? (p. 10). To answer these questions, Kahneman organized them in the form of the model diagramed in Figure 6-4.

The first feature to notice is that Kahneman's model is not a flow chart showing a linear order of information processing of the sort we offered in Figure 6-1. In Kahneman's (1973) words, it is a control diagram that simply describes the relations of influence and control

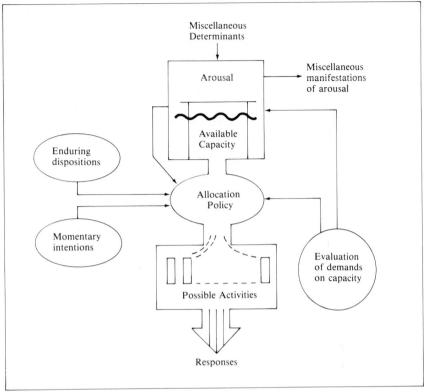

FIGURE 6-4   The basic elements of Kahneman's (1973) model of attentional allocation. (From Daniel Kahneman, *Attention and Effort*, © 1973, p. 10. Reprinted by permission of Prentice-Hall, Inc., Englewood Cliffs, New Jersey.)

between components of an overall system (p. 11). Specifically, it treats "attention" as a processing capacity, or degree of effort. Kahneman (1973) states:

> Different mental activities impose different demands on the limited capacity. An easy task demands little effort, and a difficult task demands much. When the supply of attention does not meet the demands, performance falters, or fails entirely. (p. 9)

The idea of flexibility in allocation implies that one could choose to allocate one's resources, or effort, almost entirely on just one of several *possible activities* such as processing stimulus inputs, holding their analyses in memory, or organizing a complex response. Alternatively, we could divide these same limited resources more evenly across all of these activities. The first allocation strategy would yield superior performance in one of these activities at the expense of the others. For example, deep processing of speech heard in one ear could be performed at the expense of remembering what was heard in the other ear. The second strategy would allow some success at several simultaneous activities, but no one activity would have sufficient resources for more than low level performance.

Our decision in these cases would be determined by our *allocation policy*. This allocation policy would be influenced by evaluating the *capacity demands* which are required by the various activities, our *momentary intentions,* such as a decision to focus on one conversation versus another at any given time, or our *enduring predispositions,* such as paying attention when someone says our name.

To Kahneman, available capacity is limited, but it is not necessarily fixed. When tasks become difficult and/or motivation is high, there may be an increase in physiological arousal, alertness, and effort. Kahneman's view of attention as the amount of cognitive effort we are willing to allocate to a task thus narrows the historical separation between attention in its context of a selective analysis, and attention as physiological arousal or alertness.

The wavy line in the available capacity area of Figure 6-4 was Kahneman's way of representing the relationship of level of arousal and resource availability. Generally, the higher the arousal level, within the limits of the Yerkes–Dodson law, the greater will be the capacity pool on which multiple operations could draw. For example, a state of overload in which the demands of ongoing activities exceed the available capacity could induce a compensatory increase in both arousal and capacity.

Thus, within certain upper limits, the capacity available at any one time for subsequent allocation among activities is a combined function of arousal, effort, and the demands placed on capacity by these concurrent activities. Note, however, that while Kahneman does not view capacity as fixed, he does not represent it as an unlimited resource. Increasing effort will not produce an infinite increase in resources and consequent improvement in performance. Indeed, Kahneman emphasizes throughout the limiting factor of the Yerkes–Dodson law: Too high a state of arousal can lead to stress, anxiety, and a deterioration in performance.

Within the context of the capacity notion we can now reanalyze the earlier shadowing experiments, some of which showed what appeared to be absolute gating of the unattended ear, and others which implied some degree of semantic analysis. As Lachman, Lachman, and Butterfield (1979) put the position, the shadowing studies could be reinterpreted as representing the performance of two tasks at once: doing one thing with the attending ear and another with the unattended ear. As they note, this is hardly the way filter theorists viewed the task! (p. 203).

To make their point, Lachman, et al., cite an ingenious study reported by Zelniker (1971). As people were shadowing speech heard in their unattended ear, their own voices were passed through a delayed feedback apparatus and then fed, a fraction of a second later, into their unattended ear. It has long been known that delayed feedback of one's own voice produces a general hesitation and disruption of speech which sounds not unlike stuttering (Huggins, 1968). If, as the filter theory suggests, the unattended ear is perceptually gated while concentration is given fully to the attended ear, we should expect no interference of the delayed feedback in the unattended ear on shadowing performance.

Zelniker's experiment was especially interesting in that she used both children and adults, and listening tasks which would either be easy or difficult to shadow. The easy task required simply repeating a set of numbers, while the difficult task required repeating one set of numbers while also attending to another set which followed them. Although we might be reluctant to make any predictions about the difference in performance between children and adults in this task, we would expect a difference between easy and difficult shadowing tasks. The harder the shadowing task, according to the capacity notion, the greater the amount of capacity would have to be allocated to the attended ear. Hence, the less capacity should be available for processing the unattended ear. That is, a harder shadowing task should show less "stuttering" disruption in shadowing than with the easier task. Note again a capacity model's emphasis on degree of processing as opposed to a processing–no processing dichotomy.

Table 6-1 shows a summary of Zelniker's results. As a model of capacity allocation might predict, there is a difference between "stuttering" frequency when the shadowing task was easy or difficult, and this difference holds for both the adults and the children tested. When the shadowing task was easy, subjects would appear to have involuntarily allocated their spare capacity to the unattended ear, thus processing the delayed signal with its disastrous effect. When the speech materials were harder to shadow, a greater proportion of resources would have been allocated to the attended ear leaving less spare capacity for processing the unattended, delayed, ear. The interference of this material on shadowing fluency was thus correspondingly reduced.

This experiment and its interpretation by Lachman, et al. shows the essence of a capacity expectation of an attentional phenomenon. Interpretations are based not on an attention-filtered dichotomy, but on the

TABLE 6-1 The mean frequency of "stuttering" when delayed auditory feedback was fed to the unattended ear when the shadowing task for the attended ear was either easy or difficult.
(From Zelniker, 1971. Copyright © 1971 by the American Psychological Association. Reprinted by permission.)

| | Attention Condition | |
| | Easy
Shadowing Task | Difficult
Shadowing Task |
Group		
Adults	.046	.020
Children	.124	.069

relative *degree* of processing and the relative amount of resources such processing requires.

**What Requires
Capacity?**

One of the questions we are bound to ask about capacity models.of attention is whether all cognitive operations (e.g., stimulus detection, memory storage, response execution) require equal draw on resource capacity. A second, even more fundamental question, is whether all cognitive activities require access to a single, central pool of limited capacity (Kerr, 1973).

Structural Interference and Independent Channels.   At the time of this writing there is unfortunately little consensus even among capacity theorists as to whether or not attention is best characterized as a single undifferentiated pool of processing resources for which all cognitive activities must compete. In an extreme case, for example, Allport, Antonis, and Reynolds (1972) and McLeod (1977, 1978) have argued for a *multiprocessor model* of attention. This sees a number of independent channels which can simultaneously carry on analyses in different input modalities with no interference across these separate activities. These investigators, of course, recognize that doing two things at once does usually lead to lower performance than full concentration on a single activity. This, however, they see as primarily a consequence of the effort required to keep the separate response streams from confusion, rather than as evidence that all processes require access to the same central pool of resources.

Part of our problem is that it is easy to demonstrate what seems to be simultaneous, or "parallel," operations. For example, Shiffrin and Grantham (1974) have shown that people can attend to, and detect, slight changes in three separate modalities (a faint light, a faint tone, and a weak vibration on the skin) just as easily as they can detect one. Similarly, practiced subjects in highly skilled tasks such as typing while taking dictation, or playing music while simultaneously sight-reading, can apparently learn to perform simultaneous tasks with little or no decrement (Allport, et al. 1972; Shaffer, 1975; Spelke, Hirst & Neisser, 1976). The question, of course, is whether these separate operations fail to interfere because they draw on different structures each with its own resource capacity, or whether all draw on a single pool of resources but require such minimal resources that this draw does not affect overt level of performance on other tasks. This is not an easy question to answer.

Some theorists, for example, have suggested that only response selection and execution require capacity (e.g., Deutsch & Deutsch, 1963; Norman, 1968), while the processes of perceptual analysis of the competing stimuli do not. Posner and Boies (1971) came to this conclusion using a visual–auditory divided attention task analogous to the previously described experiment by Johnston and Heinz. Let us look closely at this experiment, and how it illustrates an attempt to isolate the finer elements of attentional allocation in an empirical way.

The experiment to be described is based on an extensive series of studies conducted by Posner and his colleagues involving the task of seeing letters of the alphabet and saying simply whether they are the "same" or "different" (Posner & Boies, 1971; Posner & Keele, 1967; Posner & Klein, 1973).

In one such experiment (Posner & Boies, 1971), the subject experiences the following sequence of events. First a warning signal is presented. Then, .5 seconds later, a single letter of the alphabet is visually presented. Finally, one sec after that, a second letter is presented. The two letters might be physically identical, such as two capital letter *A*s. Alternatively, the second letter might be physically different, but have the same name, such as when the first letter is a capital *A* and the second letter is a small *a*. Our discussion will focus on this condition since it represents the one of greater complexity: the subject must identify and retrieve the letter names from memory, since it is the letter names, not merely their physical form, that must be the basis for the identity judgement.

If the subject decides that the two letters are the same (in half the cases they would be different) an appropriately marked button would have to be pressed as quickly as possible. This would be done with one hand.

At various points during the presentation sequence subjects were also required to engage in a secondary task of detecting an auditory tone. On hearing the tone, which might occur at any time, the subject was to quickly press a detection key with the other hand. In spite of the fact that these two tasks involved different modalities, it could be that both require access to the same central capacity. To the extent that this is true, the complexity of the letter-matching task should interfere with tone detection and this, in turn, should be reflected in longer reaction times to the tone stimuli.

Figure 6-5 shows a summary of their results relevant to this question. As we move along the horizontal axis beginning with tones presented just before and after the warning signal, we see that the presence of the warning reduces reaction times to tones presented just after that warning. This is precisely what Kahneman's arguments would lead one to expect as the subject becomes alerted for the presentation of the first letter. Becoming alert for the presence of the letter would increase general arousal and the availability of ready resources for all incoming information and operations. In this case, the readiness applies to tone detection as well as letter presentation.

To the extent that identifying and retrieving the name of the first letter as it occurs draws on a central resource capacity, so we would expect to see an increase in reaction times when the secondary task of tone detection was required at this critical point. Surprisingly, Figure 6-5 shows that this is not so. Reaction times to tone detection were no longer when tones were presented at this point, or even 300 milliseconds (msec) later, than when they occurred before the first letter. To Posner

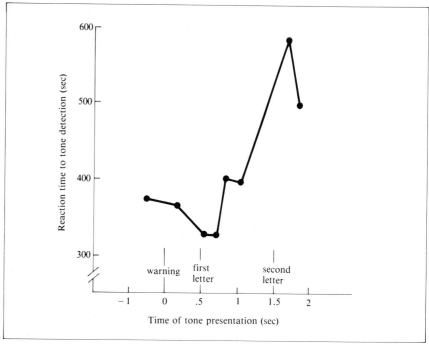

FIGURE 6-5   Reaction times to detecting an auditory tone when it occurred at various points during the course of matching visually presented letters to decide whether they had the same name identity.
(Adapted from Posner & Boies, 1971. Copyright © 1971 by the American Psychological Association. Reprinted by permission.)

and Boies, the process of identifying and retrieving the name did thus not appear to draw on central capacity.

We start to see our first increase in reaction time only when the tone occurs just before the presentation of the second letter. This would seem to imply the allocation of some resources as the subject attempts to hold the first letter in memory, or perhaps begins to visualize the second letter that he or she thinks might be seen (Posner, 1973, p. 136). This increase, however, is a small one. As we see from Figure 6-5, the really sharp increase in reaction times appear when the tone is presented shortly after presentation of the second letter. It is at this point that a response decision is presumably being made, and it is here that we see the first evidence for a really significant draw on a central capacity.

Posner and Boies' conclusion that perceptual identification of a stimulus does not require processing capacity has been strongly questioned by a number of writers for a variety of reasons (e.g., McLeod, 1978). One of the reasons to question their interpretation is the possibility that the initial identification of familiar, overlearned stimuli such as letters drew too little capacity to be reflected in a measure as relatively crude as a simple increase in manual reaction time. There seems little argument, however, that response decisions and execution, along with active maintenance of the stimuli in memory, do require access to a common pool of resources. And, if we accept Posner and Boies' interpretation, these resources must be shared whether the stimuli involve visual, auditory, or mixed presentations. The conflict between this view and the multiprocessor model is thus quite clear.

Automaticity and Capacity Allocation.   While it can be argued that all cognitive activities require some attentional capacity, those which are sufficiently well practiced may require very little. We saw an illustration of this point in Johnston and Heinz' experiment when reaction times in a secondary task became more rapid when the speech passages being shadowed became more familiar. Indeed, we certainly encounter this in everyday experience. We ordinarily have no difficulty in walking and talking at the same time, or, as in a previous example, talking while driving a car.

The term *automaticity* has been used to describe those tasks which have become so well practiced as to demand little capacity or, perhaps, to bypass the limited capacity system entirely. Such "automatic" activities have also been characterized by their speed and their performance without apparent conscious awareness (LaBerge & Samuels, 1974; Shiffrin & Schneider, 1977a).

When we think of automaticity in terms of Kahneman's emphasis on arousal and performance, however, we must reemphasize an important qualification. Very high states of arousal can go beyond the optimum level for task performance when this increased arousal results in stress, anxiety, or panic. In such cases, we can often witness a breakdown in even highly practiced skills. Norman (1976), for example, cites a report that all of the drownings of skin divers off the California coast and inland lakes in one year had one thing in common. All of the divers were found still wearing their weighted belts! Although trained to drop these heavily weighted belts to make it easier to remain on the surface when in trouble, their panic (or the cost of the belts?) seems to have overridden their training (Bachrach, 1970).

With the questions of task demands, automaticity, and capacity allocation, we now see a picture of attention which is far broader and more complex than the single-channel perceptual filter envisaged by a simple time-sharing model. Many questions, however, still remain. An important attempt to unify a number of disparate research findings within a single formulation has been offered by Norman and Bobrow (1975). They offer a way of conceptualizing the trade-off between the difficulty of the tasks themselves, and the resources we are willing, or able, to devote to their execution.

FLEXIBILITY AND TASK DEMANDS

How could apparently similar sets of experimental data lead to so many divergent theories and conceptualizations? Partly, as we have tried to suggest, paradigms which demand focused attention can easily lead to different directions for explanations than tasks which encourage a division of attention. To Norman and Bobrow (1975), however, the primary problem lay in the appropriateness of our measures and the adequacy of our paradigms to get beneath the surface of the data collected. To illustrate this point, Norman and Bobrow stress that in any task, or tasks, the level of performance we observe may be either *resource-limited* or *data-limited*.

Data-Limited versus Resource-Limited Processes

Resource-Limited Processes. As proponents of a capacity model of attention, Norman and Bobrow assume that resources are always limited. Whenever we are required to perform several operations at once, these limited resources must be proportionally allocated among them. The greater the proportional share of resources devoted to one task, the less there will be for the performance of others.

Generally, in performing some fairly complex cognitive task, we would expect—at least up to some limit—that the level of performance will improve with the amount of resources, or effort, given to that task. If we apply too few resources, or if the available resources must be shared with another task, we would expect performance to be relatively poor: The greater the proportion of allocated resources, the better should be the level of performance.

Whenever we conduct an experiment in which a continuous increase in effort, or processing resources, yields a continual improvement in performance, we can say that the task is *resource-limited:* the upper limits on the speed, accuracy, or quality of performance are set only by the amount of resources we are willing or able to apply to it.

Data-Limited Processes. There are some tasks, however, in which the stimuli we are to analyze are of such poor quality that no amount of additional resources would improve the overall level of performance. You may, for example, have had the experience of trying to follow speech on a poorly tuned radio station, perhaps further degraded by a heavy amount of static. No matter how hard you try, no matter how much capacity you may allocate, the task remains virtually impossible. In cases such as this, when the upper limit on performance is determined solely by the quality of the data, we say that the task is *data-limited*.

If you have ever tried to understand a badly tuned station, you know that there often can be an improvement in performance with additional effort. We can strain just that little bit harder, try to pick out just a few words, and then use the context to attempt some intelligent guesses about what was being said. Another way of saying this is that most tasks, even ones with a poor quality stimulus, are resource-limited up to some point: up to some point your performance is limited only by the amount of resources you are willing or able to devote. It is only beyond this point that we can say the task is data-limited.

As we think about data-limited processes, we can see that they can be represented in more than one way. The example just given relates to an upper limit on performance imposed by the quality of the stimulus itself.

Norman and Bobrow would refer to this as a task which is *signal data-limited*. We can, however, contemplate other data limits, such as those present in many of the memory paradigms discussed in previous chapters. Anyone who has ever taken a difficult examination knows that an attempt to retrieve information is, at least to some point, a resource-limited process. It often happens that when you try that little bit harder before giving up, you can remember more than you thought you ever could. But there can reach a point where the facts are just not available. The only way your performance could possibly be improved were if the memory itself were improved. Norman and Bobrow would refer to this case as *memory data-limited*.

Data-Resource Interactions. To illustrate the implications of this distinction in a more concrete way, we could plot an idealized graph which shows the level of performance we might expect to see on a task as a subject gradually increases the level of resources they devote to the task. What we might expect to see is shown in Figure 6-6. This graph shows a smooth, monotonic increase in performance level as we increase the proportion of available resources allocated to a hypothetical task. The shaded area to the right of the graph marks what must always be some upper limit on available resources, such that, in principle, performance would have to cease to improve when this level is reached.

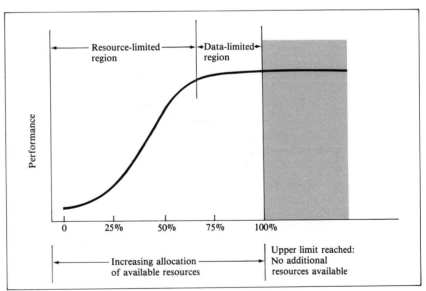

FIGURE 6-6 The performance-resource function. Performance is an increasing function of the amount of processing resources allocated within the resource-limited region. Performance within the data-limited region is independent of the expenditure of processing resources. Shaded area indicates upper limit on available resources. (Adapted from: Norman & Bobrow, 1975.)

Note, however, that our curve reaches its maximum level before this point. Even as additional effort is brought to the task, no further improvement is observed. It is at this point, Norman and Bobrow argue, that the process has ceased to become resource-limited and has now become data-limited.

In practice, one would never expect to see a performance curve continue to rise indefinitely. Any performance curve will begin to flatten as we reach a practical ceiling on performance. In other words, one cannot exceed 100% correct on an ordinary memory test, and reaction times can never become faster than allowed by physical limitations on movement speed. In principle, however, a performance curve could continue to show considerable improvement within the resource-limited range, so long as we have appropriately sensitive measures of performance. For example, a simple measurement of reaction time, or number of words correctly shadowed are both measures which can fail to reveal what might be continued improvement in the quality of performance. If we had a truly adequate measurement, however, the asymptote of any such performance function would always represent the point at which the process becomes data-limited. (Readers interested in this important question of adequacy of measurement and distinguishing between a data-limited transition and a simple "ceiling" effect are invited to read a paper by Kantowitz and Knight, 1976, which raises this issue, and the reply by Norman and Bobrow, 1976.)

In general, Norman and Bobrow argue that whenever the amount of resources allocated are less than the amount allocated at the point where performance becomes data-limited, we can say, by definition, that the process is resource-limited. Thus, by looking at performance curves such as that in Figure 6-6, called a *performance–resource function*, one could in principle quickly tell whether performance on a particular task is primarily resource-limited or data-limited. We said, however, that Figure 6-6 was an idealized graph. It was idealized in the sense that it shows hypothetical performance across the full range of degrees of effort beginning, as it were, at a zero point representing no effort at all.

In reality, one never does conduct experiments in which the subject has exerted zero effort. We always attempt to motivate our subjects to perform to at least some minimal level of effort, just as we ordinarily do not expect our subjects to give their full conceivable range of effort. We do not expect to push our subjects to the stress end of the Yerkes–Dodson curve, or to drop unconscious from exhaustion. Rather, in most experiments, we look at the middle range of effort, perhaps forgetting as we do so, what a relatively narrow range this is. We frequently, in other words, look at our subject's performance through a rather narrow window indeed.

The effects of this state of affairs in Norman and Bobrow's view is illustrated in Figure 6-7 which shows three sets of performance–resource functions as they might be observed in any experiment (the solid lines in the middle region), and as they might be in theory if we examined performance either below or above the usual range of effort (the dotted lines in the shaded areas).

Let us review what our graph shows. The picture we now have is of two shaded areas of unobserved data: one on the left representing minimal effort, and one on the right representing an upper limit on resources which cannot be exceeded no matter how hard our subject tries. What we observe in our experiment, of course, is only the middle, unshaded area: the range of resource allocation examined. Let us see what Figure 6-7 can reveal.

The upper curve, labeled *data-limited process,* would appear to show a task in which performance is independent of resources: It fails to improve even with the application of increasing resources. Seeing only this middle portion within our range of measurement, we might be erroneously inclined to assume that resource capacity is irrelevant to task performance. In the case of filter theory, we would say that the processing was either all-or-none. As we have seen, however, a task will

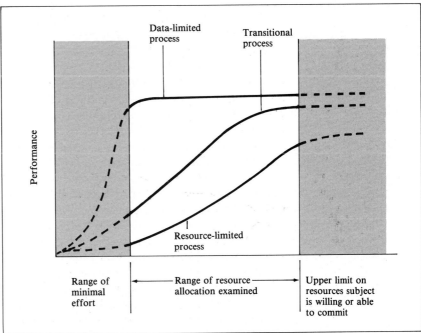

FIGURE 6-7   Observable classes of performance–resource functions. When processes are examined only over a limited range of resource allocation, some will appear to be independent of resources (because they are data-limited in the region under consideration), others will appear to require indefinite amounts of resources (because they are resource-limited within this region), and others will be in a transition between data- and resource-limited operation.
(Adapted from Norman & Bobrow, 1975.)

only show itself to be resource-limited (i.e., influenced by the amount of resources allocated) up to the point where it becomes data-limited. In the case of this top function, that point was simply reached rather quickly such that, over the area of measurement, we observe only a flat line.

The lowest curve, labeled *resource-limited process*, could equally give you the impression that limits do not exist. Except in this case, it would be the data limits which would be overlooked. It would appear that performance is limited only by the resources you are willing or able to dedicate. As we look at the shaded portion on the right, however, we can see that this curve would eventually asymptote as the task becomes data-limited; it is resource-limited only within the range examined.

Finally, the middle curve shows the idealized function as we saw it in Figure 6-6, where the *transition process*, the point at which the operation ceases to be resource-limited and now becomes data-limited, is clearly revealed within our range of measurement. Only under these ideal conditions would the full interaction between data quality and resource allocation be revealed.

As capacity theorists, Norman and Bobrow believe that operations which share the same limited resource pool will only appear to interfere with each other when the total available capacity has been exceeded. What they wish to demonstrate with this analysis is how the generality of this interaction could have been overlooked by earlier theorists. The general principle they wish to imply is a relatively simple one. The filter model assumed a failure to recall material from a nonattended ear, or even to detect the presence of a target word in that ear (e.g., Treisman & Geffen, 1967), must have been due to a total blocking or attenuation of the input from that channel. Norman and Bobrow would argue that this was an erroneous rule drawn from an extreme and exceptional case.

Let us illustrate this with the Treisman and Geffen experiment in which subjects were required to shadow speech in one ear while attempting to detect specific target words in the other ear. If we assume that the subjects considered the shadowing of the speech in the attended ear to be the primary task, we can further assume that this task drew on whatever resources were necessary for good performance. Since rapid and accurate shadowing is a rather complex activity, such a draw on available resources must have been a very heavy one. As a consequence of this heavy allocation, the resources available for operations on the secondary task (detecting target words in the other ear) would have been equal to the total available resources *minus* those devoted to the primary task. In this particular case, the low detection rates reported by Treisman and Geffen indicates that insufficient resources were available for adequate detection.

Were we to increase the resources available for performing the secondary task (e.g., by using familiar speech materials for shadowing), one might well expect to see some improvement in detecting target words in the unattended ear. This clear trade-off would be expected to appear, however, only if both tasks lie in the resource-limited region. Only within this region would we expect to see evidence of interference between these two tasks. A data-limited secondary task (one which is relatively easy and hence quickly reaches its data-limited point) would be expected to show minimal interference. A case in point is the generally high detection rate we described earlier for pure tones presented with speech in an unattended ear. The ability to distinguish between a pure tone and speech is so much easier than identifying words that the process quickly becomes data-limited. Thus, just as in the Posner and Boies letter identification experiment, high performance levels and an apparent absence of interference could lead to the erroneous conclusion that a sharing of attentional resources was not involved.

Within this framework, Norman and Bobrow also tried to show how two tasks can seemingly be performed at one time. In this context one thinks of examples of automaticity, such as holding a conversation while driving a car, or performing a well-practiced piece of music while simultaneously sight-reading. As we have seen, if tasks are sufficiently familiar they can be performed relatively automatically and hence require fewer resources which might potentially be allocated to other activities.

Early versus Late Selection: Take Your Choice

We know from our own experience that we are never fully conscious of all the sensations that continually bombard our senses. There is a limiting factor, a "bottleneck" if you like, that prevents some inputs from achieving conscious awareness and which allows others to reach this point. As we have seen, the time-sharing models of attention saw this in structural terms as a fixed, single-channel filter at the level of perception. The later capacity models were no less persuaded of the notion of a bottleneck, but they saw a flexible system which determines, perhaps on a moment to moment basis, not which stimuli are processed, but what one does with the stimuli, how deeply each is processed relative to the others.

Could one argue that there may be an element of truth in both positions? That is, could it be that attentional operations have a degree of flexibility such that one could reject a stimulus either "early" or "late," depending on which is optimal for a particular task? Can you in fact take your choice? This position has in fact recently been taken (Johnston & Heinz, 1978, 1979).

Like Kahneman and other capacity theorists, Johnston and Heinz see attention as a process which requires capacity. They further propose, however, that subjects have some strategic options in how they will handle the binding trade-off between selectivity and breadth. Early selection is one option and it would reduce the amount of information competing for our limited resources. Since selectivity itself requires capacity, however, early selection can be accomplished only at the expense of the very commodity it is designed to conserve. The trade-off, in other words, must be a tight one. The investment of capacity on early selection may nevertheless be a sound one whenever simple selection criteria can be used and sufficient residual capacity remains to satisfy any task requirements there may be for a secondary task.

Within this trade-off notion one can find a new perspective on Neisser's (1967) distinction between preattentive processes and focal attention, and also between the "early" versus "late" selection dichotomy typified by filter theories versus the typical capacity models. Rather than seeing these as competing theories of obligatory operations which are either "right" or "wrong," they could be reflections of optimizing strategies available within a highly mobile system which makes the most efficient use of limited resources in the diverse situations we frequently encounter. Here are a few examples of what we mean.

In any situation in which we simultaneously receive competing sensory inputs, early rejection of some could be employed. This would require some allocation of our processing resources. Although Posner and Boies (1971) argued that perception does not draw on capacity, selective perception surely does. Early selection, however, would allow the capacity which remains to be fully expended on the deep processing of this limited input. It is in this sense that we have a strategy which sacrifices breadth for depth.

Should the circumstances dictate, we could choose a late selection mode, in which all inputs receive some analysis, potentially to a semantic level. This strategy would be adopted whenever there is some advantage to delaying a decision as to which inputs to admit to awareness. This delay, however, could be accomplished only with expenditure of considerable capacity. Less residual capacity would be available for other operations. The more complete processing these stimuli receive, the more capacity will be absorbed.

To Johnston and Heinz, therefore, the amount of capacity available for deep processing is inversely related to the extent to which extraneous stimuli, or "secondary channels," are perceptually processed. To this, however, we should add two qualifications. The first is that some stimulus inputs may be, in Norman and Bobrow's words, *data-limited*. That is, problems of discrimination or impoverishment of data mean that some inputs may necessarily require more capacity to be processed to the same level than others. Indeed, some stimuli may not be amenable to deep processing no matter how our resources are allocated. The second qualification is the possibility that some simultaneous tasks, such as verbal versus nonverbal tasks, may draw capacity from different sources (Allport et al., 1972; McLeod, 1977, 1978; Roediger, Knight, & Kantowitz, 1977).

If we follow this logic, it could be that the experimental data used in the past to support one theory versus another may in fact have only revealed the particular strategy optimal under those experimental conditions. Thus, in the early shadowing studies, early rejection of unattended channels prior to semantic processing could have been a preferred strategy given the emphasis these studies placed on the rapid, accurate, and capacity-consuming shadowing of the attended channel. Such early rejection would have been optimal, since emphasis was always placed on keeping the channels segregated (never mixing items from one ear with the report of items from the other), and never missing a single word in the shadowing response. These activities received experimenter approval, and no resources needed to be preserved for deep or elaborative memory processing of the speech in either ear. In fact, subjects in shadowing experiments are very often as unaware of the meaning of what they had been shadowing as they are of the content of the unattended message.

We could thus contemplate a variety of circumstances which would favor either early or late selection, or broad or narrow attention. A single message, or simultaneous inputs without a shadowing requirement would allow greater capacity allocation for deep processing and the retention of the meaning of what was perceived. In those cases where divided attention between several sources or activities would be an advantage, resources would be appropriately allocated in accordance with a late selection mode.

In a similar way, the preattentive processing that Neisser proposed as a preliminary stage to focal attention may not have been a separate stage of processing. "Preattention" might simply represent an optimal strategy for situations where broad awareness would yield better success than narrow focusing. To Johnston and Heinz, there is "a continuum of attention modes and . . . this continuum is correlated with the expenditure of capacity" (1978, p. 434).

When truly engrossed in a cocktail party conversation, one might employ an early mode of selection. Very much like Broadbent's filter, we might use simple physical cues, such as voice quality or spatial localization to reject from analysis less exciting conversations. Since early rejection on the basis of physical cues requires less capacity, more is available for concentrating on the exciting conversation which is your primary focus. In such a case, as Johnston and Heinz observed, someone outside of this conversation might have to shout to get your attention.

If, on the other hand, we find ourselves in a boring conversation, we might allow a greater breadth of attention to give some degree of semantic processing to other, potentially more interesting, sources. The cost in terms of capacity would be great, but, provided the primary conversation is sufficiently dull, the cost might be worthwhile.

The thrust of these ideas should not be misinterpreted. There is selective coding from sensory memory, and not all stimuli registered in iconic and echoic memory receive full processing. The notion here, however, is that this selectivity is not on an all-or-none basis. Rather, the level of processing of these stimuli, shallow or deep, will be determined by the demand characteristics of the particular experiment or situation we pose to the subject. It is certainly the case that the number of stimulus inputs which can receive deep processing is sharply limited, if not by a perceptual filter, then by the limited capacity of our processing resources.

Our use of the term "deep" processing here is intended to imply a perceptual analysis that will lead to semantic coding and availability to memory and awareness. In the following chapter we will take a closer look at memory coding itself.

CHAPTER SUMMARY

1. *Aspects of Attention*

    A. The term attention has been used in different contexts to mean our level of physiological arousal, the degree of effort we bring to a task, the narrowness or breadth of our focus, or the selective focusing on one source of information to the exclusion of others. It was seen as an important "control process" for selecting which information might achieve some permanence in memory.

    B. Selective attention seems absolute when, at a noisy party, we remain unaware of the content of conversations other than the one in which we are engaged. The paradox, the so-called "cocktail party problem," lies in our ability to nevertheless hear our name when it is spoken in one of these previously ignored conversations.

    C. A time-sharing model of attention postulates a limited perceptual system which can only accommodate one meaningful input at a time. Simultaneous inputs can be followed only by rapidly switching attention between them to periodically sample their content. A capacity model proposes a limited pool of processing resources which must be allocated proportionally among various inputs to give some more complete processing than others.

2. *The Early Experiments*

    A. Shadowing experiments involving dichotic presentation require a subject to repeat aloud the speech heard in one ear while ignoring speech heard in the other ear. Split-span studies involve rapid presentation of simultaneous digit pairs, with one member presented to each ear. Reporting digits ear-by-ear yields higher accuracy than attempts to report them pair-by-pair.

    B. The earliest studies implied selectivity based on physical characteristics such as location or voice quality. These studies led to the notion of a filter which controls channel selection. Later studies showed an influence of context or meaning on channel selection.

3. *Time-Sharing Models of Attention*

    A. Broadbent's filter theory postulated a single-channel filter with a finite switching time that operated to allow information from only one channel at a time to be transmitted from echoic memory to short-term memory. Through access to long-term memory, the information could then receive analysis for meaning. Subjects in shadowing experiments appeared to have no memory for the unattended messages, while split-span studies implied a limit on the rate of alternating between channels.

    B. Since the content of unattended channels can often influence selective processing, a modified filter was proposed which would attenuate, rather than block, all but one channel. This would allow sufficient information for detection of especially meaningful or relevant signals occurring in unattended channels.

    C. The early split-span results can be explained in terms of organization and retrieval operations within memory, rather than the operation of a perceptual filter. Evidence has also been offered for some semantic analysis of unattended channels without conscious awareness.

4. *Capacity Models of Attention*

    A. Studies of divided attention suggest a complimentarity of performance based on allocation priorities within a limited pool of processing resources. The more resources allocated to one task, the less will be available for performance of the other. Kahneman's comprehensive capacity model proposed that available capacity can vary with our degree of arousal or effort.

    B. The possibility that all activities need not necessarily draw on a single pool of limited resources led to multiprocessor models, in which activities not involving the same cognitive structures can be carried on independently. Others have proposed that only active memory maintenance and response execution draw on resource capacity. Perceptual identification does not. Automaticity refers to overlearned, skilled responses which require minimal capacity allocation.

5. *Flexibility and Task Demands*

    A. Devoting greater effort to the processing of a stimulus improves performance only up to some maximum at which the further allocation of resources brings no further improvement. The processing of poor quality stimuli requires a greater allocation of resources before this point is reached.

    B. When performance is limited only by the resources allocated to it, the task is said to be resource-limited. When performance is limited by the quality of the stimulus, independent of the resources allocated, the task is called data-limited. Plotting performance–resource functions across a full range of resource allocation implies that earlier interpretations of shadowing experiments gave an incomplete picture by overlooking these distinctions.

C. Theorists have proposed that the attentional system contains sufficient flexibility to allow either "early" or "late" selection as optional strategies. The selection mode would depend on which represents the optimal use of resource allocation within the particular life experience or experimental paradigm.

SHORT-TERM MEMORY

TOPIC QUESTIONS

1. Approaches to the Study of Short-Term Memory.
What have been the major conceptual approaches to explaining memory for recently presented information? What sorts of questions do these approaches suggest should be asked about short-term retention?

2. The Duplex Hypothesis.
How does recall accuracy change with time over short retention intervals? What were the claims of the *duplex hypothesis* and how did it explain forgetting over short retention intervals?

3. The Capacity of Short-Term Memory.
What is a *chunk* and what is the role of this concept in explaining short-term retention? What is the relationship between *memory span* and the structural notion of a *short-term memory*? What evidence supports the distinction between the two? What alternatives? What are the difficulties in specifying the nature of coding in short-term memory?

4. The Content of Short-Term Memory.
What evidence indicates *acoustic coding* in short-term memory, but *semantic coding* in long-term memory? What is the distinction between *articulatory coding* and *acoustic coding* and what evidence was used to distinguish between these alternatives? What are the difficulties in specifying the nature of coding in short-term memory?

5. Forgetting in Short-Term Memory.
What two questions about forgetting are of interest to the Duplex Hypothesis? What conclusions were reached about the causes of forgetting from short-term memory, and what experimental techniques were used to reach these conclusions? How did these conclusions bear on the distinction between short-term memory and long-term memory?

C hapter 5 introduced the notion of "capacity limitations" as important factors restricting our ability to process information. We noted that there are definite limitations on the amount of information that can be coded at any one time, and on the rate at which information can be coded. Too much information, arriving too rapidly, seems to overload the cognitive system beyond its limits. One cannot engage in a meaningful conversation with a friend while simultaneously reading a book and mentally adding the squares of the digits of your telephone number. Just try it!

It was the realization of these limits on our ability to engage in simultaneous activities that led to the studies of selective attention described in the previous chapter. Although the way psychologists characterized these attentional limitations evolved dramatically over a 30-year period of research, the fact of these processing limits were never themselves in dispute. Throughout this same period, however, many of these same investigators were also aware of what seemed to be a second type of bottleneck in the system. In addition to a limit on processing capacity, there were also limits in storage capacity.

Imagine that you are seated quietly in a room with no distractions. All your processing resources can be devoted to a single, simple memory task. An experimenter reads aloud a list of random digits, and you must remember and repeat them back at the end of the list. How many digits can you recall without error: 5, 7, 12, 15? For most of us, the number will be about seven. From trial to trial we may remember a few more or a few less, but across many trials the average will be very close to seven.

The situation we have described is not uncommon. We engage in this sort of activity whenever we look up a telephone number and retain it just long enough to dial it. Think about your own experiences when this happens: (1) There is a limited number of digits you can hold in memory at any one time; seven can be handled, 15 cannot. (2) Your memory for the numbers seems a fleeting one; if you do not dial the number quickly, you may have to go back and look it up again. (3) Any noticeable distraction may also send you back to the directory; someone suddenly calling your name or loudly reciting another series of digits can seemingly wipe your memory clean. (4) While this recent memory is ordinarily a transient one, we can keep it alive by rehearsal. Especially when there are distractions, we repeat the number over and over to ourselves until we have finished dialing.

These characteristics are commonly referred to as those of *short-term memory,* a transient "working" memory for temporarily holding information for immediate use. This type of memory, in other words, is limited in storage capacity and duration. If we rehearse or think about the material sufficiently, it may become part of our enduring long-term memory. This happens for numbers we dial frequently, or ones like our own, which we constantly give to friends or write on endless school or business forms. Those materials we do not think about or rehearse, on the other hand, seem never to survive beyond this transient form of memory. Our goal in this chapter is to take a close look at this so-called "short-term memory."

APPROACHES TO SHORT-TERM MEMORY

To many psychologists, most notably Donald Broadbent (1958), the idea of a separate "working memory" within the total memory system seemed to have a certain adaptive quality about it. Just imagine what it would be like if we added dozens of numbers in the course of some mathematics exercise and in so doing found that we had formed a permanent memory of each and every number used in the calculation. The result would be mental chaos! There are some cases, in other words, where too good a memory would be maladaptive. For these and other reasons, the distinction between the transient, short-term storage of information versus long-term semantic storage became an active topic of research and speculation within experimental psychology. Indeed, the term "short-term memory" gained sufficient familiarity that the simple abbreviation, STM, seemed to take on a meaning of its own.

The temporary storage and use of information began to be seen as an identifiably separate function within the total memory system, and with this view, the topic of short-term memory became a distinct research enterprise. As with other topics we have discussed, however, the distinction between short- and long-term memory can be conceptualized in more than one way. These alternative views predictably led to different kinds of questions and different programs of research.

Consciousness and Primary Memory

In addition to its limited capacity, many early writers included within the notion of short-term retention a special sense of conscious awareness for recent information which is still "in mind." A telephone number you have just looked up, or words you have just heard, seem immediately present in a way that distinguishes them from other things we know, but which are not the current focus of our attention.

William James, the elder stateman of American psychology, tried to capture this difference in his distinction between *primary memory* and *secondary memory* (James, 1890). For James, primary memory was the psychological present; those events, thoughts, or perceptions that are at any moment a part of ones immediate awareness. Secondary memory represented the knowledge and information we have acquired in the past, but which is not part of our current conscious experience. That there was a distinction between primary (short-term) and secondary (long-term) memory, James (1890) had no doubt:

> The stream of thought flows on; but most of its segments fall into the bottomless abyss of oblivion. Of some, no memory survives the instant of their passage. Of others, it is confined to a few moments, hours, or days. Others, again, leave vestiges which are indestructible, and by means of which they may be recalled as long as life endures. Can we explain these differences? (p. 643)

James' question was how to conceptualize this distinction and how to derive a useful framework for its systematic investigation.

Short-Term Memory as a Structural Store

By the end of the 1940s, John Watson's behaviorism had clearly established its influence in American psychology, and with it, the concept of consciousness had all but disappeared from the research vocabulary. To be sure, memory research in the 1950s wished to understand those mental events which occurred between a "stimulus" and a "response." Thus, Watson's behaviorism no longer dominated the exploration of memory. Nevertheless, one vestige of his arguments remained; the concept of consciousness was not to be found in the models and theories of this period. Rather, as we saw in Chapter 5 memory function was divided into a series of discrete, structural memory stores, each with its own characteristics and role to play in the processing of memory information.

Figure 5-1 showed the role of short-term memory in this system as a structural entity for temporarily holding recent information selected from sensory memory and prior to its transfer to long-term memory. This *structural theory* thus claimed two different kinds of memory, or information stores beyond sensory memory: short-term memory (STM) and long-term memory (LTM). At any one time, what we remember may be "in" STM or LTM, or perhaps sometimes, in both.

This structural view of information processing led psychologists to ask questions about the capacity of these stores, how their content was coded, and how information was either lost from each store or transferred from one store to another. This general distinction between a short- and long-term memory has sometimes been called the *duplex theory*. It was beyond question the most widely accepted way of conceptualizing memory from its contemporary appearance in the 1950s up to the early 1970s.

Process Views of Memory

We have already seen examples of the differences between the *structural* and *process* approaches to information processing in memory. In the present context, the process view of information storage specifically denies that there are two distinct and separate memory systems. Rather, it claims that there are a variety of activities we ordinarily perform on incoming information. These range from the simple detection of the presence of a source of information to the more thorough interpretations of the meaning and significance of this information.

To these theorists, typified by the "levels of processing" viewpoint of Craik and Lockhart (1972), it is the kinds of activities or processes we perform with the new information which will determine how well it will be retained. While the terms "short-term" and "long-term" might still appear, they could serve only as general descriptors for the consequences of different levels of analysis within a dynamic processing continuum. The notion of an automatic "transfer" of information from one memory store to another through rehearsal was totally rejected. Instead, it was the materials' depth of processing which would determine the strength and quality of its retention.

As the structural view led to one set of questions, so the process view led to others. In this case the direction of research was shifted to the description of those mental activities which would lead to different levels of durability and retrievability of memory information. We will look more closely at this process view in Chapter 8.

The structural versus process views are in fact different orientations to the study of memory, rather than two distinct theories. There are a number of different duplex theories of memory (e.g., Atkinson & Shiffrin, 1968; Broadbent, 1958; Waugh & Norman, 1965), as well as several identifiably different process models (e.g., Bransford, McCarrell, Franks, & Nitsch, 1977; Craik & Lockhart, 1972; Shiffrin & Schneider, 1977b).

In our discussion of these orientations we will continue to concentrate on the kinds of questions that were asked and the kinds of experiments these questions inspired.

THE DUPLEX HYPOTHESIS

The beginnings of the modern study of short-term memory can be traced to two similar experiments reported by John Brown (1958) in England, and by Lloyd and Margaret Peterson (1959) in the United States. Both demonstrated that materials as simple as a single three-letter string will be forgotten within the space of several seconds if they are not rehearsed.

At the time of these reports, verbal learning research on both sides of the Atlantic was concentrated primarily on what was seen as the formation of associations between verbal elements, and the interference which often occurs among these associations. As you think about the character of these studies described in Chapters 2 and 3, you should recall their focus on the learning of long lists of verbal materials practiced over a series of many trials. Their measures of memory and forgetting spanned intervals of minutes, hours, or sometimes several days. Brown's (1958) and Peterson and Peterson's (1959) reports that verbal items can decay within seconds if not rehearsed came as something of a shock within this context. It was not primarily the rapidity of the decay that caused the stir; it was the report that this decay had occurred in the absence of associative interference.

The experiment by Peterson and Peterson (1959) can give you a good feeling for this rapid decay of unrehearsed verbal materials. On a given trial, a subject would be presented with a three-consonant trigram, such as DNP. The three letters were spoken aloud to the subject to the beat of a metronome that clicked twice per second. Immediately after the trigram the subject then heard a three-digit number presented at the same rate. At this point, the subject would have to start counting backward by threes from this number, again in time with the metronome. If, for example, the number was 832, the subject would have to begin with 829 on the first beat after the number, 826 on the next beat, and so on.

Counting backward by three's was intended as a *distractor task* which would prevent the subject from rehearsing the letters. Peterson and Peterson argued that since the distractor task involved numbers, while the retention materials were letters, retroactive interference between these materials should not occur. Thus, any memory loss would be due to the passage of time alone, rather than to response competition or any other mechanism of interference.

Over the course of many trials a variety of different retention intervals were tested by delaying the signal to recall. When the signal did occur, the subject was to cease the backward counting and try to recall the three-letter trigram. The time intervals used ranged from 3 to 18 seconds (sec) between trigram presentation and the signal for recall.

Figure 7-1 shows the then startling results obtained by Peterson and Peterson (1959). If the recall signal came as little as three seconds after the trigram presentation, subjects could recall all three consonants only 80% of the time. With only an 18-sec delay, the frequency of correct recall fell to 10%. It seemed clear from these results that the longer the subjects were required to count backwards before being allowed to recall

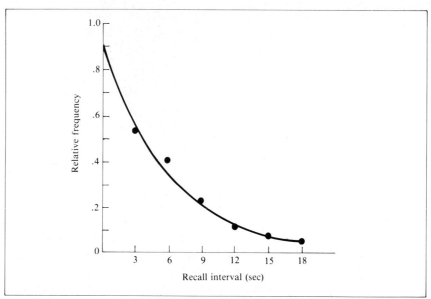

FIGURE 7-1   The relative frequency of recalling all three letters of a three-consonant trigram as a function of retention interval when this interval was occupied by backward counting to prevent rehearsal.
(From Peterson & Peterson, 1959. Copyright © 1959 by the American Psychological Association. Reprinted by permission.)

the trigram, the less likely they would be to recall the three letters. It also seemed to these investigators that this rapid loss was due to the passage of time without rehearsal, rather than to the results of associative interference.

These findings brought an immediate and sharp reaction within the field of verbal learning. For some, it initiated a search for possible sources of associative interference within the Petersons' paradigm. They could not believe that memories could be lost through time alone, no matter what the circumstances. Short-term memory as studied by Peterson and Peterson could only be the unpracticed end of a memory-strength continuum and as such, should be no less subject to the usual laws of interference (cf. Melton, 1963).

To others, such as Brown (1958) and Peterson and Peterson (1959) themselves, short-term memory seemed to be unique. Recent material will quickly and automatically fade within a very few seconds without rehearsal. The reason we ordinarily rehearse recent information, it seemed, was simply to postpone the onset of this automatic decay.

Whatever the view, this rapid forgetting in the apparent absence of competing associations sparked considerable interest in the systematic study of retention over short intervals of time. Competition versus decay not withstanding, the rate of this forgetting compared to the memory curves of more conventional studies suggested that different principles might apply to recent memories from those used to explain long-term forgetting.

The research which followed the Petersons' discovery resulted in several structural theories attempting to explain the difference between long- and short-term memory performance. The basic conception was of a memory system in which information was transferred from one form of storage to the next in a strict sequence. Chapter 5 described the first form of storage, a sensory memory. Information from this store must be transferred to a short-term store, and then to a long-term, relatively permanent store. Each of these forms of storage was thought to possess unique characteristics that would determine the character of retrieval based on this store (cf. Atkinson & Shiffrin, 1968).

Short-term memory seemed to be distinguishable from other forms of memory by (1) the rapid forgetting of unrehearsed information over short retention intervals, (2) its inability to hold more than a limited amount of information at any one time, and (3) the content of this store as inferred from the kinds of confusion errors subjects typically made in recall. These confusions seemed to be based on the sound patterns of the words, rather than their meanings. Long-term retention, on the other hand, could be (1) measured over considerable periods of time, (2) possessed effectively unlimited capacity, and (3) seemed prone to confusions of meaning.

It is important at the outset to emphasize that these basic differences have never been in much dispute. The controversy lay only in how different investigators interpreted these differences in memory over the course of time, and what caused these differences.

As we begin our discussion of the evidence on these questions, we should agree on some terms to avoid potential confusion. We will use the term short-term memory (STM) purely as a descriptive term for fairly immediate recall of recent materials, i.e., the distinction between STM and LTM refers to a purely procedural difference in the length of the retention interval required. Its use should imply no theoretical position. We will reserve the terms *short-term store* (STS) and *long-term store* (LTS) to refer specifically to the distinct structural stores envis-

The duplex theory postulated a limited capacity short-term memory that could hold only a limited amount of information. If this capacity is exceeded, some information will be lost.

aged by the duplex theory of memory. That is, we should be prepared to use the concepts of STS and LTS to explain the observed differences between STM and LTM.

THE CAPACITY OF SHORT-TERM MEMORY

Historically, writers on psychological issues have commonly taken note of limits on one's immediate awareness (see Craik and Levy, 1976 for a discussion of this early work). It was, however, George Miller (1956) who first gave shape to the contemporary view of capacity limitations in short-term memory. After reviewing the substantial literature on memory span, Miller proposed that the capacity of immediate recall is ordinarily fixed at 7 ± 2 "chunks" of information.

Miller's proposal was motivated by the fact that the number of items one can accurately report back after one presentation is relatively constant. For example, the number of unrelated words, random letters or random numbers that can be accurately reproduced after one hearing varies between five and nine (hence, 7 ± 2). On the other hand, 20 letters can easily be remembered if they can be formed into four, five-letter words. Similarly, the number of digits we can remember can be increased easily to 15 items if we recognize and retain the numbers 1, 4, 9, 16, 25, 36, 49, 64, 81 as the squares of the numbers 1 through 9.

While the number of items we can remember may be limited to 7 ± 2, the term "items" refers to subjective units based on prior learning. When the memory materials can be grouped, such as letters into words, or words into sentences, the memory span must be measured in terms of these larger groups. Miller (1956) used the term *chunks* for these subjectively defined units and his contribution, in part, was to point out that the span remains almost constant despite changes in size of the chunk. Glanzer and Razel (1974) for example, have shown that a familiar proverb can serve as a single "item" in this sense. While the memory capacity remains relatively constant, the *apparent* capacity will vary with the amount of chunking allowed by the materials and the subject's experience.

While most writers emphasized the use of logical organization to increase the usable capacity of short-term memory, intonation and pausing alone can often be quite effective. For example, given six digits to memorize, most people will spontaneously rehearse the items as two groups of three digits, each separated by a pause and distinct melodic pattern: "427316" becomes "427–316" (Bower & Springston, 1970). A common example of rhyming and melodic rhythm to create chunks is the traditional song used by children to recite the alphabet:

[(ab–cd) (ef–g)]   [(hi–jk) (lmno–p)]   [(qrs–tuv) (w–xyz)]

As Norman (1976, p. 117) describes this process, the 26 letters are broken into 3 chunks, each with 2 elements, each element with 2 units, and each unit with 1 to 4 letters.

Miller's chunking hypothesis was based on a careful review of memory span studies then available in the literature. Since that time, students of memory have developed a number of techniques which show that any given memory performance, such as memory span, can be based on more than one underlying mechanism. In the context of the duplex theory, it soon became apparent that the contribution of the short-term store (STS) to memory performance could not be unambiguously separated from that of the long-term store (LTS) (Watkins, 1974). Craik (1971), for example, concluded that the true capacity of STS was between 2.5 to 3.5 items. Recognizing that this span is much smaller than Miller's estimate of 5 to 9 items, Craik attributed the difference to the contribution of long-term memory to ordinary memory span data.

The well-known relationship between memory span and age shows why this single measure cannot unambiguously define the maximum capacity of the STS. Figure 7-2, based on data given by Hunter (1964), shows this relationship.

The average number of digits produced without error after one hearing increases systematically with age and levels off at about 7 by the mid-teens. It drops to an average of 6 in the mid-fifties. These figures, however, would be deceptive if they are taken to imply that the capacity, or "size" of a short-term store is changing with age. Belmont and Butterfield (1971) argue that the capacity of STS does not change. What changes is the way in which the information is processed. Older children and adults differ from younger children in (1) the way they attend to relevant stimuli when they are heard, (2) the use of active rehearsal to a much greater degree, and (3) the size of the chunks used in organizing the material in memory. If presentation rates are increased to prevent the effective use of rehearsal strategies, the differences in memory span between children and adults is dramatically reduced (Murray & Roberts, 1968).

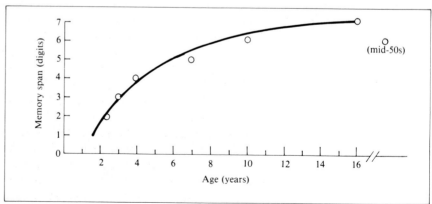

FIGURE 7-2   Average memory span for digits as a function of age. (Data from Hunter, 1964.)

This view was corroborated by studies such as that of Flavell, Beach, and Chinsky (1966), who showed that the increase in memory span for children between kindergarten and the fifth grade (approximately 6 through 10 years) is exactly paralleled by their spontaneous use of active rehearsal during a retention interval. Indeed, if nursery school children are explicitly instructed to rehearse, one can often observe a marked increase in their apparent memory span (Kingsley & Hagen, 1969). Thus, the increase in memory span with age and its decrease in old age, can often be attributable to changes in learning activities and changes in the contribution of the long-term store.

A similar logic serves to explain the very different memory spans of normal and retarded children (Ellis, 1970). The technique on which many of these inferences were based was the so-called serial position effect, which usually occurs when a list of verbal items is memorized for immediate free recall. It is assumed that the accuracy of recalling the last few items in a list (referred to as the "recency effect") is a more valid indicator of STS capacity than the accuracy of recall for earlier items in the list. Recall of early items, which the subjects have had opportunity to rehearse, reflects the contribution of LTS to the recall score. We will have more to say about this technique later, but, in this context, results suggest that the capacity of STS in retarded children is actually not much different from that of other children. For example, measures of the contribution of LTS to recall accuracy correlate more highly with a person's estimated intelligence (correlation of .72) than do measures of the STS contribution (correlation of .49) (Craik, 1971). In other words, the differences observed between the memory spans of normal and retarded children primarily reflect differences in the LTS contribution to this score.

Variables such as word length and the clustering of words together on the basis of similar sound or meaning have a dramatic impact on overall recall ability for a list of words, but not on the size of the recency effect (Baddeley, Thompson, & Buchman, 1975; Craik & Levy, 1970). That is, these effects of grouping appear to influence the long-term component of recall. As Baddeley (1976, pp. 134–135) points out, this is particularly interesting because it illustrates that the nature of the chunk in STS is dependent on the prior integration of these units. A short-term store could thus take advantage of relationships between presented items only if associative connections and integrations have already been established in this more permanent memory store.

Most investigators who subscribed to the duplex hypothesis came to agree on the question of capacity. The memory span reflects the operation of more than one storage component. Recall of material that was just presented can be from either the long-term or the short-term store. The fairly reliable fixed limit on memory span probably reflects limits on discrimination among memory traces, a process we will discuss further in the context of the distinctiveness of memory codes in Chapter 8.

However, the contribution of the short-term store to memory performance is in the range of two to four items. These items represent the capacity of this memory store and a major limitation in the learning and remembering of complex tasks.

Retrieval from Short-Term Memory

In Chapter 4 we looked at the important role played by meaningful organization in storage and retrieval from long-term memory. We saw how Bartlett viewed the dynamics of memory organization in terms of *conceptual schemata,* how network and feature models of memory organization emphasized the importance of semantic relations between memory elements, and finally, how logical inference frequently forms an essential part of the recall process.

The duplex model saw short-term memory as having a very different character. While long-term memory might be a vast store of meaningfully related concepts, short-term memory was, by contrast, of sharply limited capacity, its content kept alive only by active rehearsal. Within this framework, we are bound to be curious about retrieval from short-term memory, and how it could be studied. If we give a subject five or six digits to remember and immediately test retention, we would learn little beyond the fact that they can recall them correctly and in the correct order. If we wait too long before testing recall, all we can say is that little has been retained. Clearly, neither approach can tell us much about retrieval from short-term memory.

Some years ago, Saul Sternberg (1966, 1969a) working at the Bell Telephone Laboratories in New Jersey, developed an ingenious method for exploring search and retrieval strategies in short-term memory. He made use of a very old technique, that of the measurement of reaction times to infer something about our otherwise invisible mental activities (cf., Donders, 1868–1869; Sternberg, 1969b). Sternberg's task would require subjects to memorize a short list of digits (not unlike memorizing a telephone number). Instead of asking the subjects to recall the full list, however, the subjects were shown a single digit, a *probe* item, and were simply asked whether the probe digit had, or had not, been in the memorized list. Since the memory lists would be kept short, and the probe item was presented soon after the list had been seen, we would expect accuracy to be high. The dependent variable would not be accuracy of response, but *speed* of response.

Let us look closely at Sternberg's task, and at some of its possible outcomes. Our subject is seated in front of a visual display which will flash a series of digits, one at a time, for a duration of 1 sec each. This series of digits is called the "memory set," and from trial-to-trial the sets were varied from between one and six digits, all well within the span of short-term memory. One second after the last item in the memory set is presented, the subject is shown the probe digit. If that digit had occurred in the memory set he or she would press a lever marked "yes." If it had not been in the list, he or she would press a lever marked "no." In either case, the response was to be made as fast as possible, without making careless errors. Sternberg ensured that the probe digits were in the memory sets on half the trials only, and when they were present, that the probe digits would occur in various serial positions on various trials in a random way. Reaction times were measured from the time the probe digit appeared to the moment the subject pressed the appropriate response lever.

As Sternberg analyzed the situation, he saw at least three major operations the subject must perform when he or she sees the probe digit. First, the probe must be identified. Second, the subject must mentally scan the memory set to see if the probe digit had been presented in that list. Finally, the subject must select the appropriate response by pressing either the "yes" or the "no" lever. Regardless of how long the memory set is, the first and third stages would be the same: identifying the probe and executing the response. Each would take time, but the time required would be no greater if the memory set were large or small. Any effect of the size of the memory set would be only on the second stage: the scanning of the list in short-term memory for the presence or absence of the probe digit. One might imagine that the longer the memory list, the more time the scanning process should take. This in turn would be reflected in longer reaction times for larger memory sets.

If we now consider the scanning process itself, we can see three logical possibilities. Each has a different prediction about the relationship between reaction times and the size of the memory set.

1. *Parallel processing.* It could be that when the probe appears, the subject could examine all of the digits in memory simultaneously, or "in parallel." If this were the case, we would expect reaction times to be unaffected by the size of the memory set. If scanning in short-term memory were done in parallel, a list of six digits should take no longer to examine than a list of, say, one, three, or four digits.

2. *Serial self-terminating search.* A second alternative is that subjects might have to compare the probe with each digit in the memory set, one at a time, until the probe is found. The moment the probe is found, the subject immediately terminates the search and responds by pressing the "yes" lever. In this case, reaction times would be influenced by the number of digits the subject had to scan prior to encountering the probe. On average, the longer the list, the more digits the subject would have to scan prior to encountering the probe. You can see why this is called a *serial self-terminating search:* "serial" implies scanning the list, one digit at a time, and "self-terminating" implies that the subject will stop the search and respond as soon as the probe digit is encountered.

3. *Serial exhaustive search.* In the case of a serial search when the probe digit is not in the list, the search must necessarily be *exhaus-*

tive. That is, the full memory set must be scanned before a "no" response can be made. However intuitively unlikely, one could contemplate an exhaustive search even when a probe is encountered in the list. In such a process, our subject would scan the full set, one digit at a time, going right to the end of the list before deciding if any matches with the probe digit had been encountered. If we assume that it takes the same amount of time to scan each item in the list, the more digits in the memory set, the longer the reaction time would be. The rate of increase in reaction time with list length for "yes" responses would be exactly the same as the rate of increase for "no" responses since an exhaustive search would be occurring in both cases.

The results of Sternberg's (1966) experiment are shown in Figure 7-3, and they caused quite a stir when they were first published. The graph shows average reaction times for "yes" and "no" responses as a function of the number of items in the memory set. Note first that reaction times do increase with the size of the memory set. To Sternberg, this immediately ruled out the possibility of parallel processing, a question we will return to at the end of this section. The surprising

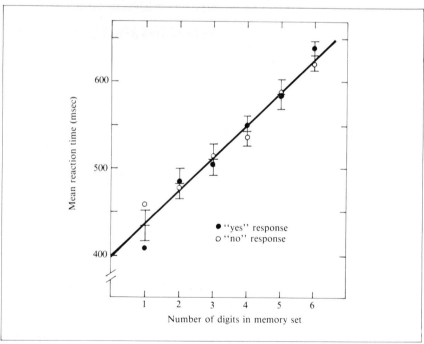

FIGURE 7-3   Mean reaction time to "yes" and "no" responses as a function of the number of digits in the memory set.
(From Sternberg, 1966. Copyright © 1966 by the American Association for the Advancement of Science.)

finding came when he observed that the "yes" responses increased with list length at exactly the same rate as the necessarily exhaustive "no" responses. Even when the probe was present, he argued, short-term memory must be scanned using a serial exhaustive search. From the slopes of the two curves, he further calculated that subjects must be able to scan memory at a rate of 38 milliseconds (msec) per digit (as one digit is added to the size of the memory set, so an additional 38 msec was added to the total response time).

To Sternberg, these results implied that the scanning operation (Stage 2) and the response decision operation (Stage 3) are quite separate. Even when the probe is encountered in the list, subjects continue to scan the full list before making a single response decision in the form of, "Were any matches encountered?" If scanning is rapid, and the decision process is slow, this scheme might well be more efficient than making a series of time-consuming decisions after each and every digit in the set is examined.

So intriguing were Sternberg's initial results that countless experiments were performed all over the country, and abroad, to either refute, verify, or extrapolate from, these findings. These studies were quick to show that the results were quite robust, with the same evidence for serial exhaustive search appearing whether one presents the memory digits one at a time or all together as a single list, or whether the memory sets or probes are presented either visually or auditorially (e.g., Chase & Calfee, 1969; Wingfield, 1973). Indeed, Sternberg's results seem to hold up even when hospitalized schizophrenics or alcoholics served as subjects. The overall heights of the curves are higher for these patients than for healthy young adults, but the slopes are surprisingly similar (Sternberg, 1975). We can infer from this that they took more time to identify the probes or to make their response decisions. The scanning process itself, however, would seem to have been the same.

Similar evidence for serial exhaustive search also appears when subjects can use chunking or other recoding strategies to facilitate the memory task. Figure 7-4 shows results of a scanning study in which up to 12 digits were given in the memory sets (Wingfield & Branca, 1970). Notice in the left-hand graph (A) how reaction times steadily increase with list length up to the point where the sets are six digits long. Again we see the similarity in the slopes for "yes" and "no" responses that Sternberg used as evidence for a serial exhaustive search. Note, however, that beyond six digits, as the memory set increases to eight, ten, and twelve digits, how reaction times systematically drop. It is easy to account for this.

If the memory set consists of only the digits 0 through 9, as they did in this experiment, it becomes more efficient for long lists to remember those digits which were *not* in the memory set, rather than those which were. For example, if the subject receives an eight-digit set, 1 4 8 2 5 0 3 9, it is far easier to remember that "7" was not in the list. The response

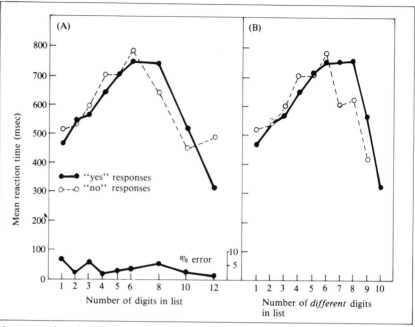

FIGURE 7-4 Mean reaction time for searching for probe digits as a function of (A) the total number of digits in the presented list, and (B) the number of *different* digits in the list. Reaction times for when the probe was present ("yes" responses) and when the probe was not present ("no" responses) are shown separately.
(From Wingfield & Branca, 1970. Copyright © 1970 by the American Psychological Association. Reprinted by permission.)

decision now requires an extra step. If "7" appears as a probe, the subject's "yes," it is in memory, would have to be translated into "no," it was not present in the *original* set. The decision process is more complex, but the need to maintain a very long list in short-term memory is eliminated. This recoding strategy would explain the downward trend of the reaction times for the longer lists. The longer the list, the fewer exclusive items would have to be held and scanned, and hence, the shorter would be the total response times.

The right-hand graph (B) shows the same data plotted as a function of the number of different digits in the list. Since in this experiment numbers were sometimes repeated in the longer lists, subjects could further minimize the memory load by dropping out the repeated digits. Using only the different digits would be all that would be necessary to perform the task. Notice how the curves for the longer lists become even more symmetrical, suggesting that this was probably what the subjects did do. (Subjects in experiments like this, incidentally, are often quite unaware of how they are doing the particular task.)

In either case, we see the similarity in slopes for "yes" and "no" responses that Sternberg used to argue for serial exhaustive search. The separation of the "yes" and "no" curves for sets beyond six digits can be attributed to the extra complexity of having to translate ''yes'' and ''no'' responses before pressing the appropriate response lever. (For similar work on memory scanning for organized lists, see also, Naus, Glucksberg, & Ornstein, 1972; Naus, 1974.)

As research progressed, however, it began to appear that serial exhaustive scanning might be limited only to the rapid scanning of memory sets for the presence or absence of a single probe. For example, when subjects are required to actually retrieve an item from memory, such as giving the name of the digit which followed the probe in the list, response times begin to suggest a serial self-terminating search process (Sternberg, 1967). Further, if we complicate the simple scanning task by requiring a subject to search for more than one possible probe at a time, one also begins to see evidence for a self-terminating search (Wingfield & Bolt, 1970).

As memory scanning research continued, heated controversy replaced the earlier certainties even about the serial nature of memory search. For example, one could contemplate parallel processing of all digits in a memory set, except where the speed of completing these stimultaneous analyses varies with the size of the memory set. If we are again confronting a limited resource system, more parallel operations would require a greater draw on resources than fewer ones, and hence, the total time to complete these analyses would be longer with longer lists. Using this and related arguments, many began to wonder whether some form of parallel processing, also known as ''direct access,'' could not be possible within these data. As interested readers can discover, this controversy is not an easy one to resolve (cf. Corcoran, 1971; Murdock, 1971; Sternberg, 1973, 1975; Townsend, 1971, 1972; Wingfield, 1973).

Controversy aside, Sternberg's studies and those which followed made an important contribution to memory research. First, they have shown how studies of reaction times can be used to make inferences about short-term memory retrieval strategies and those mental operations which may be involved in this retrieval. Second, Sternberg's paradigm was instrumental in framing the major theoretical alternatives for the ultimate explanation of short-term retrieval. Finally, for our present purposes, these studies also illustrate the spirit of a limited capacity STS, one in which items are held temporarily through active rehearsal prior to either being forgotten, or transferred to long-term memory.

THE CONTENT OF SHORT-TERM MEMORY

A very important part of the duplex theory was not only that the storage capacity of the STS was dramatically limited by comparison with the LTS, but that the character of the coding representations in these two stores were also quite different. While there was ample evidence for semantic coding in long-term retention, all of the evidence at hand seemed to imply that short-term coding was verbal or acoustic in character.

Acoustic Confusions in Short-Term Memory

Conrad (1963, 1964) was one of the first to specifically propose that the codes representing information in the two stores were characteristically different. Unlike the semantic codes of long-term memory (meanings and the relationships among words), the short-term store contained only representations of the sounds, or *phonological features* of words. His evidence came from a systematic analysis of the confusion errors people ordinarily make in tests of immediate recall.

Conrad's experiment consisted of two parts. In the first part of the experiment a group of subjects heard a large number of different letters spoken in a background of noise. The subjects' task was simply to report the letter they thought they heard after each presentation. This analysis produced no surprises. First, because of the background noise, the letters were difficult to hear, causing the subjects to make frequent errors. Second, the character of these errors were predominantly acoustic in nature: the errors the subjects made resembled the sound pattern of the letters actually presented. For example, for the letter "V," the most common error (168 cases) was to report that the similar sounding letter "B" had been heard. Similarly, for "S," the most common error (336 cases) was "F." These error frequencies for a sample of letters are shown in the top portion of Table 7-1 (A).

The interesting results came when Conrad now visually presented lists of six letters in the form of a memory experiment. After each list was presented, the subjects were to report what they remembered from the six-letter sequence. The lower part of Table 7-1 (B) shows the comparable "confusion matrix" for the visually presented letters recalled from memory. Conrad found a striking overlap in the pattern of errors made in these two cases. Just as "B" was the most common confusion error when "V" was heard in noise, so "B" was also the most common confusion error in memory (83 cases). Similarly, the most common memory error for a visually presented "S" was to report "F" (131 cases).

Although the letters in the memory test were visually presented, visual confusions did not typically occur. For example, when "P" was presented, some 281 recall errors were the similar sounding "T," while only two of the errors were the visually confusable "F." In a further analysis, Conrad also found that when visually presented letter sequences sounded alike (e.g., B, V), many more errors occurred than when they were not acoustically similar (e.g., V, S). It seemed to Conrad and many who followed him, that the predominant form of coding in short-term memory was based on the sound of the item (e.g., Wickelgren, 1965a, b, c). Subjects seemed to have identified the visually presented letters, retrieved their names, and then rehearsed these names in memory.

Acoustic versus Articulatory Coding

While the sound confusions might generally imply an "acoustic" or "phonological" code, this reference to covert verbalization implied to some the notion of a specifically *articulatory code:* a representation of

TABLE 7-1 The top matrix (A) shows the frequency with which different letters were confused with others when they were heard indistinctly with a background of noise. The lower matrix (B) shows comparable confusion errors when the letters were presented visually for later recall.
(From Conrad, 1964.)

(A) Listening confusions

Stimulus letter

Response letter	B	C	P	T	V	F	M	N	S	X
B	.	171	75	84	168	2	11	10	2	2
C	32	.	35	42	20	4	4	5	2	5
P	162	350	.	505	91	11	31	23	5	5
T	143	232	281	.	50	14	12	11	8	5
V	122	61	34	22	.	1	8	11	1	0
F	6	4	2	4	3	.	13	8	336	238
M	10	14	2	3	4	22	.	334	21	9
N	13	21	6	9	20	32	512	.	38	14
S	2	18	2	7	3	488	23	11	.	391
X	1	6	2	2	1	245	2	1	184	.

(B) Recall confusions

Stimulus letter

Response letter	B	C	P	T	V	F	M	N	S	X
B	.	18	62	5	83	12	9	3	2	0
C	13	.	27	18	55	15	3	12	35	7
P	102	18	.	24	40	15	8	8	7	7
T	30	46	79	.	38	18	14	14	8	10
V	56	32	30	14	.	21	15	11	11	5
F	6	8	14	5	31	.	12	13	131	16
M	12	6	8	5	20	16	.	146	15	5
N	11	7	5	1	19	28	167	.	24	5
S	7	21	11	2	9	37	4	12	.	16
X	3	7	2	2	11	30	10	11	59	.

the stimulus in terms of the characteristic way we would move our speech musculature in order to produce these sounds. For example, B and V share the articulatory feature of "voicing." In order to make both of these sounds we must vibrate our vocal chords. We also use the lips in producing these sounds. On the other hand, producing an S does not require either the lips or voicing. The articulation of B and V is similar while both are quite different from the articulation of an S. Thus, the memory code responsible for confusions and interference might be based on a record of articulatory patterns rather than on sound, per se.

In a later study, Conrad (1970) offered an interesting illustration of the articulatory hypothesis. His subjects in this study were all congenitally deaf students who had never heard speech, but who had nevertheless learned to speak in an understandable way. Presumably, since they had never heard the sounds of speech there is no way they could form a strictly acoustic code for letter names. Yet, when Conrad repeated his recall experiment with these students, he did find that many of them made the same sorts of acoustic errors as we saw in Table 7-1.

While many of the deaf students produced the same error patterns as his normally hearing subjects, some did not. When Conrad later interviewed the teachers and identified the students who had made the ''normal errors,'' the teachers explained that this group was also superior at using oral speech. Conrad reasoned that since these students had learned to speak without any auditory feedback, a strictly acoustic code would have been impossible. On the other hand, their ability to produce speech would have allowed for their confusion errors in recall to have been based on similarities in articulatory codes. Parenthetically, we can note that a common ''non-normal'' error for congenitally deaf subjects is in the form of visual confusions based on the physical similarity of the presented letters. These subjects apparently make use of visual coding in the absence of either good acoustic or articulatory codes (Conrad, 1972).

It could well be that normally hearing subjects can use either acoustic or articulatory codes depending on the circumstances. For example, if subjects are instructed to repeat irrelevant syllables during visual presentation of a memory list, they should be unable to form an articulatory representation of the items to be remembered. When this experiment is conducted, we find a marked drop in recall of the last items in the list (e.g., Levy, 1971; Peterson & Johnson, 1971). If the accuracy of recall for these final list items is taken as a measure of the STS contribution to memory span, and if we assume that STS stores articulatory codes, we should not be surprised to find that interfering with articulatory coding has a detrimental effect on STS storage. However, if we use the same *articulatory suppression technique* when the memory materials are presented auditorily, there is no drop in recall of the final items and acoustic confusions reappear (Peterson & Johnson, 1971). An auditory presentation apparently permits the use of an acoustic or phonological code, while the visual presentation requires participation of the articulatory apparatus in the coding process.

Coding Formats in Short- versus Long-Term Memory

Studies such as these led most investigators to conclude that STS representation is ordinarily related to the name of an item, and that the short-term component in recall can be based on either an articulatory or acoustic code representing this name. This evidence in turn became a major part of the envisaged dichotomy between short- and long-term storage with its presumed semantic system of coding.

We saw one example of this contrast in Chapter 4 where experiments by Sachs (1967, 1974) showed accurate memory for the meaning of sentences after a long delay, but poor memory for their exact wording. This was taken to indicate a preservation of the codes representing meaning in long-term retention, but more rapid forgetting of those representing the words themselves. This latter component was presumably stored in the STS, and forgotten when the semantic code for more permanent storage was formed.

Support for this coding distinction also came from studies such as one by Baddeley who showed that retention of word lists with items of similar meaning (e.g., HUGE, BIG, GREAT) typically produce more confusion errors after a 20-minute retention interval than do word lists composed of similar sounding words (e.g., MOOD, MAP, MAN). This was quite consistent with the idea that long-term retention is based primarily on semantic, rather than acoustic codes (Baddeley, 1966a,b; Baddeley & Dale, 1966).

Kintsch and Buschke (1969) showed similar effects of semantic versus acoustic similarity identified respectively with long- and short-term retention. In this case, subjects saw a list of 16 typed words presented one at a time followed by a final word which was always a repetition of one of these 16. The subjects' task was to read and remember these items, and then when the seventeenth word (called the "probe" word) occurred, to name the word that had followed it in the list. Some of the lists consisted of eight synonym pairs (e.g., POLITE, COURTEOUS) randomly ordered. Other lists consisted of pairs of words which sounded alike (e.g., KNIGHT, NIGHT) and, again, were in random order.

Kintsch and Buschke's results showed that both kinds of lists produced more confusions than lists of unrelated words, but similarity of meaning produced confusions only when subjects tried to recall items that had occurred early in the list, those presumably in long-term storage. Acoustic similarity produced confusions only in the recall of the most recent items, those presumably still held in the STS.

The appearance of acoustic confusions in recall were also interesting in showing how investigators could examine the effects of partially forgotten short-term codes (Wickelgren, 1965). These studies seemed to imply that the features of list items could be forgotten one at a time independent of each other. Confusion errors were presumably based on incomplete memory codes that retained the common features, but not the features that distinguished the error from a correct response.

These studies were less clear, however, in truly distinguishing between the type of coding employed and the presumed structure in which the storage took place. For example, we can remember a speaker's voice, presumably based on an acoustic code, for hours or days after it is first heard (Craik & Kirsner, 1974). Similarly, if we conduct an experiment in which some items are presented visually and some auditorially, we can often remember the presentation modalities of the items long after the experiment is over (Hintzman, Block, & Inskeep, 1972). Here, we have the long-term retention of sensory characteristics that does not fit the notion of either semantic or acoustic coding as envisaged by duplex theory.

To some writers, it appeared that the reason we observe semantic coding in long-term retention, and acoustic coding in short-term retention, is simply that coding the meanings or semantic relationships among items requires time, particularly with the relatively meaningless materials traditionally used in these memory studies (Baddeley & Ecob, 1970).

This latter point about the nature of the stimuli traditionally used in these studies is especially important. As we saw in Chapters 2 and 3, the use of relatively meaningless materials such as CVCs, letters, and digits, developed from a desire to study ''pure'' memory, uncontaminated by prior experience. Thus, as the duplex hypothesis developed, it built a picture based on the data available: The short-term store was, beyond doubt, primarily auditory-verbal in nature (e.g., Atkinson & Shiffrin, 1968). If studies of iconic imagery based on Sperling's (1960) work showed that visual information cannot be retained beyond 250 msec, then surely the STS must contain some representation based on the name of the presented stimulus.

As we shall see in the next chapter, visual storage in short-term memory now seems quite well established. The answer, then, may be that the emphasis on a purely acoustic STS may have arisen from the specific procedures traditionally used in its study. That is, just as the materials prevented rapid semantic coding, they also were verbal materials more amenable to linguistic rather than to visual coding.

It is in this perspective that we must view the evidence for an acoustic or articulatory code in STS. In reality, the restriction of one form of coding to each type of memory store seems unlikely. The type of coding employed for both long- and short-term retention is probably more flexible than the early presentation of the duplex theory implied.

These doubts, however, were to appear relatively late in the development of the duplex hypothesis. The duplex interpretation of the observed differences in short- and long-term memory remained, at that time, the best interpretation available. While we will develop these points later, we have one final aspect of short-term retention to consider. Perhaps the single subject to receive the most attention in the duplex theory was that of the causes of forgetting in short-term memory.

FORGETTING IN SHORT-TERM MEMORY

The demonstration by Peterson and Peterson (1959) that forgetting of recent memories takes place in a matter of seconds raised several questions about the nature of recall over these brief intervals. First of all, why was this information forgotten? Our review of associative learning studies in earlier chapters provided substantial evidence that forgetting was the result of interference from other associations. Short-term forgetting, however, seemed to take place without such competition. Brown (1958) suggested that a decay principle might operate over the short-term, while associative interference only applied to longer-term retention. This first issue, then, concerned whether decay or interference produced short-term forgetting.

A second and related issue was, for many, the primary one. It is the question of whether the difference between long- and short-term retention requires us to posit two different kinds of memory. If one set of principles can explain both phenomena, then the differences might be quantitative, rather than qualitative. In other words, short-term recall might be based on simply weaker, rather than different kinds, of memory traces.

Finally, we have the issue of the nature of the capacity limitations in immediate recall. Is this capacity limited by the interference effects of similarity and response competition, or are there only a limited number of "slots" in the short-term store. If the latter were the case, incoming information might operate to displace or "bump out" other information in order to occupy a slot. The investigations into these possibilities invariably accepted the basic distinction between short- and long-term phenomena described by William James. They differed in their interpretation of these phenomena and in what they saw as the causal variables operating in these situations.

Three major techniques were traditionally used in the study of short-term forgetting. When first devised, each seemed to provide a relatively unambiguous picture of the characteristics of the short-term store. As the methods were refined, however, each yielded results that became more difficult to interpret. These three methods made use of *distractor tasks* to prevent rehearsal, *probe recall tasks*, and *serial position effects* in free recall.

Distractor Tasks

The study by Peterson and Peterson (1959) was one of the first to use a distractor task to prevent rehearsal over short retention intervals. In their task, you will recall, subjects received a three-letter trigram followed by a three-digit number. As the number was presented, the subjects were required to start counting backward by threes, a task which presumably was a sufficient draw on resources to prevent rehearsal. As we saw in Figure 7-1, under these conditions little appeared to be retained beyond 18 sec. We also saw that the cause of this rapid loss seemed not to be due to the sort of associative interference traditionally identified with loss from long-term memory. In other words, this study of short-term forgetting seemed to imply two kinds of memory stores, a first, transient memory, for information that is only later transferred to a second, more permanent store, by rehearsal and repetition. Information was lost from the short-term store through time decay, and from the more permanent long-term store by associative interference.

Melton (1963) presented a thorough critique of this conclusion from the associationists' perspective. In reviewing several of the studies which replicated the Petersons' findings, he showed that forgetting over the short-term could be accounted for by some of the same principles used to describe long-term paired-associate learning. For example, Murdock (1961) found that increasing the number of items to be remembered increased the rate of forgetting in the Petersons' distractor paradigm. Murdock's data, along with that of Peterson and Peterson, are shown in Figure 7-5. Notice that when only one item needs to be retained there is very little forgetting over the 18 seconds of counting backward. As the number of items to be remembered increases, performance drops off rapidly. This result resembles observations in long-term forgetting: Forgetting is greater if more items are included in the list to be remembered.

To Melton, these results followed directly from the principles of associative interference; the greater number of items would be seen as increasing the total amount of interference present in the task. Also note from Figure 7-5 that three words are forgotten at the same rate as three letters. As we saw in our discussion of chunking, the rate of forgetting is affected by the number of subjective items, or number of events that are treated as units by the subject. Melton's main point, however, was that interference could have resulted from competition between the three letters of the Petersons' trigram, even if the counting task did not produce interference.

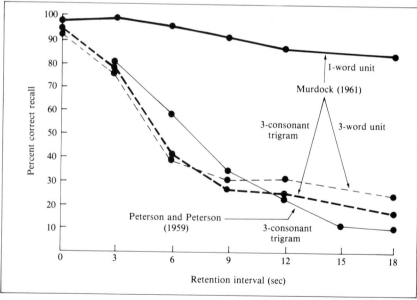

FIGURE 7-5   Percentage frequency of completely correct recall of 3-consonant trigrams (Peterson & Peterson, 1959; Murdock, 1961), and 1-word and 3-word units (Murdock, 1961).
(From Melton, 1963.)

An additional blow to the decay interpretation was provided by Keppel and Underwood (1962). These investigators demonstrated that proactive interference can be a very powerful source of forgetting even over the short retention intervals within the distractor paradigm. (Before proceeding, you might want to review the discussions of retroactive and proactive interference given in Chapter 2.)

In order to determine the effect of time on recall accuracy, the Petersons required each of their subjects to recall trigrams at each of the retention intervals in their study. If counting backward was not a source of retroactive interference, perhaps the trigrams learned on previous trials were a source of *proactive interference*. To test this possibility, Keppel and Underwood repeated Peterson and Peterson's experiment, this time plotting accuracy of recall as a function of the number of previous trials the subjects had received.

Keppel and Underwood's results are shown in Figure 7-6, and the results seemed clear. After a single trail (T-1) almost all of the subjects could recall all of the three consonants of the trigram, even with a retention interval of 18 seconds occupied by backward counting. If measured on the second trail (T-2) or the third trial (T-3), however, forgetting was clearly apparent, with only 60% correct at 18 seconds on a third trial. Loess (1964) later showed that the rate of forgetting is maximum after six trials. Increasing the number of trials beyond this point did not increase the rate of forgetting.

Keppel and Underwood (1962) explained these forgetting curves using the same principles of proactive interference we encountered in our analysis of paired-associate learning. The consonants, they argued, were

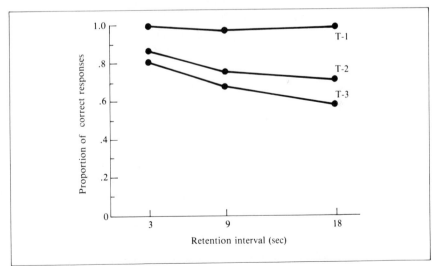

FIGURE 7-6   Retention of single consonant syllables as a function of length of the retention interval and the number of previous trials.
(From Keppel & Underwood, 1962.)

learned by the formation of an association between the three letters and the experimental setting, or perhaps some symbolic label used by the subjects (e.g., "first consonant," "second consonant," etc.). On the next trial, the new set of consonants were also associated with the same setting or label, and therefore the earlier responses were extinguished. During the retention interval, the earlier, extinguished associations would recover strength through spontaneous recovery and interfere with recall. The longer the retention interval, the more the earlier associations recovered and, therefore, the more interference they produced. This explains why there is more forgetting at the longer retention intervals in the Petersons' distractor paradigm than at shorter intervals. More trials lead to more potentially interfering associations, which is why Keppel and Underwood found more forgetting after two trials than after one.

While the Keppel and Underwood study clearly shows an effect of proactive interference on short-term retention, it did not establish the interference explanation of short-term forgetting. There are other, perhaps more plausible, explanations of what they found. For example, we could say that subjects in these experiments had to retrieve information on the basis of temporal cues. That is, while they had learned many previous trigram sets, on any given trial, they are asked to recall the "most recent" trigram that was heard. When only one trigram has been presented, retrieval of the correct information is relatively easy. However, as the experiment proceeds and more trigrams are presented, the subject may have an increasingly difficult task in selecting only the most recent consonants. At short retention intervals, when the trigram has only just been presented, there is a fairly large difference between the "age" of the most recent memory and the "age" of previous traces. As the retention interval increases, the times of occurrence of various traces become less distinct and the subject may be unable to discriminate among them on the basis of when they occurred.

For example, assume that we present the trigram RLP, have the subject count backward, and ask for recall after 4 seconds. We then wait 5 seconds between trials and present the trigram NKD. If we request recall of the second trigram after 3 seconds, recall will be relatively accurate. RLP, the first trigram, has been in memory for 12 seconds, four times as long as NKD. Thus, the two trigrams are easy to distinguish from one another. If we wait longer to require recall of the second trigram, say 9 seconds, the memory of the first trigram is now only twice as old as the most recent item. In this case the ratio is 18 seconds to 9 seconds.

According to this analysis, we could, for example, increase the value of the temporal cue simply by increasing the interval between trials. Longer intertrial intervals would increase the discriminability of the temporal differences among remembered items. In fact, when this was done, intervals exceeding 2 minutes showed no proactive effects at all (Loess & Waugh, 1967; Kincaid & Wickens, 1970). The proactive interference effect in short-term recall, then, is probably the result of a difficulty in discriminating among remembered items, a problem in retrieving the appropriate item.

A series of studies by Wickens and his colleagues (see Wickens, 1972) supports the notion that a loss of discriminability is an important factor in short-term forgetting. In one of their experiments, for example, a subject receives some set of stimuli (e.g., names of automobiles) and then counts backward for 20 sec before receiving a recall signal. Under these conditions, Wickens found that recall performance usually deteriorates as the number of trials increases just as Keppel and Underwood (1962) had found. On the fourth trial, however, Wickens changed the category of the stimulus items to be remembered to, for example, the names of birds. On this trial, recall performance again returned to a good level. Figure 7-7, taken from Wickens (1972), illustrates the kind of effect one ordinarily observes in such a study (cf. Wickens, 1973). Indeed, while in this particular study changing the category causes a rebound to just over 40% accuracy, in some experiments shift trials returned to a level of almost 90% accuracy, closely rivaling performance on the very first trial (Wickens, 1972).

Wickens (1972; Wickens, Born, & Allen, 1963) interpreted these results as showing that a category cue represented by changing from names of automobiles to names of birds, could be used to discriminate

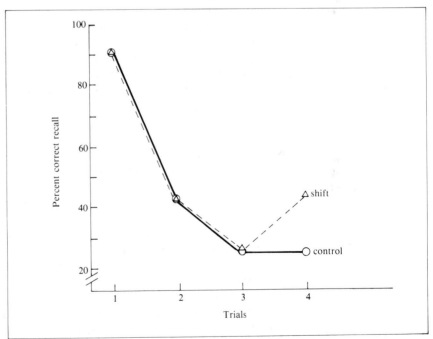

FIGURE 7-7 Release from PI effects observed when the category of the to-be-remembered items is changed on the fourth trial. The control group receives the same category of items on all trials.
(Adapted from Wickens, 1972.)

among remembered lists. For a control group having all four lists consisting of items from the same category, recall continues to fall. For this group, the time of occurrence, the "age" of the trace, remains the only dimension that can be used to retrieve the correct information.

Wickens referred to these procedures as providing a *release from proactive interference,* arguing that the category differences between the items could not have been used to improve recall unless this feature of the stimuli had been encoded in the first place. The release from PI could also illustrate that proactive interference effects in short-term retention are due more to retrieval problems than to the sort of extinction and response recovery implied by Keppel and Underwood (1962). In no way, however, do Wickens' studies imply any need to posit spontaneous decay with the passage of time to account for forgetting in short-term memory.

Wickens' emphasis on retrieval problems accounting for the effects of PI in short-term retention can be illustrated with an equally ingenious experiment by Gardner, Craik, and Birtwistle (1972). Their experiment was similar to Wickens' except that they used a shift in categories that a subject might not ordinarily notice. All subjects received four trials in the manner just described. The first three trials required retention of the names of garden flowers (e.g., rose, tulip, carnation), while the fourth trial required remembering the names of wild flowers (e.g., dandelion, daisy, crocus). One group of subjects had been warned of this subtle shift in category before the experiment began. A second group was not told of the shift until after the shift trial had been presented and they were ready to begin their recall. The final group was not told anything at all about a change in category. Both experimental groups, those warned before learning and those warned after learning, showed the release from PI effect. For these subjects, recall on the fourth trial improved dramatically over recall on the previous trial. The control group receiving no instructions about a category shift, on the other hand, showed no release.

If the proactive effects demonstrated by Wickens were due to the way in which items were originally encoded, we would expect the group who were cued before learning to show a release from PI. This group would be the only one that would have encoded the category difference, and so would have it available at recall. This would not be true of the control group or the "cue after" group. However, since the category cue improved performance when presented either before or after storage, we can infer that it is the nature of the retrieval operations that are crucial to the proactive interference effect.

These studies seem to suggest that the variables that produce effects in the distractor task are not fundamentally different from effects related to long-term retention. It seems that forgetting over the short term, at least for this task, is not substantially different in kind from forgetting that occurs over longer intervals. In agreement with this impression, several studies have shown that the distractor task can also produce retroactive interference effects on retention. As the similarity of the distractor activity and the retention materials increases, performance deteriorates (Corman & Wickens, 1968; Landauer, 1974; Wickelgren, 1965b).

Demonstrating interference effects in short-term retention does not, of course, automatically preclude the possibility of time decay as well. This is especially true for performance in the distractor task which, as Baddeley (1976) has suggested, might well be based on two separate components. One component is a very short-term memory trace that decays in as little as 5 sec, while the second is a more long-term component that is the source of the proactive interference effects we have just described.

Baddeley (Baddeley & Scott, 1971) came to this conclusion by examining the results of a large number of separate studies, each of which tested retention over various time periods for single-trial learning where no other lists or trigrams had previously been presented. While the effect was small, Baddeley and Scott did observe some forgetting in the absence of PI, up to delays of 5 sec. Beyond this point no further losses were observed. This forgetting, presumably due to the short-term component, however, was still quite small in comparison to the multiple trial losses represented by Peterson and Peterson's results.

A distractor task, it appears, can produce two effects. The first, appropriate to its intended use, is to divert resources from the target items to prevent their rehearsal. Second, however, the distracting activity can also interfere with adequate retrieval of the target items. For these reasons, a number of attempts have been made to examine recall ability under conditions which maximize the first effect while minimizing interference.

Reitman (1971, 1974) used a tone detection task to ensure minimal similarity between the target information to be remembered, and the rehearsal-preventing distractor activity. The distractor task consisted of listening to noise resembling radio static while attempting to detect a tone which would occasionally be presented in this noise background. The intensity levels of the noise and tones were kept close together to make the task of detecting a tone quite difficult. Reitman did this to make the secondary task sufficiently difficult to prevent rehearsal.

During the course of the experiment, subjects first received verbal items to be retained, and then immediately began the detection task. Performance on the detection task was compared with that of a control group that had no items to remember. Since the average detection performances of the two groups were the same, Reitman concluded that the experimental subjects had not slighted the detection task in favor of silent rehearsal, but had devoted their maximum attention to detecting the tone. Therefore, according to her reasoning, no resources would be available for rehearsal.

In the first of two studies, Reitman (1971), found no evidence of forgetting of the verbal items over a 15-second retention interval filled with rehearsal-preventing tone detection. This finding strengthened the idea that counting backward had produced forgetting because of interference due to its similarity to the to-be-remembered items. Simply preventing rehearsal with the tone detection task did not seem to produce the forgetting that time decay would predict. Similar results were obtained by Shiffrin (1973).

Reitman, of course, assumed that no rehearsal had occurred for the verbal items, since such rehearsal would presumably have drawn resources away from tone detection. As we saw, she reported that detection accuracy was as good while retaining the verbal items as in a control condition where tone detection had been the only task. As she later examined her results, however, she discovered that some subjects had in fact shown lowered detection performances during retention. It was possible, then, that these subjects had diverted some resources to rehearsing the items after all. It could have been then, that this "rehearsal" group had inflated the overall scores. Reitman was also concerned that her initial task, retention of three words, might have been too easy to reveal any decay effects which might have existed. For these reasons, Reitman (1974) conducted a second study in which she increased the number of words to five, and closely examined their tone-detection accuracy to specifically eliminate those subjects for whom there was any evidence that rehearsal had occurred.

Her analysis of the results for these subjects did show some forgetting over a 15-sec retention interval. It is true that the amount of forgetting observed (about 25%) was much less than she observed when a verbal distractor task was used (subjects had to listen for the syllable "toh" which would occur occasionally in a series of "doh's"). Nevertheless, some forgetting in the absence of interference seems to have been demonstrated. This, following Baddeley and Scott (1971), was a second demonstration of the possibility that time decay may play some role, however minor, in short-term forgetting.

Watkins, Watkins, Craik, and Mazuryk (1973) also observed forgetting of verbal items during performance of a nonverbal distractor task, although again, the amount forgotten under these conditions was much less than the forgetting observed with a verbal distractor task. Studies such as these could be used to support the idea that forgetting may be caused by decay, but it is clear that this source of forgetting is minor compared to the effects of interference.

Roediger, Knight, and Kantowitz (1977), however, have pointed out an additional problem with even these modest demonstrations of short-term time decay. It has not been demonstrated for any of these studies that the distractor tasks used necessarily drew on the same resources as required to maintain the verbal items in memory. As we mentioned in the previous chapter, there is some possiblity that different tasks may tap different attentional resources and therefore, not produce substantial interference when performed together. If rehearsal and tone detection did not require the same resources, we should not be surprised to find that little forgetting was observed in Reitman's experiment. The subjects may have been able to detect the tones at the same time as they covertly rehearsed the verbal items. The crucial test, according to Roediger et al. (1977) would be to use a distractor task which could be made to vary in difficulty. If one could then show that performance on one task systematically declined with the difficulty of the other task, this would confirm that the maintenance of memory for the words and this second task share common attentional resources.

Roediger et al. (1977) required retention of five words while subjects performed either an easy or a difficult perceptual-motor task. The task involved tapping two discs with a metal pointer in time with a flashing light. The difficulty of the task was varied by changing the size of the discs and their distance apart. If retention and the tapping task both required access to the same resources, the more difficult distractor task should require more of this capacity, and therefore, interfere more with rehearsal than the easy distractor task. As a result, recall accuracy should suffer from the now revealed effects of decay.

When they performed this experiment, Roediger et al. found no effect of task difficulty on retention. The words were retained as well when performing the difficult distractor task as when performing the easy one. From this, they concluded that the memory retaining activities did not draw on the same limited resource pool as the tapping task. Returning to the Reitman (1974) experiment, we could argue that if rehearsal and tone detection did not require access to the same resources, one should not be surprised that little forgetting occurred in that experiment. The subjects may have been able to detect the tones at the same time as they covertly rehearsed the verbal items.

Consistent with the multiprocessor view of attention described in the previous chapter, rehearsal might have a detrimental effect on tone detection, but this would be due to limits in a central mechanism that allocates resources to the various tasks or keeps the response streams from confusion. It would not necessarily mean that the tasks themselves drew on the same resources. Therefore, we must conclude that the nonverbal distractor may not have prevented mental activities that maintain verbal memory.

When first introduced, the distractor task seemed to be a relatively simple tool for demonstrating a unique character of short-term storage, the loss of information due to time decay. As we have seen, however, the task itself is considerably more complex, and its interpretation less clear, than its originators had first thought. It is certainly the case that the evidence for time decay from a STS has been seriously questioned. Indeed, most investigators have concluded that the rapid forgetting demonstrated by Peterson and Peterson was in fact due to effects of interference.

The failure to demonstrate substantial effects of decay in short-term retention does not, of course, disprove the notion that there are two kinds of memory structures, both of which lose information through interference. One view of how interference might operate in STS, as distinct from LTS, was offered by Waugh and Norman (1965) using a technique called *probed recall*.

Serial Probe Tasks

Waugh and Norman (1965) also intended to untangle the question of how time and interference influence forgetting. The distractor tasks had attempted to do this by varying the amount of time information was held in memory while preventing rehearsal with an interpolated activity. Waugh and Norman, on the other hand, intended to examine the effects of time versus interference as each was independently manipulated.

In the Waugh and Norman experiment, subjects heard a list of 16 digits. Any digit could occur more than once, but no digit was repeated twice in a row. The last digit heard at the end of a list was called the *probe* item, and was always a number that had occurred previously in the list. The probe digit was signaled to the subject by being accompanied by a tone. The subject's task was not to recall all the digits heard. Rather, he or she was to write down the name of the digit that had followed the first occurrence of the probe in the list. We can call this the "target" digit. For example, the list might be:

$$2 \quad 1 \quad 7 \quad 8 \quad 3 \quad 6 \quad 4 \quad 1 \quad 5 \quad 7 \quad 4 \quad 1 \quad 9 \quad 3 \quad 2 \quad \underline{5}$$

The final digit in the list, the probe digit, in this case is 5. The correct response would be the digit following it in the list: the digit 7.

On each trial the subject heard different lists and different probes. While the lists were always of the same length, the amount of interference was varied by using probes which would change the position of the target item in the list. Changing the position of the probe altered the number of digits intervening between the item to be recalled and the end of the list. In the example mentioned above, six items come between the target item, 7, and the end of the list (the probe item was also considered as an interfering event). In another case, using the same list, the probe 9 might be used. The correct response to this probe would be 3. Here only two items come between the target item and the end of the list. Similarly, if the probe were 8, eleven items would occur as potential interference. Recall performance was measured for each number of intervening items to determine the degree of forgetting as a function of the amount of interference.

Of course, the number of interfering items and the passage of time would vary together in this experiment. In other words, the greater the number of interfering items, the greater would be the elapsed time between the target digit and the probed recall. Twelve intervening items produce more interference than six intervening items, but a longer retention interval is also required for the earlier item. If more forgetting was produced by twelve intervening items than by six, we would not be able to tell whether this greater loss was due to more interference or the greater opportunity for time dependent decay. This is precisely the interaction that ordinarily makes it so difficult to separate the potential effects of time and interference on forgetting.

To separate these possibilities, half of the lists were presented rapidly (4 digits per second), and half were presented slowly (1 digit per second). If time dependent decay produced forgetting, one would expect better performance for the faster rates of presentation. For example, the retention interval for 12 items of interference would be 3 sec at the fast rate, but 12 sec at the slow rate. The slow rate, because it produces more time for decay, should produce poorer performance. If interference is the only factor producing forgetting, recall accuracy for both fast and slow rates should depend only on the number of interfering items and not on presentation rate.

Waugh and Norman's (1965) results are shown in Figure 7-8, and it is immediately clear that interference takes a heavy toll on short-term recall. Recall probability on the vertical axis drops from nearly 100% to zero as the number of interfering items on the horizontal axis goes from 1 to 12. The closed circles show performance at the fast presentation rate, the open circles describe the slow rate. As Waugh and Norman (1965) concluded:

> Although there appears to be a slight interaction between relative frequency of recall . . . and rate of presentation, it is clear that the effect of rate is relatively small compared to the effect of serial position. The main source of forgetting in our experiment was interference. (p. 92)

The "slight interaction" that Waugh and Norman mentioned can be seen in Figure 7-8. If you look carefully you can see that recall accuracy

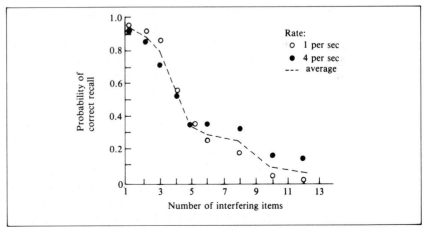

FIGURE 7-8   Probability of correct recall as a function of the number of interfering items in a probe-digit experiment for fast and slow rates of presentation.
(From Waugh & Norman, 1965. Copyright © 1965 by the American Psychological Association. Reprinted by permission.)

for the most recently presented digits (few interfering items) is slightly better for the slow rate of presentation than for the fast rate. This might possibly be attributable to coding difficulties caused by the very rapid, four-items-per-sec presentation rate. On the other hand, for the earlier items in the list (six to twelve interfering items) one sees a slight tendency for better recall for the fast rate of presentation. Several writers have seen this difference as some evidence for decay, since for any level of interference, the faster items have been in memory for a shorter length of time (e.g., Broadbent, 1971; Baddeley, 1976). These writers, however, do agree that interference takes by far a greater toll. Waugh and Norman's conclusion that interference is the primary cause of forgetting in short-term memory has thus received wide acceptance.

The case for interference and the absence of substantial decay effects in short-term memory, however, did not rule out the possibility of two memory systems for Waugh and Norman. They specifically noted the contrast between the rapid and virtually complete loss of a short-term trace over very brief intervals, with the usual forgetting rates in long-term retention. Indeed, to these investigators, the very different rates of forgetting seemed to reinforce the notion of two qualitatively different stores. They postulated that the rapid forgetting curve they obtained reflected the "displacement" of unrehearsed items from STS through interference. Rehearsal, according to Waugh and Norman, both serves to maintain items in the STS and to increase the probability of their transfer to the more permanent long-term store.

Waugh and Norman, who adopted James' use of the terms "primary" and "secondary" memory, visualized the duplex system as diagrammed in Figure 7-9. They argued that the huge amount of forgetting produced by only 12 interfering items was based on a short-term store of limited capacity which could temporarily hold items as they were presented *(primary memory)*. Because of this limited capacity, each new item that is presented has a certain probability of displacing an item already in store. Without rehearsal, items have little chance of being transferred to the long-term store *(secondary memory)*, and are therefore increasingly likely to be replaced by new information and thus "forgotten."

To be sure, interference was seen as the primary cause of forgetting in both long- and short-term memory. They agreed also that the items in the long-term store are strengthened because of the greater rehearsal they have received. The interference effects in STS, however, were seen as uniquely related to the limited capacity of this store. The resultant displacement of unrehearsed items by incoming information was a very different kind of interference from that usually associated with long-term forgetting. Waugh and Norman (1965) thus came down very firmly on the side of a duplex model of memory. Interference effects may cause forgetting in both short- and long-term memory, but the interference effects observed over short intervals was the result of different mechanisms than that over long intervals.

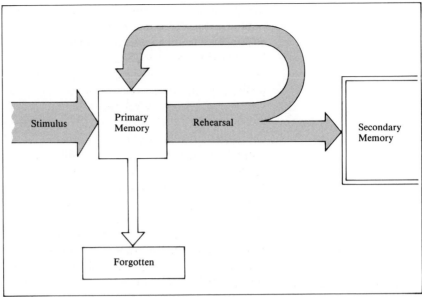

FIGURE 7-9   The primary and secondary memory system. Stimulus information enters primary memory (STS) where it is either rehearsed or forgotten after being displaced by new material. Rehearsal operates to transfer information from primary memory to secondary memory (LTS).
(From Waugh & Norman, 1965. Copyright © 1965 by the American Psychological Association. Reprinted by permission.)

Serial Position Effects

When discussing long-term memory in Chapters 2 and 3, we described the *serial position effect* in verbal learning. When subjects are asked to learn a list of 12 or 13 items, recall is usually better for the items at the beginning and the end of the list than for those in the middle. For many investigators, the duplex theory in general, and the Waugh and Norman (1965) model in particular, seemed to provide a clear structural interpretation of this well-established finding.

In order to achieve representation in long-term memory, information must be maintained in the STS by rehearsal. Because STS can hold only a limited amount of information, the items currently in this store can be "bumped" before transfer to the long-term store can occur. This view implies that the recall of the most recently presented items in a serial list are most likely to be from the STS, while recall of items earlier in the list are most likely from the long-term store. According to this interpretation, the "primacy effect" in serial learning, the good recall ability for items at the beginning of a list, is due to their having already been transferred to the long-term store through rehearsal. The "recency effect," the recall advantage for items toward the end of a list, reflects fresh storage in STS. These items have been followed by fewer interfering items, and are thus least likely to have been displaced from the limited capacity store. This theory suggested that one might be able to obtain useful data about the nature of the STS by careful study of the serial position curve.

Let us begin our analysis with the effects of rehearsal on the two ends of the serial position curve, since the argument we have just described would make very different predictions in these two cases. Specifically, we would expect that allowing greater amounts of rehearsal would affect the earlier portions of the serial position curve, which reflect recall from long-term memory, but not recall for the most recent items, which reflect recall from STS.

Figure 7-10 shows the results of an early study by Murdock (1962) which reports just this effect. The subjects in this experiment received lists of unrelated words read at a rate of either one item per second or two items per second, for lists either 10, 15, 20, 30, or 40 words long. Each list was presented just once, and was followed by a recall period in which the subjects were asked to recall as many of the words from the list as possible.

As one might expect from the foregoing argument, there were major effects of both list length and presentation rate on the early and middle items in the lists. For example, a 10-word list presented at a slower rate of one item every 2 seconds showed just under 70% recall accuracy for the first item in the list. This can be compared with the 25% accuracy for the first word of a 40-word list presented at the faster rate of one item per second. Notice, however, that neither the length of the list nor the

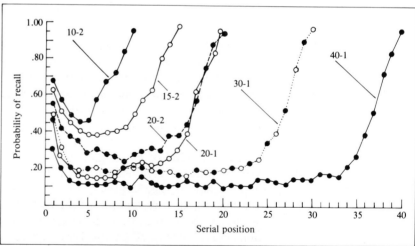

FIGURE 7-10   Serial position curves for lists of words, ranging in length from 10 to 40, presented either at a rate of one- or two-seconds per word.
(From Murdock, 1962. Copyright © 1962 by the American Psychological Association. Reprinted by permission.)

presentation rate had an effect on the later items in the lists. The accuracy of recalling the last three or four items is about the same for each curve.

List length and presentation rate are both variables which would influence rehearsal. If only a few items are presented, the subject may have time between each presentation to re-rehearse the entire list up to that point in a cumulative fashion while waiting for the next item to occur. For the longer lists, however, there would not be time for this even at the slower rate of presentation. In general, then, the longer the list, the less rehearsal we would expect each item to receive. Similarly, the faster rate of presentation would also decrease the opportunity for rehearsal as the list was being presented.

The set of curves shown in Figure 7-10, then, can be taken to represent an effect of rehearsal on LTS (the early portions of the curves), without a similar effect on STS (the recency portion of the curves). These latter items would show a uniformly high level of recall, regardless of rehearsal opportunity, because they are still "fresh" in the STS and, being at the end of the list, do not require the maintenance of rehearsal to prevent their displacement by later items.

The fact that the primacy and recency effects in a serial position curve can be manipulated independently could thus be taken to suggest that each is based on a different memory structure. Later studies were also to show that recency effects could be manipulated without producing substantial effects on the earlier portions of the curve. One can do this, for example, by filling the interval between the end of a list and a recall signal with a verbal task which would displace the most recent items from the STS. When this is done, one finds a loss of the recall advantage for items at the end of a list, an effect one does not observe simply by varying retention intervals (Baddeley & Hitch, 1974; Glanzer, 1972).

This effect of interpolated activity on the recall of final items is quite consistent with the Waugh and Norman model. Since the final list items have not yet been transferred to LTS, displacement of these items by the interpolated material causes their permanent loss. Leaving the retention interval unfilled, on the other hand, would not lead to displacement. These items are maintained in STS and recalled with good accuracy.

In fact, other studies have shown that as few as five or six items handled in a retention interval can be sufficient to displace the content of STS, consistent with the notion of its limited capacity (e.g., Glanzer, 1972). Similarly, neither the length of the retention interval nor the type of interpolated verbal materials seems to have a major influence on the recency effect, so long as the interpolated materials are verbal (e.g., Glanzer, Gianutsos, & Dubin, 1969). These effects are exactly what one would expect if the STS were predominantly verbal or acoustic in character, and if loss from this store was due to interference.

It is fascinating in retrospect to see the ingenuity with which scores of investigators nibbled away at the serial position effect, trying first one variation and then another to explore the phenomenon of recency and its implications for the duplex theory. Certainly one of the most ingenious was a study by Craik (1970) who demonstrated an effect called *negative recency* in final versus immediate recall.

Craik's study began as an apparently straightforward experiment in immediate recall. Subjects received a series of 15-word lists, and after each list was presented they were asked to recall as much of it as possible. The subjects' performance on any single list produced the now-familiar serial position curve with its marked recency effect. This effect is illustrated in the top curve in Figure 7-11 which shows the average performance levels as a function of serial position for all of the lists presented.

After ten such lists were presented, however, Craik now surprised his subjects by asking them to try to recall as many words as they could from all of the lists they had heard. The results of this "final free recall" test are shown in the lower curve in Figure 7-11. This curve represents the average accuracy of recall of the words as a function of the serial positions they occupied in the earlier lists in which they were originally presented. The results are striking. Not only does the final recall curve show an absence of the usual recency effect, but there is in fact a negative recency effect; performance tended to actually be poorer for items toward the end of the lists.

Let us assume that immediate recall of each list reflected retrieval from two separate stores, items at the beginning of the list from an LTS

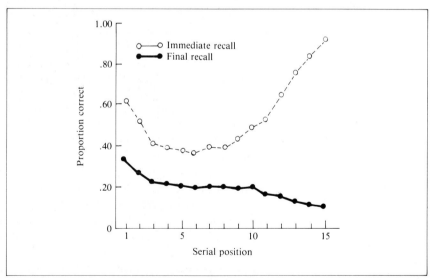

FIGURE 7-11   Serial position curves for immediate and final recall. While immediate recall shows the usual facilitation for the most recent list items, attempted final recall for all of the words presented during the experiment shows a negative recency effect.
(From Craik, 1970.)

and the most recent items at the end of the list from an STS. Since none of the subjects expected the final recall test, we can assume that the final items were recalled from the STS with no attempt to transfer them to long-term memory. Unlike the early items in the list which would have been stabilized in long-term memory, these final items could be recalled while still fresh in the short-term store. Thus, the later, final recall, test shows poorer performance for these items. These items would have been less likely to have been transferred to the LTS than the items which had occurred at the middle or the beginning of the lists.

Over the years, the serial position curve received considerable study in the context of the capacity and character of short-term memory. For example, it was an analysis of a similarity in recency effects, the STS component of the serial position curve, that led Ellis (1970) to conclude that age and intelligence had relatively little effect on the capacity of STS as compared with the utilization of this information and its transfer to the long-term store. Similarly, the studies of "articulatory suppression" by Levy (1971) and Peterson and Johnson (1971) also made use of the recency effect to experimentally manipulate the formation of articulatory codes in short-term memory. We saw how they argued that if the usual recall advantage for the final items in a list can be eliminated by verbal activity, then presumably, the effect of this activity would have been to interfere with the formation of an articulatory code.

While the duplex theory came to adopt interference as the primary source of forgetting in short-term memory, neither the notion of simple acoustic or articulatory confusions nor the displacement idea of Waugh and Norman appeared as the only explanation of how interference might operate. As investigators thought more about short-term memory in general, and the serial position effect in particular, they realized that while the phenomena we have described are consistent with a duplex hypothesis, the two-store model is not the only possible interpretation of these effects. These data could also be seen as arising from effects on retrieval strategies brought about by these various conditions.

Our discussion of temporal cues in connection with distractor tasks gave a flavor of the distinction between the strength of an item in memory (its *availability*) versus problems with its retrieval (its *accessibility*). This was seen in the argument that subjects receiving large numbers of trigrams over the course of an experiment may have difficulty in distinguishing the correct response, the last item presented, from the earlier trigrams which also have some representation in memory. This could have explained the PI effects observed by Keppel and Underwood (1962).

In a similar way, recall of items from a serial list may also involve temporal retrieval cues to distinguish each item from the others, and to distinguish these recently heard items from others already in memory. In this case, such temporal retrieval cues would be more effective for the final list items (the recency effect), and to a lesser extent for the first items in the list (the primacy effect). The appearance of Craik's negative recency effect in final recall, for example, could have resulted from a loss of this important temporal cue ordinarily available for final list items in immediate recall. The result, in other words, need not have been a consequence of effects on two different memory stores (c.f., Baddeley, 1976; Baddeley & Hitch, 1974, 1977; Bjork & Whitten, 1974).

There are many other problems with the duplex interpretation of the recency effect. For example, it can be shown that recency effects can sometimes be observed in conditions which far exceed the usual time spans associated with short-term retention. One such case is a study by Tzeng (1973) in which subjects were given a list of items for memory, but were required to count backward for 20 seconds between the presentations of each of the list items. This procedure, according to the displacement hypothesis, should have had disastrous effects on STS. Final recall of the lists nevertheless showed a recognizable recency effect.

Using a more commonplace example, Baddeley and Hitch (1977) reported that English rugby football players exhibit a recency effect in recalling the teams they had played over a series of games, even though several days may have elapsed since the last game. Either the recency effects observed by Tzeng (1973) and by Baddeley and Hitch (1977) are due to a completely different mechanism than recency effects in immediate recall, or they are both due to some common mechanism that does not involve a short-term store.

It is certainly the case that there are differences in the nature of recall over short- and long-term intervals. We have seen evidence that short-term capacity is sharply limited, that the manner of storage seems to be in the form of an acoustic or articulatory code, and that forgetting from short-term memory seems to be subject to forms of interference not ordinarily associated with long-term retention. The question, however, is whether these results necessarily derive from structurally distinct memory stores. The STS/LTS distinction is only one approach to the explanation of the STM/LTM differences. Historically, this theoretical dichotomy played an important role in sharpening our research questions and focusing interest on the issues of capacity and coding. Our appreciation of the complexity of these issues emerged primarily from experimental tests and challenges of this theory. Our next chapter gives an account of how our perspective has shifted in attempting to deal with this complexity.

CHAPTER SUMMARY

1. *Approaches to the Study of Short-Term Memory*

   A. One view of short-term memory sees recall after very brief retention intervals as supported by a distinct memory *structure* (STS) which retains information temporarily. Another approach views short-term recall as the product of a variety of different *processes* used in the course of analyzing incoming information.

B. The structural view suggests that research should focus on the characteristics of the hypothetical short-term store to determine its capacity, content, and duration. The process view leads investigators to consider the nature of the mental activities we use to analyze stimuli and the relative durability of the products of these different analyses.

2. *The Duplex Hypothesis*

A. Peterson and Peterson found that their subjects were unable to retain even three letters for more than a few seconds if this information was not rehearsed. The result was surprising because experimental work up to that point had considered such brief retention intervals of little interest. Prior work on verbal learning concentrated on the gradual build-up of associations through practice and emphasized the role of associative interference in forgetting. The Petersons' work described short-term loss in terms of time decay.

B. The duplex hypothesis claimed that short- and long-term memory differed in duration, capacity, and content. Short-term memory was a transient storage structure with a relatively limited capacity, while long-term memory held an unlimited amount of information in a relatively permanent form. Coding in long-term memory was thought to represent semantic relationships among items, while short-term memory was thought to hold acoustic representations of the items' names. The rapid forgetting found by Peterson and Peterson was attributed to decay from short-term memory before this information could be transferred to long-term storage.

3. *The Capacity of Short-Term Memory*

A. The term "chunk" was coined by George Miller to describe the subjective unit in short-term memory. He pointed out that when short-term memory was calibrated in chunks, the length of the memory span was relatively constant across a wide variety of materials. The use of the "chunk" as a metric, then, suggested that STM has a fixed capacity of 7 ± 2 items.

B. Experimental work following Miller's famous paper found the memory span to be the result of more than one mechanism. Recall of early list items represented retrieval from long-term memory, while recall of final items reflected short-term storage.

C. The distinction between short- and long-term components of the memory span was supported by studies which indicated that recall of final items in a list was relatively unaffected by variables such as age and retardation. These same variables had sizable effects on the efficiency of recalling earlier list items.

D. Studies of reaction times in memory scanning raised three possible search strategies which might be involved in retrieval from short-term memory. The three possibilities were parallel process- ing, serial self-terminating, and serial exhaustive search proc- esses. While early arguments for serial exhaustive search in short-term memory later came into question, these studies intro- duced an important experimental paradigm and set the stage for defining the parameters for alternative solutions.

4. *The Content of Short-Term Memory*

A. Errors made in the recall of recently presented sequences resem- ble errors made in auditory perception. That is, errors of recall resemble the sound of the correct response. This is true even when the mode of presentation has been visual. On the other hand, errors made after long retention intervals are usually semantic confusions.

B. The errors observed in short-term recall may be the result of either an acoustic or an articulatory code. An articulatory code implies the storage of the patterns of movement necessary to produce the sound. For example, congenitally deaf children who could not have formed an acoustic code nonetheless showed the familiar pattern of acoustic confusions in short-term recall. The degree to which this pattern appeared was related to the child's relative skill in speaking.

C. The nature of short-term coding seems to depend on circum- stances and the nature of the materials. Studies of articulatory suppression indicate that there may be a tendency to use ar- ticulatory codes for visually presented materials and acoustic codes for auditory material. The relatively meaningless materials ordinarily used in verbal learning studies may also serve to dis- courage rapid semantic coding.

5. *Forgetting in Short-Term Memory*

A. The two questions on forgetting of primary interest to duplex theorists have traditionally been first, the causes of short-term forgetting, and second, whether the nature of forgetting over long and short retention intervals requires the postulate of two qualita- tively distinct memory structures.

B. While the study of short-term forgetting using distractor tasks, serial probe tasks, and studies of serial position effects did indicate that some forgetting was due to spontaneous decay, this cause was relatively minor when compared to the effects of interference.

C. Structural theorists of memory maintained that the type of inter- ference observed in short-term memory was different from that observed after long retention intervals. Short-term interference effects were the result of a displacement effect in which new information competed for space in a limited capacity structure. Long-term interference effects were associative in nature and represented problems in the retrieval of associations.

LEVELS OF PROCESSING AND MENTAL REPRESENTATION

TOPIC QUESTIONS

1. Levels of Processing.

What were the basic elements of the original *levels of processing* view of the memory system? What factors were thought to determine how well a stimulus will be remembered? What experimental techniques were used to illustrate the "levels" notion, and what sorts of results were obtained? How does the "levels" approach interpret the earlier data on short-term versus long-term memory?

2. Elaboration and Retrieval of Memory Codes: Amendments to the Framework.

Why was the notion of *spread of encoding* added to the original levels postulate? What is *encoding specificity,* and how does it relate to the levels approach? What did the studies of "spread" of processing imply about the role of depth of processing in retention?

3. The Status of Short-Term Memory.

What conclusions were drawn about the duplex theory based on analyses of brain damaged patients suffering unique forms of memory impairment? What do we conclude about the status of short-term memory as a distinct, structural store?

4. Visual Memory.

How did early memory theory treat the idea of visual representations in memory? What conclusions were drawn from the more recent studies of picture recognition and "mental rotation?" How do easily visualizable stimuli differ on memory tests from those not easily visualizable? What explanations have been offered to account for these differences?

5. Detection in Memory: An Extended Analogy.

What is *signal detection theory,* and what are its major elements? How has detection theory been applied to the analysis of recognition memory?

Our review of the research inspired by the duplex model of memory should leave little doubt that there are differences between the character of long- and short-term retention. Each is affected to different degrees by different variables and each has different capacities. What may have emerged less clearly from these studies is whether these differences are necessarily based on different memory structures. As we saw, there were many alternative interpretations of the data and no few ambiguities that arose from the structural stores, or duplex view of memory.

LEVELS OF PROCESSING

Craik and Lockhart (1972) at the University of Toronto offered one of the major alternatives to the structural view. They suggested that memory be thought of as the product of the kinds of analyses, or *processes,* performed on the information we receive from the environment. This view proposed a fundamentally different framework for memory research. Here were the elements of their position:

1. Memory should be viewed within the context of a system of information processing which can perform a variety of analyses on stimulus information. One can see these analyses in terms of a hierarchy, or sequence of "levels," running from sensory analyses of the physical properties of a stimulus, through identification and naming of the stimulus, and finally, to the meaning of the stimulus, the relationship between this stimulus and other aspects of our knowledge. For example, "reading" a word could be seen as composed of a sequence of operations in which the visual properties of the stimulus are processed (the lines, angles, their physical relationships to one another), then a name or label is formed for this configuration, and finally, the meaning of the word placed in a context of our knowledge about this and related events. Craik and Lockhart (1972) saw this sequence as a continuum in which "deeper" processing produced progressively more meaningful information.

2. The memory trace, more properly called a memory *code,* could be viewed as a record of what processes have been carried out to analyze a stimulus. Each level of processing leaves behind a memory trace or code that represents the information produced by analysis of the stimulus at that level. Lower level, or "shallow" codes are produced by analyses which operate at the earliest levels of the hierarchy. These codes represent the physical properties of the stimulus. "Deeper" codes, which include semantic representations and associative relationships, are produced by later processing.

3. The original formulation of the "levels" view (Craik & Lockhart, 1972) proposed that deeper codes were more enduring than the more superficial shallow codes. Forgetting, then, would be a function of the depth of processing. Early, shallow codes, would be forgotten rather

quickly, while deeper codes would support relatively long-term retention. The capacity to hold recent information is limited, but not by the number of "slots" in some hypothetical structural store. Memory for a stimulus will be limited by the depth of processing that circumstances permit. If the presentation of stimulus material is rapid, and the stimuli are relatively meaningless, the subject will be restricted in the amount and kind of processing that can be performed. You will recall that structural theorists used this apparent limitation in short-term retention as evidence for the existence of a short-term store with a limited capacity and an acoustically coded content. However, these limitations may have been the consequence of studies which used meaningless materials (e.g., nonsense syllables, digits, letter strings), and which provided subjects with little time to process this information.

Craik and Lockhart saw two consequences from viewing recall as being crucially dependent on what the subject does with stimulus information. Both consequences seemed to suggest that there were more limits to the early studies of short-term memory than there are to memory itself! First, the studies of short-term memory typically observed the results of only lower levels of processing. These were manifested by, for example, the acoustic or articulatory confusions we saw in short-term retention. Their question was blunt: Does acoustic (or articulatory) coding reflect the character of an obligatory structural store intermediate between sensory and long-term memory, or is it simply a strategy employed because there is little else one can do to maintain meaningless digit or letter strings?

The second consequence follows from the first: The very impossibility of rapid deep processing of the sorts of materials used in these studies may have inflated the importance of rehearsal to the durability of a memory code. *Maintenance rehearsal* is a function we use to do things like retain a telephone number during the interval between looking it up and dialing it. If circumstances allow, short-term retention might also reveal the results of *elaborative rehearsal*. That is, if it were possible, one could perhaps use the same time interval to process information more deeply, relating it to other events, and thereby enriching the coding of the stimulus. This more complex form of rehearsal may also create more durable codes. More important, however, this form of coding is probably more typical of the kind of "rehearsal" meaningful material ordinarily receives outside of the laboratory. The distinction between maintenance rehearsal and elaborative encoding is not an either/or dichotomy. Maintenance and elaboration represent only two extremes of a variety of ways in which information can be processed.

The levels of processing view, then, claimed that memory is the record of cognitive operations that have been used to analyze the stimulus. In its earliest formulation (Craik & Lockhart, 1972), these operations were arranged in a hierarchy from shallow physical analyses to deeper semantic analyses. The differences between long- and short-term retention described earlier could thus be due to the different types of encoding that can be accomplished with different types of materials and the time available for processing over long- and short-term retention intervals. Lower level acoustic and articulatory codes are quickly lost from memory, while deeper semantic codes may be retained for indefinitely long periods of time. Practice and repetition by themselves can maintain information at a given level of processing, but to make this information more permanent requires that it be processed to a deeper level.

If we further assume that processing requires attentional resources, the depth of processing and amount remembered will thus depend on the attentional capacity devoted to analyzing the stimulus. The results we examined earlier in the context of a short-term store might therefore be explained not in terms of two structures, but as the indirect result of limitations in processing capacity and resultant depth of encoding.

The recent years since the articulation of the levels of processing view by Craik and Lockhart (1972) have produced a burgeoning of studies providing support and criticisms to their original formulation. This research led to a continuing development of the "levels" notion. Let us look at this development.

Depth of Processing and Retention

The duplex model prompted investigators to ask questions about the relative durations of the two forms of memory, their capacities, and the kinds of codes used in each. The levels of processing view led to a different set of questions. Since it is assumed that there are a variety of possible codes, investigators now became interested in the characteristics of each coding process, the durability of each of the resulting codes, and the processing capacity required for the development of these various codes.

The relative durability or "strength" of a particular code is quite a different question from those asked earlier about the usual duration of information in a particular structural store. In the levels of processing framework, how well an event is remembered is not dependent on which store contains the information. It depends instead on what the subject did with the stimulus information, how it was analyzed, and what codes were created by these analyses.

A common method used to reveal the effectiveness of different types of codes was developed from studies originally designed to investigate *incidental learning*. We saw an example of this in Chapter 4 with the study by Hyde and Jenkins (1969). In that experiment, subjects were given a list of 24 words. One group of subjects was asked to check through the list for the presence of the letter "E," another group counted the letters in each word, and a final group rated each word on its relative "pleasantness." While none of the subjects were told they would later be tested for retention of the word lists, we saw in Table 4-1 that one of these groups, the "pleasantness" raters, remembered the list quite well. Indeed, they remembered the list just as well as a control group who were specifically told to memorize the list for later testing.

The Hyde and Jenkins study showed the positive effects on retention of an orienting task which required the subjects to think about the meanings of the words ("pleasantness"), and that recall following such semantic processing can have as great an effect on retention as conscious intention to learn without this orientation (see also Hyde & Jenkins, 1973).

In a study more directly designed to provide evidence relevant to levels of processing, Craik and Tulving (1975) recruited subjects for what was described as an investigation of perception and reaction time. On each of a series of experimental trials, subjects were given a question in the form shown in Table 8-1, and then saw a word exposed for 200 milliseconds (msec) in a tachistoscope. Three types of questions were used: (1) a question about the physical structure of the word ("Is the word in capital letters?"), (2) a question about the sound of the word ("Does the word rhyme with WEIGHT?"), or (3) a semantically oriented question ("Would the word fit the sentence: 'He met a _____ in the street?'"). The words that followed each of these three types of questions would either imply a "yes" or a "no" answer. For example, question one might be followed by a word either in upper or lower case typescript (TABLE versus table), question two would be followed by a word which either rhymed with WEIGHT or did not (crate versus MARKET), and question three would be followed by a word which either did or did not fit the sentence frame (FRIEND versus cloud).

Since this was supposed to be a study of reaction times, subjects provided their answers by pressing one button for a "yes" response and another for a "no" response. They were told to give their response as quickly as possible when the stimulus word appeared. Later, and to their complete surprise, the subjects were now tested for their retention of the words they had seen in this first part of the experiment.

Before we look at Craik and Tulving's results, let us review the effects each of these orienting questions would presumably have had on

TABLE 8-1   Examples of orienting questions and stimulus words used to study the effect of depth of processing on retention performance in a later surprise recognition test. (From Craik & Tulving, 1975. Copyright © 1975 by the American Psychological Association. Reprinted by permission.)

Level of Processing	Orienting Questions	Correct Response Yes	No
(1) Physical structure	Is the word in capital letters?	TABLE	table
(2) Phonological features	Does the word rhyme with WEIGHT?	crate	MARKET
(3) Semantic features	Would the word fit the sentence: "He met a _____ in the street?	FRIEND	cloud

the processing of the words when they appeared. Each set of questions was assumed to induce a different kind of processing. A question about the typescript of a word can be answered with only the shallow processing represented by scanning the physical characteristics of the word. Determining whether two words rhyme represents processing of the acoustic/phonological characteristics of the word. Finally, determining whether a word fits a particular sentence frame involves deeper semantic processing of the meaning of the word. In terms of the levels framework, the products of these different analyses should produce different memory codes, different records of activities used in analyzing these stimuli.

Figure 8-1 shows the results of this study. The panel on the left shows the time it took the subjects to give their "yes" or "no" responses when words appeared following each question type. Whether the response was "yes" or "no," it took longer to answer a semantic question about the stimulus word than it took to answer a rhyming question, and a rhyming question took longer than the typescript of the stimulus. Deeper processing, then, seemed to require more time than shallower processing.

The panel on the right shows the results of the later surprise recognition test for the words. Consistent with the levels argument, memory for the words appeared as a direct function of the depth of processing each

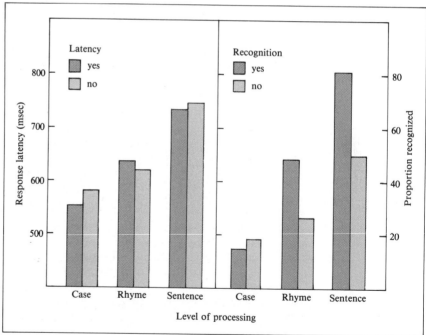

FIGURE 8-1   Mean response latency (reaction time) to answering yes and no questions about words that imply deeper levels of processing, and later recognition performance for these words on a surprise memory test.
(From Craik & Tulving, 1975. Copyright © 1975 by the American Psychological Association. Reprinted by permission.)

of the words had presumably received. Semantic processing (sentence questions) produced better recognition scores than acoustic/phonological processing (rhyme questions), while a physical feature analysis (typescript questions) was poorest. Indeed, for the "yes" words, ability to recognize increased from 15% for the case decisions to 81% for sentence decisions. This is a striking result, especially when we remember that none of the subjects had any idea that their memory for these words would later be tested. We can presume that this good retention occurred in the absence of direct rehearsal.

Task Demands and Depth of Processing

The depth of processing induced by each of the orienting questions in the Craik and Tulving study was reflected both in the time necessary to carry out this processing, and in terms of the durability of the memory codes produced by the different types of processing. One of the first questions Craik and Tulving asked, however, was whether these retention scores were due primarily to the depth of processing demanded by the task, or whether they resulted primarily from the time spent to reach these levels.

In an extended series of experiments, Craik and Tulving (1975) went on to argue that one cannot always identify the amount of time required for processing as an index of the processing depth. A semantic interpretation of a highly familiar, expected stimulus, may be achieved fairly quickly, while a structural analysis of an unfamiliar, unexpected stimulus, may require considerable time. Craik and Tulving used a variation on the experiment just described to demonstrate that it is the nature of the processing that determines retention, rather than simply the processing time.

As before, subjects thought they were participating in a perceptual reaction time study. They were asked a question, briefly saw a word in the tachistoscope, and responded "yes" or "no" by pressing the appropriate button. This time, however, the question required either a difficult low level task, or an easy semantic task. The difficult task required the subjects to determine the pattern of consonants and vowels in the stimulus word. For example, the question might be, "Does the word match the pattern Consonant–Vowel–Vowel–Consonant?" If the stimulus word that appeared was BOOK, the answer would be "yes" since it does match the CVVC pattern. We can answer this question without a semantic analysis of the word. Yet, it is still a very difficult task. The semantic orientation was typified by the question, "Does the word fit the sentence, 'He laid the _____ on the table?' ". Again, the stimulus word presented might either fit the sentence (e.g., book) or it might not (e.g., cloud).

The results were clear. While the consonant-vowel task required more time for a "yes" or "no" response than the relatively easy semantic task, the words that had been preceded by a semantic question were nevertheless remembered significantly better in a later recognition test. Craik and Tulving thus concluded that the recognition performance was determined by the nature of the processing (structural versus semantic), rather than by the amount of processing time, per se.

It might follow from this interpretation that continued maintenance of a stimulus at a lower level of processing may not substantially improve memory for the stimulus. That is, simple rote rehearsal may not ordinarily lead to substantial improvements in retention. Such rehearsal simply recirculates the information at the level of an acoustic or articulatory code. This perspective leads to a different interpretation of the results of final, versus immediate free recall than the one given in the previous chapter.

In his ''final free recall'' study, Craik (1970) presented subjects with a series of lists for recall immediately after presentation. At the end of this immediate recall phase of the study, a final free recall test was given in which subjects were unexpectedly required to remember all the words they had encountered in the earlier part of the experiment. Final free recall produced the negative recency effect we saw in Figure 7-11. The final items in each list were not as well recalled as earlier items, exactly the reverse of the superior memory for recent items found in immediate recall of the individual lists.

From the structural view, one might conclude from this study that the recent items had been temporarily held in a short-term memory store, and had been displaced by succeeding items heard during the experiment. Early items in the list, on the other hand, had received more rehearsal, and so were better recalled. The levels of processing notion inclines us to see this result as due to a difference in the kinds of processing carried out on early and late list items. Early items may be elaborated, processed more deeply and so achieve a more durable representation in memory. Items toward the end of the list may be processed only to a relatively shallow level. This shallow level permits an advantage in immediate recall but is less efficient for remembering over longer retention intervals.

Mazuryk (1974) tested this interpretation by explicitly manipulating the subjects' rehearsal strategies. He presented lists of 14 words for the subjects to learn. They were to rehearse the first 10 words silently in all cases. The last 4 words of each list, however, were to be rehearsed differently by different groups of subjects. One group rehearsed these items silently as they had the other 10. A second group rehearsed the items out loud, and a third group generated verbal associates to each of the final 4 words. Immediate recall was required for each list.

Both the overt and the silent rehearsal groups showed the typical recency effect, with final items remembered better than earlier ones. The recency effect for the group that had formed associates, however, was somewhat reduced as compared with the other rehearsal groups. It was as if this type of processing interfered with immediate recall. On the other hand, when final free recall of all the lists was required, the associates group was much superior to the other two groups on these recent items. Maintenance rehearsal, either silent or overt, produced superior immediate recall but poorer long-term recall as compared with the more elaborative strategy of generating associations. Other investigators have also found similar results for the recency and negative recency effects with shifts in rehearsal strategy (e.g., Bernbach, 1975; Watkins & Watkins, 1974).

The application of the levels of processing viewpoint to notions of rehearsal began to appear in a variety of contexts. For example, decrements in the memory performance of the elderly, very young children, and the retarded, have long been thought to reflect the rehearsal strategies used, and the attention paid to the stimulus materials (Belmont & Butterfield, 1971). Within the levels framework, we could say that the type of coding used by these groups depends on the nature of the features attended to and how this information is elaborated. Differences in strategies and attentional control will be reflected in the processes performed and, therefore, in the subject's memory for these events.

As we pointed out earlier, the usual differences in recall performance between children and adults can be reduced by explicitly instructing the children in the rehearsal operations they should perform (Murray & Roberts, 1968). Depth of processing has also been related to memory deficits often exhibited by the elderly (Eysenck, 1974). However, there still remains some controversy over whether this deficit represents processes the elderly cannot carry out due to resource limitations, or whether it involves processes they could conduct, but which they rarely do spontaneously. Craik and Simon (1980) refer to these respectively as a "processing" versus a "production" deficit.

Generally, the levels of processing notion places emphasis on encoding as a determinant of forgetting and retrieval. The quality and amount of processing has a greater role in affecting later recall than does the nature of the stimulus materials or the amount of time available for learning. Memory is seen as a record of the processes carried out during the learning experience. Information is not, according to this view, transferred between two memory structures, a short-term and a long-term store. Rather, there are a variety of possible codes reflecting the possible mental activities related to the stimulus materials.

A central feature of this argument, then, relates to the role of rehearsal. Is it the case, as previous studies seemed to imply, that rehearsal is a necessary step for transfer of information from a short-term to a long-term store? Or is repetition an optional and generally inferior strategy subjects use when circumstances discourage deep or elaborative processing? As investigators pursued this question, the levels of processing approach saw the first of several major modifications.

Rehearsal Revisited

Levels of processing interprets maintenance rehearsal as a process that keeps verbal material in immediate awareness for rapid accurate retrieval. It does not serve to increase the strength of the memory trace, or to increase the probability of transfer to a more permanent store. Craik and Watkins (1973) showed, for example, that simple repetition of items does not, by itself, increase the ease with which items are recalled after a delay. In their experiment, the last 4 words of a 12-word list were recalled either immediately or after a 20-second (sec) interval of overt rehearsal. When a surprise final free recall test was given, subjects who had rehearsed for 20 sec recalled no better than subjects who did not have the opportunity to rehearse. They concluded that maintenance rehearsal serves to recirculate the information at the same level of processing but does not increase its memorability, or "strength" (see also Jacoby, 1973; Woodward, Bjork, & Jongeward, 1973).

The original formulation of levels of processing thus made a distinction between maintenance rehearsal, which recirculates information at a given level, and elaborative rehearsal, which increases the depth of encoding by carrying out further analyses at other levels. Conclusions about the relative effectiveness of these two forms of rehearsal, however, seemed difficult to draw.

While the first rush of research within the levels of processing framework reported that maintenance rehearsal does not generally improve later free recall, other studies have reported that such rehearsal does improve memory performance when testing is done within a recognition paradigm (e.g., Woodward, et al., 1973; Glenberg, Smith, & Green, 1977; Rundus, 1977). Indeed, contrary to the early studies, some investigators claimed that under appropriate conditions maintenance rehearsal can show a positive effect even with a measure of later recall (e.g., Dark & Loftus, 1976; Nelson, 1977).

Dark and Loftus (1976) gave subjects 3, 4, or 5 words and allowed them to rehearse these words during an unfilled retention interval of from 3 to 20 sec. While the subjects were led to expect a recall test immediately after the retention interval, on some trials no immediate recall was requested. After several trials, an unexpected final free recall test was given.

Dark and Loftus' results showed that words that had been untested in immediate recall did show positive effects of rehearsal. Of these untested words, accuracy in free recall was also greater for the longer retention intervals than for the shorter ones. It would appear from this study that the longer opportunity for rehearsal did improve memory for items that were not tested in immediate recall. Dark and Loftus went on to argue that requiring immediate recall on all trials in the earlier studies had obscured this effect.

The original strong distinction between the two types of rehearsal has since been abandoned by its inventors (Craik, 1979a,b). It is evident that memory maintaining activities can take a variety of forms and that more extensive processing at a single level may increase the durability of a memory code. It is this notion of the extensiveness of processing, as opposed to depth, that provided an even more profound modification to the levels framework.

ELABORATION AND RETRIEVAL OF MEMORY CODES: AMENDMENTS TO THE FRAMEWORK

One of the central notions of the levels of processing framework of Craik and Lockhart (1972) was that deeper, semantic analyses produced codes that are remembered better than the products of "shallower," physical analyses. In the experiments we have described it was intuitively obvious what "deeper" meant. On the other hand, we know that we can retain some information about the physical aspects of a stimulus for considerable periods of time. We can, for example, recognize a speaker's voice hours after first hearing it (Craik & Kirsner, 1974). Often we can vivily remember precisely where on a page we read a certain piece of information (Rothkopf, 1971). These both seem to be relatively superficial products of shallow processing, but they can nonetheless represent enduring memories.

We encounter a variety of such problems when we try to define depth in a completely explicit way. The most important single problem was an absence of a measurement of depth of processing other than the effects it produces (i.e., better retention). It becomes hopelessly circular if we try to use better retention to measure depth of processing, while at the same time using depth of processing to explain better retention. This circularity has been criticized by several writers (e.g., Baddeley, 1978; Eysenck, 1978a,b; Nelson, 1977) and defended by Lockhart and Craik (1978) as a necessary difficulty in the development of our concept of memory. They argued that levels of processing is a fruitful conceptualization of how memory works, and that the value of this approach should be tested by its conceptual contribution regardless of the absence of specifiable variables or predictions. Nevertheless, we must deal with some of the problems encountered by this conceptualization and the modifications that developed as it attempted to gain this specificity.

Elaboration and Spread of Encoding

In the Craik and Tulving (1975) experiments we described earlier in support of the levels notion, some evidence was also obtained that questioned the simple concept of "depth" as an adequate way to describe the kinds of processing that lead to enduring memory codes. You will remember that these investigators presented their subjects with a question about a word, followed by a brief presentation of this word in a tachistoscope. Subjects responded by pressing a "yes" button or a "no" button. In general, semantic questions about the word produced slower reaction-times but better retention on an unexpected later memory test than did structural processing of the same word. In addition to these general findings, however, you may have noted that Figure 8-1 also showed that memory performance was better for words that had received a "yes" response than for words to which the subject had responded "no." If you look carefully, you will also see that the retention advantage for "yes" words was greater for the semantically processed words than it was for words that had followed structural questions.

It seems fair to assume that the words to which the subject had responded "yes" or "no" were processed to the same level for a given question. Yet, words receiving "yes" responses were better recalled. This and related data led Craik and Tulving (1975) to suggest that an additional principle, that of *spread of encoding,* would have to be used to supplement the notion of depth of encoding. In this formulation, the notion of *depth* refers to changes in the types of analyses performed on the stimulus, while *spread* refers to additional operations carried out at the same level. The concept of spread of encoding implies an enrichment of the memory code by the inclusion of features of the context in the encoding, or modification of the encoding in a way that produces a more specifiable, unique code for the stimulus.

The difference in retention between words receiving positive and negative responses could thus be accounted for by noting how the context could have been encoded in the two cases. We might, for example, have the semantic orienting question, "Does the word fit the sentence, 'He shook hands with his _____?' " If the word following this question is FRIEND, the subject can process this sentence along with the meaning of the stimulus word. In this way, the sentence frame itself would become part of the semantic processing of the meaning of the word FRIEND, and this rather enriched code would enhance memory performance. On the other hand, if the word following the question was HOUSE, the context and the word do not fit. The stimulus word would not be integrated with the sentence frame in processing.

The semantic encoding of the word FRIEND, in this view, is enriched by the presence of this context. A more elaborate and extensive code is produced than if the word were presented alone. The word HOUSE, however, does not receive this enrichment because it does not fit into the context. Even though it must be processed to a semantic level in order to answer the question, the resulting code is less extensive than for a word that was *congruent* with the sentence frame.

The difference in retention between words that had received positive and negative responses was eliminated when questions were used which supplied equally enriching contexts for both "yes" and "no" conditions. For example, the question might be, "Is the object bigger than a chair?" The word MOUSE would receive a negative response while the word TRUCK would receive a positive response. Both words receive equal elaboration of their meanings with this context, as attention is called to the size of the object in both cases. When questions and stimuli such as these were used, words receiving a negative response during the orientation task were as well remembered as words which had received a positive response (Craik & Tulving, 1975).

Craik and Tulving further illustrated the effects of spread of processing by explicitly providing different degrees of semantic context. In this case the subjects had the same sequence of events as described for the earlier experiments, but the orienting questions in all cases required judgements about whether the stimulus words fit into a certain sentence frame. The sentence frames provided, however, were different in the extent to which they elaborated on the meaning of the stimulus word. For example, the sentence frame might be simple ("He dropped the _____ ."), medium ("The old man dropped the _____ ."), or complex ("The old man hobbled across the room and dropped the valuable _____ .").

The word WATCH fits the frame in each case, and in each case the subject must process this word to a semantic level in order to answer the question correctly. The more complex frame, however, should provide a richer context for the elaboration of the meaning of the word. The greater the complexity of the sentence frame, the greater should be the effectiveness of the sentence as a retrieval cue. On the other hand, presentation of a sentence frame which does not fit the word should be a less effective recall cue regardless of sentence complexity. Here, the presentation word cannot easily be integrated with its context; the aspects of the word's meaning cannot be elaborated within the meaning of the sentence frame. Thus, a sentence frame as a recall cue would be most effective for words receiving a "yes" response, but less effective for words in negative cases. As Figure 8-2 shows, this is exactly what Craik and Tulving (1975) obtained under these conditions.

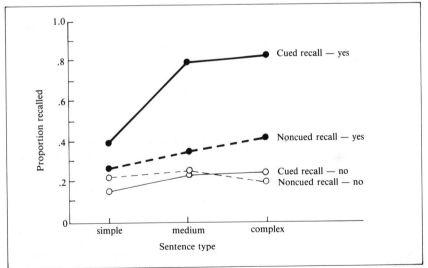

FIGURE 8-2   Recall performance for words when recall was cued by seeing the sentence frames previously associated with the words versus recall without these cues. The four curves represent those cases where the sentence frames semantically fit the words and when they did not (yes versus no), plotted as a function of the complexity of the sentence frames.
(From Craik & Tulving, 1975. Copyright © 1975 by the American Psychological Association. Reprinted by permission.)

The elaborateness, or richness of the code at a given level of processing, now became added to the notion of depth of processing as a determinant of how well a given event can be remembered.

Encoding Distinctiveness

The deeper or more elaborate the processing of a stimulus, the more likely it will be that the stimulus will later be recalled. It has been suggested that the basis for this increased ability to recall information after deep or more elaborate processing may be the increased *distinctiveness* of the resulting code. For lower level codes successive inputs are more likely to be similar to each other than are higher level codes. In listening to a lecture we may hear many similar sounding words in the course of an hour. We almost certainly hear the identical speech sounds over and over again in different words. The meaning of what the lecturer has to say, however, will be unique to that hour and that class. If you later wanted to recall what went on in that lecture, it is very unlikely that you could retrieve the exact words you heard. The words and the speech sounds do not differentiate this class from any other. On the other hand, you should recall the meaning of the lecture; that is, the product of semantic processing performed in the course of listening to and comprehending the speaker. Semantic processing makes this lecture different from other lectures in a way that shallower processing could not.

Stein (1978) experimentally varied the uniqueness of memory codes. In this study, subjects saw 24 words displayed one at a time. A single letter in each of the words was capitalized. Just before the slide with a word was presented, the subject was given an orienting question such as, "_____ has a steel blade." or "_____ has a capital I." The first question would require semantic processing, while the second could be answered by simply analyzing the typescript of the letters in the word. The first question, then, involves deeper processing than the second.

The distinctiveness of the resulting code was manipulated by increasing or decreasing the ratio of the number of semantic to typescript questions the subjects would receive. One group of subjects was asked semantic questions for 20 of the 24 words and the typescript question for only 4 words. The other group received 20 typescript questions and 4 semantic questions. The assumption was that, for each group, the type of processing used least often would produce the most unique code. That is, the subject's memory of the list would include 20 encodings of one type and only 4 encodings of the other.

In the recognition test following presentation of the 24 words, subjects showed better recognition performance for the words associated with the more unique code. Deeper encodings were still better than shallow codes, but shallow codes were better recognized when they were more unique than when they were less so. Uniqueness of the code improved recall for both types of orienting task. Stein (1978) concluded that performance on the recognition test was determined by how well the encoding operation differentiated the events from other events at the same level of encoding.

Sensory, or shallow codes may not be, then, inevitably more transient than deeper, semantic codes. Several experiments since the original levels formulation (Craik & Lockhart, 1972) have shown that the operations of sensory and perceptual analyzers can produce very enduring effects (e.g., Kolers & Ostry, 1974; Morris, Bransford, & Franks, 1977; Nelson, 1979). In particular, Kolers and his colleagues (reviewed in Kolers, 1979) have demonstrated that the perceptual encoding of the typography of a printed passage can have measurable effects on recognition memory as much as a year after initial exposure. In one of their studies (Kolers & Ostry, 1974), college students first read a series of sentences and later were required to discriminate these "old" sentences from other sentences they had not seen before ("new" sentences).

Table 8-2 outlines the design of this experiment. On first reading, half the sentences were in normal orientation (N), and half were seen inverted (I). The subjects, in other words, had to read some of the sentences upside-down. During the recognition test which followed, some of the inverted sentences had been returned to their normal orientation, while some of the originally normal sentences had been inverted. An "old" sentence, then, could appear on the recognition test in the same orientation as during the first reading (NN or II), or in a different orientation (IN or NI).

Kolers and Ostry's results showed that subjects were not only able to discriminate "old" sentences from "new" ones, but they also remembered whether the test sentences were originally seen rightside-up or upside-down. Sentences which were inverted on both first reading and at test were recognized best. This superiority of the II condition, and the subjects' ability to discriminate same from different orientations, persisted out to the longest retention interval tested—32 days.

The apparent conflict these studies seem to pose for the notion that "deeper is better," can be easily resolved. Usually it will be the case that deeper processing produces more unique or distinctive codes.

TABLE 8-2 Illustration of the experimental design used by Kolers (1979) to study the recognition of typography in order to demonstrate the potential effectiveness of perceptual cues for recognition memory. Subjects read 60 sentences, 30 in normal orientation (N) and 30 inverted (I). "Old" and "new" sentences were then presented for recognition testing shown either in the same orientation (NN or II) or a different orientation (NI or IN).

Stimulus Sentences To Be Read	Recognition Testing	
	Old Sentences	New Sentences
30 sentences with normal orientation (N)	15 normal (NN) 15 inverted (NI)	30 normal
30 sentences with inverted orientation (I)	15 normal (IN) 15 inverted (II)	30 inverted

Events at this level would be expected to be less similar to one another than the encodings at lower levels of processing. However, the effects of distinctiveness can operate at any level. Obviously, unless Kolers and Ostry's subjects had retained some representation of the superficial aspects of the stimuli, discrimination between orientations would have been impossible. In addition, the sentences which required the greatest amount of processing at a shallow level, the inverted sentences, were best remembered. From the levels of processing view, the extensive processing (elaboration) necessary produced a distinctive code at the level of visual features. Both depth and elaborateness of processing are, therefore, useful to the degree that they produce a memory code that is distinct from others (c.f., Lockhart, Craik, & Jacoby, 1976).

Encoding Specificity and Compatibility

The distinctiveness of encoding also relates to an important principle we previously mentioned, that of *encoding specificity*. The principle was demonstrated initially with paired-associate learning (Tulving, 1968a), but applies equally well to encoding that occurs during these incidental tasks and the conditions of retrieval during an unexpected recall test.

The encoding specificity principle claims that the use of cues for the retrieval of information in memory will be effective only to the extent that they are compatible with or reproduce the same encoding processes which occurred during presentation and initial encoding. In an early experiment, Tulving (1968a) had subjects learn a list of 48 paired-associates. The pairs consisted of highly associated words like AIR–PORT, BACK–LOG, and BASE–BALL. This list was practiced until the subject could give the correct responses to all of the stimulus terms twice without error. On a later recognition test following the learning trials, the subjects now saw the original response terms along with "distractors" which were also high associates of the stimulus terms. For example, not only did the subjects see the original response terms, PORT, LOG, and BALL, but they also saw PLANE, BONE, and LESS ("air-plane," "back-bone," "base-less.").

Even though the subjects had just shown perfect recall of the response terms, they showed significantly poorer retention on the recognition test. Recall, contrary to what is usually found, was clearly superior to recognition. The notion of encoding specificity implies that the encoding of the word PORT was different in the context of the word AIR than when it was later seen alone. Perhaps a different aspect of the meaning of the word is processed in different contexts (c.f., Crowder, 1976). The word AIR was a sufficient cue to reinstate the initial encoding process but the word PORT was not. The initial encoding will determine, then, how the information may be later retrieved (Thomson & Tulving, 1970; Tulving & Thomson, 1973; Watkins & Tulving, 1975).

These effects are not confined to highly associated word pairs. Light and Carter-Sobell (1970) demonstrated that a sentence context can strongly bias the encoding of a word. Subjects in their experiment were shown sentences, one at a time, and asked to read these sentences aloud, paying attention to underlined phrases. The subjects were told that these phrases would appear in a later memory test. The phrases the subject was asked to remember included such adjective–noun sequences as SWEET JAM, SKINNY DIP, and SODA CRACKER. On a recognition test following presentation of the sentences, subjects heard either the same adjective-noun pairs, or different adjectives paired with the nouns they had previously encountered (e.g., either SWEET JAM or TRAFFIC JAM; either SKINNY DIP, or CHIP DIP). There was a very large difference between recognition accuracy for nouns paired with different adjectives and those paired with the same adjectives read earlier. The same-adjective condition produced much higher recognition rates. Again, retrieval conditions are effective to the extent that they restore the initial encoding conditions.

While the initial statement of the levels of processing view emphasized the conditions of encoding (Craik & Lockhart, 1972), the results we have just described indicate that conditions of retrieval interact with conditions of encoding to produce the final level of performance. Morris et al. (1977), for example, demonstrated that the nature of the retention test contributes to the size of the levels effect one will obtain. In a typical study, such as that of Hyde and Jenkins (1969), recall that subjects whose incidental task involved a physical analysis of the stimulus remember less at final free recall than subjects who had analyzed the meanings of the words during the orienting task. Morris, et al. (1977) conducted a series of experiments in which subjects were instructed either to attend to the rhyming patterns or the meanings of a series of presented words. After this exposure, they were given a recognition test in which they were asked to pick out words that either rhymed with the stimulus words or had the same meaning. The semantic task lead to better performance on the semantic recognition test, but this was not the case when the test was for rhyming words. When the orienting task directed the subjects' attention to rhyming, they performed better on the rhyme test than on the semantic test.

Morris, et al. (1977) concluded that subjects who had performed the lower level processing (rhyming) had learned and retained information about the sound patterns of the stimulus words. Subjects who had attended to meaning retained this information, but were less adept at remembering the sound patterns. The codes formed at each level of processing, according to this view, may have been equally enduring but the testing must be compatible with encoding operations for this to be demonstrated. Unlike the original "levels" formulation, this view proposes that no one form of encoding is invariably better than others. The "best" code is the one that is most *compatible* with the particular retrieval task used to test retention (cf., Bransford, Franks, Morris & Stein, 1979; Nelson, Walling & McEvoy, 1979).

From these studies it is clear that deeper encodings are not always superior to shallower codes. On the other hand, we should stress that the Morris et al. (1977) study just described did show semantic coding with semantic testing to produce better performance than phonemic coding with phonemic testing (the rhyme conditions). That is, when the relationship between encoding and retrieval seemed to be optimal for both shallow and deeper codes, the deeper code produced the best memory performance. Several other studies have obtained similar results (e.g., Fisher & Craik, 1977; Nelson, Wheeler, Borden & Brooks, 1974).

In one of Fisher and Craik's studies (1977, Experiment 3), they biased the encoding of words in a word list by presenting a context word along with the items to be learned. The list words were presented in capital letters and were to be memorized. The context words were presented in lowercase letters. Subjects were told that the accompanying lowercase word "may help you remember." Context words either rhymed with the list word (e.g., pail–HAIL), or were highly associated to the list word (e.g., sleet–HAIL). Immediately following presentation of the list, subjects were presented with a series of retrieval cues. A cue could be one of three kinds: (1) identical to the context word seen during acquisition (e.g., either pail or sleet); (2) similar to the acquisition context (e.g., bail or snow); or (3) different from the context word (if the context was "pail," the cue might be "sleet," and vice versa). This last condition represents an incompatible or inappropriate relationship between encoding and retrieval conditions. One cue word was used for each list word.

Fisher and Craik's results are summarized in Table 8-3. The difference between Identical and Different cue conditions in the table (39% versus 19%) represents the compatibility effects predicted by the encoding specificity principle. The more compatibile the encoding and retrieval conditions, the better the recall. This was true for both rhyming and associative cues. However, with compatibility held constant, the associative, or deeper encoding was consistently superior to rhyming or shallow encoding. Even when encoding and retrieval contexts were identical, the deeper coding was substantially superior (37% versus 16%). It appears, then, that both the nature of the code (depth) and the compatibility relation between encoding and retrieval are important factors in determining memory performance.

TABLE 8-3   Accuracy of recall for words as a function of the compatibility of rhyming or associate retrieval cues to the original presentation context. (From Fisher & Craik, 1977.)

Encoding-Retrieval Compatibility	Encoding Context (% correct)		Average
	Rhyme	Associate	
Identical	24	54	39
Similar	18	36	27
Different	16	22	19
Average	16	37	

Depth and Attentional Resources

One final issue of growing importance in the development of the levels framework relates to the processes of attention and resource allocation in memory coding. We saw in Chapter 6 that the attentional resources available regulate both the amount and kind of processing that a stimulus may receive. Generally, when a task requires a simple analysis, like the detection of a tone, little capacity is required and the processing will be carried out with apparent automaticity. Deep processing, especially when the demands of the task are complicated and the stimulus materials are unfamiliar, will ordinarily require a great deal of processing capacity. There is, of course, a qualification. Complex shallow processing can require considerable resources, while little processing capacity may be required for deep processing when the task demands are simple and the stimulus material is highly familiar (e.g., detecting the occurrence of one's name).

We can illustrate the usual relationship between depth and capacity allocation with an early experiment by Eagle and Ortof (1967). Subjects were required to learn a list of words which were presented at a rate of one word every 3 sec on a tape recording. One group of subjects was allowed to devote full attention to this learning task. A second group was required to perform another task during the learning. This distractor task involved substituting digits for abstract symbols. It was intended as a complex activity which would draw processing resources away from the primary task of learning the word list. In terms of levels of processing, less capacity would thus be available for activities that analyzed and elaborated the input information.

Eagle and Ortof's results showed that divided attention was associated with an increased number of acoustic confusion errors when compared to the control group. In other words, the subjects' decreased capacity led to a shallower, acoustic level of processing than was the case for the control group which was able to devote full capacity to the analysis of the stimulus words. These two tasks, learning the words and digit–symbol substitution, appeared to draw on a common resource pool.

We should caution, of course, that not all simultaneous tasks will necessarily produce interference, either because they do not draw on a common pool of resources, or because simultaneous processing to a deep level can be accomplished without exceeding capacity limits. For example, verbal rehearsal and visual–spatial memory tasks can apparently be simultaneously accomplished without significant interference (Peterson, Rawlings, & Cohen, 1977).

Eysenck and Eysenck (1979) have attempted to measure the difference in processing capacity required by different levels of processing more directly. They also used a divided attention technique, but the expended processing capacity was measured during the encoding process. The subjects performed a secondary task (simple reaction time to the occurrence of a sound or a light) while they answered a question about a stimulus word. The questions required either deep or shallow-level processing. For example, the subject might be given the question "Edible?'' followed by a stimulus word. The task here was to respond verbally whether or not the stimulus named something edible (deep, semantic processing). In the physical coding conditions (shallow processing), subjects might be given the letter ''O'' followed by a stimulus word which either did or did not contain the letter ''O.'' In this case, they were simply to decide whether the word contained an ''O.'' The auditory or visual reaction time task occurred 100 msec after the onset of the stimulus word and required the subject to press a button to signal detection. The instructions were to give fast reaction times in the detection task, but to give the word decision task overall priority.

As we would expect from reviewing previous studies, words that were involved in a semantic classification were better recalled than words studied with a letter classification question. Answering questions about semantic category actually took less time than answering questions about the letters in the word. In other words, semantic processing for the category question required less time than the shallow processing required to answer the question about letters in the word. However, reaction times to the secondary task were longer when the subject was engaged in semantic processing than when the subject was performing shallow-level processing of the letters of the stimulus. If we take reaction time to the light or sound as an index of capacity allocation, then more capacity was being expended in the semantic task. That is, deeper processing consumed more capacity and less remained to perform the simple reaction time task, thus producing a longer reaction time.

In our review of Craik and Tulving's (1975) experiments we noted that processing time cannot be used as an index of depth. We see this again in the Eysencks' study where the semantic tasks were performed more rapidly than the shallow-level tasks. However, the predicted differences in levels did appear in the capacity or ''effort'' required to perform these different kinds of analyses. Eysenck and Eysenck do not deny that extensive practice with a particular task may reduce the capacity necessary for good performance (automaticity). The relationship between capacity and depth of processing, nonetheless, does appear to be a promising development in our attempts to understand both encoding strategies and how resources are allocated to them (Craik & Simon, 1980; Wingfield, 1980).

The last several sections have described how the levels of processing framework was modified and supplemented in response to criticism and new data. To the notion of depth of processing we have added the concepts of elaboration, distinctiveness, congruity, and compatibility between conditions of encoding and retrieval. To some researchers, these changes seem to have decreased the usefulness of the levels point of view as an orientation to memory studies (e.g., Baddeley, 1978). Other theorists deny that all of these concepts are necessary to account for the available data (e.g., Anderson & Reder, 1979; Kolers, 1979;

Tulving, 1979). On the other hand, the emphasis of the levels of processing notion on activities and operations used by people in acquiring and remembering information has come to increasingly replace the structural stores and flow diagrams with which we began the previous chapter.

THE STATUS OF SHORT-TERM MEMORY

The history of the duplex theory was a stormy one which began in the face of furious opposition from those who saw the proposal of two memory stores as adding unnecessary complexity to memory as a simple function of the strength of associations with practice. As we saw in Chapter 7, however, the duplex theory came to win the day, and, from the late 1950s through the 1960s, all evidence seemed to offer nothing but support for the duplex view. As we have also seen, however, this period of calm was soon followed by new winds which again buffeted the duplex theory. This time, under the general heading of "levels of processing," new opponents argued not that the duplex model added unnecessary complexity, but rather, that it was too simple to account for the full realities of memory!

Nowhere was this first blush of enthusiasm followed by nagging doubts more evident than in the study of brain damaged patients suffering various forms of memory impairment. It can be instructive to see how the same sets of data can be open to more than one interpretation.

Memory Deficits Following Brain Damage

Closely associated with the duplex theory were the so-called *dual-trace* or *consolidation* theories of memory based largely on the appearance of *retrograde amnesia* in animal and human subjects following a temporary disruption of normal brain activity (e.g., Glickman, 1961; Hebb, 1949; McGaugh, 1966). For example, it is commonly found that a person suffering a concussion following head injury may retain no memory for the events which occurred moments before the accident, while they have no difficulty remembering events which occurred much earlier. A pedestrian hit by a car may recall walking down the street and stepping off the curb, but then nothing until they remember waking up in the ambulance on the way to the hospital. They must surely have seen the car and experienced the momentary impact before losing consciousness, but memory for these events seem wiped clean (Russell, 1959).

Why is there no recall for those events just prior to the accident? Short-term retrograde amnesia of the sort we have just described fit nicely with the duplex theory. The immediate events were stored only in the form of a transient, easily disruptable trace in STS which had not yet had time to be transferred or "consolidated" into LTS before the disruption. Earlier events are remembered because this consolidation had already taken place.

The facts of short-term retrograde amnesia are not in dispute. Its occurrence is common following almost any temporary disruption of normal brain activity, whether this disruption is associated with a concussion, an *epileptic seizure,* or the use of *electroconvulsive shock* for the treatment of certain forms of mental disorder (Crönholm & Lagergren, 1959). The question, however, is whether such retrograde amnesia must be seen in terms of disruption of a transient short-term trace. Alternatively, we could just as easiy view it as arising from an interruption of those mental activities which would ordinarily lead to deep or elaborative processing.

Certainly the most widely cited support for the duplex hypothesis came from analyses of even more tragic cases of brain damage which were permanent, and which left unique memory deficits from which these persons never fully recovered. One of the best known of these patients was a man referred to as "Case H.M.," who, at the age of 28, had a part of his brain surgically removed for the treatment of epilepsy. This particular operation, which involved the removal of parts of the *temporal lobe* and *hippocampus,* is no longer performed. This is not because it was not effective in relieving H.M.'s epileptic symptoms. It was. The problem was that H.M. was left with a significant deficit in the ability to form new long-term memories (Milner, 1970; Milner, Corkin & Teuber, 1968).

After his operation, H.M. retained normal intelligence and an ability to remember those long-term events which occurred prior to the operation. On the other hand, the acquisition of new long-term traces was almost impossible. He could be introduced to the same person several times in one day and still have no recollection of ever having met that person before. He could not remember a simple list of numbers, nor even his new home address several years after he had moved. Yet, experiments showed that he appeared to have a relatively normal span for very immediate recall. H.M. seemed to fit well within the duplex framework. He seemed to have a normal long-term memory and an adequate short-term memory. His difficulty was in transferring information from one memory store to the other.

In fact, H.M. presented a rather more complex picture than it first appeared. For example, he would improve with practice on perceptual-motor tasks such as finger mazes (even though he would have no recollection of this practice). As we say, the picture was complex. Nevertheless, patients with brain damage such as H.M.'s were frequently used to support the duplex distinction, and this distinction seemed to make sense.

Although Case H.M. was to some extent unique, there is a tragically large group of patients who suffer a similar memory deficit associated with brain damage. That this disorder, known as *Korsakoff's Syndrome* is self-inflicted, makes it no less tragic. Korsakoff's syndrome is due to brain damage resulting from many years of chronic alcholism and the poor nutrition invariably associated with this problem. Like H.M., these patients show a fairly good ability to recall experiences which occurred sometime prior to the onset of their illness. Their ability to form new long-term memories, however, is extraordinarily poor.

Figure 8-3 shows the memory performance of a group of Korsakoff patients (amnestics) tested on immediate recall of a 10-word list. Their performance is shown in comparison with a control group of persons of similar age, intelligence, and background, but who had no evidence of Korsakoff's syndrome. As we look at the graph we see that recall accuracy for the beginning and middle part of the list, the long-term component, is clearly inferior to that of the control group. By contrast, however, we also see that the recency effect, the STS component, closely matches that of the controls (Baddeley & Warrington, 1970).

Like Case H.M., what appeared to be a selective inability to transfer information from short- to long-term memory, fit neatly within the duplex framework. Also like H.M., however, closer analyses implied a more complex picture. Baddeley and Warrington (1970), for example, found that Korsakoff errors in such experiments frequently show intrusions of items from previous lists with which they had been tested. According to a strict interpretation of the duplex view, these items should have been displaced by the new lists and hence, especially for these patients, they should have been totally unavailable for recall.

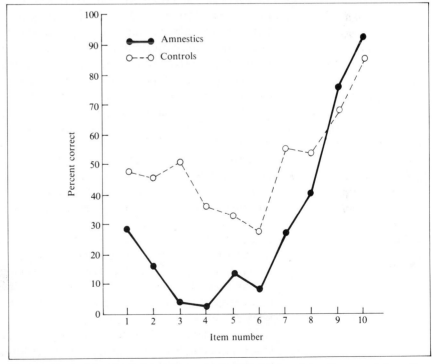

FIGURE 8-3 Mean percentage correct recall as a function of order of presentation for amnestic and control subjects with immediate recall.
(From Baddeley & Warrington, 1970.)

The Korsakoff patient does, in fact, present a mixed picture. On the one hand, these patients clearly are deficient in the formation of new memories. Like H.M., you can be introduced to them several times in the same day without their having any recollection of having met you before. At the same time, one often sees surprising islands of learning. They will often be able to tell you about salient events since the onset of their illness, such as the assassination of President Kennedy or President Nixon's resignation after the Watergate controversy. This should not minimize the extent of their deficit. While one can elicit such information with the use of cues and hints, these patients may not recognize that they have given you the correct answer, nor do they have any recollection of having learned this information in the first place (cf. Kinsbourne & Wood, 1975).

For these and other reasons, many writers began to reinterpret the Korsakoffs' difficulties in terms of an impairment of retrieval operations (Warrington & Weiskrantz, 1970), or in the formation of effective memory codes necessary for later retrieval (Baddeley & Warrington, 1973). For example, studies of the "release of PI" for these patients fail to show normal recovery when the category of the items in a final list is changed. From this, one could conclude that they failed to employ appropriate semantic coding as the lists were being presented (Cermak, Butters, & Moreines, 1974). Rather, they tend to limit their analyses to more shallow acoustic coding, which would be especially susceptible to interference (c.f., Cermak & Butters, 1972). As we saw in the previous sections, effective retrieval can only be as good as the form of initial encoding. This appears to be especially true for these patients (Kinsbourne & Wood, 1975). Indeed, there has been an increasingly common trend to reinterpret these processing deficits in Korsakoff patients within a levels-of-processing framework (Cermak, Naus, & Reale, 1976).

Other forms of memory impairment caused by specific brain damage have proven just as theoretically intriguing. Some of these appear to show a specific impairment of short-term memory itself (Saffran & Marin, 1975; Shallice & Warrington, 1970; Warrington, Logue, & Pratt, 1971; Warrington & Shallice, 1969, 1972). One of these patients, referred to as "Case K.F.", had a fairly accurate memory for day-to-day events, and could accurately recognize pictures he had seen before. On the other hand, he was almost totally unable to remember spoken verbal items. In a digit span task, for example, his recall ability averaged no more than two items, and he could frequently produce only one (Warrington & Shallice, 1969).

As one might expect from a selective STS impairment, studies of serial learning for digit and word lists for patients like K.F. show absolutely no recency effect (Saffran & Martin, 1975). On the other hand, their recall of meaningful sentences often shows paraphrases of the original sentences, or erroneous words which would fit the context.

Thus, while their short-term memory is clearly impaired (rarely could a sentence longer than four words be accurately recalled), some higher level of processing of the sentences must have occurred if they were able to give paraphrases of the original.

A similar conflict with a strict duplex interpretation comes with these patients' performance on multiple trial learning tests. K.F., for example, could recall 9 out of 10 paired-associates after 3 trials and a 6-hour delay. On a list of 10 items, while normal subjects may require as many as 9 trials for 100% recall, K.F. required as few as 7 trials. Indeed, he was able to recall 7 out of 10 items even 2 months later (Warrington & Shallice, 1969).

K.F. and similar patients seem to have a selective loss of auditory–verbal short-term memory, combined with a relatively normal long-term retention. On the one hand, this selective loss might appear to support the notion of independent STS and LTS structures. On the other hand, their impairment creates a number of theoretical difficulties for the duplex model. First, their relatively good memory for visual materials such as pictures, questions the notion of a purely verbal–acoustic short-term store. Second, the notion of long- and short-term stores implies that the route to permanent storage is through short-term storage. In particular, Waugh and Norman (1965) thought that rehearsal both renewed information in STS and resulted in transfer of this information to long-term memory. The group of clinical patients represented by K.F. seem able to bypass this process. Semantic and associative encoding can apparently occur even though measures of short-term memory indicate that very little information could have been held there while this coding took place. It is hard to reconcile this performance with the duplex ideas about the sequence of operations that result in long-term storage.

A Concluding View of Short-Term Memory

The interest in a short-term store as a repository of memory of recent events was inspired by the finding that short-term retention appeared to differ in characteristic ways from long-term retention: (1) There appeared to be relatively rapid loss of recent memories while well learned information might be retained for years; (2) the capacity for immediate recall seemed severely limited compared to the relatively indefinite capacity for permanent storage; (3) the content on which short-term memory performance was based seemed to be an acoustic representation of the stimulus, while long-term retention appeared to be based on semantic and associative relationships; (4) the principles that accounted for forgetting over long intervals did not fit the rapid loss of information that occurred when verbal material was not actively rehearsed. These findings were described in the previous chapter and remain part of the data base for our changing speculations about the nature of the human memory system.

The duplex theory of memory, that long- and short-term retention are represented by qualitatively different structures, interpreted these experimental results as evidence for the fixed characteristics of these structures. As we have seen, however, additional research has shown that more than one type of code can be used at any retention interval, and that unrehearsed material seen in a single glance is sometimes forgotten and sometimes not. These ambiguities began to blur the notion that memory performance could be explained by an inflexible sequence of operations that placed information into structural stores with fixed characteristics. The structural notion seemed too inflexible to accommodate the variety of results that could be produced under different conditions and instructions.

A process view, such as the "levels" framework, suggests that all of these findings could be products of the amount and quality of mental activities that are performed on the incoming information. Memories are perhaps better described as a record of mental operations. Emphasis was shifted from the characteristics of storage structures to the characteristics of processes used to analyze a stimulus and the processing resources necessary to carry out these analyses.

Our concluding view is intuitively related to William James' notion of the "psychological present." Short-term retention is the immediate product of our cognitive activities, rather than a "box" which merely holds memories of recent events. Because it involves the activation of structures and processes we already possess, it participates fully in the same organization as that of long-term memory. You may have noticed how this perspective dovetails with the capacity notions of attention we saw in Chapter 6. At any moment, we have a finite capacity to carry out necessary processes and the limits of these attentional resources are the major bottlenecks in our acquisition and maintenance of information.

In closing this discussion we have to admit that while the structural model seemed reassuringly clear and specifiable, the processing perspective to many seems relatively messy and ill-defined. On the other hand, a processing view is perhaps a more valid reflection of the variability and potential of what we know to be an extraordinarily complex memory system.

VISUAL MEMORY

As the duplex theory of memory became questioned, so psychologists began to break free from the accepted view of short-term memory as a purely verbal–acoustic store. The question was whether verbal coding (and verbal rehearsal) of visually presented stimuli was an obligatory operation imposed by an inability to retain visual information in memory. Verbal coding might merely represent a common and efficient strategy for dealing with the sorts of stimuli (letters, digits, CVCs) ordinarily used in the traditional studies of short-term memory.

You may be surprised to learn that established psychology for a long time doubted the common sense claim that subjects can retain and use "mental images" in the form of visual memory. Indeed, the whole concept of mental images was heavily attacked from the time of John

Watson (1913), to only a few years ago. Watson, perhaps with some justification, felt uncomfortable about accepting any theoretical construct based solely on subjects' own reports of their internal mental activities. Visual imagery, seeing a picture in "the mind's eye," is a purely internal event not easily accessible to objective test and measurement. The fact that most people report some form of visual memory could after all be nothing but the use of a visual metaphor. Describing a memory in visual terms does not itself prove that the memory is actually visual. Whether or not you agree with this skepticism, the fact is that the entire subject of visual imagery found little support either within philosophy or psychology for many decades (Ryle, 1949). Hannay (1971) offers an excellent review of these traditional, and very negative, views. As we have seen, the only form of visual memory accepted within the duplex system was the very brief, unanalyzed sensory storage associated with iconic memory.

The Early Confrontation

Ironically, the general notion of visual imagery in memory played a very prominent role in the earliest theories of memory and thought. For example, both James (1890) and Titchener (1910) accepted the proposition that sensations in any modality could form a mental impression, or "image," corresponding to that modality. James was especially impressed with the then recent reports by Galton (1883) on the subject of visual imagery.

Sir Francis Galton, himself a rather controversial figure in the study of individual differences, conducted what is probably the first systematic investigation of visual imagery. Galton's methods were primitive by today's standards as he simply used a questionnaire which asked a variety of people, from school children to artists and scientists, to form an image of their morning's breakfast table and to describe this image; its vividness, naturalness, and so forth. Interestingly, Galton found that most (but not all) of his respondents reported some form of imagery although some reported an ability to form more vivid images than others. While a strong believer in imagery, Galton was quick to point out that those who reported little success in forming vivid images seemed not to suffer from this in any observable way. Among those who reported that they could not form images of past scenes were several successful scientists and at least one artist!

It might be fair to summarize this early period in the study of imagery as a general acceptance of the idea of visual representations in memory, although this acceptance was perhaps more an act of faith than a consequence of solid empirical evidence. What experiments there were seemed consistent with the notion of imagery, but definitive proof that it was more than a visual metaphor used by subjects in their introspections was hard to obtain (cf. Bartlett, 1932).

As we have seen, by the 1960s, the notion of visual memory had all but disappeared from memory theory. We saw, for example, how Conrad (1964) showed that subjects' recall errors of visually presented letters correlated with confusions subjects made when they had to report spoken letters heard in a noisy background. It was argued that subjects implicitly name visual stimuli and then rehearse these names for retention. Indeed, the most highly developed information processing model of memory during this period, that of Atkinson and Shiffrin (1968), saw short-term memory as a purely verbal–acoustic store. To be sure, Atkinson and Shiffrin took a fairly conservative position about short-term (or long-term) storage in other modalities. They were not ready to totally reject the idea of a visual memory, but they were also not ready to accept its existence without proof that verbal encoding could not account for any such data one might obtain. As we have seen, such evidence during this period was not forthcoming.

Studies of Picture Memory and Mental Rotation

A limiting factor in any study of visual memory is the fact that most people are not trained artists. To put it most simply, asking subjects to reproduce a visual memory represents a far more difficult and uncertain task than a similar test of verbal memory. For that reason, most studies of visual memory have had to rely on indirect evidence from studies of recognition memory. When such studies have been conducted, however, their results tended to cause a considerable trauma to the verbal–acoustic notion of short-term storage.

Typical of these studies was one by Nickerson (1965) who presented subjects with a sequence of 200 photographs for 5 sec each. These were followed by an additional 400 photographs, half of which were duplicates of those originally seen, and half of which were new ones. The subjects were simply asked to indicate which pictures of this set had been seen before. His subjects' overall accuracy averaged about 95%, or recognition memory for some 190 out of the 200 pictures. This result is striking in contrast with the usual capacity measures of verbal short-term memory.

Some years later, Standing, Conezio, and Haber (1970) escalated the research by presenting as many as 2560 pictures in rapid succession for later recognition testing. Each picture was a complex visual scene which would be difficult to quickly code verbally, and each picture was presented for only 10 sec before the onset of the next one. Their subjects' recognition scores nevertheless were in the order of 93% correct, or some 2380 pictures correctly remembered. This is clearly an astonishing figure if one does not accept the possibility of some form of visual memory. It would be hard to contemplate these subjects rapidly verbally labeling each picture and retaining the verbal descriptions of these 2380 pictures. As Klatzky (1975, p. 225) put the position somewhat tongue-in-cheek, if one picture is worth a thousand words, then to store just 2000 pictures would require storing some 2,000,000 words!

It is important to note that these studies used only nonconfusable pictures throughout, such that these levels of recognition accuracy would be hard to duplicate in less ideal circumstances. Nevertheless, the superiority of recognition memory for meaningful, nonconfusable pictures has been well documented both in comparison with words (Lutz & Sheirer, 1974; Standing, 1973) and with sentences (Nelson, Metzler, & Reed, 1974; Shepard, 1967). Nor is this impressive picture memory purely a short-term phenomenon. Shepard (1967) tested recognition memory for 600 pictures after 2, 3, 7, or 120 days, finding levels of recognition accuracy of 99.7, 92.0, 87.0, and 57.7% respectively. Nickerson (1968) testing long-term recognition memory for his 200 pictures found 63% correct even when tested 1 year later.

Finding data that are hard to reconcile with a purely verbal-acoustic memory code, however, is not quite the same thing as proving that visual memory exists. For this, we must turn to other experiments specifically designed to explore this question. Certainly the best known series of studies purporting to demonstrate the existence of visual short-term codes were performed some years ago by Roger Shepard and his colleagues at Stanford University (Cooper & Shepard, 1973; Shepard & Metzler, 1971). Their experiments have been described as studies of "mental rotation."

To get a feeling for the sorts of experiments they performed, consider a task in which subjects are presented with a sequence of two letters. The first letter is always a normal letter of the alphabet, such as "R." The second letter, however, is either that letter, or a reversed, mirror-image, such as "Я." When the second letter appears, the subjects' task is to decide as quickly as possible whether it is in fact normal or reversed. Their task is to respond by pressing one of two buttons so that an accurate measure of their reaction time can be taken from the instant they see the second stimulus, to the instant of their response.

Imagine further, however, an intriguing catch to this experiment. The second letter is not always presented in its normal vertical orientation; sometimes the letter is rotated by 60, 120, 180, 240, or 300°. Thus, in order to make the decision as to whether the second stimulus is a normal or reversed letter, the subject would have to mentally rotate the letter to the vertical to compare it with his or her stored image of the normal letter.

The results of such a study are shown in Figure 8-4 (Cooper & Shepard, 1973). Below the graph are illustrations of the letter R, both normal and reversed, in its various orientations to the vertical. The graph itself shows the average reaction times to making the normal–reversed decisions. There is clearly a direct correlation between the time required for the decision and the angular deviation of the stimulus from its normal vertical orientation. Similar studies have shown that subjects' scanning, transformation and comparison of visual images require times that correspond to what we would expect if these operations were carried out on real objects (Cooper & Shepard, 1978; Kosslyn, Ball, & Reiser, 1978).

These results seem to imply that the subjects could rotate an image of the letter, that this rotation took a measurable amount of time, and that subjects mentally rotated the letters to the left or right, depending on which was the shortest route to the vertical. These results seemed to imply that subjects could form a short-term visual code, and that this code was sufficiently "real" to allow its systematic rotation. In other words, the mental rotation seemed much like a physical rotation—the whole object passes through all the positions in the rotation in a continuous fashion just as a solid object would.

We must be quite careful, however, in applying this analogy between rotating a real object in space and rotating an image "in the mind." Pylyshyn (1979) has pointed out that imagery phenomena may be influenced by our beliefs and interpretations about an object. We would not expect such factors to influence a physical rotation. For example, the physical rotation of an object in space would not be affected by the

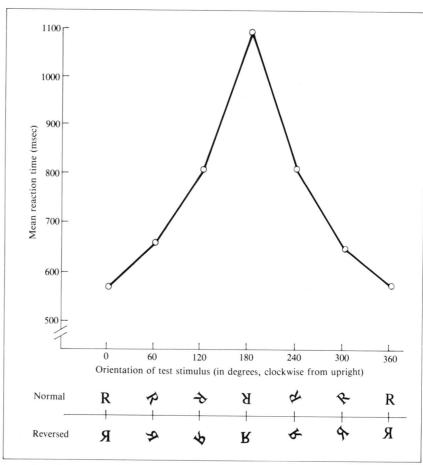

FIGURE 8-4   Reaction time to judging whether a letter stimulus is normal or reversed as a function of the degree of angular rotation of the letter from vertical. (Adapted from Cooper & Shepard, 1973.)

object's visual properties. If our analogy held up, we should be able to rotate one kind of figure as well as another. Pylyshyn (1979) has shown that the rate at which a figure is "mentally" rotated is determined in part by the amount of practice on the task, the visual properties of the stimulus, and the nature of the comparison task required. Similar findings have been obtained by Shepard and Metzler (1971) and Hochberg and Gellman (1977). These data indicate that the processing of visual images is different in important ways from simple physical rotation of a picture. Although the nature of this processing is poorly understood, it is certainly hard to reconcile the mental rotation effects with the usual verbal–acoustic recoding of visual stimuli implied by a traditional duplex theory.

Concepts of Visual Imagery

In Chapter 3 we made reference to early studies of mental imagery as a form of *mediation* in paired-associate learning. As we noted then, investigators such as Bower (1972) found that a paired-associate set such as DOG–BICYCLE could be learned and retained much better if the subject formed a mental image integrating both elements (such as the image of a dog riding a bicycle), than if simply a verbal association without imagery were attempted.

The most extensive studies of imagery, however, were conducted by Alan Paivio (1969) who, for example, reported that lists of visualizable nouns such as *cup* or *chair* are generally far easier to learn and remember than lists of more abstract, difficult-to-visualize words, such as *happiness* or *integrity*. Similar results were obtained for paired-associate learning of visualizable versus nonvisualizable words (Paivio, Smythe, & Yuille, 1968).

As reliable as such findings might be, the question of visualizability is difficult to measure directly such that one has to rely primarily on subjects' own introspective estimates. To give you a feeling for such estimates, we have listed below the average scores subjects gave six words when asked to rate them on how easy they were to image on a seven-point scale (Paivio, Yuille, & Madigan, 1968). "Seven" meant that the subjects found it easy to form a visual image, and "one" meant that it was difficult to image. Whatever the validity of these ratings, most of us would agree that they seem intuitively reasonable.

Easy	*Difficult*
Acrobat (6.53)	Abasement (2.03)
Admiral (6.20)	Advantage (2.37)
Alligator (6.87)	Allegory (2.13)

These early studies were followed by many others which were to reliably show that attempts to form visual images of presented stimuli clearly facilitates recall performance (e.g., Paivio, 1971; Paivio & Csapo, 1969).

To be sure, Paivio's experiments were hardly unambiguous proof for the existence of literal, visual imagery as a viable form of memory representation. The possibility that concrete words are better remembered than abstract ones because they are ordinarily more common, familiar words, was examined and rejected by Paivio. He reported that concrete words are better remembered than abstract ones even when they are matched for the frequency with which they occur in the language (Paivio, 1971). More difficult to test, however, is the possibility that attempts to form images of words causes subjects to think more about the meanings of the words and thus to lead to deeper and more elaborate memory codes. These codes, furthermore, need not necessarily be visual. As we have seen, deeper, more elaborate encoding could also account for their better retention.

The argument that imagery instructions might operate primarily to lead subjects to form better, more conceptually organized impressions in memory has been made by Anderson and Bower (1973). Further, some studies have shown that subjects' reports of the vividness of an image do

Mental imagery can seem very vivid to the imager.

not always correlate with the accuracy of recall, an unexpected finding if recall were truly based on a literal "picture" stored in memory (Neisser & Kerr, 1973). Also inconsistent with a literal visual image are reports that recognition memory for pictures seems independent of the visual detail these pictures offer. For example, Nelson et al. (1974) found that simple outline drawings are as easily remembered as detailed pictures or photographs on a recognition test. Perhaps most upsetting to Paivio's interpretation is the finding that instructing subjects to form visual images of words produces the same level of facilitation in blind subjects who have been blind from birth (Jonides, Kahn, & Rozin, 1975). That these subjects may have thought more about those stimuli they were asked to image is likely, and that they did indeed form some sort of image is quite possible. Whatever the form of imagery, however, we would be reluctant to call it a visual image of the sort proposed in our previous discussion.

It is certainly the case that imagery and the formation of semantic relations are closely related. For example, Reese (1965) conducted a paired-associate learning experiment with a total of 60 children ranging in age from 3 to 8 years. All of the stimuli were presented in the form of pictures drawn on 6 × 8″ cards. In one condition the children saw first a stimulus card (e.g., a picture of a cat) followed by a response card (e.g., a picture of an umbrella) and were required to learn the stimulus–response pairs through the standard anticipation method. In a second condition, however, the response cards were "compound responses" showing a single picture combining both the stimulus and response objects, such as a picture of a cat carrying an umbrella (see Figure 8-5).

Reese's results were clear in showing that seeing both the stimulus and response elements as an interaction (i.e., the cat holding the umbrella) leads to faster learning and better retention than seeing the stimulus and response items separately (i.e., first the cat, then the umbrella). Similar results have been reported for adults (e.g., Woolen, Weber, & Lowry, 1972).

As it happens, however, suggesting an interaction between the stimulus and response members seems to be the critical factor, rather than the use of pictures themselves. Simply describing the interactions verbally to the subjects (e.g., "imagine a cat holding an umbrella") works just as well as actually showing them a picture of the interaction (Reese, 1965). The function of the integrated images for Reese's subjects may thus have been to facilitate the organization of the elements. In this study, therefore, the crucial factor could have easily been the creation of a meaningful unit, as much as the use of visual imagery, per se.

Interestingly, Woolen et al. (1972) in a similar study, showed that imagery instructions produced the same advantage whether the interaction pictured is a reasonable one (e.g., a cigar resting on the edge of a piano for a CIGAR–PIANO paired-associate), or an unusual, bizarre, one (a piano smoking a cigar). This is surprising only in view of the

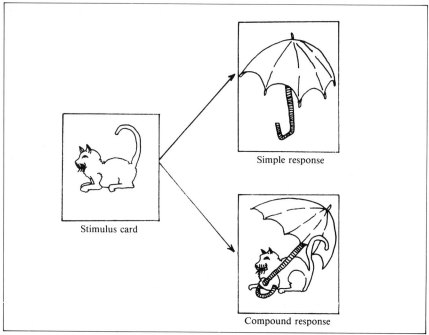

Simple response

Stimulus card

Compound response

FIGURE 8-5   A study of paired-associate learning by Reese (1965) in which children saw a stimulus card followed either by a single response picture or a compound response picture containing an image integration of both the stimulus and response elements. In both cases the children's task was to learn to give the response ''umbrella'' for the stimulus ''cat.''

generally accepted notion that imagery is an especially effective mnemonic if the image is as unique as possible (cf. Hunter, 1964). The uniqueness of the image was thought to protect the association from interference. Since no similar association existed, interference by similarity would be minimized. In fact, this apparent conflict can be easily resolved. The advantage of attempting to form a bizarre image is probably true if the subject is allowed to form a meaningful, unique relationship that has special significance for that person. The attempt to impose a unique image by Wollen et al. (1972) would thus not show the expected advantage.

The rush to imagery research also produced an imagery interpretation of a number of earlier findings not previously tied to the imagery concept. For example, Jorgensen and Kintsch (1973) examined subjects' ability to verify the truth or falsity of the sorts of propositions used by Collins and Quillian (1969) in their studies of retrieval from semantic memory (e.g., ''A fish has gills.''). Jorgensen and Kintsch's findings seemed to imply that it is easier to verify such propositions when they are more easily visualized than when they are not. In a similar way, we

saw in Chapter 4 how Begg and Paivio (1969) attempted to
studies such as Sachs' (1967) on sentence memory, or
Barclay, and Franks' (1972) study of semantic integration
forming images of the propositions and using these images in later
memory tests.

The importance of meaning, or comprehensibility in many of these
imagery studies has received considerable attention in the literature.
Goldstein and Chance (1971), for example, tested subjects' recognition
memory for pictures of snowflake patterns. Even though each of the
patterns were quite distinctive, recognition memory was fairly poor.
Unless one can give meaning to visual patterns, unless they can be
integrated within existing systems of knowledge, recall for visual stimuli
tends to be rather poor. Thus, in this single snowflake experiment, we
have the essence of the controversy reviewed in these pages. Snowflake
patterns are (a) difficult to name, (b) difficult to image, and (c) difficult to
code conceptually. We have already seen in detail how different
theorists would seize on each of these factors as "the" causal explanation for the poor memory performance, and, by inference, how stimuli
are ordinarily represented in memory (i.e., verbally, visually, conceptually). It is possible, however, that all three observations are a consequence of a single form of abstract memory. Let us look at this
possibility.

Dual-Coding versus Abstract Coding

Based on his earlier demonstrations of an apparent facilitation of memory performance with imagery, Paivio (1969, 1971) proposed a dual-code
model of memory representation which envisaged separate repre-
sentational systems in memory for verbal and visual information.
Abstract words which could not be readily imaged would be coded only
verbally. Concrete words that are easy to image would be represented
both by a verbal code and by a visual code. Imagery and verbal
processes could thus be seen as two parallel and independent codes.

Paivio thus proposed that easily imaged words show superior memory
performance based on the simple redundancy rule that "two codes are
better than one." If a stimulus has two separate representations, one
visual and one verbal, the probability will be greater that it will be
effectively retrieved. Specifically, both codes would be available for
most pictures and for concrete words. Hence, we would expect superior
recall ability for these stimuli. For materials such as CVCs or abstract
words, only verbal codes would be available and hence the relatively
poor recall performance for these materials.

There is, however, an alternative view of mental representation that
proposes that memory for pictures, or visualizable material, is based on
a more abstract representation that contains both imagelike and abstract
conceptual components (Nelson, Reed & Walling, 1976; Potter, 1975,
1976; Potter & Faulconer, 1975). The superior performance seen for
picture memory as compared with memory for words, for example,

could be due to the conceptual distinctiveness of pictures as compared with words (Intraub, 1979).

As one test of this hypothesis, Intraub (1979) replicated the picture studies of Nickerson and of Standing, Conezio, and Haber, but this time using pictures that subjects had previously shown could be named rapidly, or pictures which required some time to name. After measuring these initial naming latencies, Intraub then presented these pictures at a variety of rates which could be presumed to either allow or not allow them to be named prior to onset of the next picture in the series. Contrary to the dual-coding prediction, she found no effect of naming latency (the presumed ability of subjects to name the pictures) on later recognition testing for any of the presentation rates tested.

Other evidence could be used to suggest that memory codes for visual or visualizable stimuli are of an abstract or conceptual nature rather than separate visual and verbal codes as the dual-coding hypothesis would imply. As it happens, for example, subjects' descriptions of their visual images are often quite different in detail from a scene they are trying to recall. Furthermore, their errors are not invariably made in close spatial proximity as one would expect if a "picture" were faded or blurred in just one spot. We saw a good example of these sorts of conceptual errors in subjects' attempts to draw the floorplans of their apartments given in Figure 4-10 (Norman & Rumelhart, 1975).

For this and similar reasons, many theorists feel it is unlikely that subjects truly store picture-like images in memory (Pylshyn, 1973). Errors in recall of visual scenes, in other words, often show the same sort of conceptually based changes found for semantically processed verbal materials. In addition, further studies were to show that the abstract as opposed to concrete sentences used by Begg and Paivio were also harder to understand, a finding true for abstract versus concrete sentences in general (Holmes & Langford, 1976; Johnson, Bransford, Nyberg & Cleary, 1972; Moeser, 1974). Thus what Begg and Paivio would call a sentence which is easy to visualize, also turns out to be rated higher in comprehensibility, or ease of deep processing (Moeser, 1974).

There seems to be general agreement today that mental representations in memory are not in any way "photographs in the mind." Perhaps the closest approximation to an answer is that of Kosslyn (1975) who sees an analogy between the notion of visual imagery in memory and the way in which a computer can produce a picture on a cathode ray tube. What the computer stores are not pictures, but abstract codings which can be used to *generate* the pictures we see. In a similar way, memory representations are probably fairly abstract, modality-free conceptualizations which in turn can be used to generate an image or an image-like representation. To say that we can experience and use such an image, however, is not to say that these images are permanently stored in a picturelike way.

DETECTION IN MEMORY: AN EXTENDED ANALOGY

We have alluded frequently to the well-established fact that recognition memory typically yields performance levels higher than comparable measures of free recall. In Chapter 2, for example, we introduced this traditional finding and a common explanation of this difference, the two-stage model of the recall process. For free recall, the subject must first retrieve from memory a set of possible responses and, second, scan this set to determine which, if any, are correct or relevant responses for the task at hand. In tests of recognition memory, such as a multiple-choice examination, the first stage, a subset of responses from which to choose, is already made available to the subject. This, combined with the ability to select a correct response on the basis of partial cues, and some inflation due to guessing, is sufficient to account for higher scores in recognition testing than in free recall.

As we have seen, the subject of recognition memory is important to our understanding of memory processes as a whole. In Chapter 3 we saw how recognition testing was used by Postman, Stark, and Fraser (1968), and others, to reject the simple "unlearning" notion in favor of a retrieval explanation of long-term forgetting. Finally, recognition memory appeared again with prominence in the earlier sections of this chapter. First, we saw that the levels of processing framework began with studies of incidental learning followed by recognition testing. Recall, for example, that the "pleasantness" ratings or sentence orientations used to ensure deep processing of presented stimuli were followed by recognition testing in the form of, "Have you seen this word before?" We also saw how much of the impetus for studies of visual memory came from the studies of Nickerson and of Standing, Conezio, and Haber who reported quite extraordinary recognition memory for hundreds (Nickerson, 1965) and indeed thousands (Standing et al. 1970) of pictures presented only once in rapid succession.

As we moved to the "levels" framework in this chapter, we moved also from the earlier paradigms involving relatively meaningless CVCs, letter strings, and digit strings, to more meaningful stimuli such as words, sentences, and pictures. These are very special cases of memory: special in the sense that they involve unusual stimuli in relation to the traditional studies of memory, but special also in the sense that they tap what we might call "real" memory. In everyday experience, at least outside of the classroom, we just do not go around memorizing stimuli by rote rehearsal, nor do we "respond" to everything we encounter by giving an overt response.

A critical feature of meaningful material as experimental stimuli is the fact that subjects entering an experiment already know the stimuli; the stimuli are already in memory. If we give our subject a word list which includes the word CLOUD, our test is not whether they know what a CLOUD is (semantic memory). What we are really asking is whether they saw that word recently, whether it was in the word list they had just been given (episodic memory). Our subjects' task, whether tested by recall or recognition, is thus in reality to determine not if they "re-member" the word CLOUD, but rather, to distinguish known words just "learned" for the experiment from known words not tested in the experiment. As a matter of fact, we have known for some time that this is not always an easy task to do. Subjects will often mistakenly recog-nize an item that is highly associated with one of the stimuli. As a result they will often misrecognize these associates on a recognition test or give them erroneously in free recall (e.g., Deese, 1964).

Viewing memory performance as a function of the distinctiveness of codes and the compatibility between coding and retrieval conditions immediately yields two important implications. First, distinctive encod-ing should facilitate retrieval provided that compatible retrieval cues are utilized. Second, the recognition process ("Did I see this item in this experiment?") should be sucessful to the degree that we can distinguish this item from among other related items, and from other previous encodings of the same item. In this light, the question of recognition memory takes on a new relevance and requires further attention.

Signal Detection Theory

An important approach to understanding the recognition process comes from a field of psychology that has a longer tradition than cognitive research: the field of sensory psychophysics. In a typical psychophysical experiment, a subject hears or sees a very weak stimulus while the experimenter systematically varies the stimulus intensity. The goal is to discover the lowest intensity at which the signal becomes just detectible. This is called the *sensory threshold*. If we extend the detection paradigm to the process of recognition memory, certain similarities become appar-ent. In this case we also have a signal of variable strength. The "signal" is the memory trace, and "detection" represents the recognition process that decides whether or not a particular stimulus exceeds some "thres-hold" of familiarity.

The Psychophysical Function. When the early psychophysicists at-tempted to map sensory thresholds for human observers, they came up with what appeared to be a paradoxical finding. A soft tone, or dim light, presented at about threshold intensity would sometimes be heard (or seen) and sometimes not. If the signal were very weak subjects would of course never detect it; if it were very strong they always would. But as intensity is gradually increased from weak to strong, one does not see a sudden jump from zero detection to 100% detection. What one observes is a smooth, gradual curve, showing a gradual increase in the probability of detection. This curve, called the *psychophysical function*, is depicted in Figure 8-6.

These early investigators assumed that there must be an absolute sensory threshold which should look like the dotted-line "step" function plotted in Figure 8-6. They accounted for the observed smooth function by assuming that subjects are just poor at reporting their sensory

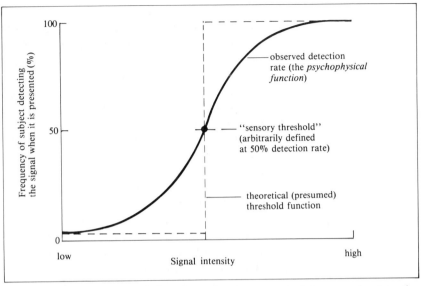

FIGURE 8-6 The typical psychophysical function, showing a gradual increase in detection rate as a function of signal intensity. The dotted-line "step" function shows the presumed absolute threshold. Based on observed data, the "sensory threshold" was arbitrarily defined as that intensity that produces detection 50% of the times the signal is presented.

experiences. Sometimes they are inattentive when a signal is presented and they miss hearing it. Sometimes they guess, and report hearing a signal that was in fact below the level of detectability. In the face of what appeared to be unreliable reporting, these early investigators arbitrarily defined the threshold as that intensity at which subjects report detecting the signal 50% of the time and miss it 50% of the time. This would be a statistical approximation to the "true" sensory threshold which they were sure existed, but which was extremely difficult to measure.

This view of the psychophysical function remained virtually unchallenged until the 1960s, when a small group of mathematical psychologists considered a fundamental reanalysis of the function. Their reanalysis was based on the revolutionary premise that there is no absolute sensory threshold for a human observer. Instead they argued that the smooth probabilistic function of the sort shown in Figure 8-6 represents the true state of affairs in sensory detection. This view was developed into a mathematical model of sensory detection known as *signal detection theory* (Green & Swets, 1966; Swets, 1964; Swets, Tanner, & Birdsall, 1961).

The Detection Criterion   To understand their analysis, consider how a decision might be affected by your expectations and the consequences of making a mistake. A classic example of these effects has been called "the sentry's dilemma." Imagine a soldier on guard in wartime who hears a noise off in the darkness at night. He could shoot at the noise and perhaps frighten away an enemy soldier who might otherwise shoot him from the darkness. At the same time, the noise might have been made by a friendly soldier who might accidentally be shot. In time of war, a frightened sentry might perceive no compromise in this situation. He may be afraid to hesitate or to call out a warning. Either option might be fatal for him. The sentry may see his alternatives as simply "shoot" versus "don't shoot."

This example was chosen because of the stark contrast between the simple shoot–don't shoot alternatives in relation to the complexity of the sentry's decision. How probable is it that the movement is an enemy soldier as opposed to a friendly one? How does he feel about the accidental shooting of a friendly soldier when his own life is in the balance? How does he feel about shooting anyone?

Thus, within the so-called sentry's dilemma we have the three elements of a detection decision: (1) the stimulus itself, in this case the ambiguous movement in the darkness, and (2) the factors affecting the sentry's decision: (a) the probability of the movement being an enemy and (b) the soldier's own notion of the consequences of his decision.

Translated into detecting a signal in the psychophysical laboratory, we have the sentry's dilema expressed as a *payoff matrix* as illustrated below:

	Response	
	"Yes"	"No"
Signal	Hit	Miss
No signal	False alarm	Correct rejection

If a signal is presented and the subject say "yes," that he or she thought they detected a signal, it is called a *hit*. If he or she says "no," it is called a *miss*. If there is no signal present and the subject says "yes" it is called a *false alarm*. If he or she says "no" it is called a *correct rejection*.

The relevance of this payoff matrix is simply this. By influencing the subject's "payoff" it turns out that we can affect his or her *criterion;* the likelihood of the subject reporting that a signal has been observed, even though the intensity of the signal itself has not been altered. The subject's criterion is called β ("beta") and its value can be calculated by a mathematical analysis of the subject's *hit rate* and *false alarm rate* for any given signal intensity over the course of an experiment. For example, if we want our subject to have a strict criterion we could pay them 10¢ for each hit, but fine them $3.00 for every false alarm. In this case, subjects would be very reluctant to report the observation of a signal unless they were very certain that one had occurred. Their false alarm rate would be very low, but of course they might miss more signals. If we wanted a more relaxed criterion, we could reverse the "payoff" with $3.00 for each hit and a fine of only 10¢ for false alarms. Under these conditions, the false alarm rate and the hit rate would go up. The subject is now biased to report that a signal had been observed and the rate of missing goes down. Such studies have been done, and these effects found (cf. Green & Swets, 1966). We hasten to point out, however, that nothing about the detection rates is conscious. As we shift our subject's criterion they honestly "hear" the signal at lower intensities. In terms of signal detection theory, the subjects' payoff, or bias, alters the subject's criterion or beta (β), and hence the likelihood of detecting a signal at any particular level of signal intensity.

Noise versus Signal Plus Noise. The subjects in the detection experiments described above appear to be treating their observations as evidence that varies in reliability. That is, the information from the subjects' senses could be ambiguous in the same way that motion in the dark was ambiguous for the sentry. In fact, signal detection theory treats an observation as evidence about the presence or absence of the signal, and this evidence in an observation can be ambiguous regarding this decision. To follow their argument, recall that the physical intensity of a stimulus is represented in the nervous system by the rate of firing of neurons along a sensory pathway. Loud sounds or bright lights are represented by rapid rates of firing, while soft sounds or dim lights are represented by slower rates of firing. The catch comes with the realization that these neural pathways are never truly silent. That is, even when there is no sensory input, there is often some level of random neural firing sometimes called neural "noise." One might think of it as "static" in an otherwise quiet system. The essence of their proposition, then, was that the detection of a weak signal at or near "threshold" must require a *statistical decision:* Is the rate of firing at that instant greater than, or equal to, the normal level of random "noise" always present when there is no sensory input?

For mathematical reasons we need not go into here, they assumed that the level of random noise is *normally distributed*. That is, at some instants, the level of firing is very low, and at other instants it is quite high. The peak of the curve corresponds to the most frequently observed rate of activity. We have depicted this *noise distribution* on the left side of Figure 8-7(A). Thus, when a signal is present, what the nervous system will reflect is a summation of the combined rate of random firing, the "noise," plus the rate of firing contributed by the signal itself. This will produce a second curve, a *signal plus noise distribution*. Such a set of distributions for a weak signal heard in a quiet background are shown in Figure 8-7(A).

According to the detection model, in other words, the subject's task is to compare the level of neural activity at any one moment with the average level of random activity always present even when no sensory

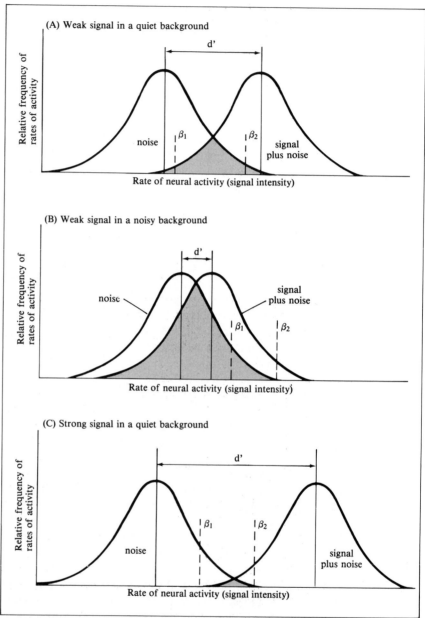

FIGURE 8-7   Three hypothetical noise and signal plus noise distributions illustrating the role of d' in sensory detection. Vertical dotted lines (β_1, β_2) represent different criteria a subject might choose in the detection paradigm.

input is present. The difference between the means of these two distributions is called d' ("d prime"). If d' is large, there will be little overlap between the distributions [see Figure 8-7(C)]. If it is sufficiently small, there is a large overlap [see Figure 8-7(B)]. The shaded portions in

Figure 8-7 represent those instants at which the total level of signal plus noise can be less than that level of activity which sometimes occurs from noise alone.

The three pairs of distributions in Figure 8-7, then, represent situations in which the evidence in an observation is more or less ambiguous. Recall, however, our previous discussion of different detection criteria. According to signal detection theory, a subject solves this problem in uncertainty by setting a criterion along the intensity dimension. If an observation produces more activity than the criterion (β), the subject reports that a signal has occurred. This signal would be "above threshold." If the observation produces a lower level of activity than the criterion, no signal is reported. This signal would be "below threshold."

We can now see how payoffs affect our criterion. The subject can set the criterion along the intensity dimension to maximize hits, leading to one form of error (false alarms), or to minimize false alarms (thus maximizing misses). For example, in Figure 8-7(C), if β is set at point β_1, no misses can occur, each occurrence of the signal will be correctly detected. However, the subject will sometimes report a signal when none occurred. This is true because there are some occasions when noise alone produces an activity level greater than the criterion set at point β_1. These occasions will lead to False Alarms. On the other hand, if the criterion is set at point β_2 in Figure 8-7(C), the subject will never make a false alarm, all occurrences of the noise alone are below the criterion. The subject will, however, still make errors. Some of the occurrences of the signal are also below the criterion and these occurrences will lead to misses. Where the subject sets the criterion, then, will depend on the costs and payoffs for these different kinds of responses.

The reliability of the evidence is represented by the distance between the two distributions (d'), the noise distribution and the signal plus noise distribution. Another way to describe this difference is to view it as the *detectability* of the signal independent of the subject's criterion. When d' is very small, there is little difference between noise and noise plus signal, and the signal has low detectability [Figure 8-7(B) is a good example of this]. Under these conditions, a subject who gets a great many hits must also make many false alarms. When detectability (d') is high, as in Figure 8-7(C), a subject need make fewer false alarms to score the same number of hits. To really understand this tradeoff between hits and false alarms, you should note for yourself what happens to these two responses as you move the criterion along the intensity dimensions of the three graphs of Figure 8-7.

To summarize the basic elements of the detection paradigm, then, a subject's detection of a signal is thought of as a statistical decision about whether or not a signal occurred. The intensity of signal (amount of evidence) necessary to report that a signal occurred is the subject's criterion (β). The criterion is determined by the subject's payoff matrix representing the consequences of hits and false alarms combined, of course, with the likelihood that a signal might occur at that particular instant. The detectability of the signal (d′) represents how reliable our observations are, independent of the subject's criterion. The accuracy of judgements and the kinds of errors depend on both the detectability (d′) of the signal, and the criterion (β) used by the subject.

The theory of signal detection did more than develop the notion of the detection of a weak signal as dependent on the strength of the signal, plus a criterion that may change from moment to moment. Its impressive feat was the development of a mathematical treatment of hit rates and false alarm rates in a typical experiment to allow one to separate that component of the detection rate which is due to the strength of the signal from that due to the subject's criterion. A good introduction to the mathematics and assumptions of detection theory for interested readers can be found in Egan and Clarke (1966). A nice discussion of the theory (without the mathematics) can be found in Marx and Hillix (1979, pp. 413–421).

Thus, the theory of signal detection is essentially a mathematical formulation which allows one to separate performance into the contributions of signal strength or sensitivity of the nervous system (d′) from the factors which determine how "liberal" or "conservative" their decision criteria will be (β). As we shall see, however, many aspects of signal detection theory can be modified to fit the recognition memory paradigm, and this trend has become quite a common one (e.g., Atkinson & Juola, 1974; Banks, 1970; Lockhart & Murdock, 1970; Parks, 1966).

Back to Recognition Memory

On one level, the operations performed in sensory detection and in recognition memory are obviously quite different. In sensory detection the subject must make trial-to-trial decisions as to the presence of a signal as distinct from simple background noise. In testing recognition memory, the subject receives a word, sentence, or picture, and is asked whether this is an "old" stimulus (one just presented in the learning set) or a "new" stimulus (one not presented in the learning set). On another level, however, there is a very strong analogy between the two situations.

In the recognition experiment there is always a certain "strength" or familiarity of the stimulus in memory, analogous to the "strength" of the sensory stimulus. That is, for English words, there is always some strength because we have seen or heard these words outside the laboratory before. Second, the subject's task of examining a recognition item and deciding whether it is "old" or "new" is also a relative judgement. As we argued previously, even a "new" item has some strength in memory, it is a word or object that the subject knows, and has seen before. The decision is whether the stimulus has been seen recently in the learning set, or some time ago in his or her past experience. The decision, then, is whether this test item is "signal" or "noise," with the difference in strength potentially translatable into d′. Finally, in both cases, factors such as likelihood and payoff can influence the conservativeness of the subject's decision criterion. This in turn would influence the false alarm or guessing rates that often inflate recognition scores. Let us see more specifically how the detection analogy might apply, and what insights it might offer.

Suppose a subject is given 10 words to learn in a memory experiment. The subject, of course, already knows these words; they are in the subject's lexicon before ever arriving for our experiment. What we are really asking our subjects to do in the memory test is to decide whether these words were encountered recently, whether they are more familiar than the words they will see as "distractors" in the recognition test. Thus, when a stimulus is presented, our subject will not say, "Do I know this word?" Of course it is known. The subject's question will actually be, "Have I seen this word recently?" In other words, is it "signal" or is it "noise?"

If we assume that the strength of recent items and not-recent items are both normally distributed, we can construct a set of curves analogous to those used in analyzing sensory detection. We can also note some criterion (β) which, when exceeded, will produce a "yes" response, indicating that the subject believes that the stimulus had just occurred in the learning set. Figure 8-8 illustrates this situation with the shaded portions to the left and right of the criterion showing the relative likelihoods of misses and false alarms.

On the whole, we would expect that the recent items, those just experienced in the memory set, would have greater relative strength or familiarity than the distractor items. Further, the more recently we have seen a particular word, the greater will be its relative strength compared with other words known by the subject, but seen less recently. This

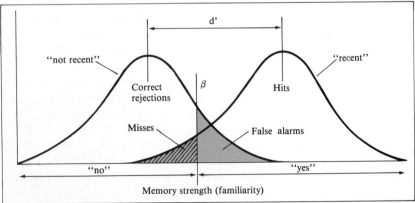

FIGURE 8-8 Hypothetical distributions for "recent" versus "not recent" stimuli in a test of recognition memory. The strength or familiarity of the item (d') combined with the subject's decision criterion level (β) will determine the likelihood of accepting or rejecting that item as belonging to a recently learned memory set.

difference would, of course, be represented by d'. From this analysis, we should not be surprised that subjects may incorrectly recognize items from prior word lists used earlier in the same experiment. The differences in strength between the words presented in the most recent list may not be that much greater than those presented in a previous list. As you can see, this is really another way of talking about the importance of temporal cues in distinguishing old items from new ones, an issue we have discussed previously in terms of theories of forgetting in long- and short-term memory.

Along the same lines, we can also see how associated words used as distractors can easily produce false alarms in the form of incorrect recognition. Receiving a particular word in a memory experiment may also boost the strength of associated words, thus making the distinctions that much more difficult.

Let us take one final example, the well-known finding that recognition testing usually shows better scores for low-frequency, or uncommon words, than common ones (Shepard, 1967; Underwood & Freund, 1970). In terms of our detection analogy, we see that both common and rare words will receive an increase in strength when they are presented in a learning set. The critical point, however, is that since the uncommon words are by definition unlikely to have been encountered recently by the subject, their appearance in a learning set would give them a dramatic increase in level of familiarity. By contrast, common words are already familiar. Their appearance in a learning set will thus produce only a minor change in their familiarity. Therefore, on the recognition test, rare words from the memory set will be relatively easy to distinguish from other rare words that may appear as distractors. Common words, on the other hand, will be easily confusable with the "noise" of other common words which may have been used that day, even if not actually presented in the learning set itself. Thus, the advantage of rare words over common ones in recognition memory can be attributed to their greater separation from the noise distribution, or d'.

As we have indicated, the theory of signal detection offers a mathematical treatment for analyzing the factors we have been discussing to this point. Readers interested in seeing how these analyses can be applied in actual recognition memory experiments can find good examples in papers by Atkinson and Juola (1974), Banks (1970), or Parks (1966).

Throughout this discussion we have used the term "strength" in distinguishing between "old" and "new" items in a recognition test. We might also examine the *distinctiveness* of encoding through the same analogy. That is, when distinguishing between "signal" and "noise," the size of d', will be greater if the test items have been given the deeper, more elaborative processing which leads to encoding uniqueness. Hence, distinctiveness, the usual consequence of deep processing, would yield higher recognition scores than shallower codes. The detection analogy still holds, but the dimension of "strength" may be expressed as a feature of trace uniqueness, uniqueness being a critical factor in recognition accuracy.

With this analogy we have come full circle. We began this book with association theory's emphasis on strength as acquired through repetition. This chapter has discussed levels of processing with its emphasis on the distinctiveness of memory codes. In the signal detection analysis of recognition, we have treated these concepts as highly related, even alternative, ways of viewing the basis of recognition judgements. Association theory placed great value on the importance of repetition for learning. The learning activities of the subject were also of primary importance to the adherents of levels of processing. However, the levels framework emphasizes the variety of possible learning activities and differences in performance produced by different activities. While interference theory emphasized similarity between stimuli as a cause of forgetting, the levels view has emphasized the distinctiveness of codes.

The later developments, then, have not so much replaced the earlier theories, as they have included them within a broader view of the variety of memory phenomena that may be produced in different contexts with different levels of skill and knowledge. Studies of rote learning and of conceptual understanding have yielded what appeared to be different results and certainly different initial explanations. The data from both types of study, however, are a consequence of the same memory system and must be encompassed by a common, integrative theory.

CHAPTER SUMMARY

1. *Levels of Processing*

   A. The levels of processing notion assumes that processing capacity is a limited, rather than a storage capacity. The processing of stimuli ordinarily go through shallow sensory analyses to deeper semantic interpretation.

   B. The most important factor determining memory for a stimulus was thought to be depth of processing achieved in the analysis of that stimulus. The records of deeper processing will, in general, be more enduring than the products of shallow processing. The nature of the processing achieved will be determined by the nature of the task, the time available, and the constraints of the stimulus materials.

   C. Demonstration of levels effects usually take the form of an incidental learning task in which the subject performs some orienting task as the information is presented. Different orienting tasks determine different levels to which the information is processed. When an unexpected recall test is given after the orienting task, different recall scores for groups who engaged in different orienting tasks is taken as evidence for a levels of processing effect.

D. The levels of processing approach explains short-term forgetting as due to the shallow level of processing that can be attained for meaningless materials over very brief retention intervals. The acoustic confusion errors after short retention intervals are also produced by the shallow nature of the codes on which recall is based. These codes represent the early phonological processing of stimulus words. Because processing resources are limited, large amounts of rapidly presented information cannot be processed to a sufficient depth to permit total recall.

2. *Elaboration and Retrieval of Memory Codes: Amendments to the Framework*

   A. *Spread of encoding* was introduced to supplement the levels of processing notion in order to account for situations in which continued processing at the same depth appeared to increase the memorability of stimulus events. Spread of encoding refers to the extensiveness, or richness of encoding at a single level.

   B. *Encoding specificity* is an additional concept which extends the levels of processing view to conditions of retrieval. Earlier, the levels of processing view had emphasized the encoding conditions as the major determinants of recall probability. Encoding specifity required that the encoding process must be reinstated at retrieval in order for recall to occur.

   C. Attempts to specify the mechanisms by which depth and spread of encoding produce their effects have led to suggestions that deeper processing increases the distinctiveness of a memory trace for that event making it easier to discriminate that trace from others.

3. *The Status of Short-Term Memory*

   A. Studies of memory deficits following specific forms of brain damage at first seemed to support the duplex theory. Later analyses showed the nature of these deficits to be more complex than first realized.

   B. While the differences between short- and long-term memories are as clear today as when William James described them, it is doubtful that they are based on distinct structures with fixed characteristics. More likely is the view that how we remember something depends on what we do with it.

4. *Visual Memory*

   A. Early research in memory theory adopted the belief that short-term retention was based exclusively on the formation of verbal–acoustic codes. The possibility of visual memory, or visual imagery, received either little attention or little support.

   B. Studies of recognition memory for large numbers of pictures presented in rapid succession began a renewed interest in the study of visual memory. These experiments were followed by studies of "mental rotation" which implied that subjects can make use of spatially distinct visual representations in memory.

C. Words and sentences which are more easily visualized in the form of a mental image are generally better retained than stimuli less easy to visualize. These data, however, could also be explained in terms of imagery instructions leading to more meaningful analyses and organized codes for these stimuli.

D. The dual-coding hypothesis accounted for the superior retention of visualizable stimuli in terms of the availability of both verbal and visual codes and the redundancy principle that two codes are better than one. Alternative explanations have centered on the likelihood of a single abstract, conceptually based, memory code which allows for the potential generation of image information.

5. *Detection in Memory: An Extended Analogy*

A. Signal detection theory was derived originally to account for the apparent unreliability of sensory detection at or near threshold intensities. Signal strength (d') would be the major determinant of detection rates, along with the subject's criterion level (β) determined by signal probability and payoff.

B. Detection theory can be extended by analogy to recognition memory experiments, where one can adopt d' as a measure of trace strength. Within this analogy, "strength" is seen as an expression of encoding distinctiveness or uniqueness, these being the critical factors in recognition accuracy.

MEMORY RESEARCH ON APPLIED PROBLEMS

TOPIC QUESTIONS

1. Eyewitness Testimony.
What are the two types of variables that influence eyewitness testimony and how might the legal system make use of information about how these variables operate? What are some of the specific variables that have an important influence on eyewitness identification of suspects?

2. Learning How to Learn.
What kinds of knowledge do people use when they plan to remember something, and how do these plans contribute to the ability to learn? How do children differ from adults in their knowledge of how to remember?

3. Strategies for Remembering.
What is the role of short-term memory in problem-solving tasks and how can these limitations be overcome? What are *mnemonics* and how can they aid learning and retention? How is "meaning" involved in the strategies we have available for remembering?

4. Individual Differences and Memory.
How do the reported cases of people with extraordinary memories compare with normal retention? What is the purpose of relating information processing concepts to ability measures? What are the major differences between young and old subjects on memory tasks and how does the *levels of processing* view interpret these differences?

5. Memory Constraints and Modern Technology.
How do capacity and storage limitations affect the learning and performance of a skill? What is the significance of biological rhythms for learning and skilled performance?

Throughout the previous chapters we have tried to illustrate the principles we discussed with examples of how they might operate in our everyday experience. It is true that many of these examples did not directly "prove" the theories they were used to illustrate. On the other hand, a theoretical idea can illuminate our common experience and make these ideas more plausible and relevant to the explanations of how we function. Further, it has been argued that research is most likely to produce a successful theory when it begins with a practical problem (Broadbent, 1971). Accordingly, the sections of this chapter discuss a range of information processing problems—from the classroom, to the courtroom, to industrial settings. Our sample will not simply describe an application of the facts and theories discussed in previous chapters. The relationship between laboratory, academic psychology, and the kinds of investigations we explore here is ideally more like siblings than any one being the "parent" of the other. Much of this work uses concepts, frameworks, and methods that also characterize less applied research. But if these concepts and methods are useful in applied settings, the study of "natural" phenomena also feeds back to keep the theoretical enterprise in touch with what must be explained, the behavior of human beings in action.

In our brief sampling of applied memory research, we will look first at problems of assessing and improving the accuracy of eyewitness testimony in the courtroom. Second, we will turn to the development of memory skills in children. The development of these skills, as you will see, is critical to the child's ability to benefit from study and instruction. A third section explores common strategies employed to deal with the information processing constraints of attention and short-term memory.

While these issues are common across individuals and are of general concern to theory and practice, equally important is the issue of individual differences among us in the rate and quality of learning. In the fourth section, therefore, we discuss illustrative research which has attempted a more specific description of these differences in terms of elementary stages of information processing. The final section takes our discussion to a broader context: how we, as information processing systems, can adapt to being part of a technologically oriented society.

EYEWITNESS TESTIMONY

One of the most dramatic situations in which memory plays a critical role is in the courtroom. Eyewitness testimony is often the most influential evidence that can be introduced in a legal proceeding. Since the witness has already perceived and encoded the event in question, the problem for the legal system is to obtain the most accurate possible account of the witnessed events. However, you are aware from previous chapters that the report of a meaningful event often goes beyond what was presented. Embedded in a subject's recollections are inferences from what actually happened, reconstructions that fill in the gaps, and sometimes actual distortions of the information that make the whole episode more consistent and comprehensible to the observer. Research in memory should provide law enforcement personnel, lawyers, judges, and juries with an adequate context in which the accuracy of eyewitness testimony can be evaluated. It should also provide suggestions and advice that will optimize the collection of reliable information about the witnessed event.

Parallel to these two questions, Wells (1978) has proposed that one can distinguish two kinds of variables that influence eyewitness testimony: *Estimator variables* that cannot be changed in an actual criminal case, and *system variables* that can be altered to maximize potential accuracy in real cases. For example, characteristics of the suspect and the severity of the crime are both estimator variables that can affect the accuracy of an observer's report. However, these are circumstances over which the police and the courts have no control. Investigations of how estimator variables affect the nature of the testimony can only serve to inform the court about the relative reliability of different witnesses in different situations.

In other words, a psychologist might testify that less confidence should be placed in testimony regarding one type of crime than in testimony about some other type of crime, or in one type of witness relative to some other type of witness. The jury might then take this information into consideration in evaluating the evidence they have heard. Investigations of estimator variables could be used, then, primarily to increase or discount the credibility of particular testimony.

Research on estimator variables has had the effect of generally increasing skepticism about the reliability of all eyewitness testimony (Buckhout, 1974). That is, since these extraneous variables seem to have substantial effects on the accuracy of report, some researchers have argued that all witness reports are inherently unreliable and, therefore, require extensive corroboration by other evidence. It is unlikely, however, that this opinion will measurably reduce the importance of eyewitness testimony for juries and judges in actual cases. Wells (1978) argues that a more useful effort for the psychologist would be the discovery and measurement of situational factors that can be altered to produce more accurate and reliable reports. As we noted earlier, the factors that can be altered in the legal system to increase the potential accuracy of the report are called *system variables* (Wells, 1978).

System variables are aspects of the procedures used in actual cases which may have effects on the recall accuracy of witnesses. For example, the kind of lineup used to identify a suspect may lead to false recognitions of innocent people, just as the kind of questions asked during interrogation of the witness may introduce distortions into the testimony. Knowledge about system variables could provide the legal system with means to ensure the most accurate, reliable information possible. Understanding of both estimator and system variables is necessary to permit a proper evaluation of eyewitness testimony as a memory performance. During the last decade applied research on these two dimensions has increased dramatically. Now that we have defined these variables and provided a few examples, we can examine this research in more detail.

Estimator Variables

The recognition of persons has been the focus of much of the research involving estimator variables. Unfortunately, the results of this work do not allow a great deal of optimism about our ability to recognize someone after a single encounter. For example, Patterson and Baddeley (1977) found that there was a significant drop in the accuracy of recognition for photographs of faces when the pose or expression of the person to be recognized was different at the time of testing than it had been during presentation. There was a further, and much larger, drop in correct recognition when the test face was disguised by adding or taking away a beard, glasses, or changing the hair style, something any criminal could easily do. In addition, the degree of confidence that a witness has in the recognition judgement does not appear to be a good predictor of the accuracy of that judgement (Deffenbacher, Brown, & Sturgill, 1978). Their research showed that witnesses were just as confident when they were wrong as when they were correct.

As we would expect from previous work on retention intervals in memory experiments, eyewitness identifications decrease in accuracy with time (Lipton, 1977). A witness who saw a film of a simulated crime and was then called back to identify the suspect one week later, would be less likely to make a correct identification than a witness who had seen the film only a day prior to the recognition test.

As mentioned earlier, the accuracy of recognition is also affected by the seriousness of the crime and the degree of violence involved. Leippe, Wells, and Ostrom (1978) found that witnesses were more accurate in identifying a suspect from a photograph when the stolen object in a staged crime was worth $50 than when the object was worth $1.50. However, if the subject did not know the value of the stolen object until 60 seconds after the theft, the value had no effect on later recognition of the suspect. That is, for the value of the stolen object to produce an effect on recognition, the value had to be known at the time of the crime.

It further turns out that seriousness of a crime in terms of violence produces different effects on memory than seriousness in terms of how much was stolen. Clifford and Scott (1978), for example, found that there was a large decrease in witness's ability to remember details of violent incidents in a film clip as compared to less violent incidents. The seriousness of the crime, as measured by the value of the object stolen, produced opposite effects to the seriousness of the crime, as measured by the degree of violence involved.

An interpretation of these findings may be suggested by our review of attention and coding in previous chapters. On the one hand, the ''importance'' of the event may determine the capacity and time devoted to encoding the information, and the depth to which one analyzes the perceived event. On the other hand, one may reallocate processing capacity to something else when the result of encoding provokes emotional upset or annoyance. During a robbery we might, for example, focus our attention on how we are going to get home without car keys, or in trying to remember how much money was in a wallet rather than the face of the robber or the kind of car the robber drove. The variability of recognition judgements under these circumstances may reflect the flexibility of the cognitive system and its sensitivity to the ''meaning'' of events to us as individuals.

The relationship of the race of the witness to the race of the suspect can sometimes also qualify the accuracy of recognition judgements. Studies have often shown that white witnesses discriminate more accurately among white suspects than they do among black suspects. Black witnesses on the other hand, show only a small difference in their recognition judgements for black versus white faces (Cross, Cross, & Daly, 1971; Elliott, Will, & Goldstein, 1973). Some investigators have even claimed a small sex difference, with female witnesses both less accurate overall than males and also better at discriminating among female suspects than they are at discriminating among males suspects (Deffenbacher et al. 1978).

These differences in accuracy among witnesses might well represent differences in their familiarity with other groups and the amount of practice they have had in encoding differentiating characteristics of individuals in these groups. Therefore, in evaluating the testimony of a particular witness, it may be necessary to consider the history and experience of the witness as well as the race and sex of the witness.

One clue to the group differences may be the work of Bower and Karlin (1974) who found that face recognition was more accurate if the subject had engaged in ''deep'' processing at the time of presentation. In their study they asked one group of subjects to make judgements about physical features of the faces in a set of photographs (e.g., size of the nose). Another group of subjects made judgements about more ''psychological characteristics'' (e.g., honesty, friendliness). The group making the judgements about psychological characteristics was more accurate in a later recognition test of these photographs. It may be that witnesses differ also in their readiness to perform deeper analyses on the faces of individuals in other groups. The stereotypes we hold of members of other groups substitute for the deeper processing we perform when we encounter members of our own group. This may, in fact, be a good example of how a stereotype inhibits thinking.

All the variables we have mentioned (length of the retention interval, crime seriousness, numbers of previous encounters with the suspect, similarity of the suspect's appearance in the original observation to the suspect's appearance during recognition testing, and witness characteristics) are beyond the control of the legal system. These studies can only enter into the legal process as qualifications to the testimony of particular witnesses about a particular event. Furthermore, these qualifications are based on the average scores of groups of subjects in simulated situations and, therefore, may not apply to the individual witness in an actual case. Nevertheless, most of this work cautions us about the vulnerability of any memory performance to error and distortion. In legal proceedings in which a person's very liberty may rest largely on the report of a witness, we must be particularly careful in assessing the likelihood that this report is accurate.

System Variables

The Lineup. As any of us who watch TV know, a common procedure used in attempting to identify the suspect in a crime is to show the witness a series of photographs, or "mugshots." If someone is identified at this stage, the witness may then be asked to pick this individual out from among others in a "lineup." From previous discussions of recognition, you know that the similarity of the people in the lineup to one another will affect the ability of the subject to pick out the individual previously identified by photograph. For example, in an obviously absurd case, if the photograph identified was a male and all the other people in the lineup were female, the identification judgement would be biased toward the one male. Selecting this individual would not really tell us very much about the witness's ability to identify the suspect. To be sure that the witness does in fact base recognition on memory of characteristics that differentiate the suspect from other individuals, the lineup must contain people who are at least superficially similar in appearance to the previously identified suspect.

In addition to the type of distractors present in the lineup, beliefs about the presence or absence of the suspect in a particular lineup also affect the accuracy of identification. If the witness is told that the suspect is in the lineup, there is a greater likelihood that a false recognition will be made than if the witness were told that the suspect might or might not be in the lineup (Hall & Ostrum cited in Wells, 1978). The belief that the suspect is in the lineup may encourage the witness to guess, or to use a less stringent criterion for recognition. As we saw in the previous chapter, either of these strategies would lead to a higher proportion of false recognitions.

The nature of the lineup is a variable that is under the control of law enforcement officials. From what we have learned about recognition tests, we can advise these officials that in order to validly assess the accuracy of a witness's testimony, individuals in a lineup should be at least superficially similar to each other. It will also decrease the likelihood that someone will be wrongly identified if there is more than one lineup and the witness is told for each that the suspect may or may not be present. These are procedural steps that the legal system can easily take to improve its assessment of the memory of a witness.

The Mugbook. The procedure of exposing witnesses to a mugbook may also introduce bias into the later judgements of a lineup (Brown, Deffen-

A police lineup should include "distractors" as similar to the physical appearance of the suspect as possible.

bacher, & Sturgill, 1977). As you may recall from discussions of retroactive and proactive interference, subjects who have heard different items on different trials may have difficulty in discriminating whether a particular item was just heard or belonged to an earlier list. That is, they may recognize an item as having been heard before, but be unable to judge whether it was in the last list presented, or in some previous list. Similarly, the witness who has looked over a mugbook may have an analogous difficulty. When confronted with several people in a lineup, they may fail to realize that the individual is familiar because they were seen in a photograph in the mugbook, rather than because that individual was the one observed at the scene of the crime.

In the study by Brown et al. (1977), subjects saw five strangers and were told that they would later be asked to identify these individuals in a lineup. One group of subjects was then asked to look at a series of photographs that included some of the people they had just seen as well as some new people. All the subjects were then asked to pick out the original five strangers from a lineup that included these five people, some individuals seen only in photographs, and some people never seen before. "Suspects" who had been seen in the mugshots were more likely to be identified than "suspects" whose photographs had not been seen. However, the witnesses also falsely identified a substantial number of people in the lineup who had been seen only in mugshots. In fact, the witnesses were just as likely to identify someone seen only in the mugshots, as they were to identify someone seen only during the original presentation. Clearly, seeing a photograph of a person increased the probability that the person would be identified, whether or not the person was actually one of the original suspects. This is obviously no less true for photographs of an accused person we may have seen in a newspaper.

Questioning the Witness.   Questioning of witnesses is a third procedural aspect of obtaining eyewitness reports that has stimulated research interest. It seems clear from this work that the kind of questions asked influences not only the witness's answer to that question, but also the nature of the witness's entire report. For example, Loftus and Palmer (1974) showed subjects a film of a traffic accident. They then questioned subjects about what they had seen. One group of subjects was asked "How fast were the cars going when they *hit* each other?" Another group was asked "How fast were the cars going when they *smashed into* each other?" The group who heard the phrase "smashed into" gave much higher estimates of speed than the group who heard the word "hit." The way the question was phrased, therefore, biased the witness's answers. This single question, however, did more than simply change the answer to a single question. When both groups were called back 1 week later to answer a series of questions about the film, the group who heard the "smashed into" version of the question was more likely to answer "Yes" to the question "Did you see any broken glass?" There had been no broken glass in the original presentation. The phrasing of the question one week earlier had a clear effect on how subjects remembered these events.

Even more worrisome, witnesses seem unable to correct their reports even when told they may have been misled. Loftus, Miller, and Burns (1978) performed an experiment similar to the one described above. In this study, one of their questions suggested that a road sign in a filmed accident had been a YIELD sign. Although the sign in question was a STOP sign, nevertheless, subjects who received the misleading information were more likely to choose YIELD when asked to pick out the sign they had seen. These subjects did not alter their choices even after they were told that they may have been provided with misleading information in the earlier questions.

Loftus and her colleagues have argued from this evidence that the misleading information is actually incorporated into the memory for the witnessed event. That is, the false information does not simply provide an interpretation of what is remembered, but it directly alters what is remembered. The message of this research is that an investigator must be very careful in eliciting eyewitness reports. It may be extremely difficult or impossible to undo the effect of even a single leading question.

Researchers who have been concerned about the dynamics of police interrogations have found that asking any specific questions at all can often reduce the accuracy of the report. Lipton (1977) had subjects view a film of a staged murder and then asked for a description of what had been seen. Subjects who were allowed free recall without questioning were the most accurate in their reports. Over 90% of the information provided by these subjects was correct. Subjects who were asked leading questions or multiple choice questions were considerably less accurate. However, the more specific questions produced a greater amount of information. That is, questioning elicited responses, but these responses were not always reliable descriptions of the event.

There appears, therefore, to be a tradeoff between the amount of information the subject reports and the accuracy of that information. Dent (1978) studied 10- to 11-year-old children who saw either a film or a live staged incident of a parcel being taken from a classroom. When the children were asked to give reports of this incident those who were allowed to freely report what they had seen without questioning produced more accurate, but less complete, reports than did children who were directly questioned about specific parts of the event. The effects of the questions seemed to especially distort the descriptions of people. The questions, however, had less of an effect on their descriptions of what actually happened. Again, accuracy was sacrificed for completeness when subjects were closely questioned about the incident.

In a second part of her study, Dent (1978) showed that experienced interviewers do not necessarily elicit superior reports; they are simply better able to distinguish accurate from inaccurate information. In this study, an incident was staged in a 4th-grade classroom and reports of this incident were solicited from the children. The interviewers were either experienced in working with children (three policemen and three teachers) or professionally inexperienced (four parents and two youth workers). Neither of the groups of interviewers had seen the incident and were told only that a bag had been taken from the classroom. The experienced interviewers obtained significantly more total information from the children than did the inexperienced interviewers (although not all of this information was correct). Furthermore, the experienced interviewers' reconstructions of the actual events were generally more accurate than those of the inexperienced groups. The skill of good investigators, apparently, is not necessarily an ability to elicit reliable information. Rather, it is an ability to discriminate the accurate from the inaccurate. In this study, the interviewers' experience with children had somehow "tuned" them to cues that indicated the reliability of a given piece of a child's report.

These studies of interviewing represent system variables since they imply that an interviewer can affect the accuracy of a witness's report by the kind of questions that are asked. The study of interviewers in particular poses interesting questions about how a skilled professional (e.g., police officer, psychotherapist, personnel specialist) learns to distinguish accurate from inaccurate information and what cues are being used to make this discrimination. The answers to these questions would have implications about how interviewers might be trained to improve the quality of information obtained from witnesses and the inferences made from this information. The interaction between psychology and the justice system is just beginning to be recognized as a fruitful and mutually beneficial field of study. The study of eyewitness testimony represents one facet of this collaboration, but a particularly important one.

LEARNING HOW TO LEARN

Learning and remembering are, in part, skills. These skills are not analogous to the factual knowledge and theoretical formulations such as you may acquire from reading this book. You acquire skill in remembering from your everyday experiences, at home, at work, and at school. Schools in particular place a great emphasis on your ability to remember. Whether or not we consider the situation ideal, it is nonetheless the case that "good" students are those who are most accomplished in the exercise of the skill of learning and remembering.

In studying this text, for example, you no doubt went through a variety of activities that are related to what you want to learn. You may have underlined in the text or taken notes, reread the important sections, tried to find logical or associative relations among the main points of a chapter, and tested yourself. Your underlining or notetaking segregated the most important information from information of lesser importance; your rereading and relating parts to each other were learning strategies; your self-testing monitored the success of these activities. Your intention to learn required that you performed these activities and your understanding of the structure of the material helped you to direct your efforts appropriately.

In addition to acquiring skills that prepare you for later remembering, you have also learned certain skills that are related to remembering itself. You have learned that some retrieval cues are better than others and that different "search" strategies are appropriate to answer different kinds of questions. For example, suppose you wanted to remember how you spent the day after your first exam last year. How would you go about it? What information would you want to help you in remembering? You know that the date of the exam probably would not help much. The time of day might help if you could remember last term's schedule. A list of your courses might prompt you to remember the different course requirements of each class and allow you to infer which one gave the first exam. The point here is that you go about remembering in a systematic way. You know what kinds of information may help you to remember and what kinds of information probably will not be of much use. Retrieval strategies and the selection of retrieval cues are skills we learn through experience and practice. When very young children are asked questions about past events, they give up if the answer does not come immediately to mind. They do not know the appropriate strategy to "search" for an answer. Indeed, they are not even aware that such strategies are necessary.

The skills of learning and remembering that the child usually acquires as the result of experience and schooling can be applied across a variety of tasks. Part of the skill is, in fact, in analyzing a task to determine what is required. The generality of these skills makes them of obvious significance for the psychology of memory. However, as we have noted many times, the type of theory one holds suggests the types of questions asked and studies undertaken. The associationist theory of memory dealt with these problems only indirectly through notions of "mediational processes"; the more cognitive, structural models saw changes in memory performance over time as being the result of "capacity changes" or changes in "organization" through chunking and rehearsal. Study of the development of memory skills and their coordination has, therefore, a relatively recent origin.

Knowing About Remembering

The practical knowledge acquired about our own memory capacities and what we must do to remember has been dubbed *metamemory* (Flavell & Wellman, 1977). The general topic of metamemory has attracted increasing interest because it is, in fact, the question of what subjects know about how they remember.

The kinds of knowledge that make up metamemory can be divided into three categories, each of which represents knowledge about a particular aspect of the task or learning situation. These categories are: (1) knowledge about your own characteristics that are relevant to remembering, (2) knowledge about differences among tasks that are important to how they are remembered, and (3) knowledge of strategies and rules that are useful in remembering (Flavell & Wellman, 1977).

The first category of metamemory, knowledge of our own characteristics, comprises our attitudes as well as knowledge about our capacities and abilities. You know what things are relatively difficult for you to learn and what things are relatively easy. For example, courses requiring verbal reasoning and written expression may be easier for you than courses in mathematics. You may have discovered that you learn more efficiently by listening to someone explain something and asking questions than you do by reading about the topic. You are aware that you can hold a telephone number in your head while dialing, but if you want to retain that number more permanently you must write it down. These examples relate knowledge of your own characteristics and capacities to the situations in which you must acquire and make use of information. This knowledge, in part, will determine what you choose to learn and how you go about it.

Our knowledge of the differences among types of learning tasks is the second category of metamemory. Examples of such knowledge include knowing that we may be able to recognize a person's name if we hear it, even though we cannot recall the name; knowing that it is easier to remember the sense or meaning of a conversation than it is to remember the exact words used to express this meaning; knowing that it is more difficult to learn lists of unrelated items (for example, state capitals) than it is to learn the same number of items related to each other in some meaningful way (for example, as the words of a sentence). In short, we know what characteristics of a memory task may present special difficulties (amount of information, similarity of items, etc.) and what aspects of a task may make it particularly easy (relationship to past learning, organization, etc.).

Finally, we also possess knowledge about strategies of learning and remembering. In the example given in the beginning of this section, trying to recall your first exam last year by searching for other related information, we pointed out a couple of alternative retrieval strategies. In effect, you would be selecting particular retrieval cues to aid in the recall of a desired piece of information. The most appropriate strategy for retrieval will depend on the type of question asked. Trying to recall "when" a particular event occurred, rather than "where" it occurred would lead to searches for different sets of cues. Learning what strategies are appropriate for different kinds of questions requires experience with trying to remember in a variety of situations.

Metamemory represents implicit knowledge, knowledge that we do not ordinarily articulate, but that nevertheless has effects on our memory performances and on how we go about making plans to remember. This concept is an important and interesting one for several reasons. First, it suggests, in a way that our earlier analyses did not, how our beliefs and attitudes related to memory may affect our performance. For example, it is not uncommon to hear a student say that they "just cannot learn math." There seems to be a stereotype in our culture that some individuals are poor in mathematics and only others are likely to excel. A person's notion that they are unable to master mathematical concepts is usually mistaken and more likely acquired from subtle social communication than from realistic feedback about performance on mathematical tasks. However, holding this belief prevents them from having the kinds of experiences that would lead to the skills and knowledge enabling them to exercise their abilities. We may, then, have false beliefs that inhibit the acquisition of certain metamemory skills. With a change in our cultural stereotypes, many individuals are finding that beliefs based on the expectations of others are poor substitutes for feedback from your own performance.

A second, and perhaps more important, implication of the concept of metamemory is that we might be able to improve the efficiency of learning and memory performance by explicitly teaching these higher order skills. Difficulties in learning, when viewed from the perspective of metamemory, may not reflect limitations in the capacities or abilities of the learner. Rather, they may represent deficiencies in what the learner knows about differences between learning tasks and about the different kinds of strategies that can be used to learn and remember. For this suggestion to pay off, of course, we must know much more than we now do about the strategies and discriminations used by effective learners. At present we have only a relatively basic analysis of what people know about the operation of their own memories and how this knowledge develops.

What Children Know About Knowing

Young children, having had limited experience with learning situations know very little about their own characteristics related to memory, about learning strategies, or about tasks. For example, when asked to remember a string of digits for a few seconds, 5-year-olds do not rehearse these items during the retention interval. As a result, their memory performance is usually quite poor. However, if these children are specifically instructed to repeat the numbers in order to remember them, they can easily perform this maintenance activity and improve their recall score as a consequence (Flavell & Wellman, 1977). These children have a *production deficiency,* that is, they fail to use a strategy spontaneously even though they are capable of doing so. Production deficiencies are to be contrasted with *process deficiencies* in which the individual is incapable of executing some activity because they do not possess a process or capacity which is necessary for the execution of the activity (Craik & Simon, 1980). The children who did not rehearse possess the required capacities; they simply are not aware that they will forget if they do not repeat the memory items. They are deficient in what they know about memory.

The naivete of young children about their own memories can sometimes be quite surprising. For example, in an experiment by Yussen and Levy (1975), preschool children did not seem to realize that there is a limit to their own memory span. Children were first asked to estimate how many items they could recall correctly without error. They then heard strings of nine or ten items and were asked for immediate recall after each list. Of course, none of the children of any age group were able to recall all of the items in a ten-item list. After a few practice trials on this simple task, the children were asked again to guess the number of items they would be able to recall correctly on the next trial. Eight-year-olds adjusted their estimates to be consistent with their performance on previous trials. Some preschool children, on the other hand, persisted in predicting that they would get all the items correct in the next string. Their inability to recall the items from previous trials was not understood as a reflection of a limitation in their own capabilities.

The handicap imposed by ignorance about the limits and parameters of one's own memory performance also extends to learning tasks. Flavell Frederichs, and Hoyt (1970) asked children to study a set of items until they were certain that they could recite the whole list perfectly. The children were given three trials in which they studied the materials as long as they wished and then attempted to recall. Children 7 to 10 years old usually performed perfectly on each of the three trials. Younger children, 4 to 6, were considerably less accurate. In addition, the performances of the younger children did not improve over the three trials. Their failure to recall the material on earlier trials did not lead them to change what they did in a way that would lead to improved performance. The younger children, then, did not properly assess their own readiness to recall. They were apparently unaware of the cues or methods used by older children in monitoring the extent to which they had adequately learned the lists of items.

This finding may have a familiar ring to even the college-level student. Many of you have had the impression that you "knew the material" only to find that your grade on an exam seemed to indicate otherwise. This work with children seems to imply that such experiences may be the result of a problem in self-monitoring, and in the selection of inappropriate cues to determine the state of your own knowledge. An important task in the study of metamemory is to determine the conditions that indicate effective learning has taken place, that is, to answer the question, "How do we know that we know?"

Another dimension of metamemory on which developmental changes have been observed is the child's knowledge of task requirements. For example, Brown and her colleagues (e.g., Brown & Smiley, 1977, 1978; Brown & Campione, 1978; Brown, Smiley, & Lawton, 1978) have studied changes in children's sensitivity to the "structure" of a set of learning materials. One sense in which a text or paragraph has structure is in the relative importance of its parts or sentences. If we are going to efficiently learn from our reading, we must be able to distinguish what is important from what is merely illustrative or peripheral to the main points. Brown and Smiley (1977) had students rate the relative importance of each element of a story. College students ordered these elements into four levels of importance, from most to least relevant to the theme. Seventh graders separated these same elements into three levels of importance. Fifth graders saw only two levels of importance, and third graders made no reliable distinctions at all. Clearly, then, these groups of students differed in their sensitivity to the "importance structure" of the story. For the college students, the story was composed of several distinguishable levels; for the third graders, each element in the story was as important as any other.

Brown and Smiley (1977) further found that this difference in discriminating the relative importance of story elements had consequences for how students spent their time studying the story when they were told they would be required to recall it. When given repeated opportunities for study and recall, college students improved their scores on "important" elements over trials; however, their scores on "unimportant" elements were much the same from trial to trial. Students who had failed to perceive a difference in the importance of the elements also failed to exhibit this differential pattern of improvement over trials. The recall improvements for the young children were not significantly related to the importance structure of the story. Presumably, the college students used their study opportunities to concentrate on a limited part of the text selected for its importance. Younger subjects, who did not perceive this structure, could not orient their study activities appropriately.

The perception of structure in prose materials and the coordination of attention and study with this structure is, then, an important part of learning to study. The development of these abilities is, of course, related to the development of our knowledge in a particular area. If you are studying a very complex text of which you have little or no prior experience, you might well have difficulty in separating what is important from what is merely illustration and example. In this case, we would expect your study behavior and later recall to resemble the pattern of some of the younger children in the study described above. As you grow more familiar with the concepts and their relationships in a new field, your ability to discriminate the structure of a text would increase, and the efficiency of your studying would increase accordingly. Knowledge of the structure of a set of learning materials is part of the knowledge of task requirements. This knowledge requires experience and practice for its acquisition.

Knowledge of structure also affects our efficiency at selecting appropriate retrieval cues for later recall. For example, in another of Brown's studies (Brown et al. 1978), students were asked which elements of a story they would like to have available at the time of recall to help them remember the story. The choices of cue made by the younger children displayed no clear pattern, but, on the first trial, college students chose as cues those elements that had been rated as the most relevant to the main theme. As in the previous study, students were now given the opportunity to study and were then tested using the retrieval cues they had chosen at the beginning of the session. After this recall experience, the subjects were again given the opportunity to select another set of retrieval cues that they thought would be most useful in recalling the story.

Cues chosen by the younger children were unrelated to their recall experience. They were just as likely to choose one of the cues used on the earlier trial as they were to choose some other cue. However, the choices of college students shifted as a result of the earlier recall trial. These students had chosen the most important elements for retrieval cues on the first trial, but after one recall attempt they preferred items that had been rated as intermediate in importance. They had discovered from their attempted recall that they could remember the major elements in the story without cues. The intermediate level of importance had produced more recall errors than the most important elements. The choice of recall cue was, then, more flexible and sensitive to experience for older students than for younger ones. The grade school children were both less sensitive to the importance structure of the story and less sensitive to the information provided by their own errors in attempting recall.

The differences we have described among age groups represent differences in the knowledge each of these groups has about their own memory performances, the factors that limit these performances, and the strategies that can be used to improve performance. Our descriptions of these differences in metamemory do not specify the necessary conditions for change. Individuals of the same age can also differ in their awareness of limitations in memory, in their understanding of task characteristics, and in the sophistication of their learning and retrieval strategies. One of the promises of research in this area is that we may eventually specify these differences in skills and plans to remember, and the conditions necessary to produce such knowledge (cf. Flavell, 1979). We might then be in a position to teach quite general learning and memory skills that could be applied across a wide variety of educational situations.

STRATEGIES FOR REMEMBER-ING

We are still a long way from that ideal of science fiction that has us effortlessly acquiring great stores of knowledge by the ingestion of a "memory pill," or by the reception of this information through a direct electrical link from our brains to an omniscient computer. The application of what you have learned about memory might be expected to result in an increase in the effectiveness and efficiency with which you acquire and retrieve information, but it will not do away with the requirement for motivated effort. In fact, the work discussed in the preceding chapters suggests that relatively passive reading or study is inherently inefficient. As you have noted, successful remembering seems to be the result of a complex set of activities. Even what one learns incidentally, without any anticipation of later recall, is determined by the kind of processing we perform on the material. What is learned and how well it is learned depends on how we pay attention, how we encode, and how we interpret information.

Intentional remembering is a kind of problem solving task in which a successful solution is the result of your understanding of the goals of the problem and the various means you have at your disposal for achieving these goals. The strategies and techniques used to increase the effectiveness of learning and remembering are those which, first, permit us to circumvent some of the constraints of our own memory systems.

Overcoming Short-Term Memory

Many types of tasks require that we retain information in memory while we perform some additional operations. In doing a multiplication problem in your head, say 16×8, you have to store an intermediate result while you complete the rest of the computation. Also of this type are logical problems that require us to remember a set of premises while we deduce some conclusion. In both these problems we are limited in what we can achieve by the capacity of short-term memory. If the size of the intermediate result in a mental calculation, or the amount of information in a set of premises exceeds the short-term capacity, we "lose our place" in the problem and fail to obtain the correct solution.

There are people who seem to show truly prodigious talents for such tasks. They can, for example, multiply ten-digit numbers in their heads, or take the cube root of a large number without the aid of pencil and paper. However, studies of these individuals (e.g., Hunter, 1978) do not indicate the possession of an extraordinarily large short-term memory. Rather, they have learned strategies that permit them to shift the burden of mental work from short- to long-term memory.

If we analyze the tasks performed by "mental calculators," we find that these tasks place three different kinds of demands on memory: (1) remembering the methods necessary for calculating certain problems (e.g., multiplication, division), (2) remembering logical and numerical equivalents (e.g., the multiplication tables), and (3) remembering where work was left off (e.g., the intermediate results of the calculation) (Hunter, 1978). Only the third type of demand involves short-term memory; the others represent long-term knowledge acquired over a lifetime of practice.

The expert in mental calculation has minimized the demands on short-term memory by minimizing the need for intermediate results. For example, you may know the multiplication table to 12×12. It would not be unusual for an expert mental calculator to know this table into the hundreds or thousands. For these individuals, multiplying 136×172 would not involve the laborious process of "carrying" and remembering the intermediate result. The mental calculator need only retrieve the numerical equivalent of 136×172 from long-term memory in the same way as you retrieve 49 as the numerical equivalent of 7×7. An individual, then, who seems able to perform impossible mental calculations does so through a "trick." The problem for this person is mainly one of retrieval from long-term memory rather than one of maintaining large amounts of information in short-term storage.

The ability to perform a wide variety of tasks is affected by limitations on short-term retention. For example, Whimbey and Ryan (1969) found that the ability of college students to solve reasoning problems was highly correlated with the students' digit span. Subjects who had lower scores on tests of reasoning, also were able to remember fewer digits after a single presentation. Whimbey and Ryan argued that the correlation between digit span and reasoning abilities indicated that performance on the reasoning task was limited by the capacity of short-term memory. However, as we noted in Chapter 5, memory span is not a good indicator of the capacity of STS.

In fact, the so-called "immediate memory span" does not correlate well with accepted measures of short-term store capacity such as Waugh and Norman's (1965) method of estimating STS from the recency portion of the serial position curve (Martin, 1978). On the other hand, the digit span does seem to reflect a subject's ability to maintain the order of a series of items (Martin, 1978). Therefore, while Whimbey and Ryan may have been mistaken about the precise nature of the constraint on reasoning ability, their hypothesis that short-term factors reflected in the digit span were a limiting factor in reasoning performance seems fully justified.

The reasoning problems studied by Whimbey and Ryan (1969) required a decision about the truth or falsity of a conclusion drawn from a set of premises. This is sometimes called *syllogistic reasoning*. The classic example of this type of problem is: "All men are mortal. Socrates is a man. Therefore, Socrates is mortal." Solution of this problem requires that we hold the premises in memory while we assess the validity of the conclusion. An important part of this task is to maintain the structure of the problem. That is, one must not confuse the conclusion with the premises. One way to decrease the load on memory in this situation is to change the way in which the premises are represented. For example, the syllogism above can be represented in the form of a Venn diagram shown in Figure 9-1.

This diagram analyzes the syllogism into "sets" of elements. The larger circle represents the set of all elements possessing the common property "mortality." "Men," the medium circle, is a subset of this larger set, that is, all the elements that possess the property of being human are also elements of the set of mortals. Socrates, the smallest circle, is an element of the subset "men." Representing the syllogism in this way permits the student to chunk the premises into a single spatial unit and to assess the validity of the conclusion from this representation.

Whimbey and Ryan (1969) tested the effectiveness of this strategy for decreasing memory load. After preliminary measurement of digit span and reasoning abilities, they taught their subjects to use Venn diagrams of the sort shown here to represent premises and conclusions of a syllogism. With training and some practice, subjects could visualize these diagrams and use them to represent the problem without actually producing a drawing. Following the training, subjects were retested for

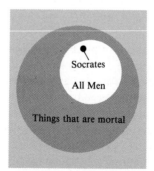

FIGURE 9-1   A Venn diagram of the syllogism: "All men are mortal. Socrates is a man. Therefore, Socrates is mortal."

reasoning and digit span. The correlation between performances on these two tasks was no longer present.

After training, in other words, digit span no longer predicted a subject's ability to solve reasoning problems. Changing the way in which the problem was represented permitted subjects to chunk information and, thereby, decreased the load on memory. Since the recoded information represented the problem structure in an integrated way, the technique had, in effect, removed one of the factors that previously limited performance on these problems.

Mnemonics   The improvement of memory and retention, as you may have gathered from our examples, consists of improving the subjective organization and understanding of the materials studied. The improvement in remembering is, thus, an indirect effect of the time and effort spent in organizing. For example, the rapid mental calculators we described had to devote considerable work to acquiring numerical equivalents and knowledge of number patterns. Similarly, the subjects of Whimbey and Ryan (1969) initially had to learn about Venn diagrams, how these diagrams could represent syllogisms, and, finally, how these diagrams could be used to solve reasoning problems. The changes in performance that resulted from these efforts was not due to an increase in the short-term capacities. Rather, the short-term limitation on performance was effectively bypassed by changing the organization of the chunk.

Chunking is the most basic level of organization because it involves changes in the subjective unit of memory. We noted several examples of chunking in earlier chapters (e.g., the sing-song rhyme used to recite the alphabet, and the rhyme used to remember the number of days in each month). Each of these served to organize a relatively arbitrary list of items into a smaller set of subjective units. The schemes for the alphabet and for the days of the month were special cases used only in recalling this particular information. There are more general schemes used to organize and remember any list of unrelated items. These organizational schemes are called *mnemonics*.

The use of mnemonics is very old, and certainly psychology can take no credit for their invention. In ancient Greece, part of a young aristocrat's training in oratory involved the use of mnemonic techniques. This was a method for insuring that all points in a public speech would be remembered, and remembered in the correct order. To commit a speech to memory, the speaker might typically use the *method of loci*. As in the other examples we have discussed, some preliminary work was required. First, it was necessary to become very familiar with a place, for example, one's own home or a public building. When the various parts of this place and their relationships to one another were clearly established in memory, the student was ready to learn the speech.

In the course of learning, the student imagined walking through the rooms learned earlier. At each point in this journey the trick would be to visualize placing some of the information required in the talk into, or beside, some notable element in the room. The information was deposited, in order, as the walk proceeded until each part of the speech had been associated with a particular locus on the walk.

To recover this information, the student would imagine the same journey through the rooms, this time retrieving the information from each locus. The order of the speech was preserved by the order of the objects and elements on the walk. Speakers could retain their place in a speech by simply remembering where in the journey they had left off. The walk through a familiar place, then, supplied a ready-made framework for recalling the chunks of the speech. The method of loci is, of course, as usable today as it was 2000 years ago. You might try it yourself.

A similar mnemonic, of more modern origin, is the well-known "one is a bun" rhyme we described in Chapter 3. To use this device, the student must first learn the following little poem: "One is a Bun; Two is a Shoe; Three is a Tree; Four is a Door; Five is a Hive; Six is Sticks; Seven is Heaven; Eight is a Gate; Nine is a Line; Ten is a Hen."

As with the method of loci, this rhyme provides the framework for ordered recall of a list or group of items. Assume that you are going Christmas shopping and want to remember a list of purchases to be made in a particular order, something like–suitcase, pajamas, toaster, kitchen clock. To use the mnemonic to commit this list to memory, you would form an interactive image of each item in the list with an item in the rhyme. For example, you might imagine a bun with a handle and clasps like a suitcase ("One is a Bun"), a disembodied pair of pajamas wearing shoes ("Two is a Shoe"), a tree being toasted in a giant toaster ("Three is a Tree"), an animated alarm clock standing in your door ("Four is a Door"), and so forth. Retrieval of these items is then cued by going through the rhyme. For example, "one" serves as a cue to summon up the bun turned suitcase.

There are several different types of mnemonics. The two we have just described are based on imagery of the sort previously described. There are also mnemonics based on mediation, story construction, and word construction. There are a variety of books and courses available on how to improve one's memory (e.g., Cermak, 1976; Higbee, 1977; Lorayne & Lucas, 1976). The need for such aids is reflected in the ever increasing popularity of these books and their authors. Harry Lorayne, for example, has frequently demonstrated his mnemonic system on television. Most of us have made use of these techniques at one time or another, though perhaps without actually calling them "mnemonics." Gruneberg (1973), for example, found that 53% of a sample of 141 psychology students had used some kind of mnemonic in preparing for their examinations. The favorite among these students was the so-called "first-letter" mnemonic.

To use the first-letter technique, one takes the first letter of each item in a list to be learned and then inserts vowels and other letters as necessary to form a word. This word can then be remembered as a single chunk. When recall is necessary, you retrieve the chunk and decode it into the appropriate items. The Christmas list mentioned earlier (suitcase, pajamas, toaster, kitchen clock) might be coded as SPecTaCle. The technique is a popular one and several special cases have been invented to remember special information. For example, many school children have learned to remember the names of the Great Lakes that separate Canada from the U.S. as HOMES (Huron, Ontario, Michigan, Erie, and Superior).

The advantage of mnemonic techniques over simple rote repetition is in the organization and chunking they supply. These advantages are particularly well documented in the case of second-language learning (Atkinson, 1975). Students in Atkinson's program studied using a "keyword" mnemonic. First, the student generated an English word (the keyword) which sounded like the foreign vocabulary item they wished to learn. An association was easily formed between the vocabulary word and this English word on the basis of acoustic similarity. Next, the student formed an image of the keyword and the appropriate English translation of the vocabulary item in interaction. This phase is the same as that described for the "One is a Bun" method above. For example, the word "chien" means "dog" in French. A similar sounding word that might function as the keyword in English is "chin." The student would then imagine a dog licking someone's chin. The image would be retrieved on the next occasion that the word "chien" was seen, and the image could be used to decode the correct translation "dog."

According to Atkinson (1975), this mnemonic serves only as an initial "crutch" in the learning of foreign language vocabulary. With continued practice, a direct association is built between "chien" and "dog" (see Figure 9-2). However, the indirect route of acoustic association followed by imagery mediation can be more rapidly formed and serves as an aid in the acquisition of word meanings.

Students taught by this method consistently do better than students who are given no mnemonic instructions. Even six weeks after the training, students in the keyword group recalled 43% of the English translations, while the control group, who used rote rehearsal, recalled only 28%.

Atkinson (1975) also reports some interesting information about optimum conditions for use of this technique. For example, active involvement of the subjects seemed to be quite important. Students did better when they supplied their own images linking the keyword to the English translation of the foreign item. Generation of the image by the subject was more effective than cartoons, words, or phrases supplied by the experimenter. In our discussion of imagery in Chapter 8, we noted that the "meaningfulness" of the interactive image may be greater for

FIGURE 9-2 Steps in using the keyword method for foreign language vocabulary learning:
1. Vocabulary item: *chien* (''dog'')
2. Find acoustic associate: ''chin''
3. Form an interactive image: a *dog* licking someone's *chin*.
4. Retrieve English equivalent from image: *chien* → ''dog''

the subject if it is generated from their own knowledge. This involvement has been a continuing theme throughout this chapter: Preparing for recall or recognition requires an active effort, some skill, and imagination. In this section we have discussed some of the skills and techniques used in ''brute memory'' tasks, the memorization of lists and arbitrary relationships. The extraction of organization and meaning from texts, what you are doing right now, requires more sophisticated and less understood skills.

Meaningful Organization   Mnemonics are obviously useful devices for the acquisition and retention of information which has no inherent organization of its own. In our examples, the relationship between words and their meanings is as arbitrary as the particular names of the Great Lakes. The most valuable and significant learning we ordinarily do, however, modifies existing knowledge and changes in major or subtle ways how we think about the world. Meaningful learning is thus related to what we already know. The material is processed ''deeply'' in terms of the concepts and categories that comprise our understanding of the materials. Mnemonics are less useful here and may, in fact, be counter productive to the extent that they may allow us to overlook these true relationships.

The Construction of Meaning. We are inclined, by and large, to learn those things that are useful to us, the information necessary for the distinctions and discriminations that are meaningful and significant for our transactions with the world. In other words we learn selectively from our environment. Mere exposure, even massively repeated exposures, is not sufficient to produce learning if resources are not allocated for their analysis. For example, imagine for a moment what a penny looks like. What is written on the "head" side? Whose head is it? What direction is he facing? Where is the date on the coin? Each of us has seen pennies, probably many times a day for many years, yet, most people have a difficult time answering these simple questions.

Nickerson and Adams (1979) asked subjects to provide information about the appearance of the U.S. penny in several different formats. In their first experiment, they merely asked subjects to fill in the appropriate visual features for heads and tails on two blank circles provided for this purpose. Subjects performed very poorly, both at recalling the correct features and at placing them correctly when they were recalled. Of the eight features scored by Nickerson and Adams (1979), only 4 out of 20 subjects got as many as half the features correct.

In another study, subjects were given a drawing of the head side of a penny. Each subject was asked to decide whether the drawing they saw was a correct reproduction. If not, they were to describe what was wrong with the drawing. There were 15 of these drawings in all. As you can see from Figure 9-3, one of these versions was accurate while, for the others, a particular visual feature was omitted, mislocated, or added. Four out of the eight subjects who were given the accurate reproduction identified it correctly. Of the subjects who correctly judged other draw-

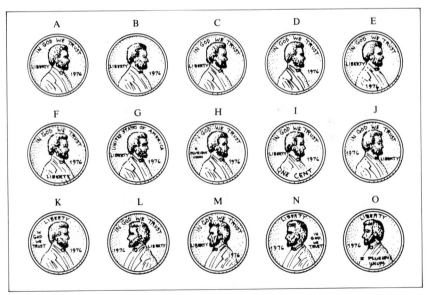

FIGURE 9-3   Fifteen drawings of the head of a U.S. penny used in a recognition study. Which of these pictures is correct?
(From Nickerson & Adams, 1979.)

ings to be inaccurate, very few were able to specify what was wrong with the reproduction. They knew "something" was wrong, but they could not say exactly what it was. In a final experiment, a new group of subjects was simply asked to select the correct representation from among the 15 drawings of Figure 9-3. Only 15 out of 36 subjects chose the correct drawing as their first choice. The moral of this story is that mere exposure to a visual stimulus is not sufficient to establish a reliable representation in memory. In the case of the penny, we have learned what is necessary to distinguish this from other coins, but little more.

These results of Nickerson and Adams (1979) contrast sharply with our discussion of other studies of visual recognition. Shepard (1967) and Standing (1973) found that subjects could recognize hundreds of pictures after a single exposure. Nickerson and Adams argue that the relative meaningfulness of the stimuli play a major role in explaining the difference between these studies. Look at the drawings on Figure 9-3 and note that almost all of them seem to be "acceptable" pennies. This is because there is no inherent logic in how these features are arranged on the face of a coin. The penny is certainly a meaningful object. However, how the visual features are related to each other, and even the particular visual features present, are relatively arbitrary. The pictures used by Shepard and Standing, on the other hand, were of meaningful, real-world scenes.

This notion of meaning fits neatly into our discussion because in studying a text you are not simply trying to commit the information to memory as you might in the case of the Christmas list in our earlier example, or in learning the names of the Great Lakes. In reading a text, you are trying to extract meaning, and to comprehend what the author has to say. Auble and Franks (1978) demonstrated that this "effort after meaning" is a significant learning activity, more important perhaps than the repetition and elaboration that follows understanding. Using a paradigm similar to that of Bransford and Johnson (1972) described in Chapter 4, but for a different purpose, they presented their subjects with sentences that, by themselves, were incomprehensible. For example, a subject might hear "The party was stalled because the wire straightened" or "The street was full of holes because the turning stopped." The sentence was followed by a cue word, either immediately, or after a 5-second delay. The cue supplied a context that made the sentence intelligible; for example, "corkscrew" for the first sentence and "cement mixer" for the second. Recall was required either immediately after the cue, or after another 5-second delay.

Auble and Franks (1978) found that it was more effective to provide 5 seconds before the cue than 5 seconds after. In other words, subjects must have exerted some effort to comprehend the material when the cue was delayed and this effort improved retention. Subjects who had time to rehearse and elaborate the material after they understood it, that is, after the cue, showed no improvement in recall. Both these groups, of course, did better than subjects who never heard the cue at all, i.e., who had no basis for understanding the sentences. This supports the earlier conclusions of Bransford and Johnson (1972). However, in this context, we want to emphasize that memory is the result of skilled activity, the learner's effort to comprehend.

Some of the activities used by successful learners have been described by Bransford and his colleagues at Vanderbilt University (Bransford, Stein, Shelton, & Owings, 1980). In a summary of several studies, they contrasted the learning skills of academically less successful fifth graders with their more successful peers. One of the tasks required of both groups of children was to provide a continuation or elaboration of a sentence. For example, a child might be presented with a sentence like, "The tall man used the paintbrush." The student was then to provide additional words for this sentence that would help in remembering it. Children who had been identified as successful students chose to elaborate the sentence in ways that made the concepts relevant to each other. Such an elaboration might be, "The tall man used the paintbrush to paint the ceiling." Students who had been less successful academically, chose to elaborate the sentence in relatively arbitrary ways that did not clarify the relationships between concepts (e.g., "The tall man used the paintbrush to paint the chair."). The difference in these strategies was reflected in a later memory test. Students who had elaborated the sentences in a nonarbitrary way were more successful in answering questions ("Who used the paintbrush?") than were students who had simply added irrelevant facts. You may be reminded here of the Craik and Tulving (1975) study in Chapter 8 in which sentence frames were used to provide elaborative coding. Only frames that were relevant or *congruent* with the word's meaning proved helpful for later recall.

Bransford and his group suggested that the difference between successful and unsuccessful learners involves the questions students ask themselves while studying, and the meaningful elaborations such questions provoke. They have shown that the less successful learners described above can become more expert in their coding strategies. They did find that direct instruction, providing examples and pointing out the difference between related and unrelated facts, did not seem to help. What did work, was forcing the children to themselves directly confront the relationships expressed in a sentence. When they did this by asking the children about the relevance of the relationships, a change of strategy was induced and improvement in memory performance followed. For example, a sentence to be learned might be, "The kind man bought the milk." The experimenters might ask the child what being kind had to do with buying milk. Was it just as likely that a mean or angry man might buy milk? This questioning was intended to lead the child to see the arbitrariness of the relationships in this sentence. At the next stage of questioning, the experimenter might ask the child why a kind man might buy milk. If the child replied, "Because he was thirsty," further questioning pressed the child to evaluate this response (e.g., "What does being thirsty have to do with being kind? Wouldn't a mean man buy milk when he was thirsty?"). After receiving practice and this kind of prompting on several sentences, the children were able to generate the appropriate questions themselves, and generate appropriate elaborations that created relevant relationships among the concepts of a sentence. This intervention succeeded dramatically in increasing these students' scores on a memory test for new material.

The differences observed in these studies, then, appeared to involve the students' attention to the relevance, or arbitrariness of relationships among facts, and the use of their own knowledge to generate relevance and meaning. The same differences might be found among more advanced students in the questions they ask themselves and the elaborations they generate for the facts of a text. For example, in our earlier chapters we spent some time describing the concepts of *retroactive* and *proactive* interference. You also put in some time in trying to learn these concepts. You may recall your own approach to studying these definitions. One approach to learning these concepts would be to try to memorize definitions and associate them to the correct names. Here, the words "retroactive" and "proactive" might as well be "x" and "y." The relationships between the name and the definition is arbitrary. Another strategy would be to ask yourself what "retroactive" means and how this meaning relates to the procedures used in the retroactive paradigm. Rereading and repetition are unlikely to generate the required relationships.

Studies of Notetaking.   A more familiar situation in which understanding and effort to comprehend play some role is in the classroom lecture. There are several studies that seem to show that lectures are not optimal methods for communicating information. For example, Goolkasian, Terry, and Park (1979) and Kintsch and Bates (1977) found that important points are often no better recognized than unimportant details. Kintsch and Bates, in fact, found that jokes and extraneous remarks from lectures were better remembered than major topic statements.

The absence of a difference in memory for important and unimportant elements resembles the immature pattern of memory performance observed by Brown and Smiley (1977) for young children. When we discussed those studies of metamemory, we noted that very young children apparently do not appreciate the structure or organization of a set of materials and, therefore, do not apportion their attention and study time to best advantage. Perhaps students in a lecture are inclined to be relatively passive listeners who rely on their immediate exposure to the lecture materials and understanding of only each isolated element to suffice for later retention. They have not exerted the effort to see the overall structure of these elements.

The results of a study on notetaking seem to suggest that some such interpretation may be appropriate. Peper and Mayer (1978) pointed out that notetaking can potentially serve two functions: First, it can simply serve to store the information for later review and study; second, it can serve to aid the subject in encoding the meaning and organization of what is heard. The fact that the student must paraphrase and organize the material in order to take notes may encourage a more elaborate and richer encoding than might be the case if the student merely listened to the lecture. In their study, Peper and Mayer (1978) had students watch a videotaped lecture for later testing on its content. One group of subjects took notes while another did not. Both groups were given a recall test of what they had retained of the lecture materials. The non-notetakers did better at recalling technical symbols and examples. The notetakers, on the other hand, recalled more ideas about the major concepts in the lecture and showed more intrusions of concepts that were relevant but had not been specifically mentioned by the lecturer. It would appear that the process of notetaking helped students to actively organize the material and integrate it with what they knew. Listening without notetaking produced a relatively literal memory for salient details of the lecture but little assimilation and organization of this material.

You should not interpret the Peper and Mayer study to indicate that notetaking ought to be elaborate and detailed. In fact, the reverse appears to be true. Howe (1970) has shown that more "efficient" notetakers, that is, those who express more ideas in fewer words, retain the material better than note takers who express these ideas in greater detail. Howe's conclusion is similar to the one we described above. A student who thinks about, and relates the content of a lecture to previous knowledge, can organize this information meaningfully and label it with a brief retrieval cue. This organization can be accessed later through the cue much as cues were used to access categories in our previous discussion of organization in free recall. This is why borrowing other people's notes from a missed lecture will usually be less useful than if you had taken your own notes.

The student who tries to take literal, detailed notes, can do so only by allocating capacity to this activity. Literal, word-for-word notetaking is like shadowing, and the results are the same. Little capacity remains for the deep processing of the information.

Once again, we are reminded that the construction of memory is an activity. The subjects of Peper and Mayer may indeed have performed differently had they been trained to take notes in the most advantageous way, that is, advantageous for organizing and assimilating the information. Various study techniques have been invented to facilitate the acquisition of organization and meaning when reading a text. Perhaps the most well known is Robinson's (1946) SQ3R Method. These letters stand for activities the student is directed to use in extracting the meaning of a reading assignment.

The first step in Robinson's method is to Survey the assignment. The student is to quickly examine the chapter or section, not reading the material, but looking at the headings, lead sentences, boldface or italicized words, searching for cues that would identify the main ideas in the section. After surveying the reading assignment the student should have a good idea of what the author is going to talk about, a framework or context in which to place later reading.

The second step requires that the student turn each heading of the text, or each lead sentence in a paragraph into a Question. Here the student works to determine what information is to be extracted from each portion of the reading. The third step is to actually Read the text in order to answer the questions that you have formulated. Having formed a question, the student can read with purpose and anticipate what will be said, rather than passively without knowing what will come next. In the fourth step, the student Recites the answers to the questions by writing out a brief synopsis of the answer. The written answer should be simple and brief, more of a retrieval cue than a paragraph, and these notes should be written without referring back to the text. These four steps are then repeated for each section of the reading. When all the reading had been completed, the student then Reviews this material by again reciting the answers to the questions formulated in the previous steps. The five stages of the SQ3R Method—Survey, Question, Read, Recite, and Review—are thus designed to ensure that a structure is discovered, relevant information is related to this structure, and that progress and achievement of these goals is continuously self-monitored.

As you can see, this is a very active process of digging information out of a text, not at all the passive experience that most of us are inclined to call ''reading.'' The object is to build an organization, to see the author's design, and use this organization as the scaffolding on which to build our own understanding of the material. The effort required by this method and its relation to memory might be summarized by a paraphrase of Whimbey and Whimbey's (1975, p. 116) definition of intelligence: We can say that memory requires paying careful, skilled attention to the analysis of structure.

INDIVIDUAL DIFFERENCES AND MEMORY

The central focus of interest in this text has been on principles that can be generalized across tasks and across people, the ''laws'' that describe how the memory system works. We also know, however, that there are large differences among individuals in the speed and accuracy with which they accomplish a given information processing task. The views presented in earlier chapters have implications for the potential sources of differences among individuals as well as implications for how one would go about looking for these differences. Theorists and experimentalists of the last decade have devoted increasing attention to analyzing individual differences in the context of information processing models. We offer in this section only an introduction to two of the many areas in which such research is being pursued. Our sampling includes the huge area of ''mental abilities,'' and the analysis of aging effects on memory.

An Extraordinary Memory

There are several studies of individuals who have developed extraordinary memory abilities, quite beyond what we ordinarily mean when we say that someone has a "good" memory. Perhaps the most famous of these reports is that of S., a man studied by the Russian neuropsychologist A. R. Luria (Luria, 1968). S. was in his late 20s when he first approached Luria and asked to have his memory tested. Luria was astounded to find that this young man could recall without error a list of 70 items after only a single presentation. He could as easily recall the list in reverse order, or enter the list and begin recall at any point cued by the experimenter. To memorize these items, S. required only that there be a brief delay of 3 or 4 seconds between words during presentation. In later testing it was found that S. could recall such a series a week, a year, and even 16 years after that single encounter. Faced with an apparently unlimited memory, Luria gave up the attempt to measure S.'s capacity and began a qualitative analysis of his memory performance, a study he pursued on and off for almost 30 years.

S. did not rely primarily on mnemonic devices or any of the ordinary types of mediation we have discussed. Rather, he reported that he continued to "see" the information that had been presented to him, or that this information had been transformed into visual images that he could later decode for recall. After being presented with a large matrix of numbers, for example, he could "read off" the columns, the rows, or the diagonals on command. He could revive this information and perform the same feat 1 month later without any intervening study. Although he possessed some control over these images, he had great difficulty in preventing their occurrence in situations that did not call for literal memory. The occurrence of these images, in fact, interfered in some cases with his understanding of a conversation or passage that he read. During a period of his career when he worked as a stage performer, entertaining people with his fantastic abilities, his greatest problem was to find a way to forget the information acquired in one performance to avoid confusion with information heard in later performances.

S. also possessed a peculiarity of perception called *synesthesia*. A sensation or experience in one modality gave rise to experiences and sensations in other modalities as well. For example, sounds for S. produced experiences of light, color, and sometimes touch and taste. Words, numbers, letters, and voices all had visual and tactile qualities that distinguished them from one another. "Two," for example, had something about it that was flat, rectangular, and gray. He reported that words and sounds were recognized by this whole complex of feelings, images, and sense impressions. In a conversation with one of the psychologists who studied him, S. once remarked, "What a crumbly, yellow voice you have" (Luria, 1968, p. 24).

When asked to memorize a series of items, S. used a strategy similar to the one we have discussed as the method of loci. He would imagine himself on a walk down a familiar street. As images were elicited by the items in the list, he would distribute these images along the way in his mental walk. To recall, he would retrace his journey, picking up the images and translating them as he went. The errors S. occasionally made resembled errors of inattention and perceptual confusion more than the interference effects we have come to expect in long-term memory. For example, on one occasion S. omitted the word PENCIL from his recall of a list. When this omission was pointed out to him, he explained that the image of PENCIL had been placed next to a fence on his imaginary walk. During his retrieval of the images in the list, the pencil had blended in with the lines of the fence and he had passed by on his walk without noticing it.

Over the course of Luria's study, S. changed his system in response to the demands placed on him by his work and the tests invented by the psychologists. His images, for example, were made larger relative to the background against which he deposited them. An extremely large PEN-CIL was less likely to be lost against its background. The memory images also became less detailed and so less distracting. In addition, he developed a technique of breaking verbal information up into its constituent meaningless sounds, and attaching an image to each of these parts. With this technique, he could learn long stanzas of poetry in languages he could not understand, long lists of nonsense syllables, and meaningless mathematical formulas. These materials could be recalled 8 years after a single presentation.

Although his feats of memory were quite beyond what most of us could accomplish, S. seemed incapable of using logical, abstract kinds of organization that would be quite obvious to the average college student. When a list that he had learned contained several birds' names, he did not cluster the items from this common category in his recall, nor could he selectively recall the items in this category. On another occasion when digits in a list followed some obvious progression (e.g., 1, 2, 3, 4, 2, 3, 4, 5, 3, 4, 5, 6), S. did not notice, and memorized these items as if they had been random digits. In addition, the meaning and coherence of a passage in a text or a story was sometimes obliterated by the flight of images evoked by isolated words. His thoughts were arrested and distracted by vivid but irrelevant detail. He himself remarked that his understanding was limited to those things he could concretely visualize.

His tremendous memory, in fact, appeared to be more of a handicap than an advantage to his personal and professional development. The compelling vividness of his imagery sometimes seemed to blur the distinction between thought and reality. Luria reports, for example, that in seeking a strategy to enable him to forget certain images, S. wrote down the unwanted images and burned the paper in his stove. These images were so vivid, in other words, that he thought it necessary to physically destroy them.

Although the abilities possessed by S. are exceedingly rare, some children also exhibit dramatic imagery with which they are able to recall highly detailed scenes as if they still had the actual event before them (Gray & Gummerman, 1975; Leask, Haber, & Haber, 1969). This so-called "photographic" or *eidetic* imagery appears to be much different from the constructed and elicited images used by S. For example, G. W. Allport (1924) reported a study of English schoolchildren in which a complicated street scene was displayed in the form of a storybook picture for 35 seconds and then withdrawn. Some of the children were able to describe this scene as if "reading off" the information from a literal image. A few of these children could spell out the name of a street that had appeared in the picture even though this street name was a 13-letter German word and the children knew no German!

These images, then, appeared to be some type of visual persistence phenomenon that maintains a copy of the experience, unlike S.'s images which were elicited by the visual experience, but were not necessarily literal records of that experience (e.g., seeing the word "green" evoked the image of a green flowerpot). Eidetic images can apparently endure for prolonged periods of time, sometimes days, or even weeks (Stromeyer & Psotka, 1970) and seem to maintain all the information in the original experience. The occurrence of these images in some children and its extreme rarity among adults has led to the speculation that this form of memory is displaced by verbal thinking and linguistic skills as these are learned in school and prove more useful for abstract thinking (Richardson, 1969, p. 40).

Other extraordinary memories have occasionally been reported in the literature (e.g., Hunt & Love, 1972; Hunter, 1977). Though perhaps not so phenomenal as the case of S., these individuals represent one extreme of the spectrum of individual differences in memory performance. They also illustrate that the ability to remember is not the same as the ability to understand, that is, remembering is not equivalent to our commonsense concept of "intelligence." Although S. was very good at solving difficult problems for which a concrete visual approach was appropriate, he was quite poor on much simpler problems that required conceptual or logical solutions. How, then, can we relate intelligence and memory?

Abilities and the Functions of Memory

One of the perennial problems of psychology has been to describe and measure individual differences in ability. Most of this effort has taken the form of test development and analysis. The field of test development, *psychometrics,* has evolved into a highly sophisticated, mathematical area of study, with impressive accomplishments. This is not, of course, a merely theoretical exercise. If we can isolate and measure human abilities, we can use this information in predicting the potential performance of job candidates, the effectiveness of training programs, the probability of success in college, and so forth. Valid and reliable measures of ability would have large economic and practical consequences.

However, even with satisfactory measures of ability, the testing strategy can carry us only so far in understanding of the human system. If we were to assess an individual's standing on some ability relative to others, the test score would not explain the difference between this individual and others. The score merely describes the difference. It is also of interest to know how this individual differs from others in the way information is processed, the operations that presumably underlie performance on the test. Knowledge about individual differences in information processing can have both theoretical and practical significance.

First of all, theories about information processing are not really separable from theories about individual differences. If two tasks, for example, are believed to require the same kinds of elementary information processing, then performance on these tasks should be correlated, that is, people who do better on one task should also do better on the other (Underwood, 1975). On the other hand, if performance on one task does not predict performance on the other, this would imply that separable and independent processes were involved in the two tasks. Individual differences, then, can be used to test our hypotheses and extend our knowledge about information processing in general.

Second, an understanding of individual differences in information processing has practical significance because such knowledge is prerequisite to the design of effective strategies of intervention. If test performance does predict, for example, the probability of academic success, we may be able to use knowledge of processes underlying test performance to diagnose deficient skills more specifically and invent programs which remediate or compensate for the deficiencies. There have been several recent attempts to analyze ability measures in terms of the concepts of information processing (e.g., Hunt, 1978; Kirby & Das, 1978; Sternberg, 1977; Yen, 1978). This is a large and complex area of which we can hope to give only the flavor.

Hunt and his associates (Hunt, 1978; Hunt, Frost, & Lunneborg, 1973; Hunt & Lansman, 1975; Hunt, Lunneborg, & Lewis, 1975) have attempted to describe the "mechanics" of information processing which might contribute to performance on tests of verbal ability. Hunt (1978) describes such tests as refecting two kinds of processes: first, processes requiring knowledge that has been acquired through the experiences of a lifetime, and, second, purely mechanistic processes whose operations are independent of the specific information that is processed. One of these mechanistic processes, for example, is "decoding" in which an external stimulus activates highly overlearned information in long-term memory such as in retrieving the name of a familiar word in response to a printed representation of that word.

The measure of individual differences in decoding used by Hunt was a task invented by Posner and Mitchell (1967). We saw this technique outlined in Chapter 6 in relation to capacity allocation in attention. In this task, two letters are flashed on a screen side by side and the subject must indicate as rapidly as possible whether these letters are the same or different. In one condition the subjects receive *physical identity* instructions, that is, they are to respond SAME only if the two letters are physically identical to one another (e.g., AA). The second condition requires a *name identity* judgement; subjects are to respond SAME only if the two letters have the same name (e.g., AA or Aa). For the college population that ordinarily participates in these studies, name identity decisions require 75 to 80 milliseconds longer than Physical Identity decisions. The shorter time for Physical Identity judgements is expected on the grounds that, in this condition, the physical representations of the symbols can be directly compared. Name Identity, however, requires that both symbols be decoded to retrieve the name before a comparison can take place. Theoretically, then, the difference between response times under Physical and Name Identity instructions reflects the amount of time taken up by extra decoding steps necessary to access the name of the letters.

Differences between name and physical identity response times for several groups are displayed in Table 9-1. Of greatest interest are the three university groups since these can be most directly compared. The "high-verbal" university students were those who scored in the top 25% of their college group on a standardized test of verbal abilities. The "low verbal" students were those who scored in the bottom 25% on this test. Note that the low verbal subjects required longer decoding times than the high verbal subjects. The increase in decoding times for each group as you read down the table is presumed to reflect slower access to

TABLE 9-1 Average differences in response time between name identity and physical identity conditions in a letter-matching task for various groups of subjects. (From Hunt, 1978. Copyright © 1978 by the American Psychological Association. Reprinted by permission.)

Group	Difference between Name-Identity and Physical Identity (msec)
High-verbal university students	64
Normal university students	75–80
Low-verbal university students	89
Young adults not in a university	110
Severe epileptic adults	140
Adults past 60 years of age	170
10-year-old children	190
Mildly mentally retarded schoolchildren	310

long-term memory, that is, slower activation of the relevant names. Of course, there is not a perfect correlation between measured verbal ability and decoding time as measured in the letter matching task. Hunt does argue, however, that part of the difference in verbal abilities is accounted for by differences in the speed with which individuals can retrieve codes from long-term memory.

Hunt's research group found that subjects who had scored in the upper 25% on the verbal ability measure differed from those scoring in the lower 25% on several other standard memory tasks. High verbals, for example, showed greater release from proactive inhibition, faster acquisition of a list of paired associates, and superior performance on the Peterson short-term memory distractor task. The pattern of results obtained suggested to Hunt et al. (1975) that tasks which best discriminated between low and high verbals were those that required (1) rapid decoding of a symbol, and (2) the maintenance of ordered information in short-term memory for a brief period of time. These conclusions are, of course, only the tentative hypotheses offered at the beginning of our analysis of the relationships between information processing and intelligence. It is the goal of this research both to isolate the elementary operations that are reflected in ability measures and to describe the consequences of these differences. Eysenck (1977) has suggested, for example, that the greater speed with which high verbals access long-term memory may result in deeper and more elaborate processing of the input by these individuals.

The value of tests, as we mentioned earlier, is their ability to predict something about future behavior, for example, academic success, or job performance. If performance on tasks involving elementary information processing can predict test performance, then, we assume, differences in information processing can also predict the behavior of interest, academic success, or job performance. However, our research efforts could take a more direct route. We might try to relate our information processing analyses to the real-world behavior that we would like to predict. For example, Kahneman, Ben-Ishai, and Lotan (1973) wished to analyze driving skill among commercial truck drivers. Subjects in their experiment monitored one of two messages presented dichotically, one message to each ear. A cue that occurred periodically was a signal to continue monitoring the same message, or to shift to attending to the other ear. The investigators found that the accuracy with which the truck drivers were able to report the first few items of the new message after a switch, was related to their safety records on the road. That is, safe driving presumably had something to do with the subjects' ability to focus in on a new source of information. The same ability appeared to relate to flying performance. Military combat pilots were better able to refocus their attention under these conditions than were noncombat pilots (Gopher & Kahneman, 1971).

Elementary information processing tasks performed in the laboratory do, then, relate to concrete skills and more abstract ability measures.

This relatively new research enterprise, the analysis of mental ability, promises to be an interesting and valuable extension of the study of learning and memory.

Aging and Memory

Researchers who have examined the differences between young and old people on learning and memory tasks have, until quite recently, assumed that they would find a continuing decline in performance with age (Schaie & Gribbin, 1975). The research problem, given this assumption, was to chart the nature and course of this "irreversible decline." In fact, memory research which has used age as a variable has usually found decrements in the performance of older as compared to younger subjects. However, there are several difficulties in interpreting the results of these studies as consequences of the aging process. The elderly may also differ from younger subjects in general health and their motivation to participate in laboratory tasks. If we can isolate qualitative changes in memory processes, we may then differentiate age-related changes in these functions from the quantitative decline in health status and motivation that is secondary to our interest.

Contemporary research on the relationship between age and memory has generally taken this qualitative approach (e.g., Poon, Fozard, Cermak, Arenberg, & Thompson, 1980) and the result has been a variety of findings that, at least tentatively, describe the differences in processing that produce differences in performance levels between young and old. Investigators have found, for example, that there are comparatively small differences in short-term retention as measured by the recency effect in free recall, the distractor task of the Petersons, or the ordinary memory span (Craik, 1977b). In addition, little age decline has been observed in how subjects use the metamemorial skills described earlier (Lachman, Lachman, & Thronesbery, 1979). However, there are large differences between age groups on paced tasks, tasks requiring divided attention, and on recall as opposed to recognition tests of retention (Schaie & Gribbin, 1975). In addition, these effects appear to be larger when the presentation is visual than when the presentation is auditory. The deficiencies observed in elderly subjects, then, appear to be problems in the processing of recent episodic memories and may be related to age declines in processing capacity.

Eysenck (1974) and Craik and Simon (1980) have examined these secondary memory deficits from the levels of processing perspective. In Eysenck's study, different groups of subjects each performed one of four different orienting tasks on the items in a list of unrelated nouns. One group counted the number of letters in each word, another responded with words that rhymed with each list item, a third group generated appropriate adjectives for each list word, and a fourth group rated the vividness of the imagery elicited by each list item. After these incidental tasks, all subjects received an unexpected free recall test of the list items. Eysenck found that young and old subjects did not differ on the amount recalled after letter-counting or rhyming. Both young and old subjects had better recall after the "deeper" orienting task of generating adjectives and images, but the improvement with depth was greater for the young than for the old subjects. Eysenck concluded that deeper semantic processing was imparied by age, but shallower processing ability remained intact. This suggests, then, that the elderly have a *processing deficit* that prevents the deeper encoding of information. Shallow encoding leads to less distinctive memory traces, and therefore a greater difficulty in discrimination among traces at the time of recall.

Craik and Simon (1980) supported the conclusion that elderly subjects are less likely to use semantic processing, but noted that this deficit may be due to a decrease in processing resources. In their view, deeper processing is more difficult and requires more effort than shallow processing. If resources are limited, there may be a decrease in the extent to which such processes are utilized. In support of this notion, Craik and Simon cite an experiment in which young and old subjects were asked to make either a "case" (capitals versus small letters), rhyme, or category decision about items in a list of nouns. An unexpected free recall test after this incidental task produced the same effects as found by Eysenck (1974). That is, older subjects did about as well as younger subjects after the shallow processing task (rhymes and case decisions), but showed poorer performance after semantic processing (category decisions). However, when retention was tested by recognition rather than recall, the age differences disappeared.

Craik and Simon (1980) argued that accurate memory performance requires appropriate processing at both encoding and retrieval (encoding specificity). Older subjects are less likely to perform deep processing of list items but can be induced to do so by an orienting task. The resulting increase in the durability of traces did not show up in Eysenck's study because the elderly are also less likely to process retrieval information to a deep level. As a consequence they do poorly on free recall. When this retrieval problem is alleviated by providing a recognition test, access to the more elaborately coded item is permitted and the benefits of semantic coding are available for both young and old subjects. This argument implies that the elderly have a *production deficit,* that is, under ordinary circumstances older subjects would process information less deeply than younger subjects because greater resources are required for deeper coding. When, however, a task explicitly requires semantic encoding, older subjects are capable of this processing if sufficient time is provided.

The levels of processing framework also suggests why elderly subjects differ from younger ones primarily on longer-term memory for recent events. As we noted in our discussion of levels in Chapter 8, short-term retention tasks usually represent the retrieval of relatively shallow acoustic or articulatory codes. If the elderly normally code materials to this level, there should be relatively little impairment in their performance on short-term retention tasks. This interpretation is supported by the finding that after learning a list of words, older subjects find phonemic cues (the first two letters of a word) more helpful to their recall than semantic cues (synonyms). For younger subjects, the relative effectiveness of the types of cue are reversed (Craik & Simon, 1980). Older subjects, then, profit more from cues providing access to relatively shallow, acoustic codes than they do from semantic cues.

One of the stereotypes of professors and older people is that they are absent-minded, that is, they lose track of the immediate context of a conversation, or a sequence of events. Craik and Simon's argument suggests that the underlying cause of such incidents may be the same in both cases. That is, not enough resources are being devoted at that moment to the semantic integration of context and immediate experience. In the case of someone who is preoccupied with other matters (the professor), resources have been allocated to other tasks and little remains to allow for deep processing of the context. In the case of the elderly, limited processing of context may be due to a diminished pool of resources available to allocate to this task.

For example, Craik and Simon (1980) presented young and old subjects with sentence frames containing words that were to be retained for later recall (e.g., "The highlight of the circus was the clumsy BEAR" or "The lock was opened with the bent PIN.") On a cued recall test, subjects received as a retrieval cue either the specific adjective used in the sentence frame (e.g., "clumsy" or "bent") or a general descriptive cue (e.g., "wild animal" or "fastener"). The specific adjective was the more effective retrieval cue for younger subjects, while the general descriptive term proved more effective for older subjects.

The younger subjects, according to Craik and Simon, had processed the sentence context along with the word. As we noted in reviewing the work on elaboration of coding (Craik & Tulving, 1975), such processing should lead to a highly distinctive, durable trace of the experience. In addition, because the sentence is specific to this word, the sentence also provides relatively efficient access to these traces (encoding specificity). On the other hand, older subjects apparently did not integrate the context in this way. They encoded PIN and BEAR just as they might have if these words occurred in isolation. As a consequence, their retention was relatively poor and the most effective retrieval cue was the word's general meaning, rather than the context in which it had been experienced.

Again, deeper processing is assumed to require greater effort, more resources than shallow processing. In support of this assumption, Eagle and Ortoff (1967), for example, found that divided attention tasks were associated with increases in phonemic errors, a shallow code. Thus, when resources are divided between more than one message, the depth of processing performed on each message decreases. It is of interest here that divided attention impairs the performance of the elderly more than it impairs performance for younger subjects. This suggests that the elderly have fewer resources to share among competing tasks.

However, the generalization that deeper processing requires greater resources must be tempered by a consideration of the subject's *expertise* (Bransford et al., 1980). Deep processing that involves a highly practiced skill may be automatized to the point that it requires very few resources. Murrell and Humphries (1978) found, for example, that, as we would expect, the "shadowing" performance of naive subjects declined with age. However, when the investigators used subjects who were professional translators, highly practiced at performing translations of speeches as they heard them, no age decrements in shadowing were observed. Older translators performed as well as younger ones. Presumably these subjects' great skill compensated for the decrease in resources with age.

We have described in some detail only one of the information processing hypotheses offered to explain age related changes in memory performance. Others include less rapid access to information in long-term memory, less rapid perceptual processing, and increased cautiousness (Schaie & Gribbin, 1975). We have chosen to discuss what we can call the "diminished resources hypothesis" in this section because it illustrates very well the strategy of seeking qualitative differences in performance and using these to make inferences regarding the underlying changes that accompany the aging process. This hypothesis also suggests that the elderly are not incapable of memory performance equal to that of younger subjects. They may on occasions which permit use of their greater skills, or when supporting conditions are properly maintained, exhibit performance levels equal to or better than younger subjects.

MEMORY CONSTRAINTS AND MODERN TECHNOLOGY

Our discussion of human memory and its determinants has portrayed memory as a complex system. Memory is not simply the repository for the accumulation of information. The utilization of memory is also an integral part of larger systems of work, transportation, communication, education, and many more. As our society and our technologies become more complex, it becomes of greater concern that these larger systems are designed to ensure the best fit with human capabilities. Technology, now and in the future, must take psychology into account.

The field of experimental psychology that has been most concerned with the adaptation of technology to human capabilities is a discipline that has variously been called *human factors, human engineering,* or *ergonomics*. Human engineering is an applied discipline in the sense that the origin of the problems considered is in the "real" world; problems, for example, in the design of machinery, control systems, work schedules, and training to optimize the interaction of the human element with other parts of the system. The extent to which a system fulfills its function, is productive and efficient, does not depend on either the human being or other parts of the system in isolation. It depends also on the capacities of each, and on the quality of their interaction. In this section we will discuss some problems of human engineering involving particular systems and broader considerations that apply to several kinds of systems. Our starting point is the view presented in Chapters 7 and 8 of the human as a limited capacity processing system.

Capacity and Processing Limitations

A particularly frightening example of failing to take human engineering into account came to light in the retrospective analysis of "human operator errors" that contributed to the accident and shutdown of a nuclear power station at Three Mile Island in Pennsylvania in March 1979 (Marshall, 1979). At this power station, there were numerous alarms and indicators that could alert the station operators of any system malfunctions. However, the number of alarms that could potentially be triggered by events or conditions that departed from the optimal was much too large to permit adequate response or judgement by the human operator. If multiple alarms went off, presumably the operators would have to decode the meaning of these alarms and make some decisions regarding the priorities with which this information should be handled. In the first few minutes of the accident, more than 100 alarms went off. Even during "normal" operation it was not uncommon for more than 50 alarms to operate. The indicators that signaled off-normal conditions were sometimes red, sometimes white, sometimes amber, or green depending on the particular system that was monitored.

In addition to the number of indicators and the different kinds of coding and decoding required, some of the important indicators that had to be monitored were out of sight of the operator on the other side of the control console. Clearly, the inconsistent coding, the number of indicators and their positions would overload the human system. Among the various indicators was one which monitored the steam generation system. This system boiled dry within the first 2 minutes of the accident and ceased to relieve the reactor of excess heat. Failure to "notice" the condition of the steam generation system immediately was one of the major operator errors cited by the later report.

The design of this power station, then, had not adequately taken into account, at least for emergency situations, the limited capacity of the human information processing system. The human operator had not been adequately integrated into the control system of the plant's operation. While none of these problems caused the accident, they may have contributed to its severity and could certainly have been avoided by proper consideration of the capacities and limits on human performance. In fact, some analysis of the human factors problems in reactor control and maintenance has been performed from a human engineering perspective (Whitfield, 1970).

As this example makes clear, the role of the human processing system is not simple. If a particular signal is expected, it may take an operator .2 seconds to begin a proper response. By far the greatest portion of this time is consumed in the processing of the information in this signal and decisions about the proper course of action. Very little time is taken to register the signal, or in signaling the muscles to move once the decision has been made. If the situation involves several signals requiring different responses, the time to process the signal's information and make decisions increases dramatically. If, in turn, these signals are difficult to discriminate from one another, and/or the response must be made with great precision and accuracy, the processing time is increased still further. In addition, when several signals must be dealt with at once, a running memory must be kept of what has been done and what is currently being done. Understanding of current conditions must be constantly ''updated.'' Remembering outdated information may, in fact, interfere with the ability to monitor the most recent state of affairs (Bjork & Landauer, 1978).

While this description of the human operator's performance can be applied to the complex monitoring and control of a nuclear power station, it is also applicable to the performance of more mundane skills like driving a car (Poulton, 1971). In the early stages of driving, the person must respond appropriately to a variety of signals from the road and from the automobile itself. Since, at this stage, the relationships among signals and responses are not well learned, the initiation of a response may require considerable time and resources. If another signal should occur during the time the system's capacity is occupied in processing and decision making, the learning driver may be in trouble. In addition, the beginning driver has not completely learned to differentiate among various responses, so the consequences of each behavior must be carefully monitored in case correction is required. The response of the car to the behavior of the driver is itself another signal that must be monitored and responded to. Beginning drivers at this stage feel overwhelmed. Driving teachers often report that they must keep an eye on the road for the students at times when they become overloaded.

After considerable practice at driving, much of the work becomes automatized. The responses of the car to movements of the driver are now permanent patterns stored in long-term memory. The execution of this pattern need only be monitored occasionally to ensure that operations do not depart significantly from what is expected. The most relevant sources of information have been localized and the most appropriate responses to each is now also part of a program in long-term storage. We need no longer consciously tick off the variety of things that must be done to make a left-hand turn: let up on the accelerator, operate turn signal, turn wheel, etc. Much less of our processing resources need be devoted to processing decisions in these tasks and we can, as a result, carry on a conversation, answer questions, notice window displays as we drive along. The increases in spare capacity that occur as a result of greater skill can be objectively described by measuring the accuracy of question answering (Brown, 1966) and changes in visual search and scanning patterns (Mourant & Rockwell, 1972) that occur with practice.

Under extremely difficult driving conditions the demand for resources may markedly increase, even for highly practiced drivers. Under these circumstances, processing capacity is again taken up with time consuming decision processes and continuous monitoring of the consequences of our own behavior. More favorable conditions permit the highly overlearned schema to run out automatically with only occasional monitoring to check for possible malfunctions and violations of expectations.

The engineering psychologist in these situations might be regarded as a specialist in human error. Errors in control situations will inevitably occur; human beings are fallible creatures. The psychologist must analyze the components of the task, the frequency, and nature of the errors in order to suggest modifications and training that will improve system operation. Reduction of error is, of course, one goal. Since, however, it is unlikely that errors will be reduced to zero, other goals include minimizing the consequences of errors on system operation, improvement of error detection, and the facilitation of corrective feedback into the system.

For example, the launching of a rocket powered missile involves a fairly lengthy series of steps. The control systems are designed in such a way that appropriate steps must be executed in a particular invariant order. Pushing the wrong button at the wrong time will produce no effect. The consequences of error have been minimized by the design of the controls. In other cases another approach may be more feasible. For example, no matter how many times you exhort yourself to take the keys out of the ignition before you leave your car, you do sometimes forget. Automobiles now have an audible alarm that sounds whenever the door is opened and the keys are still in the ignition. This device allows you to detect your error and correct it before the keys have been locked in the car. Finally, systems can be designed to facilitate the correction of errors. Electric typewriters now come equipped with a correction ribbon so that a mistake in typing can be eliminated by merely backspacing and typing over the error. Office computer systems promise to make this editing and revision of written material even easier. Each of our examples is comparatively simple, but each involves a problem in the interaction of people and machines. Each is a problem in which the capabilities and limitations of human operators are important considerations.

There are many similar types of problems that require "fitting" the system to the human subsystem. Think of, for example, walking into a supermarket determined to get your money's worth. You are deluged from all sides by uninformative adjectives—"Family Size, Economy

Size, Giant Size''—boxes of cereal, laundry detergent, ketchup. Without some standardization, the task of comparison shopping would require a formidable amount of information processing. ''Unit pricing,'' however, is an attempt to ease the burden on resources and accommodate the structure of pricing to the structure of our abilities. Each item receives, in effect, two prices: one for the total quantity in the package and the other, a cost per unit. You can, thus, easily determine that the ''Family Size'' of Brand X is cheaper per ounce than the ''Economy Size'' of Brand Y. You can shop more accurately, more quickly, and you do not need a calculator.

Storage limitations, in addition to capacity limits, pose some problems for our interaction with technology. In our discussion of short-term memory, we used the familiar example of telephone dialing. If you have looked up a new number in the directory and proceeded to the telephone, a distraction or a random thought that disrupts your rehearsal may send you back to the telephone book to try again. The seven digits that make up a telephone number in the U.S. are very close to the span of immediate memory. The phone number consists of the three digits that identify the local exchange and four digits that specify a particular phone within that exchange. The total load on memory may be somewhat reduced by the fact that the local exchange numbers are common to several different phone numbers and, therefore, we may have stored this number in long-term memory related to the name of a particular community. Nevertheless, errors and ''wrong numbers'' are frequently the result of problems with retaining the necessary information over even the short interval necessary to complete the dialing.

The technology of telephones has, in fact, undergone several changes to accommodate the human user. Touch telephones, for example, allow one to enter a telephone number much more quickly since you do not have to wait for the dial to return after dialing each digit. The more rapid entry of the number decreases errors that may have resulted from short-term forgetting.

One might use familiarity with local exchanges to improve the ease of retaining phone numbers generally. As noted earlier, we will often have the local exchange number in long-term memory. This is also true of the area code. The digits, then, that are most vulnerable to short-term forgetting are those digits that identify the unique phone within an area. Dialing these numbers first, followed by the local exchange and area codes, would minimize forgetting of the unfamiliar unique code. Shepard and Sheenan (1965) tested this notion and found that both the time necessary to complete the dialing and errors in dialing were reduced by rearranging the order in which these parts of the telephone number were dialed.

In the last few years telephone systems have offered additional services that further reduce the short-term memory load. For example, you may now subscribe to a ''speed dialing'' service. Subscribers to this service select for speed dialing a group of telephone numbers that they are likely to call frequently and for which rapid access would provide a considerable convenience. Each of these numbers is assigned a code, a single digit corresponding to each phone number. The code and the corresponding phone number are entered into the computer that controls switching for the local exchange. Thereafter, the subscriber to speed dialing need only enter a single digit on the telephone in order to call any number on the coded list.

The adaptation of the telephone to the limits of the human user is not only a matter of convenience. The errors produced by a lack of fit between the instrument and its operator lower the efficiency of the communications system and, summed over millions of telephones, can be very costly.

Sleep and Biological Rhythms

While the capabilities and limitations of the human component in a system must play a major role in system design, we should also be aware of the fact that these capabilities and limitations are not constant; they vary for a given individual over time and conditions. Our activities at work and at play are superimposed on a set of biological cycles called the *circadian rhythms* (Colquhoun, 1971). The physical processes of the body alter in a regular pattern that corresponds to our behavioral pattern of sleep and activity. The majority of us are awake and active during the day and sleep during the night. However, there are large numbers of people on nightshifts at industrial plants and military installations who reverse this pattern. There are also increasing numbers of people who travel across time zones and thereby encounter a cycle of day and night shifted from the one they just left. Given the number of people whose pattern of activities is different than the ordinary day/night pattern, it is of some interest to consider how biological rhythms affect our ability to function, and whether these rhythms can adapt to the demands of work and global travel.

Perhaps most intriguing in the context of work and ''jet lag'' are the variations in performance and memory within the 24-hour cycle. Performance of timed tasks appear to vary in parallel with the bodily cycle. Figure 9-4 shows changes in reaction times to rapidly naming colors as a function of time of day. Also shown in this figure are the changes in body temperature over the same time period. Body temperature is often taken as a rough approximation to the level of physiological activity. Note that the temperature and performance changes are inversely related: as body temperature goes up, reaction times go down. In fact, the correlation between body temperature and performance was a very significant $-.89$ (Kleitman, 1963).

In addition to its effects on speed of response, time of day also influences short- and long-term retention. Figure 9-5 shows accuracy of answering questions about a 1500-word magazine article immediately after reading the article. The curve indicates that immediate memory for

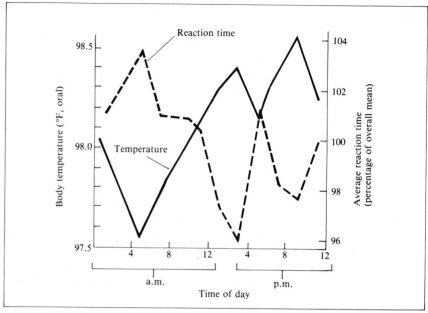

FIGURE 9-4 Relationship between subjects' body temperature over the course of a day, and their average reaction time in a color-naming task. Average speed of response shows a high inverse correlation with subject body temperature.
(Adapted from *Sleep and Wakefulness* by N. Kleitman. Copyright © 1973 by the University of Chicago Press. Reprinted by permission.)

prose passages seems to decline from a maximum in the early morning to a minimum in the late evening. Longer-term retention, on the other hand, appears to be affected in the opposite direction. For example, Folkard and Monk (1978) found that when recall was delayed for one week, recall scores were higher for subjects who had originally read the passage in the afternoon (3 p.m.) than for subjects who had read the passage in the morning (9 a.m.).

The effects of daily cycle on human performance are usually related to the concept of "arousal" or "alertness" (Colquhoun, 1971) which was mentioned in the context of our discussion of attention (Chapter 7). According to this interpretation of the circadian rhythm, arousal level parallels the temperature curve plotted in Figure 9-4, with arousal minimal sometime around 4:00 in the morning and maximal around 8:00 in the evening. However, it does not appear to be the case that this increase in arousal over the course of the day represents simply an increase in the efficiency or speed of information processing. Rather, investigations of the effects of arousal have found that as arousal changes there are qualitative changes in the nature of processing.

For example, how you deploy attention in a complex task is partly determined by your level of arousal. In most tasks, like driving a car, the operator must monitor several conditions (e.g., gas gauge, speedometer, oil temperature, condition of the road ahead). Attention is allocated to these monitoring tasks in proportion to the relative probability that they will provide information (Hamilton, 1969). You look more often at the speedometer than at the gas gauge in driving your car; you look more often at the road ahead than at your speedometer. In these cases, attention is allocated in proportion to the relative probability that important information will appear from each of these sources. Hamilton, Hockey, and Rejman (1977) found that increased stress (arousal) did not simply decrease efficiency in a monitoring task. Rather, increase in stress increased the tendency to pay attention to dominant sources of information. In our example, under arousal or stress, the attention allocated to the road ahead may be more than proportional to the relative probability of observing something important from that source. The attention allocated to this source may then decrease the resources available for processing information from alternative sources of information such as the speedometer.

The effect of arousal on memory also appears to be qualitative. For example, recall of the order of a set of items actually is improved by increases in arousal while free recall, in which items may be recalled in any order, is impaired by increases in arousal (Hockey, 1978). Also,

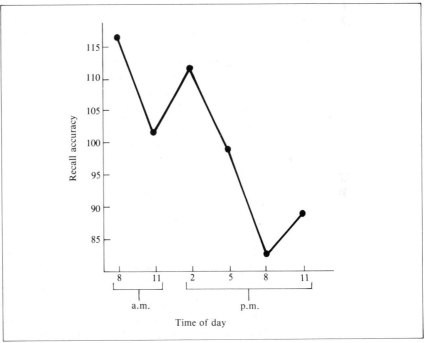

FIGURE 9-5 Immediate memory for a prose passage as a function of time of day. (From Folkard & Monk, 1978. With permission from *Practical Aspects of Memory*. Copyright © 1978 by Academic Press, Inc., London, Ltd.)

change in arousal with time of day appear to have very small or zero effects on immediate recall of auditory material, but when the same material is presented visually there is a decline in immediate memory performance over the course of the day (Jones, Davies, Patrick, & Camberpatch, 1978). The Yerkes–Dodson Law mentioned in Chapter 6 is a useful overall summary of arousal effects on performance. The law states that each task has an optimal level of arousal for most efficient performance, and that the optimal level will vary with task difficulty. There will also be an effect on the nature of the performance, the kinds of errors and improvements, dependent on the kind of task and the kinds of processing required. Obviously, these effects of daily rhythms of arousal are of considerable importance to the workplace since they suggest that performance will vary with time of day and the effect of time of day will interact with the type of task. Some tasks may be efficiently performed in the morning while others will be performed more effectively in the afternoon. Of concern is not only the design of tasks and equipment to increase productivity and efficiency, but also to prevent accidents and insure the safety of the worker on the job.

We have been discussing the circadian rhythm as if these effects were wired into the organism and immutable. Of course, this is not the case. The human organism is highly adaptable. The arousal cycle can shift with the circumstances of work and, often, resources can be mobilized to overcome the effects of stress and arousal. Wilkinson (1964) for example, found that subjects could maintain an efficient performance despite prolonged sleep deprivation if the task was interesting to them. In addition, when workers change to a nightshift, their circadian patterns alter by moving the maximum and minimum peaks to accommodate the new pattern of sleeping and waking (Colquhoun, Blake, & Edwards, 1968).

Adaptability of the pattern is an important consideration in scheduling work. Some scheduling arrangements alternate nightwork among people in order to share the inconvenience of a schedule which is out of synchrony with the rest of society. However, these alternating scheduling arrangements are inefficient since they do not allow enough time for adaptation of the cycle. Under normal working conditions, even with a "stabilized" nightshift, the 24-hour pattern does not completely reverse, probably because cues available from the environment are still tuned to the normal routine (e.g., light and dark). Studies which completely isolate subjects from the outside world have been able to produce a complete reversal of the normal pattern (Aschoff, 1969). The 24-hour cycle itself is apparently the result of environmental "tuning." When subjects are isolated from all time of day cues a slightly longer, 25-hour cycle emerges (Dement, 1974).

Eventual accomodation to the pattern also occurs when a person flies across time zones. Klein, Bruner, Holtmann, Rehme, Stolze, and Steinhoff (1970), for example, have studied adaptation of pilots flying from the U.S. to Europe and back. Testing their subjects in a simulator, they found that complete adaptation on all performance measures of flying efficiency required more than a week. Interestingly, there was slower adaptation to flights from the U.S. to Europe than from Europe to the U.S. As Klein et al. point out, this may have been because the U.S. to Europe flights that they studied involved night flying time and so resulted in a loss of sleep. The implication would seem to be that arrival in a new time zone in the evening would be more favorable for adaptation than arrival during the day. Even though the travelers may not be ready to sleep, beginning the adaptation at this point would be easier than beginning during the activity portion of the cycle.

The effects of biological rhythms on performance and memory can be quite large, as much as 10 to 20% of a total performance score. They are also an increasingly important consideration in our technological society as it becomes necessary to maintain the operation of our complex industrial and transportation systems throughout the 24 hours of the day.

As you can see from the variety of examples in this section, human engineering has a prominent role to play in describing the optimum integration of the human component in the operation of systems. The considerations brought to bear on practical problems include not only abstract descriptions of human information processing discussed in earlier chapters, but also the analysis of concrete tasks, the effects of levels of skill, stress, fatigue, motivation, and differences among individuals. Although human engineering, as we noted in the introduction to this section, is classified as an "applied" discipline, it involves more than the simple application of theoretical principles. In fact, the purely theoretical psychologist in the academic laboratory may overlook mechanisms and capacity limitations that become apparent only when one examines the human processing system "in action" coping with a problem, or task, in everyday life. Thus, the applied setting becomes the source of new insights and theories about human functioning and a testing arena for theories and ideas derived from laboratory work. Although this reciprocal influence has sometimes been less than ideal, we believe that the interaction will become more frequent and more profitable as psychologists increasingly become interested in justifying the value of what they have learned.

CHAPTER SUMMARY

1. *Eyewitness Testimony*

   A. The variables that affect eyewitness testimony can be usefully divided into estimator variables and system variables. Estimator variables are characteristics of witnesses and conditions of observation that predict the accuracy of witness reports. Information regarding the operation of these variables can be used to estimate the relative credibility of witnesses in the courtroom. System variables are aspects of investigative and courtroom procedures that affect the testimony of the witness. The legal system can use information about these variables in ways that increase the likelihood of accurate witness reports.

B. Estimator variables that influence suspect identification include the time elapsing since the event was witnessed, the seriousness and violence of the events, the racial and ethnic identity of the witness and suspect, number of previous encounters with the suspect, and similarity of the suspect's appearance on the occasion of the observation and the time of identification. System variables include the biasing of familiarity with mugshots, the similarity of non-suspects to the suspect in a lineup or a group of photographs, prior knowledge that the suspect is in the lineup, leading questions during interrogation, and the experience of the interrogators.

2. *Learning How to Learn*

A. Metamemory is knowledge about personal characteristics, tasks, and strategies that is relevant to remembering. These forms of knowledge affect what you choose to learn, how effort and attention are applied to different tasks, and the level of sophistication and skill shown with alternative modes of learning.

B. Very young children lack the experience which is the basis of knowledge about remembering. Children younger than eight, for example, appear deficient in their knowledge of when rote rehearsal is appropriate, their own limited capacities for short-term retention, the use of internal cues to predict later recall, selection of appropriate retrieval cues, and coordination of learning activities with the structure of materials.

3. *Strategies for Remembering*

A. Short-term retention serves as a "working space" in problem-solving and thinking; it holds data on which we are working as well as the results of intermediate steps in our progress toward a solution. Consequently, our ability to solve problems is limited, in part, by the amount of information we can retain actively during the interval that we are working on the problem. Some of this burden on short-term retention can be relieved by memorizing equivalencies and transformations. The storage of the latter information in long-term memory eliminates the need to compute these transformations in active memory. The short-term burden can also be reduced by a chunking strategy which decreases the capacity necessary to maintain the information.

B. Mnemonics are highly learned schemes or structures that, when associated to information you wish to remember, can function as a set of retrieval cues preserving the order of the information and improving recall.

C. Mere exposure, even very frequent exposure, to a set of stimuli is insufficient to produce efficient remembering. One of the most important strategies for remembering appears to be an effort to understand and organize the material you are trying to learn.

4. *Individual Differences and Memory*

   A. Extraordinary memory abilities seem to represent an exaggeration of some normal ability, an exceptionally vivid and compelling imagery, or great adeptness in the invention of pattern or organization. Some of the talents displayed by these individuals involve the exercise of learned skills, but the core of these talents seem to reflect unique characteristics of the person that are not well understood. These individuals are a diverse group whose memory abilities are not necessarily reflected in other intellectual accomplishments.

   B. The measurement of individual differences in elementary information processing can provide a testing ground for hypotheses regarding the basis of task performance and hypotheses about the separability of information processing stages. Success in this enterprise may also lead to methods providing specific diagnoses of information processing deficits as well as strategies of remediation and compensation.

   C. There are considerable age differences in performance on tasks with time constraints, tasks requiring the division of resources, and those that require recall from long-term episodic memory. The levels of processing framework interprets these differences as due to a diminishing of resources with age. The smaller pool of resources available to an elderly person affects the depth to which information is ordinarily processed. They are less likely than younger subjects to engage in semantic, elaborative processing and less likely to integrate contextual information with their processing of current information. The result is a less distinctive memory code and less efficient use of retrieval cues.

5. *Memory Constraints and Modern Technology*

   A. As a skill is being learned, decisions regarding the appropriate response to varying sources of information require considerable resources. Resources are also required at this stage to monitor the consequences of behavior and provide corrective feedback where necessary. As learning progresses, many of these stimulus/response relationships are automatized and the capacity demanded by the task decreases. However, the structure of the environment plays a crucial role in the ease of learning and in determining the final level of resource commitment required after learning is complete. The number of signals that must receive attention, the discriminability of these signals, the precision with which the response must be executed, the amount of information that must be stored, and the retention interval required all affect the ultimate level of task performance that can be achieved.

B. Circadian rhythms, the daily patterns of physiological change in our bodies, appears to have different effects on different kinds of information processing. Short-term retention, for example, is better in the morning while long-term retention is better when the material has been learned in the afternoon. These effects are usually related to the concepts of "arousal" and "stress." As measured by body temperature, arousal is at a minimum in early morning and a maximum for most people in the late evening. Changes in arousal over the course of the day are correlated with changes in performance over the same period. These changes, in turn, are of importance for the scheduling of educational tasks, work requirements, and the arrangement of work shifts.

REFERENCES

Adelson, E.H. Iconic storage: The role of rods. *Science,* 1978, *201*, 554–546.

Allport, D.A., Antonis, B., & Reynolds, P. On the division of attention: A disproof of the single channel hypothesis. *Quarterly Journal of Experimental Psychology,* 1972, *24*, 225–235.

Allport, G.W. Eidetic imagery. *British Journal of Psychology,* 1924, *15*, 99–120.

Anderson, J.R. *Language, memory and thought.* Hillsdale, N.J.: Lawrence Erlbaum Associates, 1976.

Anderson, J.R. Arguments concerning representations for mental imagery. *Psychological Review,* 1978, *85*, 249–277.

Anderson, J.R., & Bower, G.H. Recognition and retrieval processes in free recall. *Psychological Review*, 1972, *79*, 97–123.

Anderson, J.R., & Bower, G.H. *Human associative memory.* Washington, D.C.: Winston, 1973

Anderson, J.R., & Bower, G.H. A propositional theory of recognition memory. *Memory and Cognition,* 1974, *2*, 406–412.

Anderson, J.R., & Paulson, R. Representation and retention of verbatim information. *Journal of Verbal Learning and Verbal Behavior,* 1977, *16*, 439–452.

Anderson, J.R., & Reder, L.M. Negative judgements in and about semantic memory. *Journal of Verbal Learning and Verbal Behavior,* 1974, *13*, 664–681.

Anderson, J.R., & Reder, L.M. An elaborative processing explanation of depth of processing. In L.S. Cermak & F.I.M. Craik (Eds.), *Levels of processing in human memory.* Hillsdale, N.J.: Lawrence Erlbaum Associates, 1979.

Anderson, R.C., & Myrow, D.L. Retroactive inhibition of meaning discourse. *Journal of Educational Psychology Monographs,* 1971, *62* (1).

Anderson, R.C., Spiro, R.J., & Montague, W.E. (Eds.). *Schooling and the acquisition of knowledge.* Hillsdale, N.J.: Lawrence Erlbaum Associates, 1977.

Anisfeld, M., & Knapp, M.E. Association, synonymity and directionality in false recognition. *Journal of Experimental Psychology,* 1968, *77* 171–179.

Aschoff, J. Desynchronization and resynchronization of human circadian rhythm. *Aerospace Medicine,* 1969, *40*, 844–849.

Atkinson, R.C. Mnemotechnics in second language learning. *American Psychologist,* 1975, *30*, 821–888.

Atkinson, R.C., & Juola, J.F. Search and decision processes in recognition memory. In D.H. Krantz, R.C. Atkinson, R.D. Luce, & P. Suppes (Eds.), *Contemporary developments in mathematical psychology* (Vol. 1). San Francisco: Freeman, 1974.

Atkinson, R.C., & Shiffrin, R.M. Human memory: A proposed system and its control processes. In K.W. Spence & J.T. Spence (Eds.), *The psychology of learning and motivation* (Vol. 2). New York: Academic Press, 1968.

Auble, P.M., & Franks, J.J. The effects of effort toward comprehension on recall. *Memory and Cognition,* 1978, *6*, 20–25.

Ausubel, D.P., Stager, M., & Gaite, A.J.H. Retroactive facilitation in meaningful verbal learning. *Journal of Educational Psychology,* 1968, *59* 250–255.

Averbach, E., & Coriell, E. Short-term memory in vision. *Bell System Technical Journal,* 1961, *40*, 309–328.

B

Bachrach, A.J. Diving behavior. In *Human Performance and SCUBA Diving.* Proceedings of the symposium on underwater physiology. Chicago: The Athletic Institute, 1970.

Baddeley, A.D. The influence of acoustic and semantic similarity on long-term memory for word sequences. *Quarterly Journal of Experimental Psychology,* 1966, *18*, 302–309. (a)

Baddeley, A.D. Short-term memory for word sequences as a function of acoustic, semantic, and formal similarity. *Quarterly Journal of Experimental Psychology,* 1966, *18*, 362–365. (b)

Baddeley, A.D. *The psychology of memory.* New York: Basic Books, 1976.

Baddeley, A.D. The trouble with levels: A reexamination of Craik and Lockhart's framework for memory research. *Psychological Review,* 1978, *85*, 139–152.

Baddeley, A.D., & Dale H.C. A. The effect of semantic similarity on retroactive interference in long and short-term memory. *Journal of Verbal Learning and Verbal Behavior,* 1966, *5*, 417–420.

Baddeley, A.D., & Ecob, J.R. Simultaneous acoustic and semantic coding in short-term memory. *Nature,* 1970, *227*, 288–289.

Baddeley, A.D., & Hitch, G.J. Working memory. In: G.M. Bower (Ed.), *The Psychology of learning and motivation* (Vol. 8). New York: Academic Press, 1974.

Baddeley, A.D., & Hitch, G.J. Recency re-examined. In S. Dornič (Ed.), *Attention and performance VI.* Hillsdale, N.J.: Lawrence Erlbaum Associates, 1977.

Baddeley, A.D., & Scott, D. Short-term forgetting in the absence of proactive inhibition. *Quarterly Journal of Experimental Psychology,* 1971, *23*, 275–283.

Baddeley, A.D., Thompson, N., & Buchman, M. Word length and the structure of short-term memory. *Journal of Verbal Learning and Verbal Behavior,* 1975, *14*, 575–589.

Baddeley, A.D., & Warrington, E.K. Amnesia and the distinction between long- and short-term memory. *Journal of Verbal Learning and Verbal Behavior,* 1970, *9*, 176–189

Baddeley, A.D., & Warrington, E.K. Memory coding and amnesia. *Neuropsychologica,* 1973, *11*, 159–165.

Bahrick, H.P., & Bahrick, P.D. A re-examination of the inter-relations among measures of retention. *Quarterly Journal of Experimental Psychology,* 1964, *16,* 318–324.

Banks, W.P. Signal detection theory and human memory. *Psychological Bulletin,* 1970, *74,* 81–99.

Banks, W.P., & Barber, G. Color information in iconic memory. *Psychological Review,* 1977, *84,* 536–546.

Barnes, J.M., & Underwood, B.J. "Fate" of first-list associations in transfer theory. *Journal of Experimental Psychology,* 1959, *58,* 97–105.

Barrett, T.R., & Ekstrand, B.R. Effects of sleep on memory: III. Controlling for time-of-day effects. *Journal of Experimental Psychology,* 1972, *96,* 321–327.

Bartlett, F.C. *Remembering: A study in experimental and social psychology.* Cambridge: Cambridge University Press, 1932.

Begg, I., & Paivio, A. Concreteness and imagery in sentence meaning. *Journal of Verbal Learning and Verbal Behavior,* 1969, *8,* 821–827.

Belmont, J.M., & Butterfield, E.C. Learning strategies as determinants of memory deficiencies. *Cognitive Psychology,* 1971, *2,* 411–420.

Benson, K., & Feinberg, I. The beneficial effect of sleep in an extended Jenkins and Dallenbach paradigm. *Psychophysiology,* 1977, *14,* 375–384.

Bernbach, H.A. Rate of presentation in free recall: A problem for two-stage memory theories. *Journal of Experimental Psychology: Human Learning and Memory,* 1975, *104,* 18–22.

Bjork, R.A., & Landauer, T.K. On keeping track of the present status of people and things. In M.M. Gruneberg, P.E. Morris, & R.N. Sykes (Eds.), *Practical aspects of memory.* New York: Academic Press, 1978.

Bjork, R.A., & Whitten, W.B. Recency-sensitive retrieval processes. *Cognitive Psychology,* 1974, *6,* 173–189.

Bobrow, D.G. Dimensions of representation. In D.G. Bobrow & A.M. Collins (Eds.), *Representation and understanding: Studies in cognitive science.* New York: Academic Press, 1975.

Bobrow, D.G., & Norman, D.A. Some principles of memory schemata. In D.G. Bobrow & A. Collins (Eds.), *Representation and understanding.* New York: Academic Press, 1975.

Bobrow, S.A., & Bower, G.H. Comprehension and recall of sentences. *Journal of Experimental Psychology,* 1969, *80,* 455–461.

Boring, E.G. *A History of experimental psychology.* New York: Appleton-Century-Crofts, 1950.

Bousfield, W.A. The occurrence of clustering in the recall of randomly arranged associates. *Journal of General Psychology,* 1953, *49,* 229–240.

Bousfield, W.A., & Cohen, B.M. The occurrence of clustering in the recall of randomly arranged words of different frequencies of usage. *Journal of Genetic Psychology,* 1955, *52,* 83–95.

Bousfield, W.A., & Puff, C.R. Clustering as a function of response dominance. *Journal of Experimental Psychology,* 1964, *67,* 76–79.

Bousfield, W.A., & Sedgewick, C.H. An analysis of sequences of restricted associative responses. *Journal of General Psychology,* 1944, *30,* 149–165.

Bower, G.H. A selective review of organizational factors in memory. In E. Tulving & W. Donaldson (Eds.), *Organization of memory.* New York: Academic Press, 1972.

Bower, G.H., Black, J.B., & Turner, T.J. Scripts in memory for text. *Cognitive Psychology,* 1979, *11,* 177–220.

Bower, G.H., & Karlin, M.B. Depth of processing pictures of faces and recognition memory. *Journal of Experimental Psychology*, 1974, *103*, 751–757.

Bower, G.H., & Springston, F. Pauses as recoding points in letter series. *Journal of Experimental Psychology*, 1970, *83*, 421–430.

Bowling, A., Lovegrove, W., & Mapperson, B. The effect of spatial frequency and contrast on visual persistence. *Perception*, 1979, *8*, 529–539.

Bransford, J.D., Barclay, J.R., & Franks, J.J. Sentence memory: A constructive versus interpretive approach. *Cognitive Psychology*, 1972, *3*, 193–209.

Bransford, J.D., & Franks, J.J. The abstraction of linguistic ideas. *Cognitive Psychology*, 1971, *2*, 331–350.

Bransford, J.D., & Franks, J.J. The abstraction of linguisitc ideas: A review. *Cognition*, 1972, *1*, 211–249.

Bransford, J.D., Franks, J.J., Morris, C.D., & Stein, B.S. Some general constraints on learning and memory research. In L.S. Cermak & F.I.M. Craik (Eds.), *Levels of processing in human memory*. Hillsdale, N.J.: Lawrence Erlbaum Associates, 1979.

Bransford, J.D., & Johnson, M.K. Contextual prerequisites for understanding: Some investigations of comprehension and recall. *Journal of Verbal Learning and Verbal Behavior*, 1972, *11*, 717–726.

Bransford, J.D., & McCarrell, N.S. A sketch of a cognitive approach to comprehension: Some thoughts about what it means to comprehend. In W.B. Weimer & D.S. Palermo (Eds.), *Cognition and the symbolic processes*. Hillsdale, N.J.: Lawrence Erlbaum Associates, 1975.

Bransford, J.D., McCarrell, N.S., Franks, J.J., & Nitsch, K.E. Toward unexplaining memory. In R. Shaw & J. Bransford (Eds.), *Perceiving, acting, and knowing*. Hillsdale, N.J.: Lawrence Erlbaum Associates, 1977.

Bransford, J.D., Stein, B.S., Shelton, T.S., & Owings, R.A. Cognition and adaptation: The importance of learning to learn. In J. Harvey (Ed.), *Cognition, social behavior, and the environment*. Hillsdale, N.J.: Lawrence Erlbaum Associates, 1980.

Breitmeyer, B.G., & Ganz, L. Implications of sustained and transient channels for theories of visual pattern masking, saccadic suppression, and information processing. *Psychological Review*, 1976, *83*, 1–36.

Briggs, G.E. Acquisition, extinction, and recovery functions in retroactive inhibition. *Journal of Experimental Psychology*, 1954, *47*, 285–293.

Briggs, G.G., & Kinsbourne, M. Visual persistence as measured by reaction time. *Quarterly Journal of Experimental Psychology*, 1972, *24*, 318–325.

Broadbent, D.E. Speaking and listening simultaneously. *Journal of Experimental Psychology*, 1952, *43*, 267–273.

Broadbent, D.E. The role of auditory localization in attention and memory span. *Journal of Experimental Psychology*, 1954, *47*, 191–196.

Broadbent, D.E. *Perception and communication*. London: Pergamon Press, 1958.

Broadbent, D.E. *Decision and stress*. New York: Academic Press, 1971.

Broadbent, D. E. Relation between theory and application in psychology. In P.B. Warr (Ed.), *Psychology and work*. Baltimore, Md: Penguin Books, 1971.

Broadbent, D.E., & Gregory, M. Stimulus set and response set: The alternation of attention. *Quarterly Journal of Experimental Psychology*, 1964, *16*, 309–312.

Brown, A.L., & Campione, J.C. Training strategic study time apportionment in educable retarded children. *Intelligence,* 1977, *1,* 94–107.

Brown, A.L., & Campione, J.C. The effects of knowledge and experience on the formation of retrieval plans for studying from texts. In M.M. Gruneberg, P.E. Morris, & R.N. Sykes (Eds.), *Practical aspects of memory.* New York: Academic Press, 1978.

Brown, A.L., & Smiley, S.S. Rating the importance of structural units of prose passages: A problem of metacognitive development. *Child Development,* 1977, *48,* 1–8.

Brown, A.L., & Smiley, S.S. The development of strategies for studying texts. *Child Development,* 1978, *49,* 1076–1088.

Brown, A.L., Smiley, S.S., & Lawton, S.Q.C. The effect of experience on the selection of suitable retrieval cues for studying texts. *Child Development,* 1978, *49,* 829–835.

Brown, E.L., Deffenbacher, K.A., & Sturgill, W. Memory for faces and the circumstances of an encounter. *Journal of Applied Psychology,* 1977, *62,* 311–318.

Brown, I.D. Subjective and objective comparisons of successful and unsuccessful trainee drivers. *Ergonomics,* 1966, *9,* 49–56.

Brown, J. Some tests of the decay theory of immediate memory. *Quarterly Journal of Experimental Psychology,* 1958, *10,* 12–21.

Brown, R.W., & McNeil, D. The "tip of the tongue" phenomenon. *Journal of Verbal Learning and Verbal Behavior,* 1966, *5,* 325–337.

Bryden, M.P. Order of report in dichotic listening. *Canadian Journal of Psychology,* 1962, *16,* 291–299.

Buckhout, R. Eyewitness testimony. *Scientific American,* 1974, *231,* 23–31.

Bugelski, B.R. Presentation time, total time and mediation in paired associate learning. *Journal of Experimental Psychology,* 1962, *63,* 409–412.

Byrnes, D.L. Memory search of dichotically presented lists of digits. *Bulletin of the Psychonomic Society,* 1976, *8,* 185–187.

Byrnes, D.L., & Wingfield, A. Retrieval time and decay of information in dichotic memory. *Perceptual and Motor Skills,* 1979, *48,* 831–839.

C

Calkins, M.W. Association. *Psychological Review,* 1894, *1,* 476–483.

Campbell, F.W., & Wurtz, R.H. Saccadic omission: Why we do not see a grey-out during a saccadic eye movement. *Vision Research,* 1978, *18,* 1297–1303.

Ceraso, J. The interference theory of forgetting. *Scientific American,* 1967, *217,* 117–124.

Ceraso, J., & Henderson, A. Unavailability and associative loss in RI and PI. *Journal of Experimental Psychology,* 1965, *70,* 300–303.

Cermak, L.S. *Improving your memory.* New York: McGraw-Hill, 1976.

Cermak, L.S., & Butters, N. The role of interference and encoding in short-term memory deficits of Korsakoff patients, *Neuropsychologia,* 1972, *10,* 89–95.

Cermak, L.S., Butters, N., & Moreines, J. Some analyses of the verbal encoding deficit of alcoholic Korsakoff patients. *Brain and Language,* 1974, *1,* 141–150.

Cermak, L.S., Naus, M.J., & Reale, L. Rehearsal strategies of alcoholic Korsakoff patients. *Brain and Language,* 1976. *3,* 375–385.

Chapman, L.J., & Chapman, J.P. *Disordered thought in schizophrenia.* New York: Appleton-Century-Crofts, 1973.

Chase, W.G., & Calfee, R.C. Modality and similarity effects in short-term recognition memory. *Journal of Experimental Psychology,* 1969, *81,* 510–514.

Cherry, E.C. Some experiments on the recognition of speech with one and with two ears. *Journal of the Acoustical Society of America,* 1953, *25,* 975–979.

Cherry, E.C., & Taylor, W.K. Some further experiments on the recognition of speech with one and with two ears. *Journal of the Acoustical Society of America,* 1954, *26,* 554–559.

Chow, S.H., & Murdock, B.B. Concurrent memory load and the rate of readout from iconic memory. *Journal of Experimental Psychology: Human Perception and Performance,* 1975, *2,* 179–190.

Clifford, B.R., & Scott, J. Individual and situational factors in eyewitness testimony. *Journal of Applied Psychology,* 1978, *63,* 352–359.

Cofer, C.N. On some factors in the organizational characteristics of free recall. *American Psychologist,* 1965, *20,* 261–272.

Cofer, C.N. Constructive processes in memory. *American Scientist,* 1973, *61,* 537–543.

Cofer, C.N., Chmielewski, D.L., & Brockway, J.F. Constructive processes and the structure of human memory. In C.N. Cofer (Ed.), *The structure of human memory.* San Francisco: Freeman, 1976.

Cole, R.A., & Scott, B. Toward a theory of speech perception. *Psychological Review,* 1974, *81,* 348–374.

Collins, A.M., & Loftus, E.F. A spreading activation theory of semantic processing. *Psychological Review,* 1975, *82,* 407–428.

Collins, A.M., & Quillian, M.R. Retrieval time from semantic memory. *Journal of Verbal Learning and Verbal Behavior,* 1969, *8,* 240–247.

Collins, A.M., & Quillian, M.R. Does category size affect categorization time? *Journal of Verbal Learning and Verbal Behavior,* 1970, *9,* 432–438.

Collins, A.M., & Quillian, M.R. How to make a language user. In E. Tulving & W. Donaldson (Eds.), *Organization in memory.* New York: Academic Press, 1972.

Colquhoun, W.P. *Biological rhythms and human performances.* New York: Academic Press, 1971.

Colquhoun, W.P., Blake, M.J.F., & Edwards, R.S. Experimental studies of shift work I: A comparison of "rotating" and "stabilized" 4 hour shift systems. *Ergonomics,* 1968, *11,* 437–453.

Conrad, R. Acoustic confusions and memory span for words. *Nature,* 1963, *197,* 1029–1030.

Conrad, R. Acoustic confusions in immediate memory. *British Journal of Psychology,* 1964, *55,* 75–84.

Conrad, R. Short-term memory processes in the deaf. *British Journal of Psychology,* 1970, *61,* 179–195.

Conrad, R. Short-term memory in the deaf: A test for speech coding. *British Journal of Psychology,* 1972, *63,* 173–180.

Conrad, R., & Hull, A.J. Information, acoustic confusion and memory span. *British Journal of Psychology,* 1964, *55,* 429–432.

Cooper, L.A., & Shepard, R.N. Chronometric studies of the rotation of mental images. In W.G. Chase (Ed.), *Visual information processing.* New York: Academic Press, 1973.

Cooper, L.A., & Shepard, R.N. Transformations on representations of objects in space. In E.C. Carterette & M.P. Friedman (Eds.), *Handbook of perception: Perceptual coding* (Vol. 8). New York: Academic Press, 1978.

Corballis, M.C. Rehearsal and decay in immediate recall of visually and aurally presented items. *Canadian Journal of Psychology,* 1966, *20,* 43–51.

Corcoran, D.W.J. *Pattern recognition.* Harmondsworth: Penguin, 1971.

Corfield, R., Frosdick, J.P., & Campbell, F.W. Grey-out elimination: The roles of spatial waveform, frequency and phase. *Vision Research,* 1978, *18,* 1305–1311.

Corman, C.N., & Wickens, D.D. Retroactive inhibition in short-term memory. *Journal of Verbal Learning and Verbal Behavior,* 1968, *7,* 16–19.

Corteen, R.S., & Wood, B. Autonomic responses to shock-associated words in an unattended channel. *Journal of Experimental Psychology,* 1972, *94,* 308–313.

Craik, F.I.M. The fate of primary memory items in free recall. *Journal of Verbal Learning and Verbal Behavior,* 1970, *9,* 143–148.

Craik, F.I.M. Primary memory. *British Medical Bulletin,* 1971, *27,* 232–236.

Craik, F.I.M. Depth of processing in recall and recognition. In S. Dornič (Ed.), *Attention and performance VI.* Hillsdale, N.J.: Lawrence Erlbaum Associates, 1977 (a).

Craik, F.I.M. Age differences in human memory. In J.E. Birren & K.W. Shaie (Eds.), *Handbook of the psychology of aging.* New York: Van Nostrand Reinhold, 1977 (b).

Craik, F.I.M. Human memory. *Annual Review of Psychology,* 1979, *30,* 63–102. (a)

Craik, F.I.M. Levels of processing: Overview and closing comments. In L.S. Cermak & F.I.M. Craik (Eds.), *Levels of processing in human memory.* Hillsdale, N.J.: Lawrence Erlbaum Associates, 1979 (b).

Craik, F.I.M., & Kirsner, K. The effect of speaker's voice on word recognition. *Quarterly Journal of Experimental Psychology,* 1974, *26,* 274–284.

Craik, F.I.M. , & Levy, B.A. Semantic and acoustic information in primary memory. *Journal of Experimental Psychology,* 1970, *86,* 77–82.

Craik, F.I.M., & Levy, B.A. The concept of primary memory. In W.K. Estes (Ed.), *Handbook of learning and cognitive processes: Attention and memory* (Vol. 4). Hillsdale, N.J.: Lawrence Erlbaum Associates, 1976.

Craik, F.I.M., & Lockhart, R.S. Levels of processing: A framework for memory research. *Journal of Verbal Learning and Verbal Behavior,* 1972, *11,* 671–684.

Craik, F.I.M., & Simon, E. Age differences in memory: The roles of attention and depth of processing. In L.W. Poon, J.L. Fozard, L.S. Cermak, D. Arenberg & L.W. Thompson (Eds.), *New directions in memory and aging: Proceedings of the George Talland memorial conference.* Hillsdale, N.J.: Lawrence Erlbaum Associates, 1980.

Craik, F.I.M., & Tulving, E. Depth of processing and the retention of words in episodic memory. *Journal of Experimental Psychology: General,* 1975, *104,* 268–294.

Craik, F.I.M., & Watkins, M.J. The role of rehearsal in short-term memory. *Journal of Verbal Learning and Verbal Behavior,* 1973, *12,* 599–607.

Crönholm, B., & Lagergren, A. Memory disturbance after electroconvulsive therapy. *Acta Psychiatrica Neurologia Scandinavica,* 1959, *34,* 283–310.

Cross, J.F., Cross, J., & Daly, J. Sex age, race and beauty as factors in the recognition of faces. *Perception and Psychophysics*, 1971, *10*, 393–396.

Crowder, R.G. Waiting for the stimulus suffix: Decay, delay, rhythm and readout in immediate memory. *Quarterly Journal of Experimental Psychology*, 1971, *23*, 324–340.

Crowder, R.G. Representation of speech sounds in precategorical acoustic storage. *Journal of Experimental Psychology*, 1973, *98*, 14–24.

Crowder, R.G. *Principles of learning and memory*. Hillsdale, N.J.: Lawrence Erlbaum Associates, 1976.

Crowder, R.G., & Morton, J. Precategorical acoustic storage (PAS). *Perception and Psychophysics*, 1969, *5*, 365–373.

Crowder, R.G., & Prussin, H.A. Experiments with the stimulus suffix effect. *Journal of Experimental Psychology Monographs*, 1971, *91*, 169–190.

Crowder, R.G., & Raeburn, U.P. The stimulus suffix effect with reversed speech. *Journal of Verbal Learning and Verbal Behavior*, 1970, *9*, 342–345.

Cudahy, E., & Leshowitz, B. Effects of contralateral interference tone on auditory recognition. *Perception and Psychophysics*, 1974, *15*, 16–20.

D

Dallett, K.M. "Primary memory": The effects of redundancy upon digit repetition. *Psychonomic Science*, 1965, *3*, 237–238.

Dallett, K., & Wilcox, S.G. Contextual stimuli and proactive inhibition. *Journal of Experimental Psychology*, 1968, *78*, 475–480.

Dark, V.J., & Loftus, G.R. The role of rehearsal in long-term memory performance. *Journal of Verbal Learning and Verbal Behavior*, 1976, *15*, 479–490.

Darwin, C.J., Turvey, M.T., & Crowder, R.G. Auditory analogue of the Sperling partial report procedure: Evidence for brief auditory storage. *Cognitive Psychology*, 1972, *3*, 255–267.

Davis, R., Sutherland, N.S., & Judd, B.R. Information content in recognition and recall. *Journal of Experimental Psychology*, 1961, *61*, 422–429.

Deese, J. Influence of inter-item associative strength upon immediate free recall. *Psychological Reports*, 1959, *5*, 305–312.

Deese, J. From the isolated verbal unit to connected discourse. In C.N. Cofer (Ed.), *Verbal learning and verbal behavior*. New York: McGraw-Hill, 1961.

Deese, J. *Principles of psychology*. Boston: Allyn and Bacon, 1964.

Deffenbacher, K.A., Brown, E.L., & Sturgill, W. Some predictors of eyewitness memory accuracy. In M.M. Gruneberg, P.E. Morris & R.N. Sykes (Eds.), *Practical aspects of memory*. New York: Academic Press, 1978.

Dement, W.C. *Some must watch while some must sleep*. San Francisco: Freeman, 1974.

Dent, H.R. Interviewing child witnesses. In M.M. Gruneberg, P.E. Morris, R.N. Sykes (Eds.). *Practical aspects of memory*. New York: Academic Press, 1978.

Deutsch, J.A., & Deutsch, D. Attention: Some theoretical considerations. *Psychological Review*, 1963, *70*, 80–90.

Dillon, D.J. Intervening activity and the retention of meaningful verbal materials. *Psychonomic Science*, 1970, *19*, 369–370.

Dilollo, V. Temporal integration in visual memory. *Journal of Experimental Psychology: General*, 1980, *109*, 75–97.

Dilollo, V. Temporal characteristics of iconic memory. *Nature*, 1977, *267*, 241–243.

Donders, F.C. [On the speed of mental processes.] In W.G. Koster (Ed. and trans.), *Attention and performance II.* Amsterdam: North-Holland, 1969. (Reprinted from *Acta Psychologica, 1969, 30.*)

Dooling, D.J., & Lachman, R. Effects of comprehension on retention of prose. *Journal of Experimental Psychology, 1971, 88,* 216–222.

Dooling, D.J., & Christiaansen, R.E. Episodic and semantic aspects of memory for prose. *Journal of Experimental Psychology: Human Learning and Memory, 1977, 3,* 428–436.

Doost, R., & Turvey, M.T. Iconic memory and central processing capacity. *Perception and Psychophysics, 1971, 9,* 269–274.

Dresher, B.E., & Hornstein, N. On some supposed contributions of artificial intelligence to the scientific study of language. *Cognition, 1976, 4,* 321–398.

E

Eagle, M., & Leiter, E. Recall and recognition in intentional and incidental learning. *Journal of Experimental Psychology, 1964, 68,* 58–63.

Eagle, M., & Ortoff, E. The effect of level of attention upon "phonetic" recognition errors. *Journal of Verbal Learning and Verbal Behavior, 1967, 6,* 226–231.

Ebbinghaus, H.E. *Memory: A contribution to experimental psychology.* New York: Dover, 1964. (Originally published 1885; translated, 1913.)

Efron, R. Effect of stimulus duration on perceptual onset and offset latencies. *Perception and Psychophysics, 1970, 8,* 231–234.

Efron, R. An invariant characteristic of perceptual systems in the time domain. In S. Kornblum (Ed.), *Attention and performance IV.* New York: Academic Press, 1973.

Egan, J.P., & Clarke, F.R. Psychophysics and signal detection. In J.B. Sidowski (Ed.), *Experimental methods and instrumentation in psychology.* New York: McGraw-Hill, 1966.

Ekstrand, B.R. Effect of sleep on memory. *Journal of Experimental Psychology, 1967, 75,* 64–72.

Ekstrand, B.R. To sleep, perchance to dream (about why we forget). In C.P. Duncan, L. Sechrest, & A.W. Melton (Eds.), *Human memory: Festschrift for Benton J. Underwood.* New York: Appleton-Century-Crofts, 1972.

Elliot, E.S., Wills, E.J., & Goldstein, A.G. The effects of discrimination training on the recognition of white and oriental faces. *Bulletin of the Psychonomic Society, 1973, 2,* 71–73.

Elliot, L.L. Development of auditory narrow-band frequency contours. *Journal of the Acoustical Society of America, 1967, 42,* 143–153.

Ellis, N.R. Memory processes in retardates and normals: Theoretical and empirical considerations. In N. Ellis (Ed.), *International review of research in mental retardation* (Vol. 4). New York: Academic Press, 1970.

Empson, J.A.C., & Clarke, P.R.F. Rapid eye movements and remembering. *Nature, 1970, 227,* 287–288.

Eriksen, C.W., & Collins, J.F. A reinterpretation of one form of backward and forward masking in visual perception. *Journal of Experimental Psychology, 1965, 70,* 374–351.

Eriksen, C.W., & Collins, J.F. Some temporal characteristics of visual pattern perception. *Journal of Experimental Psychology, 1967, 74,* 476–484.

Erwin, D.E. Extraction of information from visual persistence. *American Journal of Psychology, 1976, 89,* 659–667.

Erwin, D.E., & Hershenson, M. Functional characteristics of visual persistence predicted by a two-factor theory of backward masking. *Journal of Experimental Psychology,* 1974, *103, 2,* 279–254.

Estes, W.K. Structural aspects of associative models for memory. In C.N. Cofer (Ed.), *The structure of human memory.* San Francisco: Freeman, 1976.

Eysenck, M.W. Age differences in incidental learning. *Developmental Psychology,* 1974, *10,* 936–941.

Eysenck, M.W. *Human memory: Theory, research and individual differences.* Oxford: Pergamon, 1977.

Eysenck, M.W. Levels of processing-a critique. *British Journal of Psychology,* 1978, *60,* 157–169.(a)

Eysenck, M.W. Levels of processing: A reply to Lockhart and Craik. *British Journal of Psychology,* 1978, *69,* 177–178.(b)

Eysenck, M.W., & Eysenck, M.C. Processing depth, elaboration of encoding, memory stores, and expended processing capacity. *Journal of Experimental Psychology: Human Learning and Memory,* 1979, *5,* 472–484.

F

Fisher, S. The microstructure of dual task interaction. 1. The patterning of main-task responses with secondary-task intervals. *Perception,* 1975, *4,* 267–290.(a)

Fisher, S. The microstructure of dual task interaction. 2. The effect of task instructions on attentional allocation and a model of attention-switching. *Perception,* 1975, *4,* 459–474.(b)

Fisher, R.P., & Craik, F.I.M. The interaction between encoding and retrieval operations in cued recall. *Journal of Experimental Psychology: Human Learning and Memory,* 1977, *3,* 701–711.

Flagg, P.W., Potts, G.R., & Reynolds, A.G. Instructions and response strategies in recognition memory for sentences. *Journal of Experimental Psychology: Learning and Memory,* 1975, *1,* 592–598.

Flavell, J.H. Metacognition and cognitive monitoring: A new area of cognitive-developmental inquiry. *American Psychologist,* 1979, *34,* 906–911.

Flavell, J.H., Beach, D.R., & Chinsky, J.M. Spontaneous verbal rehearsal in a memory task as a function of age. *Child Development,* 1966, *37,* 283–299.

Flavell, J.H., Fredrichs, A.G., & Hoyt, J.D. Developmental changes in memorization processes. *Cognitive Psychology,* 1970, *1,* 324–340.

Flavell, J.H., & Wellman, H.M. Metamemory. In R.V. Kail & J.H. Hagen (Eds.), *Perspectives on the development of memory and cognition.* Hillsdale, N.J.: Lawrence Erlbaum Associates, 1977.

Folkard, S., & Monk, T.H. Time of day effects in immediate and delayed memory. In M.M. Gruneberg, P.E. Morris & R.N. Sykes (Eds.), *Practical aspects of memory.* New York: Academic Press, 1978.

French, J.W. The effect of temperature in the retention of a maze habit in fish. *Journal of Experimental Psychology,* 1942, *31,* 79–87.

G

Galton, F. *Inquiries into human faculty and its development.* London: Macmillan, 1883.

Gardner, J.M., Craik, F.I.M., & Birtwistle, J. Retrieval cues and release from proactive inhibition. *Journal of Verbal Learning and Verbal Behavior,* 1972, *11,* 778–783.

Gilson, E.Q., & Baddeley, A.D. Tactile short-term memory. *Quarterly Journal of Experimental Psychology,* 1969, *21,* 180–184.

Glanzer, M. Storage mechanisms in recall. In G.H. Bower (Ed.), *The psychology of learning and motivation: Advances in research and theory* (Vol. 5). New York: Academic Press, 1972.

Glanzer, M., Gianutsos, R., & Dubin, S. The removal of items from short-term storage. *Journal of Verbal Learning and Verbal Behavior*, 1969, *8*, 435–447.

Glanzer, M., & Razel, M. The size of the unit in short-term storage. *Journal of Verbal Learning and Verbal Behavior*, 1974, *13*, 114–131.

Glass, A.L., & Holyoak, K.J. Alternative conceptions of semantic memory. *Cognition*, 1974, *3*, 313–339.

Glenberg, A., Smith, S.M., & Green, G. Type I rehearsal: Maintenance and more. *Journal of Verbal Learning and Verbal Behavior*, 1977, *16*, 339–352.

Glickman, S.E. Perseverative neural processes and consolidation of the neural trace. *Psychological Bulletin*, 1961, *58*, 218–233.

Glucksberg, S., & Cowen, G.N. Memory for nonattended auditory materials. *Cognitive Psychology*, 1970, *1*, 149–156.

Godden, D.R., & Baddeley, A.D. Context-dependent memory in two natural environments: On land and underwater. *British Journal of Psychology*, 1975, *66* 325–332.

Goldstein, A.G., & Chance, J.E. Visual recognition memory for complex configurations. *Perception and Psychophysics*, 1971, *9*, 237–241.

Goolkasian, P., Terry, W.S., & Park, D.C. Memory for lectures: Effects of delay and distractor type. *Journal of Educational Psychology*, 1979, *71*, 465–470.

Gopher, D., & Kahneman, D. Individual differences in attention and the prediction of flight criteria. *Perceptual and Motor Skills*, 1971, *33*, 1335–1342.

Graesser, A., & Mandler, G. Recognition memory for the meaning and surface structure of sentences. *Journal of Experimental Psychology: Learning and Memory*, 1975, *104*, 238–248.

Gray, C.R., & Gummerman, K. The enigmatic eidetic image: A critical examination of methods, data and theory, *Psychological Bulletin*, 1975, *82*, 383–407.

Gray, J.A., & Wedderburn, A.A.I. Grouping strategies with simultaneous stimuli. *Quarterly Journal of Experimental Psychology*, 1960, *12*, 180–184.

Green, D.M., & Swets, J.A. *Signal detection theory and psychophysics*. New York: Wiley, 1966.

Griggs, R.A., & Keen, D.M. The role of test procedures in linguistic integration studies. *Memory and Cognition*, 1977, *5*, 685–689.

Gruneberg, M.M. The role of memorization techniques in finals preparation: A study of psychology students. *Educational Research*, 1973, *15*, 134–139.

H

Haber, R.N. Where are the visions in visual perception? In S.J. Segal (Ed.), *Imagery: Current cognitive approaches*. New York: Academic Press, 1971.

Haber, R.N. & Nathanson, L.S. Post-retinal iconic storage? Some further observations on Park's camel as seen through the eye of a needle. *Perception and Psychophysics*, 1968, *3*, 349–355.

Haber, R.N., & Standing, L. Direct measures of short-term visual storage. *Quarterly Journal of Experimental Psychology*, 1969, *21*, 43–54.

Haber, R.N., & Standing, L. Direct estimates of apparent duration of a flash followed by visual noise. *Canadian Journal of Psychology*, 1970, *24*, 216–229.

Hall, J.F. Learning as a function of word frequency. *American Journal of Psychology*, 1954, *67*, 138–140.

Hamilton, P. Selective attention in multi-source monitoring tasks. *Journal of Experimental Psychology*, 1969, *82*, 34–37.

Hamilton, P., Hockey, B., & Rejman, M. The place of the concept of activation in human information processing theory: An integrative approach. In S. Dornič(Ed.), *Attention and performance VI*. Hillsdale, N.J.: Lawrence Erlbaum Associates, 1977.

Hannay, A. *Mental images: A defense*. New York: Humanities Press, 1971.

Harris, R.J., & Monaco, G.E. Psychology of pragmatic implication: Information processing between the lines. *Journal of Experimental Psychology: General*, 1978, *107*, 1–22.

Hart, J.T. Memory and the feeling-of-knowing experience. *Journal of Educational Psychology*, 1965, *56*, 208–216.

Hebb, D.O. *The organization of behavior*. New York: Wiley, 1949.

Higbee, K.L. *Your memory: How it works and how to improve it*. London: Prentice-Hall, 1977.

Hintzman, D.L., Block, R.A., & Inskeep, N.R. Memory for mode of input. *Journal of Verbal Learning and Verbal Behavior*, 1972, *11*, 741–740.

Hoagland, H. A study of the physiology of learning in ants. *Journal of Genetic Psychology*, 1931, *5*, 21–41.

Hochber, J., & Gellman, L. The effect of landmark features on ''mental rotation'' times. *Memory and Cognition*, 1977, *5*, 23–26.

Hockey, R. Arousal and stress in human memory: Some methodological and theoretical considerations. In M.M. Gruneberg, P.E. Morris, & R.N. Sykes (Eds.), *Practical aspects of memory*. New York: Academic Press, 1978.

Hockey, G.R.J., Davies, S., & Gray, M.M. Forgetting as a function of sleep at different times of day. *Quarterly Journal of Experimental Psychology*, 1972, *24*, 386–393.

Holen, M.C., & Oaster, T.R. Serial position and isolation effects in a classroom lecture simulation. *Journal of Educational Psychology*, 1976, *68*, 293–296.

Hollingsworth, H.C. Characteristic differences between recall and recognition. *American Journal of Psychology*, 1913, *24*, 532–544.

Holmes, V.M., & Langford, J. Comprehension and recall of abstract and concrete sentences. *Journal of Verbal Learning and Verbal Behavior*, 1976, *5*, 559–566.

Hovey, H. B. Effects of general distraction on the higher thought processes. *American Journal of Psychology*, 1928, *40*, 585–591.

Hovland, C.I. Experimental studies in rote-learning theory. II. Reminiscence with varying speeds of syllable presentation. *Journal of Experimental Psychology*, 1938, *22*, 338–353.

Howe, M.J.A. Using students' notes to examine the role of the individual learner in acquiring meaningful subject matter. *Journal of Educational Research*, 1970, *64*, 61–63.

Huggins, A.W.F. Distortion of the temporal pattern of speech: Interruption and alternation. *Journal of the Acoustical Society of America*, 1964, *36*, 1055–1064.

Huggins, A.W.F. Delayed auditory feedback and the temporal properties of speech materials. *Zeitschrift fur Phonetik, Sprachwissenschaft und Kommunikationsforschung*, 1968, *1*, 54–60.

Hunt, E. Mechanics of verbal ability. *Psychological Review*, 1978, *85*, 109–130.

Hunt, E., Frost, N., & Lunneborg, C. Individual differences in cognition: A new approach to intelligence. In G. H. Bower (Ed.), *Psychology of learning and motivation* (Vol. 7). New York: Academic Press, 1973.

Hunt, E., & Lansman, M. Cognitive theory applied to individual differences. In W.K. Estes (Ed.), *Handbook of learning and cognitive processes: Introduc-*

tion to concepts and issues (Vol. 1). Hillsdale, N.J.: Lawrence Erlbaum Associates, 1975.

Hunt, E., & Love, T. How good can memory be? In A.W. Melton & E. Martin (Eds.), *Coding processes in human memory.* Washington, D. C.: Winston, 1972.

Hunt, E., Lunneborg, C., & Lewis, J. What does it mean to be high verbal? *Cognitive Psychology,* 1975, *7,* 194–227.

Hunter, I. M.L. *Memory.* Baltimore: Penguin Books, 1964.

Hunter, I.M.L. An exceptional memory. *British Journal of Psychology,* 1977, *68, 155–*164.

Hunter, I.M.L. The role of memory in expert mental calculations. In M.M. Gruneberg, P.E. Morris, & R.N. Sykes (Eds.), *Practical aspects of memory.* New York: Academic Press, 1978.

Hyde, T.S., & Jenkins, J.J. Differential effects of incidental tasks on the organization of recall of a list of highly associated words. *Journal of Experimental Psychology,* 1969, *82,* 472–481.

Hyde, T.S., & Jenkins, J.J. Recall of words as a function of semantic, graphic and syntactic orienting tasks. *Journal of Verbal Learning and Verbal Behavior;* 1973, *12,* 471–480.

I

Intraub, H. The role of implicit naming in pictorial encoding. *Journal of Experimental Psychology: Human Learning and Memory,* 1979, *5,* 78–87.

J

Jacoby, L.L. Encoding processes, rehearsal, and recall requirements. *Journal of Verbal Learning and Verbal Behavior,* 1973, *12,* 302–310.

James, W. *Principles of psychology.* New York: Holt, 1890.

Jenkins, J.G., & Dallenbach, K.M. Oblivescence during sleep and waking. *American Journal of Psychology,* 1924, *35,* 605–612.

Jenkins, J.J. Mediated associations. In C.N. Cofer & B.S. Musgrave (Eds.), *Verbal behavior and learning.* New York: McGraw-Hill, 1963.

Jenkins, J.J., Mink, W.D., & Russell, W.A. Associative clustering as a function of verbal association strength. *Psychological Reports,* 1958, *4,* 127–136.

Jenkins, J.J., & Russell, W.A. Associative clustering during recall. *Journal of Abnormal and Social Psychology,* 1952, *47,* 818–821.

Jensen, A.R. Spelling errors and the serial position effect. *Journal of Educational Psychology,* 1962, *53,* 105–109.

Johnson, M.K., Bransford, J.D., Nyberg, S.E., & Cleary, J.J. Comprehension factors in interpreting memory for abstract and concrete sentences. *Journal of Verbal Learning and Verbal Behavior,* 1972, *11,* 451–454.

Johnston, W.A., & Heinz, S.P. *It takes attention to pay attention.* Paper presented at the meeting of the Psychonomics Society, Boston, November 1974.

Johnston, W.A., & Heinz, S.P. Flexibility and capacity demands of attention. *Journal of Experimental Psychology: General,* 1978, *107,* 420–435.

Johnston, W.A., & Heinz, S.P. Depth of nontarget processing in an attention task. *Journal of Experimental Psychology: Human Perception and Performance,* 1979, *5,* 168–175.

Jones, D.M., Davies, D.R., Hogan, K.M., Patrick, J., & Cumberbatch, W.G. Short-term memory during the normal working day. In M.M. Gruneberg,

P.E. Morris, & R.N. Sykes (Eds.)., *Practical Aspects of Memory*. New York: Academic Press, 1978.

Jonides, J., Kahn, R., & Rozin, P. Imagery improves memory for blind subjects. *Bulletin of the Psychonomic Society*, 1975, *5*, 424–426.

Jorgensen, C.C., & Kintsch, W. The role of imagery in the evaluation of sentences. *Cognitive Psychology*, 1973, *4*, 110–116.

Julesz, B. Binocular depth perception without familiarity cues. *Science*, 1964, *145*, 356–362.

K

Kahneman, D. Method, findings and theory in studies of visual masking. *Psychological Bulletin*, 1968, *70*, 404–425.

Kahneman, D. *Attention and effort*. Englewood Cliffs, N.J.: Prentice-Hall, 1973.

Kahneman, D., Ben-Ishai, R., & Lotan, M. Relation of a test of attention to road accidents. *Journal of Applied Psychology*, 1973, *58*, 113–115.

Kantowitz, B.H., & Knight, J.L. On experimenter limited processes. *Psychological Review*, 1976, *83*, 502–507.

Kausler, D.H. *Psychology of verbal learning and memory*. New York: Academic Press, 1974.

Keppel, G., & Underwood, B.J. Proactive inhibition in short-term retention of single items. *Journal of Verbal Learning and Verbal Behavior*, 1962, *1*, 153–161.

Kerr, B. Processing demands during mental operations. *Memory and Cognition*, 1973, *1*, 401–412.

Kincaid, J.P., & Wickens, D.D. Temporal gradient of release from proactive inhibition. *Journal of Experimental Psychology*, 1970, *86*, 313–316.

Kingsley, P R., & Hagen, J.W. Induced versus spontaneous rehearsal in short-term memory in nursery school children. *Developmental Psychology*, 1969, *1*, 40–46.

Kinsbourne, M., & George, J. The mechanism of the word-frequency effect on recognition memory. *Journal of Verbal Learning and Verbal Behavior*, 1974, *13*, 63–69.

Kinsbourne, M., & Wood, F. Short-term memory processes and the amnestic syndrome. In D. Deutsch & J.A. Deutsch (Eds.), *Short-term memory*. New York: Academic Press, 1975.

Kintsch, W., & Bates, E. Recognition memory for statements from a classroom lecture. *Journal of Experimental Psychology: Human Learning and Memory*, 1977, *3*, 150–159.

Kintsch, W., & Buschke, H. Homophones and synonyms in short-term memory. *Journal of Experimental Psychology*, 1969, *80*, 403–407.

Kirby, J.R., & Das, J.P. Information processing and human abilities. *Journal of Educational Psychology*, 1978, *70*, 58–66.

Klatzky, R. *Human memory: Structures and processes*. San Francisco: Freeman, 1975.

Klein, N.K.E., Bruner, H., Holtmann, H., Rehme, H., Stolze, J., Steinhoff, W.D., & Wegman, H.M. Circadian rhythms of pilots' efficiency and effects of multiple time zone travel. *Aerospace Medicine*, 1970, *41*, 125–132.

Kleitman, N. *Sleep and wakefulness*. Chicago: University of Chicago Press, 1963.

Koffka, K. *Principles of Gestalt psychology*. New York: Harcourt, 1935.

Kolers, P.A. Some psychological aspects of pattern recognition. In P.A. Kolers & M. Eden (Eds.), *Recognizing patterns*. Boston: MIT Press, 1968.

Kolers, P.A. A pattern-analyzing basis of recognition. In L.S. Cermak & F.I.M. Craik (Eds.), *Levels of processing in human memory*. Hillsdale, N.J.: Lawrence Erlbaum Associates, 1979.

Kolers, P.A., & Ostry, D.J. Time course of loss of information regarding pattern analyzing operations. *Journal of Verbal Learning and Verbal Behavior*, 1974, *13*, 599–612.

Kosslyn, S.M. Information representation in visual images. *Cognitive Psychology*, 1975, *7*, 341–370.

Kosslyn, S.M., Ball. T.M., & Reiser, B.J. Visual images preserve metric spatial information: Evidence from studies of image scanning. *Journal of Experimental Psychology: Human Perception and Performance*, 1978, *4*, 47–60.

L

LaBerge, D., & Samuels, S.J. Toward a theory of automatic information processing in reading. *Cognitive Psychology*, 1974, *6*, 293–323.

Lachman, J.L., Lachman, R. & Thronesbery, C. Metamemory through the adult life span. *Developmental Psychology*, 1979, *15*, 543–551.

Lachman, R., Mistler-Lachman, J., & Butterfield, E.C. *Cognitive psychology and information processing: An introduction*. Hillsdale, N.J.: Lawrence Erlbaum Associates, 1979.

Lackner, J.R., & Garrett, M.F. Resolving ambiguity: Effects of biasing context in the unattended ear. *Cognition*, 1972, *1*, 359–372.

Landauer, T.K. Rate of implicit speech. *Perceptual and Motor Skills*, 1962, *15*, 646.

Landauer, T.K. Consolidation in human memory: Retrograde amnestic effects of confusable items in paired-associate learning. *Journal of Verbal Learning and Verbal Behavior*, 1974, *13*, 45–53.

Leask, J., Haber, R.N., & Haber, R.B. Eidetic imagery among children:II. Longitudinal and experimental results. *Psychonomic Monograph Supplements*, *1969*, *3*(Whole No. 35), 25–48.

Leippe, M., Wells, G.L., & Ostrom, T. Crime seriousness as a determinant of accuracy in eyewitness identification. *Journal of Applied Psychology*, 1978, *3*, 345–351.

Leshowitz, B., & Cudahy, E. Frequency discrimination in the presence of another tone. *Journal of the Acoustical Society of America*, 1973, *54*, 882–887.

Levy, B.A. Role of articulation in auditory and visual long-term memory. *Journal of Verbal Learning and Verbal Behavior*, 1971, *10*, 123–132.

Lewis, J.L. Semantic processing of unattended messages using dichotic listening. *Journal of Experimental Psychology*, 1970, *85*, 225–228.

Liberman, A.M., Cooper, F.S., Shankweiler, D.P., & Studdert-Kennedy, M. Perception of the speech code. *Psychological Review*, 1967, *74*, 431–461.

Liberman, A.M., Delattre, P.C., & Cooper, F.S. The role of selected stimulus variables in the perception of the unvoiced stop consonants. *American Journal of Psychology*, 1952, *65*, 497–516.

Light, L.L., & Carter-Sobell, L. Effects of changed semantic context on recognition memory. *Journal of Verbal Learning and Verbal Behavior*, 1970, *9*, 1–11.

Lindsay, P.H., & Norman, D.H. *Human information processing: An introduction to psychology* (2nd ed.). New York: Academic Press, 1977.

Lipton, J. On the psychology of eyewitness testimony. *Journal of Applied Psychology*, 1977, *62*, 90–95.

Lockhart, R.S., & Craik, F.I.M. Levels of processing: A reply to Eysenck. *British Journal of Psychology*, 1978, *69*, 171–175.

Lockhart, R.S., Craik, F.I.M., & Jacoby L. Depth of processing, recall, and recognition. In J. Brown (Ed.), *Recall and recognition*. New York: Wiley, 1976.

Lockhart, R.S., & Murdock, B.B. Memory and the theory of signal detection. *Psychological Bulletin*, 1970, *74*, 100–109.

Loeb, M., & Holding, D.H. Backward interference by tones or noise in pitch perception as a function of practice. *Perception and Psychophysics*, 1975, *18*, 205–208.

Loess, H. Proactive inhibition in short-term memory. *Journal of Verbal Learning and Verbal Behavior*, 1964, *3*, 362–368.

Loess, H., & Waugh, N.C. Short-term memory and intertrial interval. *Journal of Verbal Learning and Verbal Behavior*, 1967, *6*, 455–460.

Loftus E.F., Miller, D.G., & Burns, H.J. Semantic integration of verbal information into a visual memory. *Journal of Experimental Psychology: Human Learning and Memory*, 1978, *4*, 19–31.

Loftus, E.F., & Palmer, J.P. Reconstruction of automobile destruction: An example of the interaction between language and memory. *Journal of Verbal Learning and Verbal Behavior*, 1974, *13*, 585–589.

Lorayne, H., & Lucas, J. *The memory book*. New York: Stein and Day, 1974.

Luh, C.W. The conditions of retention. *Psychological Monographs*, 1922, *31* (3, Whole No. 142).

Luria, A.R. *The mind of a mnemonist*. New York: Basic Books, 1968.

Lutz, W.J., & Sheirer, C.J. Coding processes for pictures and words. *Journal of Verbal Learning and Verbal Behavior*, 1974, *13*, 316–320.

M

Mackworth, J.F. The duration of the visual image. *Candian Journal of Psychology*, 1963, *17*, 62–81.

Mackworth, J.F. *Vigilance and habituation*. Baltimore: Penguin Books, 1970.

Mandler, G., & Pearlstone, Z. Free and constrained concept learning and subsequent recall. *Journal of Verbal Learning and Verbal Behavior*, 1966, *3*, 1–5.

Mandler, J.M., & Johnson, N.S. Remembrance of things parsed: Story structure and recall. *Cognitive Psychology*, 1977, *9*, 111–151.

Marshall, E. Kemeny report: Abolish the NRC. *Science*, 1979, *206*, 796–798.

Marshall, G.R., & Cofer, C.N. Associative indices as measures of word relatedness. *Journal of Verbal Learning and Verbal Behavior*, 1963, *1*, 408–421.

Martin, C.J., Boersma, F.J., & Cox, D.L. A classification of associative strategies in paired associate learning. *Psychonomic Science*, 1965, *3*, 455–456.

Martin, C.J., Cox, D.L., & Boersma, F.J. The role of associative strategies in the acquisition of P-A materials: An alternate approach to meaningfulness. *Psychonomic Science*, 1965, *3*, 463–464.

Martin, E. Transfer of verbal paired associates. *Psychological Review*, 1965, *72*, 327–343.

Martin, E. Verbal learning and independent retrieval phenomenon. *Psychological Review*, 1971, *78*, 314–332.

Martin, E. Serial learning: A multilevel access analysis. *Memory and Cognition*, 1974, *2*, 322–328.

Martin, M. Memory span as a measure of individual differences in memory capacity. *Memory and Cognition*, 1978, *6*, 194–198.

Marx, M.H., & Hillix, W.A. *Systems and theories in psychology* (3rd ed.). New York: McGraw-Hill, 1979.

Massaro, D.W. Preperceptual images, processing time and perceptual units in auditory perception. *Psychological Review*, 1972, *79*, 124–145.

Mazuryk, G.F. Positive recency in final free recall. *Journal of Experimental Psychology*, 1974, *103*, 812–814.

McCloskey, M.E., & Glucksberg, S. Natural categories: Well defined or fuzzy sets? *Memory and Cognition*, 1978, *6*, 462–472.

McCloskey, M., & Watkins, M.J. The seeing-more-than-is-there phenomenon: Implication for the locus of iconic storage. *Journal of Experimental Psychology: Human Perception and Performance*, 1978, *4*, 553–564.

McCrary, J.W., & Hunter, W.S. Serial position curves in verbal learning. *Science*, 1953, *117*, 131–134.

McGaugh, J.L. Time-dependent processes in memory storage. *Science*, 1966, *153*, 1351–1358.

McGeoch, J.A. Forgetting and the law of disuse. *Psychological Review*, 1932, *39*, 352–370.

McGhie, A. *Pathology of attention*. Baltimore: Penguin Books, 1969.

McGhie, A., & Chapman, J. Disorders of attention and perception in early schizophrenia. *British Journal of Medical Psychology*, 1961, *34*, 103–116.

McGovern, J.B. Extinction of associations in four transfer paradigms. *Psychological Monographs*, 1964, *78*(Whole No. 593).

McGuire, W.J. A multiprocess model for paired-associate learning. *Journal of Experimental Psychology*, 1961, *62*, 335–347.

McKay, D.C. Aspects of the theory of comprehension, memory and attention. *Quarterly Journal of Experimental Psychology*, 1973, *25*, 22–40.

McKoon, G. Organization of information in text memory. *Journal of Verbal Learning and Verbal Behavior*, 1977, *16*, 247–260.

McLeod, P. A dual task response modality effect: Support for multiprocessor models of attention. *Quarterly Journal of Experimental Psychology*, 1977, *29*, 651–667.

McLeod, P. Does probe RT measure central processing demand? *Quarterly Journal of Experimental Psychology*, 1978, *30*, 83–89.

McNulty, J.A. An analysis of recall and recognition processes in verbal learning. *Journal of Verbal Learning and Verbal Behavior*, 1965, *4*, 430–435.

Melton, A.W. Implications of short-term memory for a general theory of memory. *Journal of Verbal Learning and Verbal Behavior*, 1963, *2*, 1–21.

Melton, A.W., & Irwin, J.M. The influence of degree of interpolated learning on retroactive inhibition and the overt transfer of specific responses. *American Journal of Psychology*, 1940, *53*, 173–203.

Melton, A.W., & Von Lackum, W.J. Retroactive and proactive inhibition in retention: Evidence for a two factor theory of retroactive inhibition. *American Journal of Psychology*, 1941, *54*, 157–173.

Merluzzi, T.V., & Johnson, N.F. The effects of repetition on iconic memory. *Quarterly Journal of Experimental Psychology*, 1974, *26*, 266–273.

Meyer, B.J.F. The structure of prose: Effects on learning and memory and implications for educational practice. In R.C. Anderson, R.J. Spiro, & W.E. Montague (Eds.), *Schooling and the acquisition of knowledge.* Hillsdale, N.J.: Lawrence Erlbaum Associates, 1977.

Meyer, D.E., & Schvaneveldt, R.W. Facilitation in recognizing pairs of words: Evidence of a dependence between retrieval operations. *Journal of Experimental Psychology,* 1971, *90,* 227–234.

Meyer, G.E., Jackson, W.E., & Yang, C. Spatial frequency, orientation and color: Interocular effects of adaptation on the perceived duration of gratings. *Vision Research,* 1979, *19,* 1197–1201.

Meyer, G.E., Lawson, R., & Cohen, W. The effects of orientation-specific adaptation on the duration of short-term visual storage. *Vision Research,* 1975, *15,* 569–572.

Meyer, G.E., & Maguire, W.M. Spatial frequency and the mediation of short-term visual storage. *Science,* 1977, *198,* 524–525.

Millar, S. Tactile short-term memory by blind and sighted children. *British Journal of Psychology,* 1974, *65,* 401–412.

Miller, G.A. The magical number seven, plus or minus two: Some limits on our capacity for processing information. *Psychological Review,* 1956, *63,* 81–96.

Miller, G.A., & Licklider, J.C.R. The intelligibility of interrupted speech. *Journal of the Acoustical Society of America,* 1950, *22,* 167–173.

Milner, B. Memory and the medial temporal regions of the brain. In K.H. Pribram & D.E. Broadbent (Eds.), *Biology of memory.* New York: Academic Press, 1970.

Milner, B., Corkin, S., & Teuber, H.L. Further analysis of the hippocampal amnesic syndrome: 14 year follow-up study of H.M. *Neuropsychologica,* 1968, *6,* 215–234.

Minami, H., & Dallenbach, K.M. The effect of activity upon learning and retention in the cockroach. *American Journal of Psychology,* 1946, *59,* 1–58.

Moeser, S.D. Memory for meaning and wording in concrete and abstract sentences. *Journal of Verbal Learning and Verbal Behavior,* 1974, *13,* 682–697.

Montague, W.E., Adams, J.A., & Kiess, H.O. Forgetting and natural language mediation. *Journal of Experimental Psychology,* 1966, *72,* 829–833.

Moray, N. Attention in dichotic listening: Affective cues and the influence of instructions. *Quarterly Journal of Experimental Psychology,* 1959, *11,* 56–60.

Moray, N. Broadbent's filter theory: Postulate H and the problem of switching time. *Quarterly Journal of Experimental Psychology,* 1960, *12,* 214–220.

Moray, N. Where is capacity limited?—A survey and a model. *Acta Psychologica,* 1967, *27,* 84–92.

Moray, N. *Listening and attention.* Baltimore: Penguin Books, 1969.

Moray, N., Bates, A., & Barnett, T. Experiments on the four-eared man. *Journal of the Acoustical Society of America,* 1965, *38,* 196–201.

Moray, N., & O'Brien, T. Signal detection theory applied to selective listening. *Journal of the Acoustical Society of America,* 1967, *42,* 765–772.

Morris, C.D., Bransford, J.D., & Franks, J.J. Levels of processing versus transfer appropriate processing. *Journal of Verbal Learning and Verbal Behavior,* 1977, *16,* 519–533.

Morton, J., & Byrne, R. Organization in the kitchen. In P.M.A. Rabbitt & S. Dornič (Eds.), *Attention and Performance V.* New York: Academic Press, 1975.

Morton, J., & Holloway, C.M. Absence of a cross-modal "suffix effect" in short-term memory. *Quarterly Journal of Experimental Psychology*, 1970, *22*, 167–176.

Mourant, R.R., & Rockwell, T.H. Strategies of visual search by novice and experienced drivers. *Human Factors*, 1972, *14*, 325–335.

Murdock, B.B., Jr. The retention of individual items. *Journal of Experimental Psychology*, 1961, *62*, 618–625.

Murdock, B.B., Jr. The serial position effect in free recall. *Journal of Experimental Psychology*, 1962, *64*, 482–488.

Murdock, B.B., Jr. A parallel-processing model for scanning. *Perception and Psychophysics*, 1971, *10*, 289–291.

Murray, D.J. The effect of white noise upon the recall of vocalized lists. *Canadian Journal of Psychology*, 1965, *19*, 333–345.

Murray, D.J. Vocalization-at-presentation and immediate recall, with varying recall methods. *Quarterly Journal of Experimental Psychology*, 1966, *18*, 9–18.

Murray, D.J., & Roberts, B. Visual and auditory presentation, presentation rate, and short-term memory in children. *British Journal of Psychology*, 1968, *59*, 119–125.

Murrell, H., & Humphries, S. Age experience and short-term memory. In M.M. Gruneberg, P.E. Morris, & R.N. Sykes (Eds.), *Practical aspects of memory*. New York: Academic Press, 1978.

N

Naus, M.J. Memory search of catagorized lists: A consideration of alternative self-terminating search strategies. *Journal of Experimental Psychology*, 1974, *102*, 992–1000.

Naus, M.J., Glucksberg, S., & Ornstein, P.A. Taxonomic word categories and memory search. *Cognitive Psychology*, 1972, *3*, 643–654.

Neisser, U. *Cognitive psychology*. New York: Appleton-Century-Crofts, 1967.

Neisser, U. *Selective reading: A method for the study of visual attention.* Paper presented at the Nineteenth International Congress of Psychology, London, 1969.

Neisser, U. Visual imagery as process and as experience. In J.F. Antrobus (Ed.), *Cognition and affect*. Boston: Little, Brown, and Company, 1970.

Neisser, U., & Becklen, R. Selective looking: Attending to visually specified events. *Cognitive Psychology*, 1975, *7*, 480–494.

Neisser, U., Hoenig, Y.J., & Goldstein, E. Perceptual organization in the prefix effect. *Journal of Verbal Learning and Verbal Behavior*, 1969, *8*, 424–429.

Neisser, U., & Kerr, N. Spatial and mnemonic properties of visual images. *Cognitive Psychology*, 1973, *5*, 138–150.

Nelson, D.L. Remembering pictures and words: Appearance, significance, and name. In L.S. Cermak & F.I.M. Craik (Eds.), *Levels of processing in human memory*. Hillsdale, N.J.: Lawrence Erlbaum Associates, 1979.

Nelson, D.L., Reed, V.S., & Walling, J.R. Pictorial superiority effect. *Journal of Experimental Psychology: Human Learning and Memory*, 1976, *2*, 523–528.

Nelson, D.L., Walling, J.R., & McEvoy, C.I. Doubts about depth. *Journal of Experimental Psychology: Human Learning and Memory,* 1979, *5,* 24–44.

Nelson, D.L., Wheeler, J.W., Borden, R.C., & Brooks, J. Levels of processing and cuing: Sensory vs. meaning features. *Journal of Experimental Psychology,* 1974, *103,* 971–977.

Nelson, T.O. Repetition and depth of processing. *Journal of Verbal Learning and Verbal Behavior,* 1977, *16,* 151–172.

Nelson, T.O., Metzler, J., & Reed, D. Role of details in the long-term recognition of pictures and verbal descriptions. *Journal of Experimental Psychology,* 1974, 102, 184–186.

Newman, E.B. Forgetting of meaningful material during sleep and waking. *American Journal of Psychology,* 1939, *52,* 65–71.

Newton, J.M., & Wickens, D.D. Retroactive inhibition as a function of the temporal position of interpolated learning. *Journal of Experimental Psychology,* 1956, *51,* 149–154.

Nickerson, R.S. Short-term memory for complex meaningful visual configurations: A demonstration of capacity. *Canadian Journal of Psychology,* 1965, *19,* 155–160.

Nickerson, R.S. A note on long-term recognition memory for pictorial material. *Psychonomic Science,* 1968, *11,* 58.

Nickerson, R.S., & Adams, M.J. Long-term memory for a common object. *Cognitive Psychology,* 1979, *11,* 287–307.

Noble, C.E., & McNeely, D.A. The role of meaningfulness (m) in paired associate verbal learning. *Journal of Experimental Psychology,* 1957, *53,* 16–22.

Norman, D.A. Toward a theory of memory and attention. *Psychological Review,* 1968, *75,* 522–536.

Norman, D.A. Memory while shadowing. *Quarterly Journal of Experimental Psychology,* 1969, *21,* 85–93.

Norman, D.A. Memory, knowledge and the answering of questions. In R.L. Solso (Ed.), *Contemporary issues in cognitive psychology: The Loyola symposium.* Washington, D.C.: Winston, 1973.

Norman, D.A. *Memory and attention* (2nd ed.). New York: Wiley, 1976.

Norman, D.A., & Bobrow, D.G. On data-limited and resource-limited processes. *Cognitive Psychology,* 1975, *7,* 44–64.

Norman, D.A., & Bobrow, D.G. On the analysis of performance operating characteristics. *Psychological Review,* 1976, *83,* 508–510.

Norman, D.A., Gentner, D.R., & Stevens, A.L. Comments on learning schemata and memory representation. In D. Klahr (Ed.), *Cognition and instruction.* Hillsdale, N.J.: Lawrence Earlbaum Associates, 1976.

Norman, D.A., & Rumelhart, D.E. *Explorations in cognition.* San Francisco: Freeman, 1975.

O

Oldfield, R.C. Things, words and the brain. *Quarterly Journal of Experimental Psychology,* 1966, *18,* 340–353.

Oldfield, R.C., & Wingfield, A. Response latencies in naming objects. *Quarterly Journal of Experimental Psychology,* 1965, *17,* 272–281.

Oltmanns, T.F., & Neale, J.M. Schizophrenic performance when distractors are present: Attentional deficit or differential task difficulty? *Journal of Abnormal Psychology,* 1975, *84,* 205–209.

Osgood, C.E. The similarity paradox in human learning: A resolution. *Psychological Review*, 1949, *56*, 132–143.

P

Paivio, A. Mental imagery in associative learning and memory. *Psychological Review*, 1969, *76*, 241–263.

Paivio, A. *Imagery and verbal processes*. New York: Holt, Rinehart & Winston, 1971.

Paivio, A. Imagery and long-term memory. In R.A. Kennedy & A. Wilkes (Eds.), *Studies in long-term memory*. New York: Wiley, 1975.

Paivio, A., & Csapo, K. Concrete image and verbal memory codes. *Journal of Experimental Psychology*, 1969, *80*, 279–285.

Paivio, A., Smythe, P.C., & Yuille, J.C. Imagery versus meaningfulness of nouns in paired-associate learning. *Canadian Journal of Psychology*, 1968, *22*, 427–441.

Paivio, A., Yuille, J.C., & Madigan, S.A. Concreteness, imagery, and meaningfulness values for 925 nouns. *Journal of Experimental Psychology Monograph Supplement*, 1968, *76*(1, Pt 2).

Parks, T.E. Signal detectability theory and recognition memory performance. *Psychological Review*, 1966, *73*, 44–58.

Patterson, K.E., & Baddeley, A.D. When face recognition fails. *Journal of Experimental Psychology: Human Learning and Memory*, 1977, *3*, 406–417.

Paul, J.H. Studies in remembering: The reproduction of connected and extended verbal material. *Psychological Issues*, 1959, *1*, 1–152.

Peper, R.J., & Mayer, R.E. Note taking as a generative activity. *Journal of Educational Psychology*, 1978, *70*, 514–522.

Peterson, L.R., & Johnson, S.T. Some effects of minimizing articulation on short term retention. *Journal of Verbal Learning and Verbal Behavior*, 1971, *10*, 346–354.

Peterson, L.R., & Peterson, M.J. Short-term retention of individual verbal items. *Journal of Experimental Psychology*, 1959, *58*, 193–198.

Peterson, L.R., Rawlings, L., & Cohen, C. The internal construction of spatial patterns. In G.H. Bower (Ed.), *The psychology of learning and motivation* (Vol. 11). New York: Academic Press, 1977.

Plath, O.E. Do anesthetized bees lose their memory? *American Naturalist*, 1924, *58*, 162–166.

Pollio, H.R. *The psychology of symbolic activity*. Reading, Mass.: Addison-Wesley, 1974.

Pollio, H.R., & Gerow, J.R. The role of rules in recall. *American Journal of Psychology*, 1968, *81*, 303–313.

Pollio, H.R., Richards, S., & Lucas, R. Temporal properties of category recall. *Journal of Verbal Learning and Verbal Behavior*, 1969, *8*, 529–536.

Poon, L.W., Fozard, J.L., Cermak, L.S., Arenberg, D., & Thompson, L.W. (Eds.). *New directions in memory and aging: Proceedings of the George Talland memorial conference*. Hillsdale, N.J.: Lawrence Erlbaum Associates, 1980.

Posner, M.I. *Cognition: An introduction*. Glenvue, Ill.: Scott, Foresman, 1973.

Posner, M.I., & Boies, S.J. Components of attention. *Psychological Review*, 1971, *78*, 391–408.

Posner, M.I., & Keele, S.W. Decay of visual information from a single letter. *Science*, 1967, *158*, 137–139.

Posner, M.I., & Klein, R. On functions of consciousness. In S. Kornblum (Ed.), *Attention and performance IV*. New York: Academic Press, 1973.

Posner, M., & Mitchell R. Chronometric analysis of classification. *Psychological Review,* 1967, *74,* 392–409.

Postman, L. A pragmatic view of organization theory. In E. Tulving & W. Donaldson (Eds.), *Organization of memory*. New York: Academic Press, 1972.

Postman, L., & Keppel, G. (Eds.). *Norms of word association*. New York: Academic Press, 1970.

Postman, L., & Rau, L. Retention as a function of the method of measurement. *University of California Publications in Psychology,* 1957, *8,* 217–270.

Postman, L., Stark, K., & Fraser, J. Temporal changes in interference. *Journal of Verbal Learning and Verbal Behavior,* 1968, *7,* 672–694.

Postman, L., & Underwood, B.J. Critical issues in interference theory. *Memory and Cognition,* 1973, *1,* 19–40.

Potter, M.C. Meaning in visual search. *Science,* 1975, *187,* 965–966.

Potter, M.C. Short-term conceptual memory for pictures. *Journal of Experimental Psychology: Human Learning and Memory,* 1976, *2,* 509–522.

Potter, M.C., & Faulconer, B.A. Time to understand pictures and words. *Nature,* 1975, *253,* 437–438.

Potts, G.R. Information processing strategies used in the encoding of linear orderings. *Journal of Verbal Learning and Verbal Behavior,* 1972, *11,* 727–740.

Potts, G.R. Storing and retrieving information about ordered relationships. *Journal of Experimental Psychology,* 1974, *103,* 431–439.

Poulton, E.C. Skilled performance and stress. In P.B. Warr (Ed.), *Psychology and work*. Baltimore, Penguin Books, 1971.

Prytulak, L.S. Natural language mediation. *Cognitive Psychology,* 1971, *2,* 1–56.

Pylyshyn, Z.W. What the mind's eye tells the mind's brain: A critique of mental imagery. *Psychological Bulletin,* 1973, *80,* 1–24.

Pylyshyn, Z.W. The rate of ''mental rotation'' of images: A test of a holistic analogue hypothesis. *Memory and Cognition,* 1979, *7,* 19–28.

Q

Quillian, M.R. Word concepts: A theory and simulation of some basic semantic capabilities. *Behavioral Science,* 1967, *12,* 410–430.

R

Rayner, K. Eye movements in reading and information processing. *Psychological Bulletin,* 1978, *85,* 618–660.

Reese, H.W. Imagery in paired-associate learning in children. *Journal of Experimental Child Psychology,* 1965, *2,* 290–296.

Reitman, J.S. Mechanisms of forgetting in short-term memory. *Cognitive Psychology,* 1971, *2,* 185–195.

Reitman, J.S. Without surreptitious rehearsal, information in short-term memory decays. *Journal of Verbal Learning and Verbal Behavior,* 1974, *13,* 365–377.

Reitman, J.S., & Bower, G.H. Storage and later recognition of exemplars of concepts. *Cognitive Psychology,* 1973, *4,* 194–206.

Reynolds, A.G., & Flagg, P.W. *Cognitive psychology*. Cambridge, Mass.: Winthrop, 1977.

Richardson, A. *Mental imagery*. New York: Springer-Verlag, 1969.

Rips, L.J., Shoben, E.J., & Smith, E.E. Semantic distance and the verification of semantic relations. *Journal of Verbal Learning and Verbal Behavior*, 1973, *12*, 1–20.

Robinson, F.P. *Effective study*. New York: Harper, 1946.

Roediger, H.L., Knight, J.L., & Kantowitz, B.H. Inferring decay in short-term memory: The issue of capacity. *Memory and Cognition*, 1977, *5*, 167–176.

Rosch, E., & Mervis, C.B. Family resemblances: Studies in the internal structure of categories. *Cognitive Psychology*, 1975, *7*, 573–605.

Rosch, E., Mervis, C.B., Gray, W.D., Johnson, D.M., & Boyes-Braem, P. Basic objects in natural categories. *Cognitive Psychology*, 1976, *8*, 382–439.

Rosenberg, S., & Schiller, W.J. Semantic coding and incidental sentence recall. *Journal of Experimental Psychology*, 1971, *90*, 345–346.

Rothkopf, E.Z. Incidental memory for location of information in text. *Journal of Verbal Learning and Verbal Behavior*, 1971, *10*, 608–613.

Routh, D.A., & Mayes, J.T. On consolidation and the potency of delayed stimulus suffixes. *Quarterly Journal of Experimental Psychology*, 1974, *26*, 472–479.

Royer, J.M., Hambleton, R.K., & Cadorette, L. Individual differences in memory: Theory, data and educational implications. *Contemporary Educational Psychology*, 1978, *3*, 182–203.

Rumelhart, D.E. Notes on a schema for stories. In D.G. Bobrow & A.M. Collins (Eds.), *Representation and understanding*. New York: Academic Press, 1975.

Rumelhart, D.E., & Ortony, A. The representation of knowledge in memory. In R.C. Anderson, R.J. Spiro, & W.E. Montague (Eds.), *Schooling and the acquisition of knowledge*. Hillsdale, N.J.: Lawrence Erlbaum Associates, 1977.

Rundus, D. Maintenance rehearsal and single level processing. *Journal of Verbal Learning and Verbal Behavior*, 1977, *16*, 665–681.

Russell, R.W., & Hunter, W.S. The effect of inactivity produced by sodium amytal on the retention of the maze habit in albino rats. *Journal of Experimental Psychology*, 1937, *20*, 426–436.

Russell, W.A., & Storms, L.H. Implicit verbal chaining in paired associate learning. *Journal of Experimental Psychology*, 1955, *49*, 287–293.

Russell, W.R. *Brain, memory, learning*. London: Oxford University Press, 1959.

Ryle, G. *The concept of mind*. London: Hutchinson, 1949.

S

Sachs, J.S. Recognition memory for syntactic and semantic aspects of connected discourse. *Perception and Psychophysics*, 1967, *2*, 437–442.

Sachs, J.S. Memory in reading and listening to discourse. *Memory and Cognition*, 1974, *2*, 95–100.

Saffran E.M., & Martin, O.S.M. Immediate memory for word lists and sentences in a patient with deficient short-term memory. *Brain and Language*, 1975, *2*, 420–433.

Sakitt, B. Locus of short-term visual storage. *Science*, 1975, *190*, 1318–1320.

Sakitt, B. Iconic memory. *Psychological Review*, 1976, *83*, 257–276.

Sakitt, B., & Long, G.M. Relative rod and cone contributions in iconic storage. *Perception and Psychophysics*, 1978, *23*, 527–536.

Sakitt, B., & Long, G.M. Spare the rod and spoil the icon. *Journal of Experimental Psychology: Human Perception and Performance*, 1979, *5*, 19–30.

Savin, H.B. On the successive perception of simultaneous stimuli. *Perception and Psychophysics*, 1967, *2*, 479–482.

Schachtel, E.G. *Metamorphosis*. New York: Basic Books, 1959.

Schaie, K.W., & Gribbin, K. Adult development and aging. *Annual Review of Psychology*, 1975, *26*, 65–96.

Schaie, K.W., & Strother, C.R. Cognitive and personality variables in college graduates of advanced age. In G.A. Talland (Ed.), *Human behavior and aging: Recent advances in research and theory*. New York: Academic Press, 1968.

Schank, R., & Abelson, R. *Scripts, plans, goals, and understanding*. Hillsdale, N.J.: Lawrence Erlbaum Associates, 1976.

Schneider, W., & Shiffrin, R.M. Controlled and automatic human information processing: I. Detection, search and attention. *Psychological Review*, 1977, *84*, 1–66.

Schulman, A.I. Recognition memory for targets from a scanned word list. *British Journal of Psychology*, 1971, *61*, 355–346.

Senders, J.W. On the distribution of attention in dynamic environment. *Acta Psychologica*, 1967, *27*, 349–354.

Shaffer, L.H. Multiple attention in continuous verbal tasks. In P.M.A. Rabbitt & S. Dornič (Eds.), *Attention and performance V*. New York: Academic Press, 1975.

Shallice, T., & Warrington, E.K. The independent functioning of the verbal memory stores: A neuropsychological study. *Quarterly Journal of Experimental Psychology*, 1970, *22*, 261–273.

Shaw, R., & Bransford, J. (Eds.). *Perceiving, acting and knowing*. Hillsdale, N.J.: Lawrence Erlbaum Associates, 1977.

Sheehan, P.W., & Neisser, U. Some variables affecting the vividness of imagery in recall. *British Journal of Psychology*, 1969, *60*, 71–80.

Shepard, R.N. Recognition memory for words, sentences, and pictures. *Journal of Verbal Learning and Verbal Behavior*, 1967, *6*, 156–163.

Shepard, R.N., & Metzler, J. Mental rotation of three-dimensional objects. *Science*, 1971, *171*, 701–703.

Shepard, R.N., & Sheenan, M.M. Immediate recall of numbers containing a familiar prefix or postfix. *Perceptual and Motor Skills*, 1965, *21*, 263–273.

Shiffrin, R.M. Information persistence in short-term memory. *Journal of Experimental Psychology*, 1973, *100*, 39–49.

Shiffrin, R.M., Craig, J.C., & Cohen, E. On the degree of attention and capacity limitations in tactile processing. *Perception and Psychophysics*, 1973, *13*, 328–336.

Shiffrin, R.M., & Grantham, D.W. Can attention be allocated to sensory modalities? *Perception and Psychophysics*, 1974, *15*, 460–474.

Shiffrin, R.M., Pisoni, D.B., & Casteneda-Mendez, K. Is attention shared between the ears? *Cognitive Psychology*, 1974, *6*, 190–216.

Shiffrin, R.M., & Schneider, W. Toward a unitary model for selective attention, memory scanning and visual search. In S. Dornič (Ed.), *Attention and performance VI*. Hillsdale, N.J.: Lawrence Erlbaum Associates, 1977(a).

Shiffrin, R.M., & Schneider, W. Controlled and automatic human information processing: II Perceptual learning, automatic attending, and a general theory. *Psychological Review*, 1977, *84*, 127–190. (b)

Simon, C.W., & Emmons, W.H. Responses to material presented during various levels of sleep. *Journal of Experimental Psychology*, 1956, *51*, 89–97.

Singer, M., & Rosenberg, S.T. The role of grammatical relations in the abstraction of linguistic ideas. *Journal of Verbal Learning and Verbal and Behavior*, 1973, *12*, 273–284.

Slamecka, N.J. Retroactive inhibition of connected discourse as a function of practice level. *Journal of Experimental Psychology*, 1960, *59*, 104–108.

Slamecka, N.J. Proactive inhibition of connected discourse. *Journal of Experimental Psychology*, 1961, *62*, 295–301.

Smith, E.E. Theories of semantic memory. In W.K. Estes (Ed.), *Handbook of learning and cognitive processes: Linguistic functions in cognitive theory* (Vol. 6). Hillsdale, N.J.: Lawrence Erlbaum Associates, 1978.

Smith, E.E., Rips, L.J., & Shoben, E.J. Structure and process in semantic memory: A featural model for semantic decisions. *Psychological Review*, 1974, *81*, 214–241.

Spelke, E., Hirst, W., & Neisser, U. Skills of divided attention. *Cognition*, 1976, *4*, 215–230.

Sperling, G. The information available in brief visual presentations. *Psychological Monographs*, 1960, *74*(Whole No. 498).

Sperling, G. A model for visual memory tasks. *Human Factors*, 1963, *5*, 19–31.

Sperling, G. Successive approximations to a model for short-term memory. *Acta Psychologica*, 1967, *27*, 285–292.

Spieth, W., Curtis, J.F., & Webster, J.C. Responding to one of two simultaneous messages. *Journal of the Acoustical Society of America*, 1954, *26*, 391–396.

Standing, L. Learning 10,000 pictures. *Quarterly Journal of Experimental Psychology*, 1973, *25*, 207–222.

Standing, L., Conezio, J., & Haber, R.N. Perception and memory for pictures: Single-trial learning of 2560 visual stimuli. *Psychonomic Science*, 1970, *19*, 73–74.

Stein, B.S. Depth of processing reexamined: The effects of the precision of encoding and test appropriateness. *Journal of Verbal Learning and Verbal Behavior*, 1978, *17*, 165–174.

Sternberg, R. *Intelligence, information processing, and analogical reasoning: The componential analysis of human abilities*. Hillsdale, N.J.: Lawrence Erlbaum Associates, 1977.

Sternberg, S. High-speed scanning in human memory. *Science*, 1966, *153*, 652–654.

Sternberg, S. Retrieval of contextual information from memory. *Psychonomic Science*, 1967, *8*, 55–56.

Sternberg, S. Memory-scanning: Mental processes revealed by reaction-time experiments. *American Scientist*, 1969, *57*, 421–457. (a)

Sternberg, S. The discovery of processing stages: Extension of Donder's method. *Acta Psychologica*, 1969, *30*, 276–315. (b)

Sternberg, S. *Evidence against self-terminating memory search from properties of RT distributions*. Paper presented at the annual meeting of the Psychonomic Society, St. Louis, November 1973.

Sternberg, S. Memory scanning: New findings and current controversies. *Quarterly Journal of Experimental Psychology*, 1975, *27*, 1–32.

Stones, M.J. Sleep and the storage and retrieval processes in humans. Unpublished doctoral dissertation, University of Sheffield, Sheffield, England, 1974.

Stromeyer, C.F., & Psotka, J. The detailed texture of eidetic images. *Nature*, 1970, *225*, 346–349.

Sulin, R.A., & Dooling, D.J. Intrusion of a thematic idea in retention of prose. *Journal of Experimental Psychology*, 1974, *103*, 255–262.

Swets, J.A. (Ed.). *Signal detection and recognition by human observers: Contemporary readings.* New York: Wiley, 1964.

Swets, J.A., Tanner, W.P., & Birdsall, T.G. Decision processes in perception. *Psychological Review*, 1961, *68*, 301–340.

T

Thomson, D.M., & Tulving, E. Associative encoding and retrieval: Weak and strong cues. *Journal of Experimental Psychology*, 1970, *86*, 255–262.

Thorndike, E.L. *Animal intelligence.* New York: Macmillan, 1911.

Thorndike, E.L., & Lorge, I. *The teacher's word book of 30,000 words.* New York: Teachers College Press, Columbia University, 1944.

Thorndyke, P.W. Cognitive structures in comprehension and memory of narrative discourse. *Cognitive Psychology*, 1977, *9*, 77–110.

Thorndyke, P.W., & Hayes-Roth, B. The use of schemata in the acquisition and transfer of knowledge. *Cognitive Psychology*, 1979, *11*, 82–106.

Thune, L.E. Warm-up effect as a function of level of practice in verbal learning. *Journal of Experimental Psychology*, 1951, *42*, 250–256.

Titchener, E.B. *Lectures on the elementary psychology of feeling and attention.* New York: Macmillan, 1908.

Titchener, E.B. *A textbook of psychology.* New York: Macmillan, 1910.

Townsend, J.T. A note on the identifiability of parallel and serial processes. *Perception and Psychophysics*, 1971, *10*, 161–163.

Townsend, J.T. Some results concerning the identifiability of parallel and serial processes. *British Journal of Mathematical and Statistical Psychology*, 1972, *25*, 168–199.

Treisman, A.M. Contextual cues in selective listening. *Quarterly Journal of Experimental Psychology*, 1960, *12*, 242–248.

Treisman, A.M. Selective attention in man. *British Medical Bulletin*, 1964, *20*, 12–16. (a)

Treisman, A.M. Effect of irrelevant material on the efficiency of selective listening. *American Journal of Psychology*, 1964, *77*, 532–546. (b)

Treisman, A.M. Verbal cues, language and meaning in selective attention. *American Journal of Psychology*, 1964, *77*, 206–219. (c).

Treisman, A.M. Monitoring and storage of irrelevant messages in selective attention. *Journal of Verbal Learning and Verbal Behavior*, 1964, *3*, 449–459. (d)

Treisman, A.M. Human attention. In B.M. Foss (Ed.), *New horizons in psychology.* Baltimore: Penguin Books, 1966.

Treisman, A.M. Strategies and models of selective attention. *Psychological Review*, 1969, *76*, 282–299.

Treisman, A.M., & Geffen, G. Selective attention: Perception or response? *Quarterly Journal of Experimental Psychology*, 1967, *19*, 1–17.

Tulving, E. Subjective organization in free recall of "unrelated" words. *Psychological Review*, 1962, *69*, 344–354.

Tulving, E. Intratrial and intertrial retention: Notes toward a theory of free recall verbal learning. *Psychological Review*, 1964, *71*, 219–237.

Tulving, E. When is recall higher than recognition. *Psychonomic Science*, 1968, *10*, 53–54. (a)

Tulving, E. Theoretical issues in free recall. In T.R. Dixon & D.L. Horton (Eds.), *Verbal behavior and general behavior theory*. Englewood Cliffs, N.J.: Prentice-Hall, 1968(b).

Tulving, E. Episodic and semantic memory. In E. Tulving & W. Donaldson (Eds.), *Organization of memory*. New York: Academic Press, 1972.

Tulving, E. Relation between encoding specificity and levels in processing. In L.S. Cermak & F.I.M. Craik (Eds.), *Levels of processing in human memory*. Hillsdale, N.J.: Lawrence Erlbaum Associates, 1979.

Tulving, E., & Madigan, S.A. Memory and verbal learning. *Annual Review of Psychology* (Vol. 20). Palo Alto, Calif.: Annual Reviews 1970

Tulving, E., & Osler, S. Effectiveness of retrieval cues in memory for words. *Journal of Experimental Psychology*, 1968, *77*, 593–601.

Tulving, E., & Pearlstone, Z. Availability vs. accessibility of information in memory for words. *Journal of Verbal Learning and Verbal Behavior*, 1966, *5*, 381–391.

Tulving, E., & Thomson, D.M. Encoding specificity and retrieval processes in episodic memory. *Psychological Review*, 1973, *80*, 352–373.

Turvey, M.T. Repetition and the preperceptual information store. *Journal of Experimental Psychology*, 1967, *74* 289–293.

Turvey, M.T. On peripheral and central processes in vision: Inferences from an information processing analysis of masking with patterned stimuli. *Psychological Review*, 1973, *80*, 1–52.

Turvey, M.T. Visual processing and short-term memory. In W.K. Estes (Ed.), *Handbook of learning and cognitive processes: Human information processing* (Vol. 5). Hillsdale, N.J.: Lawrence Erlbaum Associates, 1978.

Turvey, M.T., & Kravetz, S. Retrieval from iconic memory with shape as the selective criterion. *Perception and Psychophysics*, 1970, *8*, 171–172.

Tversky, B. Encoding processes in recognition and recall. *Cognitive Psychology*, 1973, *5*, 275–287.

Tzeng, O.J.L. Positive recency effect in a delayed free recall. *Journal of Verbal Learning and Verbal Behavior*, 1973, *12*, 436–439.

U

Underwood, B.J. The effect of successive interpolations on retroactive and proactive inhibition. *Psychological Monographs*, 1945, *59* (Whole No. 273).

Underwood, B.J. Retroactive and proactive inhibition after five and forty-eight hours. *Journal of Experimental Psychology*, 1948, *38*, 29–38. (a)

Underwood, B.J. "Spontaneous" recovery and verbal associations. *Journal of Experimental Psychology*, 1948, *38*, 429–439. (b)

Underwood, B.J. Interference and forgetting. *Psychological Review*, 1957, *64*, 49–60.

Underwood, B.J. False recognition produced by implicit verbal responses. *Journal of Experimental Psychology*, 1965, *70*, 122–129.

Underwood, B.J. Individual differences as a crucible in theory construction. *American Psychologist*, 1975, *30*, 128–134.

Underwood, B.J., & Freund, J.S. Word-frequency and short-term recognition memory. *American Journal of Psychology,* 1970, *83,* 343–351.

Underwood, B.J., & Schulz, R.W. *Meaningfulness and verbal learning.* Philadelphia: Lippincott, 1960.

V

Van Dijk, T., & Kintsch, W. Cognitive psychology and discourse: Recalling and summarizing stories. In W. Dressler (Ed.), *Trends in text-linguistics.* New York: DeGruyter, 1977.

VonWright, J.M. On selection in visual immediate memory. *Acta Psychologica,* 1970, *33,* 280–292.

VonWright, J.M. Anderson, K., & Stenman, V. Generalization of conditioned GSRs in dichotic listening. In P.M.A. Rabbitt & S. Dornič (Eds.), *Attention and performance V.* London: Academic Press, 1975.

W

Wachtel, P.L. Conceptions of broad and narrow attention. *Psychological Bulletin,* 1967, *68,* 417–429.

Wallace, W.P. Consistency of emission order in free recall. *Journal of Verbal Learning and Verbal Behavior,* 1970, *9,* 58–68.

Ward, L.B. Reminiscence and rote learning. *Psychological Monographs,* 1937, *49* (Whole No. 220).

Warrington, E.K., Logue, V., & Pratt, R.T.C. The anatomical localization of selective impairment of auditory verbal short-term memory. *Neuropsychologica,* 1971, *9,* 377–387.

Warrington, E.K., & Shallice, T. The selective impairment of auditory verbal short-term memory. *Brain,* 1969, *92,* 885–896.

Warrington, E.K., & Shallice, T. Neuropsychological evidence of visual storage in short-term memory tasks. *Quarterly Journal of Experimental Psychology,* 1972, *24,* 30–40.

Warrington, E.K., & Weiskrantz, L. An analysis of short-term memory and long-term memory defects in man. In J.A. Deutsch (Ed.), *The Physiological basis of memory.* New York: Academic Press, 1970.

Watkins, M.J. Concept and measurement of primary memory. *Psychological Bulletin,* 1974, *81,* 695–711.

Watkins, M.J., & Tulving, E. Episodic memory: When recognition fails. *Journal of Experimental Psychology: General,* 1975, *1,* 5–29.

Watkins, M.J., & Watkins, O.C. Processing of recency items for free recall. *Journal of Experimental Psychology,* 1974, *102,* 488–493.

Watkins, M.J., Watkins, O.C., Craik, F.I.M., & Mazuryk, G. Effect of nonverbal distraction on short-term storage. *Journal of Experimental Psychology,* 1973, *101,* 296–300.

Watson, J.B. Psychology as the behaviorist views it. *Psychological Review,* 1913, *20,* 158–177.

Waugh, N.C., & Norman D.A. Primary memory. *Psychological Review,* 1965, *72,* 89–104.

Weiner, W.B., & Palermo, D.S. (Eds.). *Cognition and the symbolic processes.* Hillsdale, N.J.: Lawrence Erlbaum Associates, 1975.

Weisstein, N. Metacontrast. In D. Jameson & L.M. Hurvich (Eds.), *Handbook of Sensory physiology* (Vol. 7, Pt. 4, *Visual psychophysics*). New York: Springer-Verlag, 1972.

Welford, A.T. The "psychological refractory period" and the timing of high speed performance: A review and a theory. *British Journal of Psychology,* 1952, *43,* 2–19.

Welford, A.T. Evidence of a single-channel decision mechanism limiting performance in a serial reaction task. *Quarterly Journal of Experimental Psychology,* 1959, *11,* 193–210.

Welford, A.T. *Fundamentals of skill.* London: Methuen, 1968.

Welford, A.T. Serial reaction-times, continuity of task, single-channel effects and age. In S. Dornič (Ed.), *Attention and performance VI.* Hillsdale, N.J.: Lawrence Erlbaum Associates, 1977.

Wells, G.L. Applied eyewitness-testimony research: System variables and estimator variables. *Journal of Personality and Social Psychology,* 1978, *36,* 1546–1557.

Whimbey A.E., & Ryan, S.F. Role of short-term memory and training in solving reasoning problems mentally. *Journal of Educational Psychology,* 1969, *60,* 361–364.

Whimbey, A., & Whimbey, L.S. *Intelligence can be taught.* New York: Dutton, 1975.

Whitfield, D. *A pilot survey of human factors aspects of power reactor safety and control* (rep. EDU101). University of Aston, Applied Psychology Department, Birmingham, England, 1970.

Wickelgren, W.A. Acoustic similarity and intrusion errors in short-term memory. *Journal of Experimental Psychology,* 1965, *70,* 102–108. (a)

Wickelgren, W.A. Short-term memory for phonemically similar lists. *American Journal of Psychology,* 1965, *78,* 567–574. (b)

Wickelgren, W.A. Similarity and intrusions in short-term memory for consonant-vowel digrams. *Quarterly Journal of Experimental Psychology,* 1965, *17,* 241–246. (c)

Wickelgren, W.A., & Whitman, P. Visual very-short-term memory is nonassociative. *Journal of Experimental Psychology,* 1970, *84,* 277–281.

Wickens, D.D. Characteristics of word encoding. In A.W. Melton & E. Martin (Eds.), *Coding processes in human memory.* Washington, D.C.: Winston, 1972.

Wickens, D.D. Some characteristics of word encoding. *Memory and Cognition,* 1973, *1,* 485–490.

Wickens, D.D., Born, D.G., & Allen, C.K. Proactive inhibition on and item similarity in short-term memory. *Journal of Verbal Learning and Verbal Behavior,* 1963, *2,* 440–445.

Wilkinson, R.T. Effects of up to 60 hours of sleep deprivation on different types of work. *Ergonomics,* 1964, *7,* 175–186.

Wingfield, A. Perceptual and response hierarchies in object identification. *Acta Psychologica,* 1967, *26,* 216–226.

Wingfield, A. Effects of frequency on the identification and naming of objects *American Journal of Psychology,* 1968, *81,* 226–234.

Wingfield, A. Effects of serial position and set size in auditory recognition memory. *Memory and Cognition,* 1973, *1,* 53–55.

Wingfield, A. The perception of alternated speech. *Brain and Language,* 1977, *4,* 219–230.

Wingfield, A. *Human learning and memory: An introduction.* New York: Harper and Row, 1979.

Wingfield, A. Attention, levels of processing, and state-dependent recall. In L.W. Poon, J.L. Fozard, L.S. Cermak, D. Arenberg, & L.W. Thompson (Eds.), *New directions in memory and aging: Proceedings of the George Talland memorial conference.* Hillsdale, N.J.: Lawrence Erlbaum Associates, 1980.

Wingfield, A., & Bolt, R.A. Memory search for multiple targets. *Journal of Experimental Psychology,* 1970, *85,* 45–50.

Wingfield, A., & Branca, A.A. Strategy in high-speed memory search. *Journal of Experimental Psychology,* 1970, *83,* 63–67.

Wingfield, A., & Bynes, D.L. Decay of information in short-term memory. *Science,* 1972, *176,* 690–692.

Wingfield, A., & Sandoval, A.W. Perceptual processing for meaning. In L.W. Poon, J.L. Fozard, L.S. Cermak, D. Arenberg, & L.W. Thompson (Eds.), *New directions in memory and aging: Proceedings of the George Talland memorial conference.* Hillsdale, N.J.: Lawrence Erlbaum Associates, 1980.

Wingfield, A., & Wheale, J.L. Word-rate and intelligibility of alternated speech. *Perception and Psychophysics,* 1975, *18,* 317–320.

Winograd, E. List differentiation as a function of frequency and retention interval. *Journal of Experimental Psychology Monographs Supplement,* 1968, *76,* (2, Pt. 2).

Winograd, T. Understanding natural language. *Cognitive Psychology,* 1972. *3,* 1–191.

Wiseman, S., & Tulving, E. Encoding specificity: Relation between recall superiority and recognition failure. *Journal of Experimental Psychology: Human Learning and Memory,* 1976, *2,* 349–361.

Wood, G., & Underwood, B.J. Implicit responses and conceptual similarity. *Journal of Verbal Learning and Verbal Behavior,* 1967, *6,* 1–10.

Woodward, A.E., J. Bjork, R.A., & Jongewood, R.H., Jr. Recall and recognition as a function of primary rehearsal. *Journal of Verbal Learning and Verbal Behavior,* 1973, *12,* 608–617.

Woolen, K.A., Weber, A., & Lowry, D. Bizarreness versus interaction of mental images as determinants of learning. *Cognitive Psychology,* 1972, *3,* 518–523.

X,Y,Z

Yen, W.M. Measuring individual differences with an information processing model. *Journal of Educational Psychology,* 1978, *70,* 72–86.

Yerkes, R.M., & Dodson, J.D. The relation of strength of stimulus to rapidity of habit-formation. *Journal of Comparative Neurology of Psychology,* 1908, *18,* 459–482.

Yntema, D.B., & Trask, F.P. Recall as a search process. *Journal of Verbal Learning and Verbal Behavior,* 1963, *2,* 65–74.

Young, R.K. Serial learning. In T.R. Dixon & D.L. Norton (Eds.), *Verbal behavior and general behavior theory.* Englewood Cliffs, N.J.: Prentice-Hall, 1968.

Yussen, S.R., & Levy, V.M., Jr. Developmental changes in predicting one's own span of short-term memory. *Journal of Experimental Child Psychology,* 1975, *19,* 502–508.

Zelniker, T. Perceptual attenuation of an irrelevant auditory verbal input as measured by an involuntary verbal response in a selective attention task. *Journal of Experimental Psychology,* 1971, *87,* 52–56.

NAME INDEX

SUBJECT INDEX

C 3
D 4
E 5
F 6
G 7
H 8
I 9
J 0